Bodies in Suspense

Bodies in Suspense

Time and Affect in Cinema

Alanna Thain

UNIVERSITY OF MINNESOTA PRESS

MINNEAPOLIS · LONDON

Earlier versions of chapter 2 appeared in "Funny How Secrets Travel," *Invisible Culture* 8 (Fall 2004) and in "Crime/Scene: Reanimating the Femme Fatale in David Lynch's Hollywood Trilogy," in *Aprehendiendo a delincuente: Crimen y medios en América del norte,* ed. Graciela Martinez-Zalce, Will Straw, and Susana Vargas, 85–97 (Mexico City: CISAN/UNAM and Media@McGill, 2011).

Published by the University of Minnesota Press
111 Third Avenue South, Suite 290
Minneapolis, MN 55401-2520
http://www.upress.umn.edu

Printed in the United States of America on acid-free paper

The University of Minnesota is an equal-opportunity educator and employer.

23 22 21 20 19 18 17   10 9 8 7 6 5 4 3 2 1

Library of Congress Cataloging-in-Publication Data
Names: Thain, Alanna, author.
Title: Bodies in suspense : time and affect in cinema / Alanna Thain.
Description: Minneapolis : University of Minnesota Press, [2017] |
Includes bibliographical references and index.
Identifiers: LCCN 2016022219 |
ISBN 978-0-8166-9293-4 (hc) | ISBN 978-0-8166-9295-8 (pb)
Subjects: LCSH: Space and time in motion pictures.
Classification: LCC PN1995.9.S668 T47 2017 |
DDC 791.43/6584—dc23
LC record available at https://lccn.loc.gov/2016022219

For my mom,
who gives me everything

Contents

Time Crimes, or Feeling Difference Made

The play of intensity of the ontological constellation is, in a way, a choice of being not for the self, but for the whole alterity of the cosmos and for the infinity of times.

—Félix Guattari, *Chaosmosis*

D avid Lynch's *Inland Empire* begins and ends with two images of suspense, contact points when the film spirals back on itself as a direct experience of the body in time. Space-time bends through this spiral form via two beams of light—incandescent time machines. *Inland Empire* begins with a projector's lamp arcing across a deep, soft blackness. The thick consistency of the projector's low rumble, a variant of Lynch's signature "sound baths," doubles the discrete, percussive repetitions of each

Opening Shot of *Inland Empire* (David Lynch, 2006).

individual frame change, throwing us into a machinic sonic ecology. We never see the images carried by the light; indeed, the beam itself doesn't even reach the other side of the frame, but hangs heavily as a luminous cone: a developing form. Immediately, we have an image of suspense that resists a logic of revelation in which the light's (in)visible content could resolve uncertainty and release bodily tension. Instead, suspense generates a fragile yet persistent zone of indeterminacy. When the light fails to land onscreen, other points of contact emerge, and other images surface. A record player rises from the image's murky depths through a slow dissolve, immediately doubled by the ephemeral sound waves of a radio broadcast. Through this unresolved delay of knowledge, where a neat divide between onscreen and off, seen and heard, is displaced in favor of the inbetween, delay becomes a *relay* opening onto emergence, a world without end. Thus, the film begins not by asking "What will happen next?" but with the statement that characterizes the suspenseful feeling of a body in time: *Something is happening.* The present's immediacy stretches, accruing to itself the felt force of past and future, deranging the film's eccentric temporality from its inception. As the suspensive medium of an event ecology, this light neither clarifies nor illuminates: it *immediates*.[1]

Folding back onto itself, *Inland Empire* also ends in suspense: narratively, in the irresolution of Laura Dern's baroque permutations of

Laura Dern at the end of *Inland Empire*.

character over the course of nearly three hours, and formally, with a suspended point-of-view (POV) shot. The last two shots of the film are an eyeline match that is an impossible look across time, the end point of an intensive re-viewing of the film's actions initiated by the beam of a spotlight. Left behind after the film's clichéd closure via the reunion of the Lost Girl with her nuclear family, Dern lingers on the set of *Rabbits* as a spotlight finds her. As images from the film frenetically rewind before the viewer's eyes, Dern's narrative path is eccentrically reversed to the moment of *her* first break (as Nikki in her living room), and she turns her gaze across that room to see herself on its other side. A suspended POV is also called an impossible objective shot, where the camera occupies a position unattributable to any human character onscreen. Although normally this is understood as spatial impossibility, in Lynch's films such spatial positions are almost always incompossibilities of time.[2] Suspense is the experience of this intensive embodiment, the body's own propensity to become other in time. Suspense thus names a technic for an attentive awareness to the minor form of difference that (re)constitutes a body in time, a feeling of futurity immediately impinging on the body's stability and reopening it to intensive relationality. When the film folds back on itself, the effect is not the resolution of a closed circle, but a spiral's vertiginous plunge.

Of course, this final image is not the end; as the credits roll, a reservoir of potential other stories, other parts, other bodies is revealed during the delirious choreography of the "Sinnerman" lip-syncing sequence. The credit's re-sorting of bodies and performances into their rightful place, and the bracketing of the film's world as a threshold back into the "real world," are suspended in an experience of affective contagion. This sequence's excesses occupy an ambiguous place relative to the rest of the film; its generosity testifies to the productive excess of the film's intensive embodiments. Impossible embodiments in Lynch bear witness to the potential of the body in time, in the intensity of its affective engagements.

To see oneself in an experience of auto-alterity, directly experiencing the (an)otherness at the heart of the self, as Dern does at *Inland Empire*'s end, is one variation on a figural technique I develop in this book: "double vision." Double vision is a perceptual feeling of the direct experience of time: a suspension of the present through the repetition of the past experienced as the potential of the future. I address examples of cinematic doubles to demonstrate how cinema can make us *live time* by restoring a sense of the heterogeneity of durations that compose us. I do this via a new theory of cinematic suspense that engages the legacy of Gilles Deleuze's influential work on cinema, *Cinema 1: The Movement-Image* and *Cinema 2: The Time-Image,* and his work both solo and with Félix Guattari on time in relation to the creative and "emergent alterfications" of subjectivation. This theory of suspense particularly dialogues with two claims from *Cinema 2*: first, that "there is no crime but time itself" and second, that "the direct time-image is the phantom which has always haunted the cinema, but it took modern cinema to give a body to this phantom."[3] Suspense names the incorporated effects of living time at the movies.

Bodies in Suspense explores double vision through cinematic doubling in two senses. First, I examine key films that tie the double to aberrant experiences of time, where questions of identity (Who is the double?) are effectively and affectively displaced in favor of what doubling does: becoming double as an intensive multiplicity. Reading transversally across this book's chapters, doubles and repetitions become sites for thinking a "free replay" of cinema. For example, chapters 1, 2, and 3 transversally map a triptych of films: Alfred Hitchcock's *Vertigo* (1958) and its "remakes," in David Lynch's Hollywood trilogy—*Lost Highway* (1997), *Mulholland Drive* (2001), and *Inland Empire* (2006) (serial repetitions themselves)—and Lou Ye's *Suzhou River* (2000), exploring the double as both figure and technique. Deleuze offhandedly cites *Vertigo* as one of only three films that show us how we inhabit time. I track a *Vertigo*-effect of double vision both within and across these works.

I trace in particular the figure of the duplicitous woman, simultaneously under suspicion of infidelity and literally duplicated in dual roles and the subsequent hesitation between actress and character, what Jean-Louis Comolli terms the problem of a "body too much."[4] I argue this duplicitous woman and the uncertainties she generates can be understood as a "conceptual persona," a time-image expressing the experience of becoming other than we are.[5] The duplicitous woman enters into relations and exchanges of depersonalization, what Deleuze calls the "depersonalization of love."[6] In these films, love comes to be the affective experience of time, understood as an infidelity to the self. This infidelity is what Deleuze calls "the crime of time," or as he rewords it, "There is no crime but time."[7] This contention grounds my theory of cinematic suspense, rerouting generic associations of guilt and criminality into fabulative powers and new compositions. The double vision generated by these duplicitous remakes displaces concerns of reference in favor of the cinematic event.

Second, *Bodies in Suspense* explores double vision as a methodology emerging from these films themselves, speaking directly to a cinematic logic of difference in repetition. Thus Hitchcock's *Vertigo* is explored not as a representation of the time-image, but as performing *a methodology of rereading and remaking* to activate the (reanimating) power of cinematic doubling. This methodology plays out both within narratives, as in the time-travel film *Looper* (2012) and in formal experiments, as in Christian Marclay's experimental twenty-four-hour compilation event, *The Clock* (2011), both blueprints for postcinematic time machines (chapter 4). I use this methodology of repetition as the key quality of the cinematic body; rereading, looking again, re-citation. These minor modes of change open onto affect's potential: the body, after all, is our most intimate experience of repetition, in that it is still here again and again. Yet each repetition opens onto the world of difference, each breath, each heartbeat an anarchic rhythm testifying to the incorporeal temporal dimension of the body itself. This in-consistency of an in-constant body mutes ongoing difference by everyday familiarity. These films incite a double time of "looking again," through a hesitation of recognition, through the work of remaking, and through a cut or break in the narrative (for example, the death or disappearance of a main character and her or his ambiguous reappearance: Madeleine and Judy in *Vertigo*, Fred and Pete in *Lost Highway*, Mei Mei and Mudan in *Suzhou River*, and so on) or through the reanimation of media archives harvested from databases both cinematic and corporeal. Of *Vertigo*, Chris Marker notes its apparent vertigo of space is in fact a vertigo of time.[8] Double time thus names the vertiginous effects of this invitation to look again, the differential repetition of cinema itself. But this imperative to look again also concerns a remix logic of remake and reperformance in suspense films. I trace a theory of suspense that deviates from narrative logic, deforming genre expectations and taking a lost highway rather than the royal road of narrative cinema. Looking again becomes not simply a practice of strategic rewatching that would allow an active spectator to re-sort and reorder the confusions of narrative sense that many of the films addressed here share. Instead, double vision opens onto other modes of sensation, what Brian Massumi terms "thinking-feelings."

A key aim of this book is to articulate this new model of suspense as the name of a specifically cinematic force. Force is, of course, another definition of *affect*, and this book concerns cinema studies' affective turn. A paradoxical example of cinematic repetition is the phenomenon of *anomalous suspense*: the intransigent experience of sustained levels of heightened affect experienced by audiences even in the face of a known outcome. Do our palms fail to sweat, our stomachs fail to clench as Scottie drags Judy up the bell tower again and again? Anomalous suspense is the perception of a perception, the thinking-feeling of an intensive inbetween. Its other appellation, *recidivist* suspense, binds this duplicitous feeling more tightly to the crime of time itself. A technique of intensive reviewing can become a method of capturing vision in its nascency toward figuration, for rearticulating the relation of discrete forms to their own emergence. Although engaging with suspense's history as a deeply problematic genre in film history, I also use suspense as a lens through which to explore the audience's affective responsiveness, and to pursue an expanded cinema studies rearticulating narrative and non-narrative approaches to film. This is the focus of chapter 4, which considers the productive unlivability of two very different time-travel suspense films, *The Clock* and Rian Johnson's *Looper*.

Bodies in Suspense thus employs a method that Bliss Cua Lim has termed "temporal critique," to account for this affective uncertainty as the temporal force of cinema itself; this uncertainty marks temporal critique's ethical dimension of cinema as a site for thinking otherness. Lim's *Translating Time: Cinema, the Fantastic, and Temporal Critique* explores the potential of temporal critique for developing alternatives to the homogeneous time of modernity. Todd McGowan's *Out of Time: Desire in Atemporal Cinema*, like other recent work drawing on Levinas, takes a psychoanalytical approach to cinematic temporality, arguing that the "atemporal subject" of cinema repeats the founding absence of the death drive itself, via repetition as a logic of the same. *Bodies in Suspense* shifts the terrain of this debate from the ethical to the ethico-aesthetical, the paradigm Guattari suggests is most useful for understanding how affect is a "process of existential appropriation through the continual creation of heterogeneous durations of being," focused on the germinality of cinema.[9]

In the films analyzed here, two aspects in particular foreground the aesthetic aspect of the ethics of repetition: the figure of the unfaithful woman as performer, and the reflective play with cinematic form. Puzzle films, complicated narratives, atemporal cinema—these are names given to a film form that has become increasingly popular in the past decade. My focus on the cinematic "event" as the object of temporal critique argues for an alternative model of thinking about these films, one that neither dismisses nor reorients the affective force of these dysnarratives, but values that force as an opening onto an ethico-aesthetic dimension. The value of attention to affect as a mode of temporal critique is an attentiveness to minor change, the difference that emerges in repetition; this force of affect is an alternative to an "atemporal" understanding of the problems of making sense of films with complicated relations to time. Suspense is frequently understood in cinema studies as an epistemological problem; what is the potential of this, and what new approaches to imagining a cinematic knowledge might we need? As David Rodowick argues, "Time is the event defined as the ever recurring possibility for the creation of the new." *Bodies in Suspense* offers an account of these films as such events.[10]

Last, I illustrate how this eventness plays out through the *double time* of suspense, simultaneously one of movement and stasis. This special kind of movement happens when "anomalies of movement become the central point rather than accidental or contingent."[11] In Deleuze's description of the shift from the movement-image to the time-image, bodies paradoxically seem to enter into states of stasis, first through eccentric or aimless wanderings, and then through intensive modes of stillness. Does movement disappear in the time-image, or does it become intensive, rather than extensive in nature? When Dern looks across time and catches up with herself back at the beginning of the film, what do we do with the inbetween? What persists and resists? This *figural* form of suspense is traced here via the vertiginous spiral of Hitchcock's film, and from Lynch's and Dern's reanimation of the downward spiral of a "woman in trouble" (the film's tagline) into a "play of intensity" for the "whole alterity of the cosmos and for the infinity of times."

Thinking the Event of Anotherness

In *Inland Empire*, movement through the spaces, landscapes, and architectures of the film repeatedly dissolve into the intensive transitions of moving in time. This is not an architecture of memory, or a time traveling into previously actualized pastness or chronological future. It is experienced as a zone of partial embodiments, disjunct spaces and ambiguous repetitions recomposing corporeality itself. Dern's final look across time at herself is affectively coded as a look of care; the feeling of a sustainability *because of* the intensive embodiments that the film frequently presents as terrifying, exhilarating, exhausting, and violent: the vertiginous creativity of life itself. This look is doubly articulated as human gaze and as eccentric cinematic technique, deviating shot-reverse-shot into an impossible suspense of subjective and objective point of view. Dern's own doubleness is a figural image that responds to the ethical challenge of Lynch's film: How do we get there from here without losing the potential of passage itself? This is what Félix Guattari terms the "ethico-aesthetical" question: How can we attend to the body's mattering in time, its ongoing and heterogenetic renewal of our modes of being through the experience of a becoming-other, or self-modulation? For Guattari, ethical choice is implicated in the aesthetic of anotherness: "Either we objectify, reify, 'scientifise' subjectivity, or, on the contrary, we try to grasp it in the dimension of its processual creativity. . . . This 'detachment' of an ethico-aesthetic 'partial object' from the field of dominant significations corresponds both to the promotion of a mutant desire and to the achievement of a certain disinterestedness."[12] This sensational desiring disinterestedness—namely, intensity—signals the production of new modes of subjectification. This heterogenetic self-creation is the intimate and ongoing pulse of our immanence, a pulse normally muted by familiar contours of our habituated selves by positing a subjective and corporeal stability across time. Recall that for Deleuze and Guattari, desire is never for the other or for an object, but for the assemblage (*agencement*); desire is for anotherness. Anotherness names an experience of the heterogeneity of the self in time that attends to its creative and compositional qualities. Dern's auto-alterity at the end of the film, impossibly "rhymed," simply generates a new field that exceeds the boundaries of *Inland Empire*'s narrative tendencies, in a joyful explosion of disjunctive life.

The ethico-aesthetic paradigm is driven by this anotherness, an auto-alterity both plural and singular:

> I is an other, a multiplicity of others, embodied at the intersection of partial components of enunciation, breaching on all sides individuated identity and the organized body. The cursor of chaosmosis never stops oscillating between these diverse enunciative nuclei—not in order to totalize them, synthesize them in a transcendent self, but *in spite of everything, to make a world of them.*[13]

What links the ethical and the aesthetic here is world-making (eventness) as intensive livability and creative action. The goal is to "find an emergent alterfication relieved of the mimetic barriers of the self."[14] *Inland Empire*'s cinematic ecology is almost exclusively composed of this emergent alterfication, working precisely by destabilization of mimesis: of characters, the postdigital cinematic body and the sensational experience of spectators. How do we get to the irresolute end of this film: What difference does the passage itself make? How can we take seriously the shock of contact at this fold of the images of suspense, the immediating beams of light? What of the inbetween, "an inside which is merely a fold of the outside?" How does *Inland Empire* continually reactivate, rather than resolve, its suspense? This film takes place *within* emergence and processuality: the point where the film spirals around on itself isn't a closed circuit, but rather the vibratory oscillation of an exchange, a vertigo of time.

Get there from here: the problem of suspense is that of the singular, creative difference that time makes in an art of repetition like cinema, and in the art of life itself. In *Difference and Repetition*, Deleuze describes this as eccentric time or "time out of joint": "demented time or time outside the curve which gave it a god, liberated from its overly simple circular figure, freed from the events which made up its content, its relation to movement overturned; in short, time presenting itself as an empty and pure form. Time itself unfolds . . . instead of things unfolding within it."[15] It is cinema's ability to make us *live time* that marks the emergence of a cinematic body. In this book, suspense names a technic, or cinematic idea that generates such an experience of living time. Lynch's film utterly fails as a puzzle film or database narrative, where the complications and deviations of narrative unfolding can be retroactively reordered by an "active" spectator. That recompositional logic of information and order Deleuze calls "communication," characterized by spectators or recipients who are told what they are to believe.[16] Opposed to this is the event of a cinematic idea, what Deleuze terms "counterinformation," or resistance. This resistance can be understood as the creativity, or still-acting, of the heterogenizing force of duration itself, which continually proposes the idea of "this, and what else?"

Ultimately, relation in this film remains virtual and not causal.[17] No logic of causality can determinatively explain why Dern's kiss is the key to the Lost Girl's freedom, or finally resolve her multiple incarnations relative to an original. If, as William James argues, the knower is the end of an event's becoming, an after-the-fact sense making in the light of retro-spectatorship, *Inland Empire* continues to stage the event as a different kind of light.[18] *Inland Empire* is a suspense film because it draws on the creative force of the body itself: its propensity to enter into new compositions as its power of expression. The body's becomings thus immediately belong to it; it is the nature of the body to live time as becoming. That our own bodies are semblances of stability in no way contradicts this insight; rather, this opens our experience onto the minor forms of difference that characterize the body in time.

Both the beginning and ending of *Inland Empire* emerge from a beam of light, the projector's beam and the spotlight irradiating Dern as she enters the ultimate sequence of her aberrant movements in this film. This light would be misread as transcendence or escape from corporeality. From the film's start, an indiscernibility is established between cinematic and human bodies as corporealities subject to this intensive mode of being-in-light, infusing the material/corporeal with an incorporeal dimension that is fully of the body itself. Lynch's critique of Hollywood's dream machine should not be read as a reflexive exposé of the illusion of cinema itself, but as an intensification of cinema's ethico-aesthetic powers of the false. Neither ephemeral nor illusory, these powers are the affective experience of the body in time. Light is not a medium, but an immediation.

Here, light is the intensity and indetermination of the body, made perceptible for a fleeting instant as aesthetic feeling (recall Guattari's "disinterest" that doubles a mutant desire). In Lynch's work, light is never the beam of clarifying intellect radiating from a subject to make sense of a dimly confusing world. Repeatedly, light marks passage, what Gilbert Simondon calls a "phase shift," the entry into anotherness via the immanent experience of the world as becoming.[19] Suspended in light, these images show the immediacy of relation itself, the indiscretion of objects of vision in the haze of a vibrant mattering. Light is the zone of the affective engagements of the body and the world. If in *Last Year at Marienbad* (1961), the classic "time-image" film of incompossible worlds and heterochronicities, Alain Resnais painted the crisp geometry of shadows on the grounds of the château to make a clean break between bodies and environment, it only made more apparent the impossibility of marking where light shades into its other and where bodies end. Like these captured shadows, the complex temporality and permutations of corporeality in Lynch's film fold around suspended illuminations.

In cinema, light is the suspensive medium par excellence: we doubly experience what is suspended and the *feeling of suspense* itself as emergent change. Cinematic suspense gives us the image of how we are in time, the consistency of the self becoming (an)other. I term this *immediation*: suspended (re)animation. Cinematic doubleness is not a copy of reality but the immediacy of du-*pli*-cation, the felt folding of the world. This suspendedness is neither displacement nor alienation, but an infidelity to the self, understood here as the "crime of time."[20]

The "crime of time" is a minor concept in *Cinema 2: The Time-Image*, remodeled from Jean-Louis Schefer. Schefer argued that cinema's power is to make us "live time," by giving us a being without memory; this is a purloining or theft of the spectator's body, experienced as such. Schefer rejects cinematic identification: "Here I project not a sovereign consciousness but a disguised body, dressed from the start in a *prism* of minor passions, sequences of gestures, words and lighting."[21] Here, affect is an anamorphosis of form, vibrating as a play of light and refraction. The fantastic bodies onscreen are cinema's "interior being": "as if this mosaic face, made up of flakes, dust and dots, quite simply and with no possible correction, had invaded the seated being with the immense extension of a being that *has no present*, but is still exclusively tied to the mystery and horror of Time."[22] Without memory, we experience the unlived-as-yet: "In the cinema we are dealing with a new experience of time and memory which alone can form an experimental being.[23] Schefer terms this the "enigmatic body"; Schefer's translator, Paul Smith, glosses this as "the unknown center of ourselves."[24] This enigmatic body undoes our "doxical" (conventional) self-understandings. In suggesting that the "enigmatic body" of cinema has no present, I understand this as akin to Deleuze's critique of the lived body as synthesizing and habitual in nature. This is cinema's monstrous/monstrative quality, a criminal purloining of memory.[25]

But Deleuze appropriates Schefer's "crime of time" to conclude that "there is no crime but time itself."[26] If "bad" films rely on extremes of sexuality and violence as indirect expressions of a more foundational violence, "good" films, he argues, activate these forces directly, stuttering common sense toward minoritarian expressions of anotherness. Following a similar impulse, *Bodies in Suspense* reorients the generic association of suspense films with criminality, toward such an understanding of genre films as sites of tendencies opening onto new questions of what cinematic bodies can do. Here, "suspense" films subject us to "the crime of time" as the felt force of becoming.

A reimagining of what genre films do is emerging as a key direction opened up in film studies by Deleuze's work. In books such as Amy Herzog's *Dreams of Difference, Songs of the Same: The Musical Moment in Cinema*, Tom Lamarre's *The Anime Machine: A Media Theory of Animation*, Lim's *Translating Time*, Paul Gormley's *The New-Brutality Film: Race and Affect in Contemporary Hollywood Cinema*, and Elena del Rio's *Deleuze and the Cinemas of Performance: Powers of Affection*, genre theories are reactivated via forces or tendencies: in other words, in terms of what these cinematic bodies can *do*.[27] Genre films foreground problematics of time and the body, but a Deleuzian shift takes the emphasis off archival classifications and toward a diagrammatic mode of tendencies and potential. Several key issues emerge.

The first is the idea that, as Linda Williams has argued, genre films are "films that do things to bodies."[28] This analytical emphasis makes films and bodies productive. Although suspense films have traditionally been analyzed in terms of cognitive effects (as Roland Barthes once argued, "Suspense grips you in the mind, not the guts"), there is no denying that the genre relies on bodily engagements of tension and release.[29] *Bodies in Suspense* thus asks, "What are the recompositional potentials opened up by such intensive bodily engagements?"

Second, genre films make repetition and circulation into active components of analysis. Bliss Cua Lim describes genre as "a formal, social and industrial contract to repeat and to return," opening onto temporal plurality through recirculation.[30] Although genre films may seem to operate according to a logic of the same, there is actually a motor of differential repetition underpinning their repetitive pleasures. Shifting toward genre as tendencies brings out this aspect of minor difference too often dismissed, taking seriously qualitative change. Relatedly, this circulation of the film object also addresses the heterogeneous temporalities of reception, and in *Bodies in Suspense*, the question of the remake as repetition and of the effect of repeat viewing are key to a working theory of suspense as force.

The Double Time of Affect

The critical point in *Bodies in Suspense* is that the body's affective capacity emerges directly from its ability to make sensational, via a thinking-feeling, its own relation to time. Thinking-feeling is a duplicitous sensation, a "double vision," in which our habits of perception are immediately doubled by a Bergsonian real as "the continual change of form."[31] Thinking-feeling is the name Massumi gives to the doubled experience of a perception of perception. The process of becoming as emergence amid other durations is immediately doubled by a *self-enjoyment* of this process, the event's singular arc; doubling as *duplicity*. Self-enjoyment, the qualitative *how* of its singular unfolding, does not occur at a reflexive remove; rather, it redoubles the immediacy of the event's relationality, its "immediate participation in a world of activity larger than its own." The doubling makes movement itself the differential of critical thought. Duplicity displaces the dichotomies "haunting Western philosophy," such as the subject/object divide; in place of this split is "the event."[32]

Eventness, or something happening, is explored in this book as the body that Deleuze claims the direct time-image gives to a phantom, to explore the broader question of the creative compositions of cinema, affect, and bodies. Affirming rather than rejecting the subjective/objective divide, Massumi writes that "activist philosophy affirms them otherwise, reinterpreting them in terms of events and their taking-effect. Specifically, it understands them in terms of the relaying between events, in their 'successive takings.' This makes the problem of the subjective and the objective fundamentally a question of time, as implicating a multiplicity of events."[33] The affirmation as relay or successive takings makes process itself—how do we get there from here—fully part of the event. Relay is one technic of suspense this book explores, considering how movements, gestures, and relations unfold across bodies as a heterogeneous becoming in time.

Duplicity evokes simultaneously the fold (*le pli*), the copy, and the taint of the false. Describing a generative, nonrepresentational cinema, Deleuze names this duplicity of the relational and qualitative process of becoming as "the powers of the false": "There is a point of view that belongs so much to the thing that the thing is constantly being transformed in a becoming identical to point of view. Metamorphosis of the true."[34] He calls this "immanent evaluation." Meaghan Morris has described this as the "vertigo of a critical distance."[35] Duplicity is thus a double vision of an exchange of the objective and subjective within the suspensive medium of their affective contagion.

Thus *double vision* is to see form and its immediate potential for becoming other as a blur in the image, or what Barthes called its "shimmer."[36] This suspended (re)animation witnesses not the reanimation of the same, but a suspending of the already-known in favor of the emergence of the as-yet unlived. If familiar tropes such as the vampire, the zombie, or the ghost have all been employed as figures for the uncanny otherness of the cinema, such externalizations of reanimation still keep otherness at bay. A suspended (re)animation, by contrast, activates anotherness itself not through the ambivalent recognition of an externalized other, but through "giving a body to a phantom," a sensational awareness of our own creative potential for anotherness. This double vision, hazing of the world, is the perception of both the differential relation between elements and the self-referentiality of auto-affection. In *Inland Empire*, Lynch pulls apart Hollywood's mechanics to recompose becoming, decomposing relations between parts (the projector's beam, on-screen images, audiovisuality, and so on) to amplify the felt gap within the self as the force of auto-affection. Deleuze and Guattari distinguish the mechanical and the machinic, as assemblages geared toward the mechanical production of a repeatable same versus the machinic production of something new. *Inland Empire* reanimates the dead objects of the Hollywood dream factory via the factory of the unconscious, where a lived undecidability of actress and role, of studio and city, of cinema and outside places the emphasis squarely on production itself: something is happening. Double vision thus names both the affective impact of suspense, and the pedagogical imperative of suspense films.

Reinflecting the Corporeal Turn

Bodies in Suspense is itself a double vision of contemporary cinema studies, located at the intensive inbetween of two recent theoretical concerns:

the corporeal and affective turns. These are linked by the desire to tease out a rigorous approach to the intuitive feeling that spectators are not simply passive recipients but that "something is happening." Since the early 1990s, cinema studies has turned to the body as a source of renewal, through questions of spectatorial responsiveness, sensational immediacy, and the incorporative effects of audiovisual images. *Bodies in Suspense* explores the legacy of this turn: the avenues of investigation it enabled and its underdeveloped potential by linking the corporeal turn with questions of affect. Although affect is increasingly important to cinema studies to account for the spectator's embodied experience, affect's temporal dimension is rarely foregrounded, or appears as a paradoxical problem that can only be sidelined. An affective theory of cinematic corporeality requires specific attention to the body in time, understood as its creative charge of indeterminacy.

The corporeal turn initially sought to recognize the activity of the spectator's body in relation to cinema's unique modes of representing bodies on screen. Against a presumably passive spectator immobilized before the screen, the corporeal turn brought bodies as something other than inert materiality back into the picture. Building off Williams's notion of "body genres," or "films that do things to bodies," the past twenty years have seen a growing body of work dedicated to exploring the effects of sensation in cinema. Increasingly, this work argues that when the body feels, it is not the passive recipient of a preconditioned set of sensations, but is actually *doing* something.

Thomas Elsaesser and Malte Hagener have proposed that one outcome of film theory's corporeal turn is the perception that "the cinema seems poised to leave behind its function as a medium (for the representation of reality) in order to become a 'life form' (and thus a reality in its own right)." They conclude that film theory today is a "general theory of movement: of bodies, of affect, of the minds and the senses," requiring not only new ways of new knowing, but new ontologies as well.[37] In a shift from representation to an indeterminate and emergent cinematic body, the centrality of the question of the body itself needs to be rethought. *Bodies in Suspense* proposes to think the cinematic body through anotherness as the body's temporal dimension. This project aligns with

Deleuze and Guattari's ethological imperative in *A Thousand Plateaus*: "Establish a logic of the AND, overthrow ontology!"[38] I define a body first by its relationality, its "becoming" rather than its being. Gilbert Simondon defines becoming as "a perpetuated and renovated resolution, an incorporating resolution, proceeding through crises, such that its sense is in its center, not at its origin or its end."[39] The anotherness of the body thus puts process at the center of inquiry.

To inflect a history of the corporeal turn toward an investigation of this "anotherness," I briefly revisit three foundational works from the early 1990s—Williams's "Film Bodies: Gender, Genre, and Excess" (1991), Steven Shaviro's *The Cinematic Body* (1993), and Vivian Sobchack's *The Address of the Eye* (1992)—to explore the turn away from representation toward the question of what bodies might do in cinema.[40] These works articulate several key concerns. What questions were opened up beyond representing the body? How might we sketch out a concept of the film (Sobchack, Williams) or cinematic body (Shaviro)? How did the corporeal turn attempt to displace a simple active/passive divide with a careful consideration of affect and sensation? Why did these early theories not account adequately for time as the incorporeal dimension of the body? I specifically trace how they address the question of the cinematic body as a double, identifying their key questions and understanding of the body through relationality. Finally, I read Deleuze's claim in *Cinema 2*, that modern cinema "gives a body to a phantom," as an untimely intervention in the corporeal turn. As Deleuze describes a suspended body caught up in seeing without acting, he foregrounds eventness as the doubled experience of our relationality with the world. This seeing without acting, which I call the pedagogical impulse of the time-image to "look again" (double vision), is a form of intensive repetition, a direct perception of time as a reservoir of potential. My exploration of cinema's corporeal turn is motivated by the exclusion of certain experiences of corporeal intensity as "other" to film theory. What differences are made when the corporeal turn is reinflected by the eccentric energies of temporal critique?

The corporeal turn was motivated by dual desires. On the one hand, theorists sought to reclaim spectatorial agency against a passivity ubiquitous in accounts of the film apparatus or then-dominant film theory, on the grounds of the vibrant, engaged activity of the spectator's body before the screen. On the other hand, there was a desire to pose critical questions of agency that were no longer simply about control, but about the productivity of power itself. How might attention to the body reorient questions about the "illusion" of cinema toward a more productive account of cinema's ambiguous efficacy? As Vivian Sobchack summarizes this concern: "Until quite recently, however, contemporary film theory has generally ignored or elided both cinema's sensual address and the viewer's 'corporeal-material being.' Thus, if we read across the field, there is very little sustained work in English to be found on the carnal sensuality of the film experience and what—and how—it constitutes meaning."[41] The corporeal turn proposed analytical techniques that retained spectatorial experiences of affect and feeling. Each offered an alternative framework for cinema studies; for Williams, a developing Foucauldian–Freudian hybrid of films that "do things to bodies"; for Shaviro, a Deleuzo–Guattarian focus on affect via the concept of passion; and for Sobchack, an extended reengagement with phenomenology, in particular Maurice Merleau-Ponty.

Theorizing genre films' emotional machinics, Williams's influential article "Film Body: Gender, Genre, and Excess" explored the sensational experience of cinema beyond dismissing these thrills as gratuitous excess. Laying out a theory of "films that do things to bodies," Williams aligned two (at that time) rather marginalized and suspect subjects— genre film and corporeal sensation—to ask what happens at the movies: how we are moved. The film body experienced through "body genres" is a machinic production of sensation, where we witness the effective reality of cinema itself: its ability to produce visible evidence of its workings via extra-corporeal activations of arousal (porn), terror (horror), and tears (melodrama).

Excess in genre films figures as the spectacle of a (predominantly) female body in the grip of an intense emotion or sensation, an ecstasy of a body "beside itself." This "too-close" doubling of the body through ecstatic excess names the "cultural problem solving mode" of body genres, working through a nonreproductive logic of perversion as an intensified repetition that repeats the potential of difference itself. Williams problematized standard accounts of identification in genre films, particularly around gender, as productively "fluid," especially in how "low" body genres bring all spectators into "too close" mimetic contact with the excess of women's bodies themselves, through fantasy.[42] The "as-if" bodies of these fluid and oscillating identifications point to problems of sexual difference through repetition and variation of the central problem. The utopian potential of body genres thus reopens fixity precisely through generic repetition: opening onto difference.[43]

Linking genre with the body's work and exploring of a film body of produced effects (neither simply a subjective response that boils down to personal tastes, not a passive reaction to a set of mechanical impulses), Williams's intervention highlighted how the ambiguous embodiment of cinematic sensation is bound to repetition itself. Although she returned such questions to psychoanalytic accounts of fantasy, her attention to recuperating excess and the ob/scene also took a Foucauldian turn toward the question of what such effects produce. The immediacy of excess as the body beside itself, opening onto new means of thinking-feeling through intensive repetition, showed how genre films produce minor forms of anotherness. On the one hand, the repetitive and generic qualities of these films make responsiveness habitual and familiar (mechanical). On the other hand, the machinic articulation of the spectator with "films that do things to bodies" reconfigures dualisms of activity/passivity or object/subject. Films as catalytic agents participate in a bodily productiveness that exceeds mechanical determinism. Our bodies become surprising to ourselves through feeling effects as they occur. Williams's essay opened questions of how we might think determination beyond determinism, and bring to bear the question of event as it impinges on experience.

Sharing Williams's emphasis on sensation, Shaviro's self-admitted polemic *The Cinematic Body* argued for the affective immediacy of cinema as *passion*. Against a notion of lack that defused the affective charge of the cinematic encounter, passion starts from a different place than an active/passive split. He too engages the efficacy of excess, here as the "fugitive, supplemental materiality" of the image itself: "an uncanny, excessive residue of being that subsists when all *should* be lacking." This banal subsistence is an obstinate "blankness" resisting the closure of a singular meaning. This inertness, however, is doubled by Shaviro's insistence that the effect of this excess is an "endless proliferation" or repetition, "without hope of regulation or control." Thus Shaviro's text pointed toward (without fully developing) the image's *differential* persistence "in time," the source of its uncanny liveliness that he likens to an "unburied cadaver," the "insupportable image and the figure of the unique becoming anything at all."[44]

Passion, or cinematic fascination, attends to sensation to articulate the difference between cinematic and natural perception, emerging from the "automatism of perception," the camera's mechanical recordings doubled by the spectator's subjective experience. The camera's dehumanizing perception neither invents nor represents, but only records: "This passivity allows it to penetrate, or to be enveloped by, the flux of the material world." In this ecstatic fascination, images assail our senses and register as sensation *before* we can make sense of them, in an "autonomy of affect" that requires Shaviro to redefine cinematic identification. Feminist film theorists had long challenged the fixity of identification, arguing that for female spectators, identification is frequently multiple and characterized by negotiation.[45] Shaviro taps into that tradition in suggesting that all spectators are made "restless," by cinematic identification, passionally caught in movement and stasis at once:

> The subject is captivated and "distracted," made more fluid and indeterminate, in the process of sympathetic participation. Mimesis and contagion tend to effect fixed identities and to blur the boundaries between inside and outside. The viewer is transfixed and transmogrified in consequence of the infectious, visceral contact of images.[46]

Becoming transfixed and fluid (stasis + movement) in the same instance focuses on dynamic *processes* rather than identity positions. Shaviro describes this as cinema's "similarity disorder," a proliferation of "resemblances without sense or origin."[47] This undermining of identity foregrounds the spectator's body: there is a "continuity between the physiological and affective responses of my body and the appearances and disappearances, the mutations and perdurances, of the bodies and images on screen." The bodyscreen continuity effectuates a discontinuity of the self, a cinematic "passion for otherness and a vertiginous disidentification." Defining cinema as a "kind of non-representational contact, dangerously mimetic and corrosive, thrusting us into the mysterious life of the body,"[48] the body here is less ours (possession) than a source of abject otherness. This vertiginous sense of the body's otherness is the possibility of resistance to meaning.

In 2008's "*The Cinematic Body* REDUX," Shaviro critically reappraised his original's blind spots and what he terms the confusion of the aesthetic and the political in his account. He also critiques the very immediacy of his own understandings of the affective force of cinema, stating that his claim that "images confront the viewer directly, without mediation" is "exactly wrong, because it simply sides with the literal against the figurative, or with presence against mediation, instead of rejecting the binary altogether." He reorients the force of his critique against cognitive film theory with the reminder that, *pace* William James, "the cognitive—far from being opposed to the visceral or the bodily—grows out of the visceral, and is an elaboration of it."[49] If the corporeal turn critically rethought an active/passive divide to better account for the body's activity, *The Cinematic Body* prefigures its inflection with work on affect, by emphasizing the *I feel* that precedes cognition, moving from "films that do things to bodies" toward the work of cinematic affect as "what it feels like to live."[50] Here, the affect's potential is a reservoir underpinning the tip of the cognition's iceberg.

Shaviro's "similarity disorder"[51] resonates with Deleuze's idea of the fractured subject of time-image cinema in a way directly relevant to thinking the cinematic body as doubled. Deleuze writes:

> Contrary to the form of the true which is unifying and tends to the identification of a character (his discovery or simply his coherence), the power of the false cannot be separated from an irreducible multiplicity. "I is another" (*Je est un autre*) has replaced Ego=Ego.[52]

This formula certainly refers to how subjectivity, as he writes, "is never ours." But it also evokes the sense that "I is another"—a repetition—and that what repeats is difference, *not* the same. The double is the bare repetition that invites this presentiment of the virtual, the affective force that is the thin margin of chance fraying the sharp edge of every determinate actuality. Here, time is the affection of self by self, and aberrant movement is the means by which the self as difference, not consistency, appears. A closed self opens to its *in-consistency*. The body is sensational before it is perceptive; affect is the sensation of the body's own in-consistency. Despite the focus on affect, *The Cinematic Body* does not yet read the body's fugitive materiality in these terms, as the productive force of time itself, the "incorporeal yet real" that "gives a body to a phantom."

If the body gives us, as I argue, a key experience of "anotherness" when we attune to its temporal dimension, how might we think about the specific nature of a "film body's" anotherness? Sobchack's *The Address of the Eye* asked this very question, influentially reanimating phenomenological approaches (via Merleau-Ponty) to cinema, and defining a film as "an expression of experience by experience."[53] Cinema makes art by transposing the experience of being in the world, uniquely doubling our chiasmatic embodiment.[54] For her, in film we *recognize* another subject, like us in its functional embodiment. Films make embodied sense to viewers (even prior to conscious cognition) not only as objects to be understood, but as subjective perceptions of an active consciousness.[55] Thus film is not a "window on the world" (a naïve realism), but a perception through which the spectator experiences a world via another consciousness, recognizable because it seizes the world in an *intentional* manner like our own.

Sobchack's major theoretical innovation is the concept of the "film body," a way to think relations among filmmaker, technology, and spectator, and to articulate cinematic otherness as relational. We experience cinema subjectivity doubly: we *intra*-subjectively live another's perspective of the world (though the embodied perception of the film's body) and *inter*-subjectively and reflexively experience the embodied grounds of our own conditions of perception. To this end, Sobchack sees cinematic experience as essentially *dialogic*: we experience a "double occupancy"[56] of a film body, seeing the world through the eyes of the film as another subject. This doubleness is generally not problematic in its shared, outwardly directed intentionality, unless the *film's body* stands in the way (as with self-reflexive films), displacing a smoothly functional embodiment with a disruptive "echo focus" on its own embodiment, threatening to the subject.

For Sobchack, space is the primary interpretive category of film analysis (as in the concept of double occupancy), and for understanding the film body as well:

> Directly perceptible to the viewer as an anonymous "here where eye am" simultaneously available as "here where we see," the concretely embodied situation of the film's vision also stands *against* the viewer. It is also perceived by the viewer as "there, where I am not" as the space consciously and bodily inhabited and lived by an "other" whose experience of being in the world, however anonymous, is not precisely congruent with the viewer's own.[57]

This shared space does not dissolve into absolute identification; the viewer remains able to negotiate the difference in embodied perception. In this description, one sees a central concern of the corporeal turn in film studies: a validation of the active role that the sensing spectator takes in "making sense" of the film.

Sobchack's phenomenological argument privileges the consistency of everyday, functional embodiment above aberrant or unusual experiences. The very recognizability of the film body mirrors an idealized human condition—embodied, enworlded, centered, and unmarked by fatigue, disease, and eccentricities. This model is defined by the relation of the possible and the real, not the actual and the virtual, and as such limits the virtual *potential* of both film and human body. Differential or emergent embodiment, or anotherness, remains a limit here. For example, she claims, "The film presents an analogue of my own existence as embodied and significant. It is perceptive, expressive and always in the process of becoming *that being which is the conscious and reflected experience of its own expressed history.*"[58] An idealism of conscious experience here leaves little room for the efficacy of minor difference: to become in this formulation is to become what you recognize having been. Deleuze argues that in the distinction between the possible and the real, the possible falsely occupies the place of the future, when in fact it is a retro-formation from experience. Or, as Keith Ansell Pearson puts it, "It is not simply the case that the real comes to resemble or mirror the possible but rather the other way round (the possible resembles the real),"[59] precisely because the possible is merely an extrapolation of what is already inherent in the actual. Thus the possible is *not* the new and lacks the virtual's creative, destabilizing force that does not resemble the actual. "Double occupancy" in Sobchack restricts the film body's contagious, transformative potential. Throughout this book, I reimagine double occupancy as anotherness in relation to Deleuze's eccentrically moving body of the time-image.

Sobchack's insistence on the term *film body* as "empirical, not meta-phoric,"[60] was an exciting theoretical precursor to the emergent "life form" that Elsaesser and Hagener describe. The film body as the embod-ied site of a commutation between perception and expression strategi-cally sidelined the temporality of the cinematic experience, underplaying how film is not a subject as a human is, at the cost of underestimating how difference is made when cinematic subjectivity shares the space of the spectator in the process of experiencing a film. In other words, Sobchack's film body misses the *charge* of this indeterminacy by making relationality between film body and spectator secondary to the consis-tency of primary embodiment. In effect, this preservative approach knows all too well what the film body can do. Indeed, Sobchack's turn away from the film body and toward the "cinesthetic subject" in *Carnal Thoughts* suggests the aims and limitations of a phenomenological approach. A differential cinematic intrasubjectivity also requires a consideration of the *suspended* body, the effect of the body's ongoing anotherness. In developing the anotherness of the body as a conceptual approach both enabled by, but also moving beyond, the corporeal turn, I contrast a pre-servative ethics of recognition to a generative ethico-aesthetics of time; this contrast is developed in here around, on the one hand, an experi-ence of double vision as a delay or hesitation of recognition, and on the other, through a methodological hesitation of "to see or to read?"[61]

Anotherness: Movement-Visions

How might attentiveness to time reorient the focus on sensation that characterized the corporeal turn, from the experience of the spectatorial body to the event of cinema itself? What cinema gives us is not simply a representation of bodies, but a direct, *self-referential* experience of the incorporeal dimension of the body, a "movement-vision" of our own potential in relation. Double vision is such a form of movement-vision—a perception of potential itself. Affect opens up new ways of conceiving the body in terms of its temporal dimension, both drawing on, but also reorienting Williams's ecstatic body beside itself, Shaviro's similarity disorder, and Sobchack's double occupancy as descriptions of the productive effects of a cinematic doubling. How might we reopen this double vision to temporality, rather than the spatiality of double occupancy? Massumi's concept of *self-referentiality* is an alternative way to think the work of self-reflexivity in cinema. Doubles in cinema almost always provoke self-referential potential. Although I agree with Sobchack that, given that cinema cannot be *determined* by the form of its embodiment, self-referentiality ultimately lacks a demystifying force, we should not dismiss the potentially productive "re-enchantment" that this type of attention can produce, making the body a generative problem. The corporeal turn argued for the value of analytical approaches and concerns that precisely attended to vague or ambiguous experiences, not to do away with vagueness, but to ask what difference does it make to take sensation seriously?

Massumi's distinction between movement-vision and mirror-vision helps articulate a shift from understanding the double of cinema as a fixed and spatialized representation of the world (a mirror-image) to a Bergsonian "moving-mirror" as the immediacy of the past duplicitously unrolling alongside the present. Massumi argues we never see ourselves in a mirror in the way that others see us: in movement. The result will always be a blurred vision as a failure of fixity. Mirror vision, or self-*reflectivity*, is thus always static (and thus positional). Movement vision, on the other hand, or self-*referentiality*, involves the body as subject *and* object for itself, indeterminate; it is not reflective because it includes (many) other perspectives, producing a generative blur in the image as the perception of potential itself. Massumi calls this "the body without an image [a mental picture or mirror image] an accumulation of relative perspectives and passages between them," or, *an event*. Self-reflexive films are often understood as a one-way exposure, "showing the man behind the curtain"; this interpretation omits the experience's wonder and retro-forms it as illusion. Although self-reflectivity delimits vision along a single axis of sight, based on resemblance and minimizing change, self-referentiality (anotherness) concerns questions of relation: "where movement occludes both subject and object." The viewer in movement-vision is neither subject nor object, but one with the movement; Massumi describes this as "relationality, freed from its terms,"[62] intimating difference, not resemblance.

In self-referentiality, the *giveness* of relations is directly perceived, registering first in the body's activity before it registers in consciousness. Participation *precedes* recognition of distinct subjects and object. "Chances are, when all is said and done, that the subjects and objects involved will be largely what they were in previous definitions. *Largely the same but with some difference—if only by virtue of their having come to be themselves again. They will be at least as different as last is from next.*"[63] Movement-vision, the blur in the mirror, is the direct perception of the body in time: self-referentiality doubled as the body's anotherness. Movement-vision names the experience of the time-image, giving a body to a phantom ghosting the edges of the cinematic body. I turn now to Deleuze's untimely intervention around cinema's corporeal turn, to articulate affect and the body via the anotherness of time.

Arrhythmic Encounters

Semblance and Subjectivation

Arguing that "in motion a body is in an immediate unfolding relation to its own nonpresent potential to vary," a relation that is "real but abstract," Massumi notes that "this is an abstractness pertaining to the transitional immediacy of a real relation—that of a body to its own indeterminacy." Critiquing the limits of contemporary approaches to "the body," which have frequently argued for a "concreteness" of experience to counter the decorporealizing effects of abstraction, Massumi claims the real problem is that understandings of the body are not abstract enough. Every actual body is "fringed" (a Bergsonian qualification) by an incorporeal but real dimension of the virtual, a "non-present potential to vary." "Far from regaining a concreteness, to think the body in movement means accepting the paradox that there is an incorporeal dimension of the body. Of it, but not it. Real, material, but incorporeal. Inseparable, coincident, but disjunct."[64]

The charge of indeterminacy is closely linked to the double in cinema as Deleuze conceives it, a mutual image of the actual and its immediate virtual double. To "give a body to a phantom" inverts the usual order of things; a phantom is traditionally understood as divested of corporeal form, lacking in relation to a previous wholeness, a shadow of a former self. Deleuze is not arguing, however, for a restoration of presence, but for a manifestation of the abstract yet real that "fringes" the corporeal, like a charge of static electricity made visible as your hair stands on end.

The corporeal turn in part responds to a characterization of cinematic body through lack as ephemeral or illusory. Behind Deleuze's thought of the body is the Spinozist refrain: "We do not yet know what a body can do." I use *refrain* here via the refrain function from *A Thousand Plateaus*, to describe the peculiar in-consistency of the body in time, at once our home and also our most intimate means of "going outside." The refrain repeatedly constructs an existential territory: "the great refrain arises as we distance ourselves from the house, even if this is in order to return, since no one will recognize us anymore when we come back."[65] As Lone Bertelsen and Andrew Murphie point out, refrains enable "modes of living in time, not in states,"[66] allowing us to feel ourselves becoming another. Its indetermination is that of the body's incorporeal dimension, the temporal ground of our existential territories.

Attention to anotherness shifts focus from the senses that have dominated corporeal cinema theory to addressing the immediately relational quality of cinematic events. This doubling, developed via Massumi's notion of duplicity as an "artifact of. . . immediacy," starts from a different place than a subject/object divide. It thinks the body in time as a suspended (re)animation: the felt experience of becoming other to ourselves. Cinema is what Jussi Parikka, linking a renewed sense of the body's potential to ethologies, calls a "temporal machine" of another-ness, or self-variation.[67] How does Deleuze's work develop a key legacy of the corporeal turn: de-ranging the dualisms of object/subject, active/passive? I reread Deleuze's untimely intervention in the corporeal turn to explore the suspended body before turning to a wider rethinking of suspense as a tendency in cinema history.[68]

A suspended reanimation displaces the dualism of stasis and movement in favor of intensity as a *movement in stasis*, a dwelling in potential. Deleuze and Guattari write, "Voyage in place: that is the name of all intensities, even if they develop in extension. To think is to voyage."[69] Massumi has described such suspense as a "special case of movement,"[70] through the suspension events of Australian body artist Stelarc, where he hung his body from hooks for variable durations.[71] Stelarc turned skin into a gravitational landscape, making visible what is felt but rarely perceived: the body's relation to force. The aim was to render the body "obsolete," not to lose the body, but to manifest concepts that do not preexist their expression. They exhaust a certain fixed concept of the body in order to evoke its latent potential through sensation: a solicitation of the virtual. Sensation, polarized on the one end as the virtual and on the other end as potential, is the body in passage, the very image of another-ness. The body does not visibly change in this durational image of the body's "metastable" composition of relations of speeds and slownesses. Suspension events manifest "the reality of an excess over the actual,"[72] making felt the virtual doubling (a body beside itself) of an emergent actuality. What is suspended is functionality, in a forced passivity (stasis) filled with a restless "ferment." "The 'restlessness' of the body is not 'action,' since it produces no outward effect and disengages no possibility. It is a kind of activity prior to action." Or as he later puts it, "This is the zero-degree of sensation, sensation as the zero-degree of everything a body can do. Suspended animation. . . felt futurity." This "activity prior to action" I call suspended (re)animation, the anotherness of the body in time. In this vivid movement of suspense, "the body's obsolescence is its condition of change"[73] and must be pushed to the limit, because we are well habituated to daily life. This doesn't so much make a new body as render *really apparitional* the body's ongoing emergence.

A cinematic example of suspended (re)animation can be found in the brutal belatedness of 2001: A Space Odyssey's "Stargate." It activates a derangement of the body and its relations, the long drag of Astronaut Dave Bowman's suspended animation and reawakening accelerating in a developing time-image. In The Odyssey, Odysseus returns to a home of tenuous temporal suspense, the relentless linearity mapped on his aged body held in check by Penelope's making and unmaking of her tapestry as a way to buy time.[74] Time is out of joint, the proliferation of body doubles only resolved in the last instance. Astronaut Dave's body insistently produces anotherness, first by "defeating" HAL, and rebounding with a vengeance in Bowman's auto-alterity. Stargate begins with a long psychedelic sequence down the rabbit hole, alternating between Dave's POV and the same images reflected on his visor, delaying their reception in a doubled, inassimilable perception. Within his helmet, Dave shakes violently, caught up in the unlivable quality of his actual experience.[75]

All five segments of the sequence activate a suspended (re)animation as variations of the voyage in place. The first sequence creates a vivid sense of moving in place through Donald Trumbell's "slitscan" technique, frame-by-frame animation in which the camera moves toward a long slit, framing backlit transparencies of images of nature, geometric shapes, and bands of color. The resulting image "bleeds," as vivid colors and patterns streaking past on the edge of the image, as if a train window's peripheral perspective was remapped for differently configured eyes. Intercut with freeze-frame close-ups of Dave's face, the disjunctive contrast of stasis and vivid motion is striking. In the second segment, abstract images, indifferent galaxies, primordial ooze, or the body's interior replace the slitscan animation, effects created by filming differently colored liquids and oils in a drum, literally images of suspension. Macro- and microperceptions, inner and outer space are indistinct, the human body failing to stabilize a sense of scale. In the third segment, the last of his "journey," traveling aerial shots of alien landscapes alternate with close-ups of Dave's eye in a cross contagion of bizarre coloration, rendering even definable landscapes (for example, what could be a desert, or the Grand Canyon) eerie and unrecognizable. Finally, the extreme close-up of Dave's eye reappears, each blink changing the image's tinting.

Although clearly a journey, it would be inaccurate to suggest that there is a narrative progression here; rather it is a series of irrational cuts.

Dave's eye finally restabilizes in "normal" color; we might imagine that having survived the passage, he has recovered his stable form. The fourth segment finds Dave (and his space capsule as well) in a Louis XVI-style bedroom. Shots leapfrog from one stage of life to the next in an elliptical continuity, bumping one version of Dave in favor of the next until he is an elderly, bedridden man, but always initially respecting a Bazinian *montage interdit*, with both versions of Dave visible in the same shot.[76] This begins with the close-up of the eye, followed by a POV wide shot of the bedroom from within the capsule; we hear the hollow sound of Dave's breathing within his helmet. Two exterior medium shots of the capsule follow from within the empty bedroom. We return to Dave's POV; he sees an older version of himself standing in the bedroom, outside of the capsule. Jump cuts take us into a close-up of the older version of Dave. We never return to Dave 1, and although the two occupy space simultaneously, when Dave 2 registers the younger, all trace of 1 (including his capsule) disappears; this pattern repeats four times. Each time, a subjective perspective is repeatedly established (framed by his spacesuit or the edge of his ear) and immediately evacuated, his "future" self's POV cancelling a return to the initial POV, a bumping-off of incompossible bodies through jump cuts with a brief, temporal overlap: an actualization of déjà vu. To see one's double traditionally foreshadows death; these jump cuts instead produce a suspended reanimation as a stuttering toward death.

In the final version of Dave, an old bedridden man is replaced by a fetus/starchild in a glowing, transparent bubble. The final segment bookends the film's opening shot, tracking downward from the planet in space until a left pan reveals the floating star child (on a planetary scale). Dave's untenable, mutated body has been bumped in favor of what Val Hartouni has called the "fetal astronaut" as ideal human subject.[77] The Stargate sequence makes sensible the passage from virtual to actual; its tremendous violence and de-rangement of perspectives and the double underlines that the body in time is a composition of competing speeds and slownesses. Dave's suspended animation thus becomes the spectacular suspension of the everyday, lived body, not as superhuman indifference to the body, but as an intensification of its obsolescence in "emergent alterfication."

Massumi argues that suspense is a special case of movement, where movement is not action, but "the activity before action."[78] With mounting intensity, Dave lives the effect of movement-vision displacing mirror-vision in his encounter with his own double. In this long sequence we cannot definitively resolve what we see along a single axis of sight, despite, or indeed, because of the sequence's foregrounding of POV shots. Movement-vision displaces the threatening and objectifying gaze of the other by starting from a different point than the object/subject divide. It is thus not about becoming the object of an other's gaze. Instead, the self-referentiality of movement-vision starts from the point of view of the other in me, the felt sensation of anotherness as the difference made by passage. The multiplicity of points of view in movement-vision is not an accumulation of relative perspectives, but the making sensible of the movement of change. This is the blur in (movement) vision itself.

Another name for this blur? Semblance. In *Semblance and Event*, Massumi develops the concept of semblance to describe the sensational temporality of the event itself. Semblance is "the form in which what does not appear effectively expresses itself, in a way that must be counted as real;" Massumi notes that "the importance of what doesn't appear is, of course, the past and the future." Semblance is the "lived expression of the eternal matter of fact that is time's passing." Semblance makes "really apparitional" becoming itself. We see form with and through virtual potential, blurring crisp and inert outlines with the precision of the inexact, the undoing of the point of the single axis of vision.[79] As Deleuze and Guattari note, anexactitude is "the exact passage of that which is underway."[80]

The powers of the false, as a mode of immanent evaluation rather than transcendent judgment, generates a POV so closely coupled to its object that it sparks a "becoming identical to point of view. Metamorphosis of the true."[81] This multiplicity in mutation of the object, undoing the spatialized stability of reference in favor of an eccentric POV of time, is the underwayness of the event itself. This "metamorphosis" is a "vitality affect" of sensed becoming. Semblance, despite the connotation of a second-order reality, or irreality, is not the ghostly trace of a past event, defined by resemblance. Massumi likewise points out that subject and object do not map onto knower and known, citing William James's contention that the knower is the "end of the experience's becoming." In the key films in this study, the suspension of knowedge and the refusal to identify a "knower" is consistently delayed as the film's affective motor, and its eventful openness, mattering beyond narrative resolution. The narrative form of the cinematic body itself is made "obsolete." Temporal disruption not only destabilizes narrative conventions and the work of identification on the part of viewers and of characters; objects transformed by the POV of the viewing subject acquire a lively force of metamorphosis. Objects, Massumi writes via Whitehead, are the immediate past, as "activity that has been left over in the world by previous events of change and that can be taken up by a next event for taking-in to its self-creation."[82] They retain a creative contagion in their abilty to act as lures for relation. Thus the object, which is best understood in Simondon's terms as "metastable," is both pastness (what it has been) and the opening onto the future (what it could become). The indeterminate liveliness of objects is not only the object of an immanent, revelatory power of cinema, but part of a self-enjoyment of a cinematic body as well.

With the concept of semblance, Massumi's language provocatively foregrounds the powers of the false and reroutes them away from their negative and even criminal orientation; as in Deleuze, this generative falseness names a creative recomposition. Semblance is felt when things are suspended from their utility; Massumi makes this argument in the context of redefining "interactivity" not as the ability of a subject to act upon an object, but as the duplicitous sensation of a re-worlding, the event's unfolding and the self-enjoyment of the event in an affective attunement. Conceptually, semblance comes from Suzanne Langer, when "the body is capacitated but this capacity has nowhere else to go. It's in suspense."[83] In Massumi's reading, this charging of capacity does not reflexively reconfirm what we already know, but activates the powers of the false as the emergence of the new. The self-referentiality of experiencing eventness is felt as "duplicity," yet another term laden with criminal intent. In a twist, duplicity carries the charge of "folding" (*le pli*) with the implications of the Deleuzian diagram of Foucault's folds, which cannot start from an interior/exterior divide, since the fold itself makes an interior of the exterior. Semblance and duplicity displace the connotation of a second order of representation or copying with the directly expressive powers of the false.

As Gregory Flaxman has argued, over the course of his life Deleuze abandoned the notion of the simulacrum, as "a copy without a model" and a first figure of his rejection of representation, because it "precludes" the creation of sci-phi, a genuine fabulation of the future: "The birth of the simulacrum is also the moment of its death, for its very existence renders the terms of its definition effectively meaningless: what would a 'copy' mean anymore—and why invoke a language that remains beholden to the dead model?" This shift occurs as Deleuze realizes that there is no need to "blow up" representation, because it has already failed. What we need now are reasons to believe in the world. Flaxman cites Cinema 2 to explain how the powers of the false affirm the generative force of creativity itself: "Affirmation is itself a creative act: 'to believe is to affirm the powers of fabulation, for only when we affirm the power to 'make-false' (faire-faux) do we surpass the true and the false and undertake the whole transformation of belief."[84] This re-enchantment of the world is frequently figured in Deleuze through the wasted bodies of philosophers and artists, and in Cinema 2, through the suspended body of the seer who is no longer the actor. These are the lived ravages of the crime of time, images of passage itself. In this way, Deleuze's later work figures the effects of duplicity not in terms of the degraded copies of the simulacrum, but through form doubled by affect itself.

A cinematic doubling heightens the question of time, activating the aberrant movement within a mirror-vision via affective sensation. The differential of the double can produce this estrangement, a pausing in the normal activity of perception and reaction. The verbal stumble of Rimbaud's declaration: "I is an other" ("je est un autre") activates the powers of the false, as irreducible multiplicity displacing the "form of the true."[85] Guattari's schizoanalysis approaches modes of subjectification from a psychosis that "denudes" the "ordinary modelisation of everyday existence." He writes that what finds itself fragilised, cracked up, schizzed, in delire or hallucinating when confronted with the status of the objective world, is the point of view of the other in me, the recognized body in articulation with the lived body and the felt body, these are the normalized coordinates of alterity which give their foundation to sensible evidence.[86]

How would attuning to our inherent alterity help us understand a "cinematic body" as a body in time? Cinema, long thought of as a double as representation of reality, acquires a body when the powers of the false displace the "form of the true," and the human body is no longer the standard measuring stick of relation. Deleuze reminds us that no matter how familiar it feels in its quotidian experience, cinema is not an analogue for human perception; more than one hundred years of cohabitation hasn't exhausted the potential for surprise. Cinematic perception is always doubled by the othering potential of affect.

Movement-vision must thus be reread in terms of relations of times, rather than in terms of stabilized position. Deleuze's contribution to the corporeal turn is the suspended immediated body of the time-image. This suspense is immediately double. On the one hand, it is the suspension of action that accompanies the intensity of affect itself. Rather than the lived body, its vitalism repeats as a difference or newness, even the minor form of difference that is the body in time. This passive vitalism, as Deleuze and Guattari state (via Raymond Ruyer) "is, but does not act": "the contraction it preserves is always in a state of detachment in relation to action or even to movement and appears as a pure contemplation without knowledge."[87] "What it feels like to live" thus does not immediately translate into action.

On the other hand, this passivity is also a self-creation, or self-enjoyment. Again, in *What Is Philosophy?*, Deleuze and Guattari state that "it is the brain that says I, but I is an other," displacing recognition or identification with "a state of survey without distance, at ground level, a self-survey that has no chasm, fold or hiatus escapes." Here, sensation is "pure contemplation, for it is through contemplation that one contracts, contemplating oneself to the extent that one contemplates the elements from which one originates. Contemplating is creating, the mystery of passive creation, sensation. . . . It is "enjoyment" and "self-enjoyment."[88]

Self-enjoyment is a contemplation of relation itself. Thus, there is no turning away in self-reflexivity, no separation to a critical remove. Self-referentiality produces a vertiginous distance that is an immediate doubling. It is prior to an agent, except that we have to think of this "prior" not as an ontological origin, but in terms of Deleuze's insistence that we continually rediscover duration. The unlived/relived body of cinema is neither material trace of a former presence, nor an artificial human, but its own anotherness. The past and future are made "really apparitional" as semblance, doubling the immediacy of the event itself. Semblance is thus a self-referentiality, an aberrant "movement-vision" that in Deleuze's cinema books is discussed in terms of the double, a mutual-image that includes the point of view of anotherness in me.

The double of movement-vision is de-forming, even in the minor sense of understanding objectivity (the state of being an object) as a form of persistent repetition. To live time is to be de-formed as an intensive re-composition: the identity of the thing and its difference as a double movement is figured throughout *Cinema 2* in the chapter "The Crystals of Time" as Deleuze's own suspended figure of the double. In this hesitation between the double and that of the reflection to characterize the splitting of time, we see his question "What is a mutual image?" and his response: the (unequal) exchange between an actual image and its immediate virtual double. He asks, "Should not the opposite direction have been pursued? Contracting the image instead of dilating it. Searching for the smallest circuit that functions as internal limit for all the others and that puts the actual image beside a kind of *immediate, symmetrical, consecutive or even simultaneous double.*" Almost immediately, he proposes an alternative that hesitates between double or reflection: "If we take this direction to its limit, we can say that the actual image itself has a virtual image which corresponds to it like a double or a reflection." At other times, the reflection seems to predominate to avoid an independent coexistence of the double: "It is as if an image in a mirror, a photo or a postcard came to life, assumed independence and passed into the actual, even if this meant that the actual image returned into the mirror and resumed its place in the postcard or photo, following a double movement of liberation or capture." In a footnote to that chapter, he cites a discussion of Tod Browning's work in relation to the actor as a source of this hesitation—double or reflection?—undecidably caught in a "spectacle-reality distinction": "Rather than a double, it is a matter of reflection, a reflection that exists only because of someone else's gaze, while, beneath the mask, the face lives in shadow." Last, Deleuze seems concerned to contain any independence or externality of the double by assimilating it to a reflection, citing Jean Ricadou: "The putting into abyss (*mise en abyme*) does not redouble the unit, as an external reflection might do; in so far as it is an internal mirroring, it can only ever split it in two, and subject 'it to the infinite relaunch of endlessly new splitting'"; summarizing this in a footnote: "Sabatier says: it is a reflection, not a double."[89]

This hesitation marks Deleuze's concern to avoid suggesting that the double is an external projection of an inner state, in which only one is "real." Ultimately, the double in *Cinema 2* figures the difference between self and an other, but in the gap produced when "I is an other." This splitting, however, is simultaneously a folding, best described in Deleuze's *Foucault* in terms of the affect of self by self. "Memory" names this relation, not personal memory as a "recollection-image," but "an absolute memory of the past that is preserved, but which must be forgotten in order to be rediscovered or relived": an oblivion founded in being.[90] The figure of the double is fundamentally one of disfigurement, folding the past against the future and suspending the present:

> This double is never a projection of the interior; on the contrary, it is an interiorization of the outside. It is not a doubling of the one, but a redoubling of the Other. It is not a reproduction of the Same, but a repetition of the different. It is not the emanation of an "I," but something that places in immanence as always other or a Non-self. It is never the other who is a double in the doubling process, it is a self that lives me as the double of the other: I do not encounter myself on the outside, I find the other in me.[91]

Topologically figuring the folding of the Outside as "the act of doubling in sewing: twist, fold, stop, and so on," Deleuze puts the double in suspense; the body in time is such a double as the du-*pli*-city of the folding itself.

When Deleuze states that the direct time-image gives a body to a phantom, it raises the question: What can such a body do? This question is especially urgent, given that much of the time-image is devoted to a discussion of the suspension of action. Throughout *Cinema 2*, there is a repeated evocation of the *sensation* of suspense—as an oscillation or vibration. This suspense is filled with movement at the same time that it renders movement aberrant, delaying activity. If a classic definition of suspense is "narrative withholding" as suggested by Roland Barthes in *Image-Music-Text*, something different happens in time-image films, connected to the eccentric quality of their narration. Delay becomes not just a withholding to be eventually released, but a paradoxical alternation between movement and stasis that can allow for the emergence of something unanticipated, not simply a filling in of the blank. The body is not simply fleshed out. Massumi describes the "autonomy" of affect as "a suspension of action-reaction circuits and linear temporality in a sink of what might be called 'passion,' to distinguish it from both passivity and activity."[92] This suspension distinguishes affect from emotion, defined as qualified affect; emotion contains affect's charge of indeterminacy.

Affect thinks the body in passage, not position, but this passage is deforming, producing not forms but what Deleuze calls "Figures." Not a reference to an object, as in figuration, the Figure "is a form that is connected directly to a sensation, and that conveys the violence of that sensation directly to the nervous system."[93] Here, the event is the "sensation of point of view as variation."[94] As Tom Conley puts it, "An event is a space-time in and by which the possible is pulverized. It causes a destruction of mimetic process, recovery or even memorialization."[95] Deleuze describes the Figure as a kind of spasm—a violent movement in place. In painting, this is achieved through a chiasmus of figure and ground, through eccentric elements, and through color. But in cinema, movement is no longer in the mind of the spectator, as in painting, but available onscreen. For both Schefer and Deleuze, this marks the shift from painting to cinema, especially in terms of the Figure. Schefer continues to investigate this through the figure of the monstrous. Deleuze, however, uses the figure of repetition itself as monster and monstrating, attentive to the medium itself. As Peter Canning describes it:

> What makes the image move is life-time, the feeling or intuition of being alive as "the indiscernible passage between image, the transition from one sensation to another" experimentation in affect, mutual affectations of living beings, the affects or powers of plants and minerals, means experiencing the inorganic life of things, the immanent animation of all matter-energy.[96]

This lifetime is "a" life, the impersonal.

In the corporeal turn, sensation has been one way to understand that images are more than a secondhand reality, and a return to the sensing body sought to rearrange what counts as knowledge. How should we understand that affective, sensational side of cinema? Does it adequately present the experience of a lived body, so that the spectator experiences a sympathetic vibration, a *recognition*? Or, is recognition the wrong model, subordinating difference to the logic of identity? In *Cinema 2*, Deleuze posits the body as an image, yet also repeatedly evokes mirroring in his discussion of the crystal image, in which mirror image and body are in a relationship of an undecidable exchange: a vibratory circuit or a passionate in-difference. It is not that bodies are actual and images are virtual, but the dynamic yet non-indifferent exchange creates an indiscernibility that doesn't collapse into utter indetermination. Instead, the double signals the felt splitting of time. The time-image does not represent time, but concerns how, as Jean Louis Schefer puts it, "the final reality of these images consisted in making us *live time*."[97]

How does the idea of "living time" illuminate Deleuze's claim that "the direct time-image is the phantom which has always haunted the cinema, but it took modern cinema to give a body to this phantom?" A commonsense understanding might read this as a concretization of cinema's ephemerality. Lynch's projector beam, for example, may simply visibly embody that which for too long has simply haunted cinema, its material substrate (as with Shaviro's excess of the unburied corpse): at the moment of celluloid's decline, it reanimates as zombie. However, to "give a body" in Deleuzian terms is rather to give a capacity to affect and to be affected; a body has both corporeal and incorporeal dimensions. If the incorporeal dimension of the body is its felt becoming, the indetermination of a cinematic body restores an ambiguous status to matter itself. In film studies, the affective turn emerges from the limitations of a linguistic model that could not account for the directly signaletic matter of cinema itself and the intensity of prelinguistic, precognitive sensation. Indeed, Deleuze's cinema books directly reject the idea that cinema is a language, needing to be broken down in order to understand how meaning is produced. Instead, cinema means directly as an utterable, not an utterance: "a composition of images and of signs, that is, a pre-verbal intelligible content (pure semiotics)."[98] What, then, is a method that can productively engage with this semiotics, and that participates in the cinematic pedagogy of making us live time?

Intuition as the Method of Suspense

In *Cinema 2*, Deleuze begins his analysis by evoking Bazin, but critiques him as posing a false problem at the level of a reality "out there" as the raw material of cinema, when the problem should be posed at the level of the mental as an encounter with a directly intelligible matter itself, what he terms "opsigns" and "sonsigns."[99] Deleuze gives Bazin pride of place in thinking the *false* problem of cinema, that of an (admittedly impossible) teleology that would allow "more" of the real to break through the artifice of cinema, but critiques Bazin for not attacking the real problem of cinema's direct, presentational potential, how it makes us "live time."[100] Deleuze employs a Bergsonian method of intuition to understand the *true* problem of cinema to ask, what mode of existence do different types of cinema make possible?[101] Henri Bergson proposed intuition as the best method to attend to change as an ongoing "rediscovery" of duration: our recurrent takings of time that suspend everyday experience and put us back in contact with "other durations, above and below our own."[102] Intuition "should be able to overcome the dualisms of ordinary language and, at the same time, to give a new truth to things, a new distribution, an extraordinary arrangement."[103] Crucially, it is also a method for *rediscovering* (and not merely *uncovering*) duration as the creative force of becoming. I use this last insight to clarify the "duplicity" of duration itself. Intuition rediscovers and returns to our own duration as essentially relational (freed from its terms); it returns us to the middle of things where we already are in a movement that we can only ever repeat. Intuition, as Deleuze describes it, gives us a way to understand the suspended nature of the "cinema of the seer, no longer the actor," via Deleuze's claim that time is not "in us," but rather that "we are in time." This is a duplicity of anotherness itself, the "affection of self by self."[104]

As a method, intuition is nonrepresentational; it does not double the world as copy, but rather, to borrow Simondon's term, is a *dédouble-ment* or dephasing that produces a new arrangement. This is why intuition is a *return*: "We rediscover the immediate because we must return to find it."[105] Intuition intimately relates to the Bergsonian form of time as the "pure past" preserved in its entirety, not the past in the guise of recollection-images. The Bergsonian splitting of time between a present that passes and a past that is preserved is a central preoccupation for Deleuze in *Cinema 2*, figured as the "moving mirror" of the preserved past alongside the passing present, or a "mutual image." The counter-intuitive claim that we return to, rather than start from, the immediate, avoids conflating the immediate with the present: "at every instant the movement is no more—being is not made up of presents." The simultaneity of the present that passes and the past that is preserved is the foundation of the "unforeseeable and the contingent": the virtual itself.[106] As such, intuition is the "vertigo of a critical distance" in practice, as it locates us "in the things themselves, rather than outside":

> We are separated from things; the immediate datum is not immedi-
> ately given; and yet, we cannot be separated from things by a pure
> accident, by a mediation that comes from us and concerns us only: it
> is necessary that the de-naturalizing movement be in the things them-
> selves, *that the things begin losing themselves before we lose them, that
> oblivion be founded in being itself.*[107]

I discuss the question of the "oblivion founded in being" in relation to Nietzsche's discussion of man as the animal that makes promises in *On the Genealogy of Morals* in chapter 4. Intuition, time images of the direct experience of percepts and affects, differs from an intellectual method focused on action, seen in the movement-image of the functional "perception—affection—action" circuit. As art, cinema is a direct experience of becoming itself. Deleuze and Guattari write that "by means of the material, the aim of art is to wrest the percept from perceptions of objects and the states of a perceiving subject, to wrest the affect from affections as the transition from one state to another."[108] Through a suspension of action, intuition de-ranges functionalist distinctions between subjects and objects, undoing the functional limitations of perception and placing us back in the "immediate datum."

Intuition as a method of suspense allows the zone of indeterminacy between perception and action to expand and persist. When Deleuze qualifies the cinema of the time-image as a "cinema of the seer, not the actor" (*"le voyant, non plus l'actant"*), he evokes that suspense as intuition's abyss, a return to the fundamental movement of matter itself.[109] Critically, this seer is divested of the power to act, living (or unliving) a "fracture in the 'I.'" Intuition, unlike the spatializing and distributive force of the intellect, topologizes relations; interiority is opened to the outside even as the outside is made interior through a fold. Duration, which is subjective, can be understood as not internal to the subject, but where the subject is internal to duration: "We are in time."[110] This awareness stems from the sensational intuition of other durations than our own, and the modification of our own duration in affective relation.

Thus duration is a "tension" emerging from the suspended indistinction between our own duration and that of others. The intensity of this experience is suspense as a special case of movement: the affective mode of time itself. Intuition as method of suspense attends to this tension as "the difference itself of the thing, what Bergson often calls the 'nuance.'"[111] Nuance has two senses: as a *qualitative* difference, the continual nudging of difference that is being, and its connotative sense of vagueness, an awareness that can be sensed but not measured. This vagueness is not the commonsense notion of intuition as a fuzzy concept, but a rigorous methodology: "neither a feeling, an inspiration, nor a disorderly sympathy" but a productive "felt moreness" to experience, a blur in vision.[112]

As nuance, intuition defers the distribution of identities, seeking the duplicity of difference itself: "the immediate is precisely the identity of the thing and its difference":[113]

> Intuition leads us to go beyond the state of experience towards the conditions of experience. But these conditions are neither general nor abstract. They are no broader than the conditioned: they are the conditions of real experience. Bergson speaks of going: "to seek experience at its source, or rather above that decisive turn, where, taking a bias in the direction of our utility, it becomes properly human experience."[114]

Deleuze sums this up: "to open us up to the inhuman and superhuman . . . to go beyond the human condition."[115] The body of the time-image is thus the suspended (re)animation of a body in time. "Intuition . . . is the movement by which we emerge from our own duration, by which we make use of our own duration to affirm and immediately recognize the existence of other durations, *above or below us*."[116] Above or below us: the immediacy of this recognition is figured as a suspension.[117] This affirmation of other durations via our own duration is what Deleuze calls the "affect of self by self." This suspense oscillates between two poles: the relived body as the suspension between the present that passes and the past that is preserved (and returns), and the unlived as yet as a "felt futurity," an "unexperiencing" of experience. Massumi identifies this "unexperiencing" as the paradox of the virtual:

> Imagination is the mode of thought most precisely suited to the differentiating vagueness of the virtual. It alone manages to diagram without stilling. Imagination can also be called intuition: a thinking-feeling. Not feeling something. Feeling thought—as such, in its movements, as process, on arrival, as yet unthought-out and unenacted, postinstrumental and preoperative. Suspended, looped out. Imagination is felt thought, thought only-felt, felt as only thought can be: insensibly unstill.[118]

The body of the time-image activates, through a duplicitous intuition of other durations via our own (our anotherness), the virtual, incorporeal dimension of the body. Deleuze writes, "It is through the body (and no longer through the intermediary of the body) that cinema forms its alliance with the spirit, or thought,"[119] in an intuitive overcoming of the dualism (such as body/ spirit) of ordinary language. Beyond the lived body, the body in time is the abstraction of process itself; as Massumi describes this:

> Since the virtual is unlivable even as it happens, it can be thought of as a form of superlinear abstraction that does not obey the law of the excluded middle, that is organized differently but is inseparable from the concrete activity and expressivity of the body. The body is as immediately abstract as it is concrete; its activity and expressivity extend, as on their underside, into *an incorporeal, yet perfectly real*, dimension of pressing potential.[120]

An experience of the incorporeal yet perfectly real is the body in time, in the form of this superlinear abstraction. The superlinear describes the interference effect of the nonlinearity of the narrative and experimental works explored in this book.

Remakes and Free Replays

Anotherness in Action

Chapter 1, "A Free Replay: *Vertigo* and the Spiral of Time" explores *cinematic theories of suspense* through the work of Alfred Hitchcock. I first define suspense as a special case in movement by reading affective suspense as the generative experience of "reworlding" and through narrative theories of suspense and their detours into the criminal forms like anomalous or "recidivist" suspense. Working off of the figural form of *Vertigo*'s spiral that serves as the film's refrain, I characterize suspense as the "aberrant movement" of time-images and bodies in time. This is best understood not simply in generic terms, but as tendency, the "perceptual feeling" of the body's indeterminacy. I reorient the association of suspense with narratives of criminality (and an attendant logic of truth and revelation) toward Deleuze's contention that "there is no crime but time itself." The crime of time is often figured as an ex-corporative theft of bodily control and mobility, either of the spectator's autonomy of reaction and extension into action, or through the paralytic suspense of characters on screen. This is a passional possession by affect. I ask, What are the forms of superlinear abstraction that keep *Vertigo* working as a film beyond narrative resolution? How does *Vertigo* provoke cinephilic repetition through its indistinction of body and ecology that characterizes the body in time? How does *Vertigo* figure the body itself as a time machine or recording device of indeterminate liveliness? These are questions that travel across the concerns of this book.

To answer this I explore the pedagogy of *double vision* that suspense produces. I address Hitchcock's place in contemporary debates around a post-medium condition via Thomas Elsaesser's question "Why Hitchcock now?" first via experimental remakes of Hitchcock's work such as Johan Grimonprez's *Double Take* (2009) and Douglas Gordon's *24 Hour Psycho* (1993), developing a double vision of the cliché of "Alfred Hitchcock, master of suspense" that moves from generic questions to a figural analysis of suspense via the circulation of Hitchcock's own body.[121] I explore the force of "a body too much" through the doubled body of Kim Novak as Madeleine and Judy, to open questions of the decentered intensities of actor and character, cinematic and spectator body, and the transversal arc of affect across bodies that *Vertigo* effectuates.

An exemplary text for thinking suspense as "the crime of time," *Vertigo* demonstrates the difficulties of defining suspense in Barthes's terms as that which is "made right in the end."[122] Suspense's aberrant movement is a deforming delay of meaning; the figural as the delay of lost time. Suspense's affective force activates a pedagogic dimension of remaking, repetition and reviewing opened up by *Vertigo* as a film located at the fold of the movement-image and the time-image. Alain François and Yvan Thomas describe "pure optical cinema" (time-images) as a pedagogic cinema, what I call a *free replay*, arguing that it is not attentive recognition but memory failures and failed recognitions that are the equivalent of the pure op/son sign.[123] In *Cinema 2*, and in many readings of that work, there is a supplementary move toward abstract or experimental filmmaking as the example of the "pure op/son" sign. But *Vertigo*'s pedagogy is minor difference—what it means to be "in time"; this suggests that narrative cinema can likewise be thought and taught as pure op/son signs, when the conventions of form are distorted by intensity. Here, recognition fails us in the face of what seems most familiar. This is a Deleuzian pedagogy of "doing with" rather than the mimetic and didactic relation typically affiliated with Hitchcock's work.

Hitchcock is not only regarded as exemplary of cinematic suspense, but as an expert theoretician; his understanding of suspense is constantly cited as the conventional norm. Despite this, Hitchcockian suspense in practice and in theory are very different things. I use the spiral motif found everywhere in *Vertigo* as an exemplary form of suspense as a special case of movement. For Deleuze, Hitchcock is a hinge between the movement-image and the time-image because of this suspension of action that his emergent image of thought entails; as David Rodowick puts it, "For Deleuze, to withdraw perception from action means putting it into contact with thought."[124] Hitchcock has been a critical figure in relating Deleuze's cinema books to cinema studies; the importance of his works at the close of *Cinema 1* marks a kind of break as the completion of the modality of the movement-image itself via the emergence of a relation-image. I argue, however, that this placement is significant not as a means of relegating Hitchcock to the realm of the movement-image, but because it displays the technical potential of Hitchcock's work for Deleuze. This is the second way that I read *Vertigo* in terms of cinematic doublings, as an example of what Deleuze calls a "mediator," a film that asks the spectator to "do with."[125] At the heart of this contention is Chris Marker's argument that *Vertigo* is fundamentally about the problem of a "free replay"; I argue that the demands the narrative break in *Vertigo* places on the spectator via the play of doubles and ambiguously shared modes of embodiment open precisely onto a technique of repetition that foregrounds an alternative relation to time.

Chapters 2 and 3 take off from *Vertigo*'s repetition in remakes: Lynch's Hollywood trilogy and Ye's *Suzhou River*. Both Lynch's and Ye's films remake *Vertigo*, via (sampled) content and a *Vertigo* effect of double vision and duplicity. Like Novak's double performance as Judy and Madeleine, both *Suzhou River* and Lynch's trilogy feature the same actress playing a dual role (in *Lost Highway*, Patricia Arquette plays first Renée and then Alice, in *Mulholland Drive* Naomi Watts and Laura Haring both have two versions of themselves, and in *Inland Empire* Dern is both Nikki and Sue, while in *Suzhou River* Zhou Xun plays both Mudan and Mei Mei). The nature of these characters' identities and relation to each other is a key question throughout the films. *Lost Highway* explicitly contains specific references to *Vertigo*, such as a restaging of Scottie's dream, and makes the spiral motif of Scottie's vertigo the structural element of the film as a whole. In the case of *Suzhou River*, critics have noted that the film's score is reminiscent of Bernard Hermann's "Tristan and Isolde" influenced score for *Vertigo*. Why are these more than intertextual references? I argue that both Lynch's and Ye's films respond to *Vertigo*'s suspense as demanding a Deleuzian repetition; they are a particular case of the remake as repetition.

Across these films, I return to the notion of the crime of time and the duplicitous woman as a means of addressing the question of "how we are in time." The duplicitous woman becomes a key for the figural analysis of cinematic bodies: the doubled body of the actress (Novak) in her dual role, the emergence of a "conceptual persona" between Scottie, Madeleine/Judy, and an emergent camera consciousness, and last the play of animation throughout the film. The suspenseful uncertainty these bodies generate is fundamentally a problem of time, as anomalous suspense demonstrates. I also consider how temporal critique inflects feminist film criticism in relation to *Vertigo*, and as a precursor to the consideration of the femme fatale in Lynch. His films are coming to occupy a place not dissimilar to that of Hitchcock in relation to feminist film theory in the 1980s, via the ambivalent fascination of the female lead(s). The doubled role of the actress is intimately linked to questions of cinematic form, the narrative break and what it means to get productively "lost in the medium" of the body in time.

This potential has, over the three films of the Hollywood trilogy, become the obsessively repeated focus of Lynch's work. The trilogy has made increasingly apparent the ethico-aesthetical stakes of Deleuze's claim that there is no crime but time itself. Merging the suspect criminality of the female lead with the female body as the site of criminal intent, by the third iteration of the tale, *Inland Empire*, Laura Dern's character lives (and lives through) the crime of time as intensive becoming. Chapter 2, "Into the Folds: David Lynch's Hollywood Trilogy," reads across this triptych of remakes, both as remakes of Hitchcock's *Vertigo* and, transversally, of each other. In these films, I look at immediation as becoming "lost in the medium," through a consideration of delay as a form of narrative, but more important, affective suspense. Beginning with *Lost Highway*, I read the trilogy as a whole as a kind of resonance chamber, a molecular remaking of *Vertigo* where that film's narrative break and rebeginning is replayed at the level of intensive micro-repetitions. Lynch's next two films, 2001's *Mulholland Drive* and 2006's *Inland Empire*, remake Lynch's own work, through the major narrative break and rebeginning, the doubled body/role of the female lead(s), and a meditation on our lived relation to media technologies via the figure of the unfaithful woman. Through a depersonalizing decomposition of the female actress, Lynch's trilogy intensifies the really apparitional experience of the incorporeal dimension of the body: in other words, what it feels like to live the body's own indeterminacy. I reject the contemporary categorization of these works as belonging to an emerging genre of "puzzle films" or complex narratives, in favor of an attention to the minor change of the remake as repetition, as best offering a model of the body appropriate to the work of temporal critique.

The Hollywood trilogy takes place during a "corpse time" of the already lost. Deleuze argues that in the time-image, redemption comes too late (for the individual figure), but also expresses the audio-visual image as "event." I read for this "positivity" of Lynch's critique through three things. First, I explore audiovisual architectures in the trilogy, to read passage itself in Lynch's work. Second, I return to my own definition of the figural as "getting lost in the medium," to explore the disappearance into the medium across these films, as with Fred Madison's suspension in the space of intercom message he impossibly sends to himself in *Lost Highway*. Last, I examine the femme fatale as conceptual persona in these works, reassessing this iconic figure for what her indeterminate embodiment as a cinematic force tells us about the powers of the false, an "art beyond knowledge."

Chapter 3, "*Suzhou River* and the Image of Love," examines the 1999 film *Suzhou River* from sixth-generation Chinese filmmaker Lou Ye via the relation of "promise time" and affect. The theme of sexual infidelity (real or imagined) that runs through *Vertigo*, Lynch's films, and into *Suzhou River*, I argue, can best be understood as a form of bare repetition, beneath which lies a more profound infidelity at the heart of the self. This infidelity is nothing more than time as duration. I explore the "affection of self by self" to articulate the relation between this idea and the cinematic body. I use double vision to examine the "fracture in the I" to address the problem of embodiment, memory, and selfhood in *Suzhou River*.[126] The film's engagement with the flows of global capitalism and the asymmetrical temporality of rapid change provides an important test case for the value of temporal critique. *Suzhou River* explores what Jean-François Lyotard terms an "anti-development model of time," in a way that opens onto, but also reorients current debates around the affective force of contemporary "slow cinema."[127] Its pedagogical imperative to "look again" taps into the *productive*, not merely resistant force of the body's becoming as a time machine.

Picking up on the remakings, dysnarrative twists, and indistinctions between virtual and actual in the previous chapters, the final chapter turns to the contemporary moment to explore suspense as the intensive experience of ambiguous embodiment. In Chapter 4, "Time Takings: Suspended Reanimations and the Pulse of Post-Digital Cinema," I read two recent cinematic works, one commercial, one a remix of the commercial for the museum, against each other to define the machinics of the body in time. How might time travel be a category of suspense film, in terms of the new model of suspense as affective force? How does the fabulative force of suspense, the crime of time, generate what I term an "anarchival" experience of time travel, a reanimation rather than revisiting of the past in the name of a futurity yet to come? The anarchival names the force of the anarchic archive, one intimately linked to the experience of the body in time. As suspense films as special cases of movement, these films enact alter-rhythms of anotherness through a reworking of the archive, opening onto a felt futurity. In Rian Johnson's *Looper*, I explore the heterogenic re-animations of a single life—Seth, time-traveling assassin—across the expanded corporealities of Joseph Gordon-Levitt and Bruce Willis, and the time machinics of this film's re-animations of media archives. Although Johnson's film explicitly addresses time travel as content, figurally bending form to dysnarrative permutations, Christian Marclay's recent twenty-four-hour compilation film, *The Clock*, is a new mode of suspense film, one that requires a rearticulation of the narrative/non-narrative divide as a means of renewing contemporary cinema studies. As a postdigital reactivation of the cinematic archive, *The Clock* is a suspended (re)animation in multiple ways. Displacing the camera with digital editing, and through the new multiplex of the museum as cinema's home, I use *The Clock* to explore the rearticulation of the postdigital cinematic body. If we are in a post-cinematic moment, how do we read *The Clock*: as nostalgic re-viewing or an intensification of repetition that shakes loose a new indetermination of cinema? How does Marclay's work also suspend, through affective solicitation, our own habits of memory and recognition to reopen us to the felt multiplicity of repetition? As a twenty-four-hour film of inhuman duration, *The Clock* is impossibly suspended between eternal object and lived experience, and as such, reorients questions of interactivity at the heart of contemporary debates around art in general and the specific fate of cinema as an old media.

Each of the films explored in this book considers the time machinics of cinema, which give us the intensive experience of our own another-ness as inexhaustible reservoir of potential. Feeling difference made is the experience of suspense I trace across *Bodies in Suspense*.

CHAPTER ONE

A Free Replay

Vertigo *and the Spiral of Time*

In *The Machinic Unconscious*, Félix Guattari writes, "To think time against the grain, to imagine that what came "after" can modify what was "before" or that changing the past at the root can transform a current state of affairs: what madness! A return to magical thought! It is pure science fiction, and yet. . . ." His ellipsis marks the creative suspension of reading time against the grain: a return to duration that is equally a rediscovery. This experience is immediation as cinematic event, paradoxically including the "unexperience" of the virtual itself. Massumi calls this magical form of thought "semblance," the experience of that which does not appear. Here, cinema is not simply passed through and retrospectively incorporated, but makes us "live time" as deformation or anamorphosis.[1] Against a cinema of a pure present, "the duration of passions can only be measured only by the remnants of images, not by their cinematic duration, but by the power they have to remain, repeat or recur."[2]

This figural form of analysis gets us productively lost in the medium via attention to passage itself, taking a lost highway rather than the royal road of narrative analysis. Being lost in the medium subjects us to these de-ranging effects of reading time against the grain. For Nicole Brenez, the figural explores the connection between the plastic materiality of signs and their signifying content; in this sense, as in the corporeal turn, it also concerns the ambiguous embodiments of cinematic events. The

materiality of the signifier generates a productive suspension of meaning. The figural is opposed to figuration, breaking with habitual representation to linger in the indistinction between form and content: "How
can the work rediscover its thickness, its fertility, its fragility, its characteristic density or its potential opacity, in a word, its problematic virtues?"[3] Brenez's terms—opacity, thickness, but also fragility—signal the
figural's productive and deforming delay of meaning. Rethinking film
through the generative powers of the false, she asks, "How is difference
made?," attentive to a film's "manner of event." Massumi suggests that
"an evaluation of a technique's manner of event can replace the notion
of the 'medium'"; I explore it here as a way of getting lost in the medium.[4]

Two things characterize my figural approach. This is not a question of
representing the body. Kim Novak in *Vertigo* plays two roles: Madeleine
and Judy. Their incomplete distinction, evident in a slippage between
their distinct voices in key scenes, has often been "explained" by Novak's
"failing" to successfully deliver two hermetically sealed performances.
However, the dual roles, contained in one body, and made problematic
by Novak's plastic presence (whose "insufficient talent" "contaminates"
both performances) are also a problem in the film itself. An analytics of
representation and verisimilitude only considers questions of *adequacy*,
disregarding the generativity of affective uncertainty produced by *failure*.

Second, the figural attunes us to the plastic temporality of film figures
as the unique materiality of the film as audiovisual image and the mutable, even "virtual" side of film. Figural analysis breaks with reproductive
mimesis (cinema as copy of an original reality) while opening onto a
productive mimesis as a mode of affective spectatorship bound to repetition.[5] Here mimesis produces bodies deformed by "becoming beside
themselves," attending to the specific temporality of the film body itself
as an event.[6]

In this chapter, I begin with the technics of cinematic suspense, to
ask what its "manner of event" tells us about the body in time. If Linda
Williams reads the productive excess of body genres as pedagogical technique, how does the excess of suspense go beyond generic consideration of narrative effects? A figural form of suspense, embodying both
movement and stasis, deploys perverse repetition as its manner of event,

making felt the body's own minor becoming in time. Paralleling genre theories of suspense, focused on criminality and guilt, with Deleuze's immanent re-evaluation of the "crime of time," I suggest that suspense affirms affective sensation in cinema as being as becoming itself.

Brenez characterizes the figural analysis as a repeated return to the question "The body, how do you find it?" deeply pertinent to *Vertigo*, with its games of substituted corpses and deranged sensibilities.[7] For Brenez, the body becomes an effective investigative tool as it "demesures"; beyond the obviously "unbalanced individual" (for example, psychopaths) challenging standard measurements of normalcy, the undecidability of same and other abolishes frontiers that guarantee the "impermeability" of bodies.[8] Our body, what is most intimately ours, is also a site of radical dispossession. Its ability to unmake sense makes it valuable for figural analysis.

The figural form of suspense in this chapter emerges from the spiral of Hitchcock's *Vertigo*, which, as Chris Marker reminds us, is a "spiral of time." In this form's intensive repetitions, we get lost in the medium, suspended between plastic materiality and sensible lure.[9] This spiral form (for example, the movement-in-place visual representation of Scottie's vertigo) makes repetition a double movement of the event's arc and its immediate doubling in self-enjoyment, a paradoxical experience of that which doesn't actually appear (the past and the future). William James writes, "To continue . . . is the substitute for knowing in the completed sense." When Deleuze turns toward the powers of the false, the key question of the cinema books becomes how we might come to believe again in the world. For Massumi, "Being swept up in the world constitutes a lived belief in it."[10] I explore the thinking-feeling of suspense as perceptual sensation of belief in the world, a vertiginous swept-upness, affirming a becoming that precedes and exceeds knowing.

This double vision of suspense as a knowing de-ranged by continuing constitutes a form of déjà vu, or what Bergson terms "paramnesia." A disjunction of sensation and perception, paramnesia produces the inescapable sense of having already lived a moment in time, or being a witness to one's own life. Deleuze describes the crystal-image, an indivisible unity of an actual image and its virtual image, in precisely these terms:

The present is the actual image, and its contemporaneous past is the virtual image, the image in a mirror. According to [Henri] Bergson, paramnesia (the illusion of déjà vu or already having been there) simply makes this obvious point perceptible: there is *a recollection of the present,* contemporaneous with the present itself, as closely coupled as a role to an actor.[11]

Here is Bergson's description of this moving mirror from *Mind-Energy* (1920):

Our actual existence, then, whilst it is unrolled in time, duplicates itself alongside a virtual existence, a mirror image. Every moment of our life presents two aspects, it is actual and virtual, perception on the one side and memory on the other. Each moment is split up as and when it is posited. Or rather, it consists in this very splitting, for the present moment, always going forward, fleeting limit between the immediate past which is now no more and the immediate future which is not yet, would be a mere abstraction were it not the moving mirror which continually reflects perception as a memory.[12]

The uncanny effect of this doubling is desubjectifying; as Bergson describes it: "Whoever becomes conscious of the continual duplicating of his present into perception and recollection will compare himself to an actor playing his part automatically, listening to himself and beholding himself playing."[13] For Schefer, the special effect of/at the cinema is precisely this: living two worlds at the same time—with and without memory. Cinema as an inhuman eye "without memory": Schefer takes this from Jean Epstein, who describes cinema as a "descriptive geometry of gesture." These delinked gestures hold a "profound meaning" precisely because they fail to resolve into a synthetic memory of the lived as the support of a "doxical" body. Schefer claims the only knowledge in cinema is the use of our own memory: "In the mind, memory teaches us nothing but the manipulation of time as an image, made possible by the purloining of our actual bodies" via the solicitation of our body's virtual dimension (anotherness). At the cinema, we experience an anamorphic effect of double occupancy, living two worlds at once: this recomposition of the world opens onto an "enigmatic body." Cinema is an "experimental night where something stirs, comes alive and speaks in front of us," a suspended world.[14] Our purloined bodies open us to the aberrant movement of anamorphosis itself.

This suspension, a paradoxical doubleness of intensity and immobility, is the body's anotherness. Deleuze claims Schefer's key question is

How is cinema concerned with a thought whose essential character is not yet to be? He says that the cinematographic image, a soon as it takes on its aberration of movement, carries out a suspension of the world or affects the visible with a disturbance, which, far from making thought visible, as Eisenstein wanted, are on the contrary directed to what does not let itself be thought in thought, and equally to what does not let itself be seen in vision. This is perhaps not "crime" as [Schefer] believes, but simply the power of the false.[15]

Deleuze proposes immanent evaluation as the alternative to Schefer's "crime of time."[16]

The chapters that follow read this reassessment of the powers of the false as perhaps not *crime*, starting from the twisted repetitions and guilts of Hitchcock's *Vertigo*. A crime has been committed (the murder of Madeleine Elster) that bleeds into other, more ambiguous elements of responsibility and bad conscience, tearing apart both Scottie and Judy "from within." Crime becomes suspended precisely *in time* in this film. Deleuze concludes his revision of Schefer by claiming "there is no crime but time itself"; *Vertigo*'s criminal motor is the invitation to look again, double vision as its immanent "manner of event."

The crime of time for Deleuze is linked to eccentricity of the cinematic experience of double occupancy, characterizing the *aberrant movement* of the time-image:

What aberrant movement reveals is time as everything, as "infinite opening" . . . If normal movement subordinates the time of which it gives us an indirect representation, aberrant movement speaks up for

an anteriority of time that it presents to us directly, on the basis of the
disproportion of scales, the dissipation of centres and the false continuity of the images themselves.[17]

Aberrant movement is decentered and nonphenomenological, as in the
experience (or unexperience) of paramnesia. It directly presents time
by undoing a fixed point of view on the world: "A direct presentation of
time does not imply the halting of movement, but rather the promotion
of aberrant movement."[18] The affect of suspense as movement and stasis at once produces such aberrant movement.

Affect is first the uncontainable experience of the virtual impinging
on the actual, a visceral sensation not yet identifiable as a qualified emotion.[19] David Rodowick describes affect in relation to virtual conjunctions
as "abject in the sense of objectless emotion or feeling," destroying clear
boundaries. [20] However, affect is simultaneously a productive experience
of consistency, as with particles suspended in liquid, a convergence of
elements in atmosphere that does not simply dissolve them, but hangs
their usefulness. This concerns less the discrete object suspended as
the inbetween of the body composed of speeds and slowness. Suspense
is the delay of lost time that reinvests the body and its surroundings
with potential connections suppressed in everyday functional reality,
"the reality of an excess over the actual."[21] Affect, although destructively
anamorphic to form, is simultaneously productive of transitions and
passage.

Curiously, for all of its immediate, visceral sensation, affect retains
an impersonal quality directly related to this movement between. In the
suspense films analyzed here, affective sensation is intimately bound to
identity crisis, doubled bodies, repetition, clichés, and telepresence, but
its impersonality means that confusions and dysnarratives cannot simply be explained away as the distortions of a subjective perspective.
Affect is at once vivid and singular *and* a spreading out of feeling into
nextness, a means of tapping into durations "above and below" our
own. Intensifying the feeling of the body, affects makes sensational what
Massumi calls the "singular-generic."[22] This second quality of affect, its
consistency, is "world-glue":

Affect is trans-situational. As processional as it is precessional, affect inhabits the passage. It is pre and postcontextual, pre and postpersonal, an excess of continuity invested only in the ongoing: its own. Self-continuity across the gaps. Impersonal affect is the connecting thread of experience. It is the invisible glue that holds the world together. In event. The world-glue of affect is an autonomy of event-connection continuing across its own serialized capture in context.[23]

Impersonal affect holds the world together "in event" even as it tears the individual apart. The self-enjoyment that immediately doubles the event is thus the feeling of relationality itself. The consistency of affect is always doubled by an in-consistency of the self and the body in relation to its abstract realness. This inconsistency is figured in *Vertigo* as sexual jealousy and infidelity.

If the time-image is concerned with recognizing the continuity between things, this continuity is external to the objects it connects, activated by the irrational cut or interval as absolute discontinuity. This relationality is affect's impersonality. Thus the secret of relation, of split and doubled characters, is not their internal identities, but the consistency of their connection, how their doublings produce ripple effects by warping the form of the real in a "re-worlding": "Each time we experience an event, we are nonconsciously returning to our own and the world's emergence."[24] I turn now to genre theories of suspense, to explore how suspense produces a "thinking-feeling" of re-worlding through decentered movements and the crime of time as recidivist or anomalous suspense. This last problem names the point of generic "excess" that, following Linda Williams, gives us the figure of the body "beside itself" as the experience of the body in time.

Royal Roads and Lost Highways

In "Hitchcock with Deleuze," Sam Ishii-Gonzales concludes, "Implicit in Deleuze's cinema books is not the claim that 'the power of film is now explained' but the opposite: the power of cinema remains to be thought. Is this not why we return to a filmmaker like Hitchcock over and over again? Not to delineate (or contain) the power of cinema but to discover it?"[25] Let's return, then, to "Alfred Hitchcock, master of suspense" to reopen this cliché to a double vision, moving from generic questions to the figural analysis of suspense via Hitchcock's vertiginous spiral of time.

Bridging popular entertainment and art, Hitchcock and his work have served as exemplary models for thinking cinema and suspense. If he once quipped that the audience was a mere organ to play upon, we might think this organ as ambiguously embodied: both machine and flesh. *Vertigo* best articulates Hitchcock's suspense, even as it wildly deviated from his established "contract" with the audience. Far from a passive escape from reality, Hitchcock saw suspense as a way of keeping viewers "clutching at the arms of their chairs."[26] Defining suspense as "the most intense presentation possible of dramatic situations," François Truffaut, in his Hitchcock book, writes, "The art of creating suspense is also the art of involving the audience, so that the viewer is actually a participant in the film."[27]

This involvement is often characterized in terms of spectatorial knowledge, and Hitchcock continually distinguished surprise and suspense in these terms. Surprise stems from ignorance, producing only a momentary jolt. Suspense results from an agonizing awareness and the thrilling anticipation of when this will be brought to light. He demonstrates:

Let us suppose that three men are sitting in a room in which a ticking bomb has been planted. It is going to go off in 10 minutes. The audience does not know it is there, and the men do not know it is there either. So they go on talking inanely of the weather or yesterday's baseball game. After 10 minutes of desultory conversation, the bomb goes off. What is the result? The unsuspecting audience gets a surprise. *One* surprise. That's all.

Suppose the story were told differently. This time, while the men do not know that the bomb is there, the audience does know. The men still talk inanities, but now the most banal thing they say is charged with excitement. The audience wants them to get out of the room, but they talk on, and when one finally says, "Let's leave," the entire audience is praying for them to do so. But another man says, "No wait a minute, I want to finish my coffee," and the audience groans inwardly and yearns for them to leave. This is suspense.[28]

Note that one of the functions of suspense is to manipulate the reactions of the audience as a whole, involving them so intensely that their reactions can be anticipated, even choreographed. Suspense also ruptures identification; the audience's knowledge is distinct from that of the characters onscreen, and the tension in part revolves around the anticipation of the moment of reunion.

Suspense has long been associated with the dominance of feature length narratives, what Christian Metz has termed cinema's "king's highway."[29] Mary Ann Doane identified suspense as a structuring agent in consolidating the primacy of "story time" in early cinema, by making temporality internal to a film, rather than signaling a profilmic, indexical time.[30] Suspense is associated with the "invisible," the perpetually deferred "image of the worst": "duration is energized by invisibility, by the inability to see all."[31] Through this desire to see, the spectator is distracted from the invisible at cinema's heart (for example, the blackness between frames). Subsuming this desire onto the narrative level, the film attempts to stabilize its own being. For Doane, cinema produces a temporal instability managed in two contradictory ways: first, by structuring contingency into narrative and a "time of internal temporality"; and second, by emphasizing the "eternal," of which Doane gives as an example Laura Mulvey's contention that woman as spectacle suspends the narrative.[32] Both attempt to distract the audience from the problems of contingency and record that the cinema creates, reducing the spectator's need to measure events onscreen against an external determinant. Thus suspense *should* work to bind the spectator's experience of the film to the boundaries of the film's presentation.

Narrative theories concerning suspense would seem to confirm this. In "Structural Analysis of Narratives," Roland Barthes associates suspense with the process of articulation in narrative, characterized by distortion and expansion. With distortion, narrative "ceaselessly substitutes meaning for the straightforward copy of the events recounted":

"Suspense" is clearly only a privileged—or exacerbated—form of distortion: on the one hand, by keeping a sequence open (through emphatic procedures of delay and renewal), it reinforces the contact with the reader (the listener), has a manifestly phatic function; while on the other, it offers the threat of an uncompleted sequence, of an open paradigm (if, as we believe, every sequence has two poles) that is to say of a logical disturbance, it being this disturbance which is consumed with anxiety and pleasure *(all the more so because it is always made right in the end)*. "Suspense," therefore, is a game with structure, designed to endanger and glorify, constituting a veritable "thrilling" of intelligibility: by representing order (and no longer series) in its fragility, "suspense" accomplishes the very idea of language: what seems like the most pathetic is also the most intellectual—"suspense" grips you in the mind, not in the guts.[33]

The second element of narrative is "integration," a "unity of meaning" that "prevents the meaning from dangling." Barthes claims that "in all narrative imitation remains contingent": "One could say that the origin of a sequence is not the observation of reality, but the need to vary and transcend the first form given man, namely repetition: a sequence is namely a whole within which nothing is repeated. Logic here has an emancipatory value." This seems to confirm Doane's contention that narrative works to distract the spectator from the indexical quality of film. It also replaces mere mimetic repetition with invention; narrative frees one from dependence on the real. For Barthes, narratives work at a variety of levels at once, but always in the service of what can be known; narrative is supremely concerned with the intelligible, and not the felt. We falsely interpret this "thrilling of intelligibility" as a question of the gut.

Barthes's broad view of narrative includes cinema as well as "articulated language, spoken or written, fixed or moving images, gestures, and the ordered mixture of all these substances."[34] But while he divorces narrative from referentiality, it is questionable whether his account of narrative can simply be applied to cinema without considering cinema's uniquely mimetic and indexical qualities. Thus Doane's discussion of suspense as a means of *suppressing* (not eliminating) the indexical, for example, would seem to contradict Barthes's claim. A specifically cine-matic analysis of suspense assesses whether Barthes's claim that "sus-pense grips you in the mind, not in the guts" is legitimate. Suspense in film concerns not only the mind but also the "gastro-affective," rout-ing questions of knowledge, logic, and intellect through the body. For Barthes, the intelligible is bound to narrative's characteristic inventive-ness (if not falsification); it is a higher form of knowledge. But if we follow Williams's critical reassessment of body genres, how might we rethink *apprehension* to adequately address the affective side of suspense, especially when it seems to conflict with knowing?

Edward Branigan draws on Barthes in *Narrative Comprehension and Film* to analyze cinematic forms of narrative. For Branigan, suspense is likewise a privileged means of making sense demonstrating the pur-pose of narration. He uses Hitchcock's "bomb under the table" anecdote to distinguish surprise, suspense, and mystery. His "crude definition" of suspense is "the audience knowing more than the characters." At pains to point out that cinematic texts work on a multitude of levels beyond "character knowledge," he identifies some of the problems suspense raises for thinking cinematic identification as a simple conflation of the spectator and character points of view. Not only do spectators have a "multiplicity of involvements" that produces "disparities of knowledge," these disparities also call into question the "impression that a film nar-rative is a mere photographic record of a real environment."[35]

For instance, spectators gain knowledge from non-diegetic sources unavailable to characters, such as music (challenging Metz's claim that primary identification is with the look of the camera), credits, implicit narrators, and so on. At the same time, however, Branigan's own termi-nology and analysis show the difficulty of conceiving narrative sense outside a referential framework tied to a human character conscious-ness. For example, Branigan uses the term "impossible space" to desig-nate a "position and view which no character in the diegetic world can possess."[36] Two examples of "impossible spaces" from *Vertigo* that are examined in depth include Judy/Madeleine's confession, in which the camera records her letter writing from the presence of an invisible spec-tator, a scene that breaks the shot/reverse shot structure, and the final shot of the film, a low-angle medium close-up of Scottie standing on the edge of the bell tower, the camera suspended in space that no human body could occupy.

Branigan wants to avoid a simplistic "personification" of the effect of narrative—that is to say, there is "no one" speaking—but admits that it is difficult to avoid the "anthropomorphic fiction" of a narrator. This is why his examples of narrative that do not work from the perspective of a character are especially interesting. "Impossible space" is one example; another is what he calls the "extra-fictional" level of narration, including here the credits of a film (so critical in establishing the figural form of suspense in *Vertigo* through the animated spiral form). Branigan proposes a hierarchy of narrative levels, to help explain the intransigent and mysterious phenomena of "anomalous suspense," where a person continues to feel suspense despite knowing the outcome of a story, and "anomalous replotting" in which a person wishes for a different outcome despite knowing the plot. Specifically, he identifies a "dual nature" of narrative that raises tension between two kinds of knowing. On the one hand, declarative knowledge, or "what happened," collects a series of episodes as a focused causal chain, generating an experience of time (story-time). On the other hand, procedural knowledge concerns *how* events are witnessed and known. The effect of this is that "the reader's participation in narrative is *not limited to the choice of to know or not to know,* but may assume more complex nuances within a range of epistemological contexts each of which, in turn, defines a limited form of contingency."[37]

These two forms of knowledge are epistemological boundaries in the text, associated with nominal agents such as narrators, actors, and focalizers. Branigan claims that only declarative knowledge can be seen as having true or false value; procedural knowledge is simply "instructional." But a viewer's "anomalous" suspense, even in the face of knowing the outcome, suggests that the passage to knowledge is *as* significant, if not more so, than the outcome itself. By characterizing this as anomalous, Branigan seeks to bracket the significance of this experience, undermining his own "crude" characterization of suspense. Anomalous suspense addresses the difficult question of how an audience can know and yet not know at the same time: how they might "continue to believe" as an alternative to the closure of knowing. It may also suggest that knowledge is not the only way to approach this question, beyond the "thrilling of the intelligible." Anomalous suspense is fundamentally a *problem* of repetition.

Near the end of his analysis, Branigan gives examples that suggest something different than his previous claim that there is no truth or falsity associated with procedural knowledge. Tellingly, these coalesce around questions of the body. It is my contention that in *Vertigo*, there is an overlap between declarative and procedural knowledge that causes unresolved suspense; this produces an interchange between spectator and character that is characteristic of the *cinematic event*. Branigan examines "unfocalized" information that is not tied, explicitly or implicitly, to the perception of a character. Branigan describes this as "intersubjective" or objective information "reported independently by a narrator, or appears seemingly without any mediation as a fact of some kind." This produces two possible effects: either the object is presented in itself, as a simple unmediated fact, or there is no context provided to specify POV, and thus there is no evaluative possible of ascertaining truth or falsity. This is what Branigan will call a "delayed or suspended" POV structure. This "hyperdiegetic" structure can take several forms: "the barest trace of another scene, of a scene to be remembered at another time, of a past and future scene in the film (a hybrid scene) or of a scene that is evaded and finally remains absent." But clearly there are substantial differences between these possibilities. Frequently, this "delay" is unresolved. For Branigan, this undoes the concept of an "author": "What we normally construct in the reading as an "author," therefore is only a convenient summing up—male or female, or somehow beyond gender—merely *a shorthand for a multiplicity* that satisfies our urge to name and make final in order to achieve the objective."[38] What this means is that the POV of the "impossible space" cannot ultimately be attributed to the "author" of a film. Branigan's description, though, doesn't do justice to the unease and discomfort such a structure generates in the viewer.

The indetermination of a delayed or suspended POV structure can open a space of exploration for the "perceiver" (Branigan's word) of a

film to try on various possibilities of sense, but equally works at the level
of affective sensation. Thus the "thrilling of the intelligible" regains its
connection with the "guts": "The measure of indeterminateness acts to
delay and expand the kind of searching and restructuring of prior textual
knowledge undertaken by a perceiver. . . . Indefinite reference does not
mean that we can't have specific and emotional reactions to fiction; quite
the contrary, indefinite reference may facilitate such reactions."[39]

There is a tension in Branigan's analysis around extending this indetermination to the recording of material reality that occurs in fiction
film: "Interpreting a symbol fictionally requires that one qualify the
immediacy of the symbol itself; its material presence *must not imply* an
immediate reference, nor a simple reference to something atomic, nor
indeed any reference at all, much less one that is true or false in our
familiar world."[40] For example, Branigan describes actors in fiction films
as mere "placeholders"; their profilmic reality does not interfere with
the audience's understanding and interpretation of their fictional meaning.[41] But we must consider that this indefiniteness precisely does not
preclude reference, but can make it a generative problem.

For example, Novak's body doubled in Judy and Madeleine is not only
a problem within the film's narrative, but in the spectator's experience,
a case of what Jean Louis Comolli calls "a body too much." Comolli describes the audience's difficulty in successfully maintaining suspension
of disbelief in historical films, where visual referents for characters are
preestablished in the audience's mind, as with Pierre Renoir's portrayal
of Louis XVI in *La Marseillaise* (1938). The conflict between memory and
onscreen presentation creates a "body too much." Comolli's central
problem is "how does one believe" in the effect of cinema? In nonhis-
torical films, "the character reaches us as a *bodily effect* in the image"; the
actor's body appears first as an empty mask, gradually inhabited by character. The knowledge that the character has, at best, a spectral possession of the actor's body is not a problem; Comolli suggests we accept
this with "boredom." With the "body too much" of historical fiction, the
tension between the actor's body as an empty mask and iconic referentiality is only resolvable by making the actor's body into such a problem
that it pushes the question of "how do we believe in the effects of film"

to the limit, thus producing a kind of perverse pleasure: "The certainty we always have, bearing it in mind, that the spectacle is not life nor the film reality, that the actor is not the character and that if we are there as spectators it is because we know it is a simulacrum, is a certainty we have to be able to doubt."[42]

The more difficult it is to believe, the more "it is worth managing to do so." Comolli calls this double movement "denegation , , . summarized in the well-worn expression: "I know, but all the same. . . ." However, Comolli abandons the productive force of this ellipsis, ultimately arguing that the spectator is never fooled. The historical referent "ghosts" normally smooth relation between image and actor that forms a character: "The self-evidence of the image of a body as a result of which it is seen without being seen, the apparent naturalness, the familiarity of the body are thwarted here." In the example of Renoir/Louis XVI, this ghostly effect produces such a discomfort that spectators both on- and offscreen wish fervently for the body to disappear: "Far and near, here and there, double inscription of the spectator's place in the auditorium and in the scene." This double inscription, a "denegation to infinity," remains untheorized, merely an interesting effect to be largely dismissed: "something undecidable floats around [Renoir], a blur in the image, a duplication: there is a ghost in this body. At any rate there is some historical knowledge, some referent constituting a screen for the image and preventing the actor and *mise-en-scène* from playing on self-evidence."[43] Comolli's not-entirely convincing ("at any rate") "demystification" of the haze around Renoir's body simply refocuses the double vision produced by the spectatorial oscillation between knowing and not-knowing.

What happens to the spectator in the face of this "static"? Comolli identifies the indeterminacy, even going so far as to claim it infects the "spectators" on screen, but in the end can only align himself with the spectatorial wish: "May it disappear!"[44] The ghost and the mask cannot coexist in the same body. This works conveniently in the case of Renoir's film (given the fate of Louis XVI!), but what happens when the ghost fails to be exorcised? Most important, what happens to the body? Although Comolli is primarily concerned with the question of the historical body, his discussion resonates with other instances of competing presences, such as Novak's doubled body in *Vertigo*. What precisely is the "historical referentiality" of the star body?

To return to Branigan and "actor placeholders" and other indeterminations of the line between fictional world and material substrate, part of the problem here is the idea that films are only experienced fictionally rather than as falsifying, a suggestion undermined by Branigan's own thoughtful discussion of Marker's *Sans Soleil*. The affective side of the cinematic experience cannot simply be reduced to questions of knowledge or of fictional effects:

> When a film is experienced fictionally, reference is not to the profilmic event in which a set is decorated and an actor given direction, but to a post-filmic event in which patterns are discovered through active perceiving that affects the overall structure of our knowledge. . . . The material nature of the text and its history may be relevant to, but cannot determine, reference. . . . One problem should be mentioned; if fiction may be useful to us, how do we know when to read fictionally?[45]

I don't want to exaggerate here; Branigan is only arguing that "the material nature of the text does not *determine* reference," but he underestimates the place of the material nature of film and the productive problematic of figural analysis as a disjunctive synthesis. His last question summarizes this: If reading fictionally does away with the problem of reference— how do we know when to do this? Here, Doane's reading of suspense as a disciplinary procedure can be helpful, as long as we keep in mind the other side of suspense, as a bodily experience.

Branigan ends by noting the effect of delay or suspense on the purpose of narrative, that is, to make sense: "Unusual evocations of time *permanently suspend* the parts that might otherwise form a causal unity of beginnings, middles and ends in favour of surveying a field of possibilities: a multiplicity of partially realized narratives and nonnarratives competing equally.[46] It also generates a unique experience of time, one that compresses a past that is preserved (Branigan cites Bazin's characterization of film as "change mummified") and the sense that the film exists in the present tense, into what he calls the historical present tense.

In *Vertigo*, this comes through in the unsatisfying resolution of suspense; reinterpreting the past in the light of new knowledge (that is, that Judy really was Madeleine all along) does little to resolve the urgency of the present in the film, even upon repeated viewings.

The association of suspense with an unequal, but uncomplicated *distribution* of knowledge that we find in narrative theories of suspense is often belied by another "in the guts" theory of suspense, one that works against determinable intelligibility, and which is associated with nonlinear temporality. Although the flip side of the suspense's epistemological thrust is frequently characterized as emotional, I think it is more accurate, especially considering "anomalous suspense," to see it as affective, highlighting this experience's indeterminate nature. Affect is more closely associated with a suspension of knowledge, a hesitation of action, a visceral "thrilling" of the body that circulates rather than identifiable emotion. This is the suspense of *Vertigo*, and it concerns the relationality of spectators and actors through the cinematic body itself.

Anomalous suspense is consistently a stumbling block for theories of suspense that argue that suspense is generated by an uncertainty regarding the outcome; if that is the case, how can people still feel suspense when they know the ending of a film? Noël Carroll, in "The Paradox of Suspense" states, "It is an incontrovertible fact that people can consume the same suspense fiction again and again with no loss of affect."[47] Anomalous suspense is also known as "recidivist" suspense, highlighting its perverse nature and link to "the crime of time" (of repetition).[48] In this affectively intense reliving of experience, a retracing of one's steps as aberrant movement, we hear the criminal echoes. In Hitchcock's example, the anxiety comes from the question: Will they discover the bomb in time? How then, can someone feel suspense when they already know what will happen—especially with a form like film where the outcome and performance do not change from one viewing to the next?

Proposed solutions concern knowledge and intentionality. Richard Gerrig proposes that recidivists "suppress" their knowledge of the outcome in order to reexperience the pleasure of the thrill.[49] Carroll argues that the mere thought on the part of the viewer that the (desired) outcome could fail to result provokes emotion: "Thoughts that are at variance with a person's beliefs can give rise to emotion. Thus, effectively asked to imagine—that is, to entertain the thought—that the good is at risk by the author of a fiction, the reader appropriately and intelligibly feels concern and suspense."[50] Downplaying recidivism's "perversity," Carroll renders suspense a moral question; suspense is generated only by wishing for the proper outcome (the likelihood of the "good"). This moralizing turn can, however, be detoured away from judgment to immanent evaluation by rethinking anomalous suspense as "perhaps not crime," but through the powers of the false.

In "Narrative Suspense and Rereading," William Brewer looks at the implications of anomalous suspense to test theories of suspense. He argues that it cannot be explained by either a "willing suspension of disbelief" on the part of the viewer (as in Gerrig), nor by a theory of character identification (where on a second viewing a viewer is motivated by vicarious suspense on the part of a character). He suggests a "structural-affect" theory explained by the limitations of the viewer's memory (that is, they remember the broad strokes of *what* happens, but not all the details of *how* it happens). Consistently, the affect of anomalous suspense, despite being at odds with knowledge, is held to be comprehensible and even logical. Few have looked for a solution to the problem of anomalous suspense in the affect itself; it is simply an excess that needs to be explained away. May it disappear!

One critic who seriously considers the affect of suspense is Susan Smith, in her book *Hitchcock: Suspense, Humour and Tone*. She describes tone as "two-faced: directed both towards the material but also towards the audience." Smith argues that it is too limiting to discuss suspense strictly in terms of identification.[51] Suspense is both a form of epistemic control (the traditional understanding), and a regulation of affective responses. But her own argument suggests the way that "regulation" might be overstating the extent to which suspense is a controllable element in the film.

For Smith, suspense involves three forms of address beyond identification. The first is vicarious, when we feel suspense on behalf of a character. In *Vertigo*, an example of this is when the audience is told the secret of Judy's true identity before Scottie, and we feel suspense on Scottie's behalf: "When will he find out the truth?" Smith suggests the gap in knowledge between character and here *inhibits* identification by producing distance; we identify not with the character, but with his situation. The second is shared suspense: we "fear along with the character." This occurs during the final ride to the nunnery, in which both Scottie and Judy repeat a journey they know they've taken before, and we queasily anticipate the results along with them. Again, identification with a character is not an automatic outcome; although this produces a "maximum involvement with the character's experience," this very intensity may cause the spectator to "recoil" from the experience. The final type is "direct suspense," anxiety by the spectator on their own behalf. Smith's example is the tension between wanting to look and being afraid to see in a horror movie, when suspense "cracks the scene." Examples of direct suspense are frequently what Branigan calls "impossible spaces," perspectives not associated with a character. Ultimately suspense works *against* identification and "becomes a means of placing the viewer in a much more direct, unmediated relationship to the film world. In this sense, then, identification tends to serve as a safety screen or filter shielding us from the worst effects of the suspense, only to have it withdrawn in Hitchcock's films at certain points."[52]

Smith's limitation of identification to "association with a character" makes her claim that the viewer has an "unmediated access" to the film world problematic. It lacks the nuanced description of the multiple identifications a viewer may experience beyond those that can be tied implicitly or explicitly to a character, the kind of descriptions found in Branigan's analysis, and to their own experience of immediation. However, Branigan also demonstrated the difficulty in conceiving of this type of identification, of understanding this either in terms of the unmediated (that is, the object appears as a fact) or as "anthropomorphized,"[53] an option he also rejects.

Smith is particularly interested in the nature of the "contract" between audience and film, one she argues Hitchcock repeatedly breaks. This creates a spectator who exists in a state of "suspended animation," where the "static and violent" are "two sides of the same coin": a tension between process (with its threat of incoherence, of the loss of mastery) and position (with its threat of stasis, fixity, or of compulsive repetition, which is the same thing in another form). The radical function of Hitchcock's suspense is "its ability to generate and give expression to a profound sense of audience dissatisfaction with the kind of static, fixed position of inertia so often assigned by the "'prison-house' of movies" theory to the spectator of classical Hollywood cinema."[54] Smith's analysis reflects a familiar problem: How can the audience be in the know—about the material nature of film, it is only an illusion, and so on—and yet still be radically subject to the effects of film? To know, and yet not know, or wish not to know—this is problem dramatized in *Vertigo*, where Scottie, dressing up a complete stranger as his dead lover, can only respond with bafflement to his self-deception.

Like Branigan, Smith tackles anomalous suspense, claiming, "If we are generally less prone to such manipulation on subsequent viewings, the impact of our initial experience of a film like *Vertigo* or *Psycho* means that we are never allowed to feel completely aloof from the characters' own more fallible ways of apprehending their narrative worlds."[55] Hence anomalous suspense reinforces a relation to character that is broken by the unequal distribution of knowledge; although Smith doesn't specifically argue this, this relation is more akin to the "two-facedness" of tone, less a question of subjectivity than of the inbetween that reconfigures the self.

Smith's emphasis on the "emotional strand" of suspense, and the *problems* it poses for knowledge, is an important corrective for any understanding of cinematic suspense. Although she disentangles suspense from identification with characters, her discussion approaches Truffaut's definition of suspense, where viewers are themselves made characters in the film. Rather than emotion, though, I argue we should understand affect as this aspect of suspense, especially in its anomalous form. To define suspense strictly in terms of knowledge or to simply subsume affect under knowledge is clearly insufficient in the context of Hitchcock's films. What happens to the "phatic function" of suspense, speech used to share feelings or to establish a mood of sociability rather than to communicate information or ideas, where semantics become less important than expression, that Barthes dismisses by claiming that "all will be made right in the end"? If suspense relies on a rupture of identification as association with character, where does this mood of "sociability" come from, and to whom does it pertain? Is it simply a failed suspense narrative if this doesn't occur, or does this demand a different investigation of "procedural knowledge," where the "how we know" in film requires a rethinking of the film body itself? We might think the phatic function of suspense through the direct presentation of relation itself. It creates a problem of one's relation to oneself, one's own anotherness. In suspense, as in body genres more generally, we feel the primacy of relation itself, beyond its terms. For this reason, I claim suspense gives us an experience of the body in time, as the direct perception of our participation in an event.

In *Semblance and Event*, Massumi describes "gift-giving" as a "suspension-event," an "incorporeal envelope of sociality":

> The relation is a suspension of the particular definitions of the terms in relation. If it is real as they are, its reality is of a different order: an implicit order, of ready-to-be-things folded eventfully into each other. If the implicit order is of the order of an event, then like every event, really-next–effects will unfold from its happening: to be continued.[56]

He summarizes this as "transition takes precedence." To think suspense this way takes excess as a generous gift, rather than as waste (May it disappear!). It is also to understand what falls out of structure in the incorporeal terms of relation itself, what doubles the material support with a "holding-up/holding-together, integral unseen medium of suspension."[57] If Schefer approaches the crime of time through Epstein's "dismembered" gestures, Deleuze's decriminalization turns instead to the productive force of aberrant movement itself. I look at an example of such aberrant movement in the form of cinephilia to discuss a figural form of suspense, the givingness of gesture itself.

Cinephilia

L'Amour Fou *as Aberrant Movement*

The corporeal turn sought to bring the body into cinema theory to address the relation between spectator and screen. Through the untimely meditations of Deleuze's second cinema book, and considerations of affect and event in the work of Massumi, I use semblance to describe the suspended nature of the cinematic body, through self-referentiality or its capacitation of the body prior to action. This intensive suspense, a "special case of movement," is the body's anotherness in time made sensational. In *What Is Philosophy?*, Deleuze and Guattari describe art as a bloc of sensation, a cut in the world that depends neither on the conditions of its creation nor on the mind of the beholder. In their list of moments that art preserves, we hear an echo of cinephilia's primal scene: the wind in the trees of the Lumières's *Baby's Teatime* (1895):

> The young man will smile on the canvas for as long as the canvas lasts. Blood throbs under the skin of this woman's face, the wind shakes a branch, a group of men prepare to leave. In a novel or a film, the young man will stop smiling, but he will start to smile again when we turn to this page or that moment. Art preserves, and it is the only thing in the world that is preserved. It preserves and is preserved in itself (quid juris?), although actually it lasts no longer than its support and materials–stone, canvas, chemical color, and so on (quid facti?). The young girl maintains the pose that she has had for five thousand years, a gesture that no longer depends on whoever made it. The air still has the turbulence, the gust of wind, and the light that it had that day last year, and it no longer depends on whoever was breathing it that morning.[58]

The autonomy of art replies on suspended origins, lifting off from bodies and transmitting as force what Deleuze terms "resistance," rather than communication, in "Having an Idea in Cinema." As bloc of sensation, affect is ambiguously embodied in gesture itself. Paralleling the corporeal turn, the mid-1990s saw a renewed interest in cinephilia emerging from questions of preservation and cinematic ephemerality of the digital turn. Cinephilia foregrounded issues of the activity of the spectator before the screen, the problematic of repetition, and the affective force of cinema's effective reality. How might we read cinephilia as the aberrant movement of suspense, an incorporeal dimension of the cinematic body?

In *The Emergence of Cinematic Time,* Doane identifies a contemporary "elegiac" cinephilia as the indexical's disruptive trace of a profilmic real: a standard presentation of cinephilia as an "eruption" of the real speaking immediately to the spectator. Cinema's photographic substrate, with its temporality of "too soon" (arresting action before completion) and "too late" (capturing a moment that for the spectator will always be past) generates a "posthumous shock" via the photograph's "uncanny impossible instant." This uncanny doubleness, however, is "rectified" by the film's reinscribed duration, forcibly refocusing spectators on the "now" of screen time. "The ease and obviousness of cinematic movement are deceptive," disguising film's reconstituted temporality. Cinematic "re-animation," then, is essentially false and mendacious; as she puts it: "The cinematic image does not speak its own relation to time" because it obscures its own recording of time "outside itself." Cinephilic moments are fleeting eruptions of contingency that can provide relief from this, grounded in the image's photographic base. "It is this intense and privileged relation to contingency, assured by photographic indexicality in the abstract, which can be loved, this time as lost."[59]

Paul Willemen's 1994 essay "Through the Glass Darkly: Cinephilia Reconsidered" privileges the term "cinephilic" moment "because of its overtones of necrophilia, of relating to something that is dead, past, but alive in memory," characterized by a productive obscurity, around what escapes representation. Its excess takes the form of a sensational resistance, not as activity, but a pausing. Cinephilia is "like emotion," but: "it is not strictly emotional, but it has the same vagueness with which one uses emotional terminology." That vagueness, emerging from cinephilic repetition, stems from "overlap of a mode of understanding and a mode of experiencing."[60] Echoing the corporeal turn's interest in affect's disruption of conventional knowledge though excess, cinephilia also evokes the potential (virtual excess) made perceptible through Bergsonian intuition.

In Willeman, cinephilia's repetition remains underdeveloped; though "singular, unique, unrepeatable," the cinephilic moment is necessarily repeatable, not least via the cinephile's obsessive return to it. But this repetition is not incidental: it is how difference is made. At one point,

Willeman describes cinephilia as a "serialization of moments of revela-tion," he evokes serialization without delving into its paradoxical parallel with revelation (uniqueness). But in the cinephilic moment, the "spark" that "shocks" the viewer, the spectator "can go back time and again and re-consume it almost ad infinitum," without any loss of affect. It is essen-tially a suspended moment, mimetically actualizing the pressure of the virtual through the form of repetition. Willeman writes, "Cinephilia de-mands a gestural outlet": "the excess experienced needs an extra, physi-cal ritual, a gesture."[61] The generative force of the cinephilic moments is contagiously capacitating, a pure gesture without utility.

In Willemen's earlier work on cinephilia, "On Reading Epstein on *Photogénie*," cinephilic repetition is uncanny.[62] *Photogénie,* Louis Delluc's notoriously obscure attempt to account for cinema's alchemical trans-formations of reality (as the production of cinephilic moments)[63]

> invariably refers to something that has dropped away, something that falls ceaselessly through the net, no matter how fine the mesh. . . . "The difficulty then becomes the fact that it is no longer possible to get rid of it; nothing is more cumbersome than that scoria which does not fit into any order. . . . That object is lost and yet as present as a dead person is to his relatives, no matter how ceremoniously he has been buried."[64]

This description resonates with Barthes' writings on photography and with Shaviro's cinematic body as "unburied cadaver." Willemen redemp-tively reads Jean Epstein's cinephilia as an misguidedly impressionistic but intuitive version of a cinematic truth of scopophilia and a structure of split belief: in short, fetishism.[65] But Willeman overlooks two elements. First, the genuine strangeness of cinematic perception, largely figured as visual for Epstein in terms of the camera "eye," but also evoked in the image of the Bell and Howell camera as a "metal brain."[66] Though Epstein wrote while cinematic "codes" were still being established, it remains true today. At 3-D films audiences are still compelled to reach out for an object they know is not there. Second is the movement at the heart of Epstein's description, Willemen's "gestural outlet." In repetition,

Willemen sees the "false" movement of fetishism, not the falsifying "special case of movement" that is suspense.

Leslie Stern's "I Think, Sebastian, Therefore . . . I Somersault: Film and the Uncanny," draws a different cinephilic connection between cinematic repetition and movement. Epstein helps her think the uncanny movement between viewer and image to explain her own obsessive feeling that, in a scene from *Blade Runner* where android Pris springs into life "like a human missile" in the very moment before her death, space and time is reconfigured when "her bodily momentum is transmitted and experienced in the auditorium as bodily sensation." A living doll, Pris is already uncanny; but this resemblance is doubled by the nonsensuous similarity of movement itself. This is the "gestural outlet" of cinephilia that can only repeat, and not simply refer or represent. Pris launches a cinephilic moment as a suspensive time lag, stretching the present:

And it all happens so swiftly, this transformation of a body in space and time, that my bodily response lags behind. It's like what happens when you are in a lift and suddenly without warning it drops—instantaneously the movement of the lift is in you. There is a lurching in the pit of your stomach. But something more happens when you witness the somersault—as the figure becomes again ordinary, returning to an upright position the momentum remains in your body as a charge, a whoosh, a sense of exhilaration—the effect persists, the fear and exhilaration, the frisson.[67]

The figure onscreen may re-become ordinary but the change effectuated in the spectator continues to work precisely through an aberrant experience of time. Recall Massumi's contention that "relationality is already in the world and that it registers materially in the activity of the body before it registers consciously." Participation precedes and exceeds recognition. It is not the analogical recognition of movement, but the deformation of passage that contaminates the spectator in an "instanciation of the cinematic body": "a body that simultaneously moves (through human agency) and is moved (mechanically, through cinematic means)."

Space and time are reconfigured by the movement in a double becoming. This produces a self-referentiality or movement-vision where rather than simply identify with character "we are drawn into the situation of indeterminacy, of the passing present, the instability and fragility of presence, the discontinuity of the body."[68] The indeterminacy between sensation and perception is a gap that undoes the spectator as much as the object. Stern rejects identification as the means of taking one out of oneself; there is not sufficiently an "I" to identify. In this instance, cinematic mirroring concerns the movement between: more Alice's looking glass than self-reflection. The double or anotherness of the body is difference, generatively displacing the original.

Stern explicitly links this to a cinematic death drive that repeats potential (when what repeats is difference), reconfiguring of the classical conception of death as the singular moment par excellence. The key to this, as in Epstein, is time: the rendering of a passing present/presence that destabilizes the lived body but doesn't absent it as loss. The space between sensation and cognition I call "immediation," because I want to work with a particular form of delay (through repetition and suspense) but also to highlight the affective immediacy that undoes reference and position. The cinephilic moment lives in that indeterminacy. I turn now to a closer look at the relation between death and cinema in terms of the singular and the repeatable, through a discussion of suspense in relation to the work and body of Alfred Hitchcock, and to *Vertigo*, where the singularity of death is suspended in the doubled death of Madeleine/Judy.

In a 1980 issue of *Cahiers Du Cinema*, "Les monstresses," dedicated to reflections on film stills and publicity photos, Alain Bergala reads a black-and-white publicity still for *Vertigo* under the title "Les Deux Mortes."[69] Jimmy Stewart sits in a high-backed armchair, his head turning in intimation of a presence behind him. In his arms is Novak as Madeleine; eyes closed, she leans into his chest and presses her lips to his, as he turns away. Her blonde hair and pale skin fade out in the contrasty black-and-white image, giving her a ghostly quality echoed in her pose of slipping away, "returning to her fatal elements, the waters of the drowned where she is suspended." Behind Stewart is Novak as Judy, in a harsh profile looking not at him, but straight ahead into the distance. Where

Madeleine's face is ethereal, Judy's is sharp and contoured, dark hair and heavy, harsh make-up; Bergala describes her as a mannequin. Stewart hesitates between the rigidity of matter and the ephemerality of spirit, in an image less of three individuals than of a movement among them. This trick photograph foregrounds the role of the medium: a hesitant suspension of recognition. As Bergala puts it, "We search in vain for the merest trace of life in this image: James Stewart, corseted in his prosthetic chair, rigid in gesture and look, is seized between the two deaths, the white and the black."[70] For Bergala, this image contracts *Vertigo* and "does away the vibration of time" of the photograph's "too soon, too late":

> By its obstinacy in cutting itself off from all photographic believability, this image succeeds in producing a certain truth of film, something like a chemical truth. In the appearance of these figures in this photograph, there is a constituent time lag (décalage) which seems impossible to reintegrate; since the image of the man has arrived at its optimal development, to this nuanced gradation of gray which supposedly produces the best sense of the real in photography, the image of the blonde woman, with its large areas of undetailed white, appears as though latent, insufficiently revealed, while the image of the brunette, inversely, seems already too hard, too contrasty.[71]

Bergala's description fascinatingly elides the image as figure, a "chemical" truth of gradation, with the figures themselves. Like Schefer's close-up as a "mosaic face, made up of flakes, dust and dots," Bergala attends to medium to undermine figuration in favor of an enigmatic body. This special affect of "cinematic truth" can be understood as the powers of the false. The "best sense of the real" is undercut by "les deux mortes" as a "décalage": displacement, break but also time lag, reanimating the frieze-like quality as an image of suspense.

A suspension of life is frequently evoked in figures of the cinematic body, as reanimated forms or half-lives: ghosts, vampire, mummies, cyborgs. For Andre Habib, cinema's articulation of the lived body's temporality with the "objective time" of material objects produces a new regime of images: "mutants, ghosts, monsters, wasted figures, cunning mechanisms. . . .The narrative is nothing but a cover, the finery that tries to veil this time made visible."[72] Narrative movement as "illusion of life" is, according to Habib, only window dressing on a corpse, a distraction that hides the dead body of film. His argument echoes Doane's, for whom the movement of the narrative as developed in early cinema served to sever film from "speaking its relation of time,"[73] in a consolidation of screen time as primary.

What happens when the "false movement" of the narrative fails, and we have instead the falsifying experience of aberrant movement? What if instead, another type of movement forms—suspense as a special case of movement—to give rise to (as yet) unlived bodies? If aberrant movement produces a suspended body, it is only the lived body that is suspended. In semblance's "charging up," the intensive movement in place of suspense signals a reservoir of potential via "vitality affects."[74] The reanimation of film exceeds illusion; it generates a re-lived body (anotherness) as the more to life itself, the creativity of the body in time.

A Free Replay

The Ethico-Aesthetics of Vertigo

> The monument's action is not memory but fabulation.
> —Gilles Deleuze and Félix Guattari, What Is Philosophy?

Hitchcock has become another name for cinematic specificity, a legacy of the New Wave critic–auteurs who saw in his films a signature penned with a caméra-stylo, and of a popular conception of Hitchcock as master manipulator of the cinematic image, invulnerable himself to its effects. Yet such a conception overlooks how Hitchcock not only made intensive use of other media, but often did so via his image rather than his cinematic skills. Think, for example, of his introductions to television's Alfred Hitchcock Presents, the signature-image of his iconic (and self-drawn) caricature, or the publicity stills and cardboard cutouts of the man used to market his films, moves bringing him closer to someone like William Castle than Bergman or Resnais. This extra-cinematic circulation of Hitchcock's body as carefully controlled image is subversively exploited in Johan Grimonprez's experimental collage film *Double Take* (2009), where Hitchcock's doubles are caught up in a deadly world of Cold War televisual media (from news footage of Cold War meetings to old coffee commercials). Woven through the film's collage is a rewriting of Tom McCarthy's story "Negative Reel," in which a 1962 Hitchcock encounters his older double from 1980 (the year of Hitchcock's death) and ultimately murders this future self. McCarthy's tale, the double of a story by Borges (itself double), rewrites and rehinges an earlier version, where Hitchcock encounters his younger 1922 self while filming *Topaz*.[75] In *Double Take*, 1980 Hitchcock says to his Cold War counterpart, "It is the destiny of every medium to be devoured by its offspring," lamenting cinema's decline at the hands of television. However, Grimonprez's deployment of a proliferating set of doubles in an intermedial zone suggests less a banal Oedipal narrative of artistic succession than the generative uncertainties of transmedial reproduction. Hitchcock's ambiguous embodiments, contagious and crossing boundaries, not only characterizes Grimonprez's use of Hitchcock as a figure, but also a reading of Hitchcock beyond his famously closed worlds.[76]

Grimonprez's film is itself a double of a double, of the gallery film of his 2005 installation *Looking for Alfred*. This work explored Hitchcock's film walk-ons, restaged through procuring multiple Hitchcock dopplegängers (professional and nonprofessional), and the visual evocation of Hitchcock's exact contemporary Magritte, whose blank, dapper everyman echoes Hitchcock's own persona. The film unfolds in a condensed scenario of a closed world (spiraling around the interior of a large gallery) of Hitchcock's films come to murderous life, featuring a blonde woman who revengefully poisons him and gorily devours the birds he used to torment Tippi Hedren.

Against the sterility of a Baudrillardian simulation, the virtuality made apparent in *Double Take* is fully real, as in Borges's *Garden of Forking Paths*. The past doesn't allegorize or mirror the present, but is reanimated in incompossible worlds. *Double Take* is sensible to the effects of repetition as generator of difference. Hitchcock's "walk-ons" on TV and in film are the main source material, such as the famous opening to *Alfred Hitchcock Presents*, in which Hitchcock's shadow meets up and merges with Hitchcock's abstract profile; this static outline receives and is absorbed by the shadow self, then becomes the "live" intro. Grimonprez's examination of "360 minutes of Hitchcock performances which have hardly been examined at all in Film Studies," quickly reveal an obsession, familiar to any Hitchcock fan, with mistaken identities and doubles.[77] As Hitchcock asks himself in McCarthy's script, "What makes you think there are only two of us?"

The stability of symmetrical doubles is undermined by an emphasis on their intensive inbetween; the double serves to stage aberrant experiences of time and space. Hitchcock's familiar form amplifies the undecidable contradictions here, which open onto what Thomas Elsaesser describes as "a battle . . . about the reality status of each: the world of Hitchcock/Hollywood and the world of history/memory. . . . It is not always certain which will win," a battle he describes as "the power of cinema to define our reality." Hitchcock's body, ambiguously doubled by his "blond female assistants" (the actresses) is a lure that Elsaesser terms "immersion." The walk-ons become "walk-ins," opening up a brief écart where "the world on screen is 2-D but Hitchcock's world invites us to think it in 3-D . . . to gratify an almost bodily urge to enter into it." This is dubbed the "Scottie syndrome"—impossible embodiment as perceptual lure—generated by a doubling that produces for Elsaesser a "hauntology of realism and reference." This figural effect, an incommensurable exchange opened between seeing and reading (he cites Magritte's *Ceci n'est pas une pipe*) is a "thrilling of our perceptual norms and habitual expectations" provoked by Hitchcock's ambiguous embodiment.[78]

In *Double Take,* Cold War image clichés (for example, Khrushchev banging his shoe during his speech) are suspended. Grimonprez's work confirms W. J. T. Mitchell's intuitions about the contemporary "pictorial turn" of our image-based era, where "magical thinking" about the illusion of moving images (as in the concept of cinematic fetishism) is reassessed in light of their ambiguous embodiment: "The subjectivized object in some form or other is an incurable symptom." He suggests Marx and Freud as guides on how to understand, not overcome, such magical thinking; Hitchcock might also be such a guide. Mitchell suggests contemporary image culture should engage in a "paleontology of the present," which both accurately describes Grimonprez's work and indicates the necessity for a complexification of image time beyond stabilized relations of past and present.[79] Ending with Donald Rumsfeld's notorious performance "art piece" "There are Known Knowns," Grimonprez's film is more than simply a metacommentary or allegory of history repeating itself. Hitchcock's ambiguous embodiments perform a heightened awareness of time, a continual crumbling of the ground of the present in the face of a "past that is preserved." Here, memory is not the most personal possession of a subject, but that which continually takes the subject outside of herself. When Hitchcock meets his former self, he asks him to call up a memory only they would know as evidence; the refusal to do so is taken as stronger proof of identity than any fixed memory-image ever could.

Grimonprez's film partakes in a new archival sense in which cinema's preservative and closed world is complicated and infected by the "liveness" of television itself, demanding circulation. If, as Grimonprez cites from Hitchcock, the length of a film is directly related to the endurance of the human bladder, television has no such time, but works via the artificial respiration of a continually building and deflating suspense. As Hitchcock puts this in an intro: "Tonight as a special attraction we shall present some television commercials. I knew you'd like that. They will be injected at various points in the picture to keep you from getting too engrossed in the story."[80]

A contemporary return to Hitchcock as what Žižek calls "the mirror of cinema studies" has both made Hitchcock's work into the image of another world inaccessible to us, but also a figure whose newness has only been recognized in retrospect.[81] Elsaesser asks, "Why Hitchcock now?," provoked by the uncanny proliferation of critical texts and cinematic remakes of Hitchcock's work in the past two decades. This concern is echoed in Žižek's question: "Is there a proper way to remake a Hitchcock film?" Žižek suggests Hitchcock's multiple endings of his films "allow us to insert Hitchcock into the series of artists whose work forecast today's digital universe," where "we seem to be haunted by the chanciness of life and the alternate versions of reality."[82] Patricia Pisters has argued that cinema since the 1990s confirms Hitchcock as a visionary generator of images that prefigure contemporary neuroscience: his cinema of mental relations, nonrepresentational, offer us an image of the brain as a screen.[83] As Rodowick writes, time expresses that "only retrospectively do we recognize the emergence of the new."[84]

Elsaesser dates the contemporary canonization of Hitchcock as artist, not simply filmmaker, to the exhibition *Hitchcock and Art: Fatal Coincidences* (2000).[85] Its unforgettable opening room mixed the funeral and the fetishistic, testimony to the extra-cinematic liveliness of image-objects, a direct descendant of Hitchcock's shot of the gloves in *Psycho*. A single prop from each film was displayed in a darkened room, encased in glass on a rectangular base, spot lit on a velvet pillow. The exhibit assembled found works of art thematically connected to Hitchcock (such as Millais's *Ophelia* as Madeleine's precursor), contemporary artwork that engaged and reimagined Hitchcock, and objects from Hitchcock's films. Although the set designed by Dali for *Spellbound* seems at home in the museum, the status of objects such as the shower room from *Psycho* seemed at that time less secure. Laura Mulvey has read this opening room as a bittersweet elegy for cinema's spectacular aging body, its threat defused by time itself. She sees cinematic corpses on display; devoid of onscreen animation, their banality only highlights the deadened vitality of cinematic fetishism. "It was impossible not to remember that nothing looks better than when made from light and shade," she writes in *Death 24x a Second,* characterizing cinema as a form of ghostly half-life.[86]

In that rethinking of cinema's relation to time, Mulvey described a "cinema of delay" effectuated by digital technologies, which allow us to intervene in and slow down cinema. The effect is double: both a corpsing of the pseudo-liveliness of narrative cinema and the captured image of a ghost as visible trace. In her work, the phantom haunting cinema does not gain a body, but only ever refers back to lost bodies, real and phantasmatic: the indexical trace, the material substrate or the uncanny home of the mother's body. For Mulvey, the suspension events of the cinema of delay renders narrative cinema obsolete, but only through the work of revelation, uncovering what was already there. Douglas Gordon's *24 Hour Psycho,* for example, a replay of Hitchcock's film at around 2 frames per second, generates for Mulvey a meta-indexical effect, revealing what is "not there in the original *as screened* but [what] can be revealed within it," as if the event of screening itself was not part of the cinematic body and its eventness.[87] This logic of *revelation* functions as a form of tender autopsy for Mulvey, where the secret of cinema is the corpse. As with Sobchack's feeling-knowing, difference is not made by the encounter itself.

Mulvey cites Amy Taubin's claim that Gordon's film "opened up a Hollywood genre movie to aesthetics of slow motion and thus to the traditions of the avant-garde film."[88] From genre to avant-garde: this is how Mulvey recuperates body genres' excesses via intellectual suspense. The double time of Gordon's film parallels a now-ness of conventional projected flow and an obscured then-ness of registration; the not-yetness of a suspension event is not part of this experience. Gordon's public meditation on private spectatorship self-reflexively opens up passive spectatorship (here, Mulvey again echoes the questions of the corporeal turn). While admitting that the viewer of Gordon's work is, like the cinema spectator, unable to intervene in the projection's flow, she nonetheless identifies this as a break with a dying cinema, a "point of no return." Spectators of Gordon's work might well be inspired to try this interactivity "at home."[89] Collapsing photography and cinema through her emphasis on the photogram and its essential stillness, as if slow motion was a halfway point between photography and film, Mulvey attempts to guarantee for the viewer what Barthes felt cannot exist in film—the punctum—and to maintain spectatorial control, despite the fact that even if *24 Hour Psycho* gives you more time to contemplate each image, it is *still* prescribed by flow. A paused image on screen is a form of duration through repetition. In Gordon's hypnotic endurance event, no different nature opens up before the spectator's eye. Instead, the spectator's individual freedom is increased as the opportunity to think and know, rather than be thought by the impulsive and compulsive movement of narrative as illusion. Interactivity for Mulvey is less the sensation of "continuing" to believe in the world, the suspense of indetermination, than a mode of spectatorial control, one she has been tracing across her entire career. Questions of the body and cinematic temporality are at the heart of this enquiry. While her work echoes a key concern of the corporeal turn, namely the activity of the spectator before the screen, she turns away from the productive indistinctions of an emergent cinematic body. An excess of sensation is displaced in her work in favor of control, mediated by a cinephilic urge that must be kept in check.

If Hitchcock has become a kind of shorthand for cinematic specificity, Mulvey's work has made the Hitchcockian woman its star thanks to "Visual Pleasure and Narrative Cinema."[90] Mulvey reads *Vertigo* as "cut to the measure of male desire" with its split between an active, increasingly sadistic and determining male gaze, embodied in the character of Scottie (where "the narrative is woven around what Scottie sees or fails to see") and the Woman as icon, with Judy embodying both the fetishistic (her exhibitionism in the first half of the film) and the masochistic (her despairing willingness to let herself be made over in her own image in the second half) qualities that characterize the woman in classical cinema.[91] For Mulvey, the camera's "look" is bound to the perspective of the male character, emphasized by the camera's fidelity to Scottie save during the letter writing scene.[92] Cinema's ideological effects are produced through codifying and controlling the spectator's gaze, automatically producing knowledge of the world. "Identification between spectator and screen-protagonist closes up necessary or remaining gaps between form and content. (For instance, Hitchcock reconciles his extravagant and unusual use of cinema with the demands of convention, involving the spectator through suspense)."[93] For Mulvey, the spectator is *not* sufficiently distracted by Hitchcock's daring use of cinematic devices to lose the narrative thread; rather, the narrative successfully keeps the spectator in place.

Mulvey's work consistently calls for techniques to break spectatorial fascination and reveal the workings behind cinema's parasitic liveliness. What does tracing suspense across this work tell us about bodily obsolescence in the suspension-event of the cinematic encounter? Classical cinema minimizes spectatorial distancing by involving them in the form through narrative, hiding the film's body and its construction, though this can be interrupted by spectacle as when the woman's body "suspends" narrative. Ultimately, though, this suspense lacks genuinely disruptive potential as it is a visual pleasure, not an intellectual one. Conventional narrative suspense is exemplified by Hitchcock's films, where images inexorably follow each other according to the needs of story, and where plot resolves questions of knowledge. What causes Scottie's fatal fascination with Judy? She was Madeleine all along—Novak's doubled presence is not an interpretive problem. In opposing visual and intellectual pleasure, Mulvey fails to account for the bodily affect of cinema as producing a real effect. If Sobchack rereads sensation as a form of knowing, Mulvey's work subordinates this too-closeness of encounter to a knowing that depends on distance.[94] In *Death 24x a Second*, Mulvey returns to the spectacle of "Novak," but even the cinema of delay she describes, activated by a fetishistic "suspension of narrative," only operates according to a revelatory logic: "As an indexical icon, however, the star is ultimately an undifferentiated part of the photographic image, its apparatus and its ghostly trace of reality."[95] In *Fetishism and Curiosity*, Mulvey links the apparatus and female body through the figure of the carapace—an insect's hard shell, protecting the vulnerable and disgusting inside.[96]

Mulvey valorizes the formalist, intellectual suspense of avant-garde cinema. This differs from Barthes's "thrilling of the intelligible" in that it does not "make everything right in the end." Epistemological uncertainty, as with the dreamlike structure of *Un Chien Andalou*, suspends interpretation; this produces a film that means "beyond" the boundaries of screen time. Avant-garde viewers (as with classical theories of suspense) hold superior knowledge, but here divorced from character knowledge and unpredetermined. Such suspended knowledge never "meets up" with the film itself; its satisfaction is in the spectator's enhanced understanding.

Working from a psychoanalytic perspective, Mulvey is concerned with cinema's ability to render material the excess of "fears, anxieties and desires" that haunt our lives, to use "the indexical aspect of photography to slip in and out of the visible world and find concrete images for those realities of emotion that cannot be seen, while being often *excessively* felt."[97] Mulvey's cinema of delay harnesses excessive feeling, transforming it into knowledge through revelation. The figure of a cinema for delay resembles more sadistic Detective Ferguson than the broken-down, sci-phi Scottie of Deleuze, where delay does not reveal, but expands the circuits of connection to allow for the emergence of the *unthought*.

Motivated by the spectator's freedom as control, it is curious that Mulvey's reading of *Vertigo* is not more nuanced, where the ultimate interventionist spectator so clearly suffers. Scottie is persistently perplexed at his desire to remake Judy; when she asks, "Why are you doing this?" (despite knowing his motivation), his only reply is "I don't know." How might we understand them as "not knowing," and what difference would that make? Compelled to achieve perfect likeness, Scottie's demeanor suggests that in reanimating Madeleine through Judy, he himself is being animated. His open-eyed acknowledgment of the impossible scene change in the 360-degree shot admits a loss of control at the moment of his putative triumph. Beyond Comolli's denegation, which makes the spectator a clear-eyed participant in her or his own duping, Scottie's not-knowing is affective. This not-knowing is shared too by the spectator as the suspension of felt belief, and *Vertigo* both demonstrates the fragility of such belief and its potential of repetition itself. Simply knowing is not enough: Scottie does not reveal that he knows, but elaborately recreates/relives the scene of Madeleine's death.

This reliving differentiates Mulvey's revelatory approach from my theory of suspense as anotherness, "at least as different as last is from next." Mulvey rereads *Psycho* to develop a theory of the cinematic body "in time"; in each case, the body is a corpse. The obsolete body revealed is industrial narrative cinema, "showing its age" at its material base and through deadened objects on display in the museum. In *Psycho* she finds only an "essential stillness," of the photogram as the secret heart of cinema, downplaying the fact that the film's most spectacular bodies are Janet Leigh, corpse-to-be, and the "grinning skull corpse" of Mrs. Bates; neither inspire a calm meditation on essential stillness. Both are in fact spectacular "reanimations" of an ambiguous embodiment. Mrs. Bates is "reanimated" by swinging lightbulb and spinning chair; this movement is not illusory, but a direct image of the relation that produces liveliness itself, a time-image of her "persistence" in Norman and as a body producing effects and affects. Janet Leigh's unblinking eye, source of countless debates over whether this was a still image, animated, or an actual shot in duration, is shocked into life *as a moving image* by the drop of water. Mulvey reads this as *exposing* cinema's material base that underpins the apparent distinction between stillness and motion; in doing so, she undoes the difference made by suspense itself. There is no "exposing the medium" that would lay film to rest. In Hitchcock, death always plays a spectacular role, but in terms of the narrative function. Mulvey compiles a list of films that "end with or threaten death by falling as a public spectacle."[98] *Vertigo* is not among them.

How might we activate a double vision of Hitchcock, to reread the body of Judy/Madeleine in *Vertigo* as a special affect/effect against a revelatory logic? Mulvey's pensive spectator, "halting the image or repeating sequences" in a cinema of delay, "can dissolve the fiction so that the time of registration can come to the fore," here understood as referential time.[99] The pensive spectator is *self-reflective*, stabilizing relations of vision and undoing the automatism of perception that narrative cinema imposed. The contagion of affective suspense, though, is *self-referential*, asking the spectator to account for the difference made in engagement. To take a different example, what is the pedagogical perception of a Hitch- cockian replay like Jim Campbell's *Illuminated Average #1*? This work is a single still image, generated from a scan of every frame of the film, then "stacked" as a digital archive of all the film's visual data translating movement into average brightness and contrast values. The center of the image is almost completely burnt out, while recognizable images such as a lamp emerge around the edges. The result holds in tension two kinds of figurations: images of light and images of things. A revelatory reading might, for example, read the blankness at the heart of the image symptomatically, as the condensed image of an effect of white faces at the center of the screen. This "revelation" of what passes as invisible to the naked eye, such as "whiteness" as the attractional lure of industrial Hollywood cinema, is fully part of the reality of this image. But it does not determine what we see here. Campbell's work is a figural image, a hesitation between seeing and reading, and to "see through" this sus- pense foregoes a set of questions around the nature of temporality itself, the image of the body in time.

A return to Hitchcock rediscovers duration, the vitality affects that persist in his work. I read *Vertigo*'s figural form of suspense to ask, What is the obsolescence of the body produced in the suspension-event of *Vertigo*, in a way that reframes the discourse of dead ends, death, and impossibility? How does repetition reanimate as *different* the closed world of this film via potential? How do remakes amplify the differential of repetition as a vitality affect of the original object, the film itself? Many commentators have called *Vertigo* a tale of death; screenwriter Samuel Taylor jokingly suggested it be called "To Lay a Ghost." Ambiguous embodiments as indeterminately material yet sensationally effective are the desiring-motor of the film itself.

The story of Orpheus and Eurydice, the woman who dies twice, echoes Scottie's fatal obsession for Madeleine; the film's tragic ending seems to confirm cinema as an art of death. Maurice Blanchot writes in "Orpheus' Gaze" of the desire for the outside as the destructiveness of double vision:

> By turning toward Eurydice, Orpheus ruins the work, which is immediately undone, and Eurydice returns among the shades. When he looks back, the essence of night is revealed as the inessential. Thus he betrays the work, and Eurydice, and the night. But not to turn toward Eurydice would be no less untrue. Not to look would be infidelity to the measureless, imprudent force of his movement, which does not want Eurydice in her daytime truth and her everyday appeal, but wants her in her nocturnal obscurity, in her distance, with her closed body and sealed face—wants to see her not when she is visible, but when she is invisible, and not as the intimacy of a familiar life, but as the foreignness of what excludes all intimacy, and wants, not to make her live, but to have her living in the plenitude of her death.[100]

But the force of repetition in *Vertigo*, unfaithful to any notion of an eternal identity, proposes a double vision of looking-again, linking cinema as an art of (nonincidental) repetition and the body's anotherness in time. *Vertigo* is a film that demands rewatching and remaking. If repetition brings about death, again, the film as a whole exceeds the narrative closure to intimate the presence of something else. Death itself is characterized by repetition. In *Anti-Oedipus,* Deleuze and Guattari state, "The experience of death is the most common of occurrences in the unconscious, precisely because it occurs in life and for life, in every passage or becoming. *It is the very nature of every intensity.*"[101] A return to Hitchcock should be measured by the double vision of desire, where the crime of infidelity is displaced by the proliferation of doubles as the anotherness of bodies in time.

A Cinema of the Seer

We first see "Scottie" pursuing a criminal across the rooftops of the city. The tension builds as they leap between buildings until Scottie misses his mark and falls, clinging desperately to the edge. As he glances over his shoulder at the ground below, we see the first use of the "vertigo shot" designed by Hitchcock, a simultaneous forward zoom and reverse tracking shot, which creates a sickening impression of movement and spatial distortion while also remaining in place: the very definition of suspense as a special case of movement. The world stretches around and away from Scottie; he no longer moves within it. When a fellow officer reaches down to help, he loses his balance and plunges to his death. As

Scottie (James Stewart) hanging at the end of the opening of *Vertigo.*

the sprawled body of the fallen officer lies below, a frozen pinwheel spiral, Scottie is left hanging; we never see his rescue and he remains suspended over the abyss for the rest of the film, unable to effectively take action.

Plagued by acrophobia, Scottie retires. An old acquaintance, Gavin Elster (Tom Helmore), contacts him for help solving the puzzle of his wife Madeleine's (Kim Novak) increasingly erratic and self-destructive behavior. Listening to Elster's tale of Madeleine's unconscious possession by the spirit of a long dead relative, Carlotta Valdez, Scottie agrees to follow her. Elster arranges for Scottie to see Madeleine that evening at Ernie's restaurant; from the first glance, Scottie is enraptured, his pursuit less professional than an illicit desire.

In a remarkable sequence of twelve minutes with no dialogue, Scottie follows Madeleine about her unremarkable life, until she drives out to the Palace of the Legion of Honor and spends hours enthralled before a painting of Carlotta, still as a mannequin. Scottie sketches visual resonances in this *tableau vivant*: Madeleine's posy of flowers mirrors that of Carlotta, their hair is tied back in the same spiral form. Each resemblance is traced through a tracking shot, not a cut, emphasizing both the similarities and the charged space between, until an unmatched shot of Carlotta's necklace.

Scottie steps out of the shadows when an entranced Madeleine throws herself into San Francisco Bay and he saves her. Madeleine awakens in his apartment, wary, confused, but hardly suicidal; she flees before he can fully indulge his desire. The next day he follows her again; she leads him back to his own doorstep. Their growing intimacy is shaded by Madeleine's fear of possession by Carlotta. She wafts in and out of trances; in the forest, among the sequoia trees (ever green, ever living), she languidly traces the rings of a felled tree. "Here I was born, and here I died," she says, and the "I speaks, but I is an (ambiguous) other."

Madeleine is frightened by a dream; Scottie, a pragmatist who, to help her shake off the past, recognizes the setting of a dream she describes as the San Juan Bautista mission, a museum of California's Spanish past. He convinces her that upon visiting the site in the flesh, she'll be free of the haunting past: "You'll finish your dream." Once there, they confess their love and share a passionate kiss, but Madeleine breaks the embrace to race up the bell tower stairs. Scottie, overwhelmed by vertigo, watches helplessly as she falls to her death.

A listless coroner's inquest rules the death an accident; though Scottie is not found criminally liable, the coroner's pointed references to his "inadequacy" only reinforces his guilt. Scottie repeats Madeleine's dream as a terrible nightmare, falling first into the open grave, and then, in a suspended reanimation, falling through the air. He awakens in abject terror, catatonic. A damaged Scottie leaves the hospital, endlessly retracing his steps and continually glimpsing traces of Madeleine in the women around him. When he sees Judy Barton's (Novak's) uncanny resemblance to Madeleine, he becomes obsessed with recreating his lost love. Following her home, he presses this seeming stranger for a date. She finally agrees and closes the door on him; the camera abandons Scottie to stay with her as she writes an unsent confession that she and Scottie's Madeleine are one and the same. Elster's mistress, she posed as Madeleine, knowing Scottie's vertigo would prevent him from stopping her phony leap off the bell tower. Not Judy, but the real Mrs. Elster fell that day.

Abandoned by Elster, half in love with Scottie, she can't live with herself and so begins to (re)live as Madeleine. With increasing demand, Scottie overrides Judy's limp protestations and remakes her as Madeleine down to the last details of hair and dress. After a brief period of domestic bliss, Scottie finally discovers the truth; dressing for dinner, Judy slips and puts on Madeleine's locket, from Carlotta's portrait. Flashing back to his previous views of the necklace, Scottie realizes but doesn't reveal that he has been duped. The audience, already in on Judy's secret, doubles their suspense as Scottie takes Judy as Madeleine back to the bell tower. Judy recognizes his intent but protests her ignorance as Scottie, freed from vertigo by his angry certainty, forces her up the stairs. He bitterly accuses her of allowing Elster to "make her over," to "rehearse her" and "train her" to be Madeleine, setting Scottie up as the "made-to-order witness," oblivious to the irony. Atop the tower, Judy confesses, but as she kisses Scottie, she is frightened by the sudden appearance of a nun; she loses her balance and falls. The film ends abruptly, with a

The impossible objective shot that ends *Vertigo* (Alfred Hitchcock, 1958).

brief shot of Scottie posed in the bell tower window, arms spread as in flight, again suspended over the fall.

Vertigo, often described as hallucinatory, was called a "filmed dream" by Truffaut.[102] Despite the containment of the most extravagant elements as either exterior to the narrative (the credit sequence), or explained as hallucination or dream, this oneiric quality saturates the whole film. Marker writes:

> There are many arguments in favor of a reading of the second half of *Vertigo* as a dream. . . . The entire second half would be nothing but a delirium, and the double of the double is revealed at last: we were convinced that the first part was the truth, but it was the lie of a perverse spirit, the truth was in the second—but if, in the end, it really was the first part that was true, and the second the lie of a sick spirit? So what we can accuse of being too overloaded, too outrageously expressionist in the nightmare images which precede the clinic are a ruse, an additional red herring to hide from us that the fantastic film that will occupy us for another hour, has assumed the appearance of a realist film to better mislead us—with the exception of the brief moment. . . . The change of scene during the kiss, which in this perspective takes

on a new meaning, that of the lost confession, the revealing detail, the crazy blink across the fixed gaze, like that which sometimes reveals madness.[103]

Vertigo folds around the undecidable proximity of dream and reality. The suspense of *Vertigo* is this feeling of moving from the criteria of true or false to a double vision of the mutual image of actual and virtual, displacing a simple opposition. For Marker, *Vertigo* demands reviewing, in the light of the first, but simultaneously generates double vision, with no once and for all. Any stabilizing confession is lost; criminality persists and insists as a crime of time.

Derangements of narrative sense amplify the figural elements of the film, a cinematic embodiment as movement-vision. In his remake of *Vertigo* in *Sans Soleil*, Marker repeatedly activates a doubled vision, mimetically replaying the vertigo effect by presenting and then blurring a series of stills from Hitchcock's film. Peter Wollen finds a clue to *Vertigo*'s effect in Donald Spoto's biography of Hitchcock, in the green tint of Scottie's and Judy/Madeleine's encounters:

> During the editing [of *Downhill*, 1927], Hitchcock instructed the lab technicians to tint a pale green the scenes of Novello's delirium when his health fails. He remembered, from his earlier playgoing, the green stage-lights for the appearance of ghosts and for the world of fantasy, and he now employed a primitive monochrome—instead of the conventional blurring of the edges—to suggest a hallucinatory state of mind.[104]

The coloration returns in *Vertigo* to amplify the ghost story. Although Madeleine's possession is just a lure to frame Scottie for murder, the entire film plays off possession's duality: ghostly haunting and material object. On the one hand, possession takes over a body "by a phantom," thrusting aside "I" by an other. We see this in Madeleine's trances, her rapture before Carlotta's image, her seeming inability to control and recall her own movements, her involuntary leap into San Francisco Bay, and her continuous slipping away from Scottie's grasp. Scottie likewise is possessed by the memory of Madeleine, best seen in his elaborate dream of falling into the grave. Possession requires an uncanny detour from the self; as Tania Modleski notes, Scottie's pursuit of Madeleine leads him home, immediately *unheimlich*.[105] For Modleski, the uncanny in *Vertigo* is linked to femininity's threat to the "fullness of being"; the repressed possibility for man that woman is essentially a construct. If that is the case, so is man: what is repressed is the nothingness at his core of masculine identity.

The counterbalance to spiritual possession, a displacement from one's own body, is an overemphasis on the material: possession as object. This is the usual criticism of Scottie's treatment of Judy as a living doll for his own amusement (though it's a grim pleasure at best): dressing her up, changing her hair without a thought for the "real" Judy within. The body of Novak becomes the flash point for these questions, treated as a special effect. Like Modleski, although from a different perspective, I argue for Vertigo's more ambiguous gender division. Scottie also experiences this dual possession, controlled as much as he controls; his posture in the film's final image resembles nothing more than a puppet whose strings have been cut.

"There Are Things You Haven't Told Me"

Hitchcock made a critical choice when supervising the screenplay's adaptation, insisting that the film's key secret be revealed to spectators, though not to Scottie, with a third of the film yet to go. This remains controversial; Samuel Taylor felt it was mishandled, and many viewers remain puzzled by the decision.[106] Taylor argued that Judy's "real identity" should have been made explicit in a scene with Elster after Madeleine's death:

> If I were writing that scene now, I would have had her bring him (Elster) all the clothes he'd given her and say "Here, I don't want them anymore." So that the necklace would have had that much more importance later on. It's the one thing she did hold on to.[107] But the best thing about this kind of scene is that *you would have had a much stronger feeling of the humanity of the girl*.[108]

Taylor's concern for Judy's character, against Hitchcock's implied disregard for her humanity, is echoed in much feminist criticism of *Vertigo,* where Judy is seen as sacrificed to the ends of both the male characters in the film, and those of Hitchcock himself.

Andrew Sarris agreed with Taylor, noting, "It would have helped the audience's reaction to and feeling about Stewart. What you feel is that he's excessively silly and romantic instead of a victim. . . . It would have also suggested the possibility that he has some sense that she may not be dead."[109] Taylor replied:

> Well, that urge, that inner obsession is very important. I think that the thing that made me think of it when I was watching the picture today was that I wanted *more body for the girl* and that scene that I just thought of *would have given her more body* and helped the picture tremendously. Kim Novak was alright in the picture. But think about the possibility of Ingrid Bergman in the role, and the depth of emotion in this picture would be so tremendous that you would be overpowered by her.[110]

Taylor's might easily have talked about "fleshing out" Judy's character. One key criticism of the film is that "real women" are overlooked in favor of images, fantasies, and ghosts. A "real" woman is killed (Madeleine Elster); but her loss is unacknowledged and unmourned.[111] Judy meets a similar fate; Scottie is persistently disinterested in her history. Judy *is* insufficiently realized in the film, and the question of body has a great deal to do with it. Novak's performance was "alright," but failed to create two distinct characters; her Judy doesn't register fully, making only a passing impression on Scottie, and presumably on the audience. Taylor argues that Novak's poor performance failed to separate the characters: "If we'd had a brilliant actress who really created two distinctly different people, it would not have been as good. She seemed so naïve in that part, and that was good. She was always believable. There was no 'art' about it, and that's why it worked so very well." Thus the "happy accident" of casting and the "non-acting abilities," as Taylor puts it, of Novak causes the character indistinction. Incapable of "expressing"

two characters, Novak's body stands in the way instead of functioning merely as a "mask" or "placeholder." "Reality" wins out over art and
artifice.

One has only to think of the close-ups of Bergman in Hitchcock films
such as *Notorious* and *Spellbound,* her ability to convey inner states through
facial expression, in contrast to Novak's profile close-ups, posed rather
than expressive, to understand Taylor's distinction. Tag Gallagher places
Novak's dual role in the category of what he calls Hitchcock's "theoretical women," where concepts are emphasized at the "expense of human
reality"; he places Scottie in the same position.[112] To what extent, though,
is the slippage between the two roles a function of an experience of a
different type? When Sarris suggests Taylor's revision would have made
the audience question whether Scottie knew Madeleine wasn't dead,
he raises an epistemological problem: the film becomes a more effective detective story. The suspense of the letter scene works otherwise.
A clear distinction between Madeleine and Judy would also equally distinguish between the living and the dead; in this ambiguity, felt but not
rationally explained, the true suspense as affective indetermination of
Vertigo lies.

Other viewers of *Vertigo* have taken the letter-writing scene not as
an awkward misstep, but as the film's key. Modleski argues the scene
inaugurates a split between the audience's identification with Scottie
(until then, undivided) and with Judy, reflecting a larger pattern of oscillating identification between masculine and feminine elements in the
film. Robin Wood writes that in this scene "One become uncomfortably
aware of the director behind the camera telling her 'Now do this, now do
that.'" For Doug Tomlinson, beyond the question of Hitchcock's legendary cruelty toward his actresses: "This scene is crucial in its function
as a *reflexive, demystifying exposé* of both Judy Barton and Kim Novak as
actresses responding to directorial demands. . . . Here the performance
is controlled so as to signify the extent to which all her actions are controlled."[113] Tomlinson is unperturbed by the glimpse of the director that
Wood found ineffective; both Judy and Kim Novak are equally effective
reflexive puppets whose "bad performance" is a strategic demonstration
of Hitchcock's total mastery. Similarly, Scottie is often read as Hitchcock's

stand-in, his reshaping of Judy mirroring Hitchcock's famous make-overs of his leading ladies. Although the scene is undeniably stagey, Tomlinson underestimates the ambiguous nature of directorial authority in Vertigo. If Vertigo is a commentary on film itself, then the director as auteur is shown to be subject to suspense as well.

From Mind's Eye to Brain

In Deleuze's cinema books, Hitchcock hinges the movement-image and the time-image.[114] Though most of Hitchcock's work tended toward a completion of the movement-image—a cinema in which time is spatialized, where narrative unrolls through perception, affection, and action, and where cuts between images are suppressed according to the overall arc of the narrative—Deleuze argues that some of Hitchcock's films, including Vertigo, were already in the realm of the time-image, where perceptions become unhinged from actions and time is no longer subordinated to the completion of an action.[115] In Vertigo, two crucial scenes capture the oscillating suspension of the time-image; first, the simultaneous track and zoom of Scottie's crippling vertigo, and second, when Judy first appears as the newly reconstructed Madeleine. Thomas Wall writes, "Judy walks toward Scottie but she is divided into two distinct/indistinct doubles which refer to each other and chase each other in an endless circuit which forms an autonomous never-existing entity *neither simply from the past nor simply in the past*. . . . Judy emerges from the bedroom from out of time, not space."[116] This crystal-image does not actualize a memory, but occurs in the *indeterminacy* between the virtual and the actual. Compare the spatiotemporal bleed of this time-image to a later actualization of a recollection-image, when Scottie, seeing Judy in the mirror, recognizes Madeleine's necklace, and uncovers the deception. In that moment, the oscillation of identity is halted and actualized by a flashback, and this finally frees him into taking action. Scottie's actions, however, do not satisfyingly resolve the suspense of the film. The necklace as image is a thread pulled taut to connect and resolve narrative elements, especially how various bodies relate to each other. Previously this relationship was mystical and ghostly (both in the film and for the spectator, unsure how to manage the double vision of Judy as

Madeleine, and of Novak). The necklace as object stands in for and replaces all the troublesome bodies, including that of the ghostly Carlotta,
unifying their corporeal and temporal dispersions.

When Madeleine is first shown entranced before Carlotta's portrait,
the film etches a series of connections between real woman and image.
A close-up of Madeleine's posy on the bench tracks upward to a close-
up of Carlotta's identical posy; ditto Madeleine and Carlotta's spiral
chignons. Then: a close-up of Carlotta's necklace, but no correspond-
ing camera movement binds it to Madeleine. This shot remains suspended until Scottie's revelatory flashback, where the connective unity
of the tracking shots between Carlotta and Madeleine is replaced by the
intellectual resolution of narrative suspense. The initial "tracing of the
connections," though tied to Scottie's secret observation of Madeleine,
is also explicitly for the viewer; while we know Scottie is watching
Madeleine, and can interpret these shots as being Scottie's POV, they
differ from Scottie's previous observations of Madeleine in their explicit
attention to detail and in camera movement. They signal what Deleuze
terms "camera consciousness," defined by the mental connections it
can make.

Echoing Truffaut's comment that "the art of creating suspense is also
the art of involving the audience, so that the viewer is actually a participant
in the film," Deleuze notes that in time-images, the involvement works
both ways.[117] Using the incapacitated Scottie as an example, Deleuze
asks, "If one of Hitchcock's innovations was to implicate the spectator
in the film, did not the characters themselves have to be capable—in a
more or less obvious manner—of being assimilated to spectators?"[118]

Hitchcock had begun the inversion of this point of view by including
the viewer in the film. But it is now that the identification is actually
inverted: the character has become a kind of viewer. He shifts, runs
and becomes animated in vain, the situation he is in outstrips his
motor capacities on all sides, and makes him see and hear what is no
longer subject to the rules of a response or action. *He records rather
than reacts.* He is prey to a vision, pursued by it or pursuing it, rather
than engaged in an action. [119]

At the same time, the subjective/objective distinction "tends to lose its importance, to the extent that the optical situation or visual description replaces the motor action."[120] Nowhere is this more apparent than in the 360-degree shot of Scottie and the perfected transformation of Judy into Madeleine. As they kiss, Scottie is *not* lost in the moment, but opens his eyes and *registers, without reacting to,* the change in location, temporal and spatial, that surrounds them. Though he has actively pursued this re-creation, at the moment itself he is immersed, aware (of his position as spectator) and yet incapable of active intervention. Scottie's reaction (registered by nonresponse, as there is no cutaway to a close-up on Stewart's face) is deliberately ambiguous. For one thing, in pure op/son situations, the oscillation between the virtual and the actual is indeterminate, and the subjective/objective distinction is less significant because of the felt splitting between experience and memory, the "really apparitional" of past and future. Neither traditional narrative suspense, the imbalance of knowledge between spectator and character resolved in the end, nor Mulvey's enigma, an intellectual suspense requiring a turn away from the film and a determining revelation, this indeterminacy is the affective temporality at the heart of the film body and of the spectator's experience of participating in continuing. "I know, but all the same," says Comolli, wanting a spectator who is active, not fooled for a moment, always knowing even when they choose to believe.[121] Scottie's ambivalent registration, where knowledge is insufficient in the face of affect, is also the spectator's problem: film feels real, it affects us in real ways, and our "knowledge" is not secured, even when the lights come on and we leave the theatre.

In this cinema of the time-image, "everything remains real, but between the reality of setting and that of motor action there is no longer a motor extension established, but rather a dreamlike connection through the intermediary of the sense organs," as if "the action floats in the situation. . . ."[122] In the situation's suspense, there is also a continual vertiginous movement. This subjectless affect of suspense results not only from the proliferation of body doubles, but from the doubling action of the cinematic body itself: immediation, or the duplicity of semblance. As in figural analysis, attention to medium doesn't "reveal the mechanism" but gets at the new possibilities that the time-image offers. In *Vertigo*, this is most clearly expressed through the use of special effects, and the special "affect" of Novak's doubled role. Suspense delays spectatorial reaction via the feeling of potential; at the very end, the spectator remains caught up in the irresolution and tension of Scottie's fall.

The "suspended" shot of the necklace, only finally determined by Scottie's flashback, is a mastering of his (and our) temporal vertigo; except, like the recidivism of anomalous suspense, it persists. Suspense's excess marks the film's pedagogical revision of the movement-image as time-image, through the perversion of narrative from dysnarrative to the powers of the false. Žižek writes, "Hitchcock occupies a key place in Deleuze's cinema theory, that of the intermediary figure in the passage from movement-image to time-image."[123] But I argue that "Hitchcock's body" is less an intermediary than what Deleuze terms a "mediator," a pedagogue of return and repetition. This is how we can understand Hitchcock's untimely return in the form of double vision: the perceptual feeling of what does not appear, namely time itself. As a "hinge" between cinematic forms, Hitchcock's lesson is to look again at form through time. Mediators, Deleuze writes, allow us to connect through the invitation to "do with," entering a field of forces as a surfer enters a wave.[124] Likewise with cinema, we do not simply identify with the discrete forms of characters, but enter into a world of relations, not to the mirror world onscreen, but through the production of a movement-vision, a felt field of relationality.[125] This is what Schefer means when he says cinema makes us "live time," and why in Hitchcock's films, the suspense of the double is not simply the ghost as trace, but the ambiguous embodiment of felt relation, a return to or rediscovery of durations "above and below" our own.

The distinctive value of Hitchcock as a figure who asks us to "look again" is effectively demonstrated by Patricia Pisters's comparison of Žižek and Deleuze via *Vertigo*: Žižek's representation of impossible desire versus Deleuze's immanent evaluation of the film as a meta-cinematic rhizomatic "network of relations between virtual and actual images." The result, Pisters suggests, is that we arrive at very different understandings of "the idea of the subject and its relation to images and to the world."[126] Hitchcock's films for Deleuze mark the emergence of a camera consciousness of mental relation and connections, in which the spectator is a participant in a game of relation. Although Hitchcock has traditionally been read in terms of control and agency, attending to temporality via modes of subjectivation reveals a different sense of agency. We do not *have* but *participate* in agency; this is the interactive dimension of the occurrent arts or the cinematic event expressed as semblance.[127]

Pisters notes Deleuze's disinterest in the personal psychodrama of Hitchcock's Catholic upbringing, with its attendant scenarios of guilt and perversion that Žižek finds so relevant. In reading *Vertigo* through the difference time makes in the subject, guilt is displaced by a crime of time. Pisters contrasts a Žižekian motor of desire as lack to a Deleuzian desire to connect and increase our power to act. Time becomes both challenge and potential in this respect: "The indetermination and insecurity that time brings to the subject are not the negative limits of desire and knowledge, but are precisely that which brings about ongoing movements of thought: the gaps in our knowledge are needed to continue living and thinking."[128]

The model of the brain is opposed by Pisters to that of the eye. Through double vision, though, I reanimate the senses' embodied temporality, to ask how we might have a vision of "that which doesn't appear" to rearrange the common-sense homology between camera consciousness and human body, as Branigan's "impossible objective shot" both relies on and exceeds (makes obsolete) a human body. Double vision is a free replay of immanence itself, when seeing through time reanimates the world and its potential. This is the significance of delay for Deleuze, why the character of the time-image is a seer, no longer an actor. It likewise concerns the subjective/objective indistinction; a reimagining of cinematic objectivity is crucial here to "see form through time," to feel the contagious mutability of objects themselves.

Immanent evaluation drives this mode of thought. Rejecting the symbolic realm, the free replay of cinema's ambiguous embodiment activates a double vision of the directly signaletic, naming the relational game spectators participate in, first by possession (the ghost story, but also the "spiritual automaton of cinema") and then by the lively materialism

of the cinematic body, its forms and colors. I briefly read a key example
that Pisters also analyzes to illustrate this form of time in action. The
first time Scottie sees Madeleine in Ernie's restaurant is singled out
by Žižek as an example of camera consciousness. I read that scene as
activating a spiral of *refreshing double vision* that makes the body eccentric, a slow and careful spin of the spiral of time as felt relation, a tenta-
tive feeling out of becoming. This *spiral turn visually figures suspense,*
invites dizziness as a delirious recomposition of multiple temporalities.

For Pisters, this scene's "impossible objective shot" of Madeleine that
feels like a POV (especially given that the entire sequence has been staged
for "Scottie's eyes") gives the spectator a special place beyond identification. The critical revelation of Madeleine, where she poses for identification for the first time, is a moment when Scottie has turned away from
her approach. However, from the moment Madeleine rises up from the
table, movement does not stop, only contagiously leaps from camera to
characters and is simultaneously the movement of different temporal
registers. She halts behind his back, and we see what Scottie does not.
She briefly poses in profile, facing screen left and then turning to screen
right (signaling her duplicity, evocatively, through an elegantly performed
mug shot).

Jean Paul Esquinazi reads this as a "crystal image" of Madeleine in a
virtual, not actual, perception, containing all the layers of time (Judy,
Madeleine, and Carlotta) at once. However, I stress that it is not simply
that Scottie doesn't look at Madeleine that makes this a crystal-image;
the elaborate *choreography* of this scene is vertiginous in effect, a gesture
that leaps across bodies. As Madeleine approaches, Scottie turns away,
and she catches the force of his movement in the turn of her head. Scottie doesn't catch up with Madeleine in the present, but they participate
in an expended temporal field of potential. The circular movement opens
onto the "spiral of time," staging relation across incompossible bodies
and competing temporalities, and as the ritualistic gesture of refreshing doubled vision, where perception is caught up in the spiral form of
movement. (In *Lost Highway,* Lynch restages this effect in a scene I will
discuss as a "magic moment.") The effect for Pisters is that "the spectator is no longer invited to identify, but to think and make connections

between the different images. It is now the model of the brain, the rhizomatic mental connections that it can make and the way it thinks time, that are important."[129] The model of connection, the felt force of relation, underpins the ambiguous and generative embodiments of Hitchcock's return.

"What Makes You Think There Are Only Two of Us?"

Vertigo is a film often described as subjective and personal, both from an auteurist point of view and from Scottie's. This subjective sensibility comes through as simultaneously strangely impersonal and passionately intimate; Scottie is a man rent in two by time, standing beside his own actions and watching himself. When he sends Judy into the bathroom to fix her hair as the final gesture of transformation, he performs a curious ritualistic shuffle, reactivating the first sight at Ernie's (including his turn away) in what seems like self-deception. Rather than fixing his eyes on the prize, he walks to the window, and lit by the neon-green glow beaming into the room from another temporal dimension (the sequoia forest), he slowly turns away from the bathroom, lowering himself into a seat, then immediately back up and around, refreshing his own double vision with an intensive movement in place, performing the spiral of time.

Scottie spirals through time in *Vertigo*.

In *Vertigo*, the audience lives the film through Scottie's eyes, but character perspectives are persistently doubled by a camera consciousness that is not exactly other to Scottie (as in Esquenazi's suggestion that the shot of Madeleine at Ernie's is a virtual image for Scottie), but an ambiguously embodied anotherness. Rendered through impossible objective shots at key moments, and in the noted shift in character focalization from Scottie to Judy two-thirds of the way through the film, this anotherness is emphasized in Lou Ye's "remake" of *Vertigo*, *Suzhou River*, in which the "impossible objective" point of view becomes a character in the film, albeit one that remains suspended from view throughout.

As an exemplary text for thinking suspense as "the crime of time," *Vertigo* demonstrates the difficulties of defining suspense in Barthes's terms as that which is "made right in the end." All is not made right: although it resolves suspense at the level of narration and harmonizes knowledge between viewer and character, the ending leaves us hanging. The brief final shot, snatched away before the viewer has a chance to absorb it, suspends viewer and character (Scottie) in a pose of "recording without registering," a delay of impression. In *Vertigo*, suspense is a special case of movement, embodied in the film's spiral forms, and as a suspension of reference and of knowledge. This is suspense as immediation: as the form of reanimation, passing through death as exhaustion, but also as the intimation of something new.

Like Stelarc's suspension events, the cinematic body of *Vertigo* enacts the body's obsolescence in two senses. The first is through the wasted figure of the "seer, not the actor," and the contagious effect of this wasting disease on the viewer, via Hitchcock's innovative swapping of viewer and character. Flaxman identifies this as the side effect of the speculative disease of "sci-phi"; those who travel to the outside return wasted because a certain fixed concept of the body has been rendered obsolete. No wonder Marker reanimates *Vertigo* at the heart of his sci-phi film about the unlivable intensity of time travel, *La Jetée*. Second, *Vertigo* travels through an obsolescence of the movement-image itself, rendering movement aberrant, de-ranging narrative with the suspensive force of the *tableau vivant* or the *espace quelconque*. If Hitchcock closes the circle on the movement-image in *Cinema 1*, we immediately rediscover him as a filmmaker of time-images, when the circle becomes a spiral form of suspense.

How does *Vertigo* do this, when it points to the madness of reliving the past, what Marker describes as the attempt to "defeat time where its wounds are the most irreparable, to revive a dead love"?[130] Scottie's obsessive repetition of the past is doomed to fail, but in this failed repetition suspense is not resolved, but becomes a clearing for something else. Writing on *Vertigo*, Marker titles his article "A Free Replay": this is not a replay "free of the past," Scottie's bitter wish to Judy as he prepares to reenact Madeleine's death. Marker identifies that "freedom" as the male privilege embodied in Gavin Elster, whose marginal mechanics unfurl events that exceed stabilities of gendered identifications. The liveliness of *Vertigo* opens onto another free replay, one that can only pass *through* the replay as the gamble of a suspended (re)animation, what Nietzsche calls the "dice throw." Classical narrative theories of suspense rely equally on the idea that suspense stems from an uncertainty regarding outcome, and by the necessary resolution of that uncertainty. When suspense persists, a problem arises, as in "anomalous suspense." Suspense is also a problem for theories of identification, and the status of the spectator. Last, suspense is a problem for knowledge itself. It is in suspense as affective, as a "special case of movement" that *Vertigo* is exemplary.

In "Suspense and Its Master," Deborah Knight and George McKnight single out *Vertigo* as a special case of suspense that aligns the cataphors ("advance references," a signal of something to come) characteristic of suspense with the inevitability of Greek tragedy.[131] Future events complicate sense of time; the future intrudes on the present with the force of the past (that which will have happened). Cataphors are artifacts of the future, frequently making sense only retroactively. They see Carlotta's necklace as a cataphor in *Vertigo*, but also Madeleine herself: when Judy reincarnates as Madeleine in the bell tower with the vibrating modulation of her voice slipping between characters, her appearance signals her predetermined fate. In doing so, however, they overlook the continuing suspension that the body of Madeleine generates *throughout* the film. In the uncertainty of recognition that her figure generates throughout

(Judy? Madeleine? Carlotta? Kim Novak?) and in the modulation of identity she embodies, she figures a cinematic body as "unlived, as yet." Thus it is futile to ask, "Who is the real woman?," between Judy and Madeleine; her every appearance frays the fabric of everyday space-time.

Scottie too exists in a state of suspense when the role of viewer and actor are interchanged. Scottie swaps places not only with the spectator, but with Madeleine as well; the film is less a detective story of discovering a true identity than a sci-phi productive suspension of identity. Accordingly, the most significant cataphors in *Vertigo* are a triptych of *looks*, each during a kiss between lovers. These are looks not into off-screen space, but into time, and as such, cannot be fully resolved. In *Vertigo*, the true and the false are replaced with the virtual and the actual; in their exchange the cinematic body is rendered really apparitional. What we feel as "subjective" in *Vertigo* is less Hitchcock's personal vision or character focalization than the indetermination of semblance, as the "lived abstraction" of the body's anotherness.

Affective Cartographies

Vertigo was adapted from *D'entre les morts (From amongst the Dead, or The Living and the Dead)*, by *Les Diaboliques* authors Pierre Boileau and Thomas Narcejac, who wrote the novel deliberately targeting Hitchcock.[132] Hitchcock struggled with producing a filmable script until Samuel Taylor was brought on board. Rather than refer to the novel, Taylor developed a script from Hitchcock's notes, locations, and reveries. Hitchcock had made a tonal map of sites in and around San Francisco, but these empty spaces lacked a motivating storyline. As Donald Spoto describes it: "What [Hitchcock] did see was a series of *tableaux vivants*— scenes in an old cemetery, in a redwood forest, at a mission church, in an old stable, at a museum."[133] The figural force of these *tableaux vivants* persists in the finished film; characters are repeatedly seized by immobility within the film's set-pieces.

For Eleanor Kaufmann, the *tableau vivant* is a self-referential gesture that condenses the relation of mobility and immobility in Deleuze's cinema books: "life giving itself as a spectacle to life; of life hanging in suspense."[134] Kaufmann draws on Lyotard's acinema to articulate the suspended gestures of the tableau vivant as a perverse erotic economy, a tension between the "narrative movement" and an "irruptive, excessive alternative." Its doubled gesture expresses the double vision that *Vertigo* inspires, its excess of suspense. What is pictured is intensity itself, a cinematic perversion that makes visible what is normally invisible. Lyotard terms this a "sterile movement," opposed to the reproductive logic of dominant cinema; what is produced is only pleasure's intensity.[135] In this way, the *tableau vivant* is a privileged solicitor of *cinephilic* repetition. Amy Herzog notes that perversity drives the *tableau vivant*: "The body expresses resistance in successfully co-habitating these incommensurate positions at once, perhaps because it does so in ways that are often disturbing and threatening."[136] This threat comes from the immediate duplicity of the simultaneous lure of identification, with frozen bodies excessively presented for the gaze, and the disjunctive refusal to settle into dominant coordinates of identity precisely through the perverse stretching of time. The suspended indistinction between movement and immobility thus self-referentially produces perversion as an intense pleasure, its sterility unspent on narratological logic.

The original power of these *tableaux vivants* often overwhelms the storyline by the oneiric quality of the setting, and individual personalities dissolve into their surroundings. A ghost story, *Vertigo* exploits the haunting quality of "giving a body to a phantom," both via the audiences' perception of Novak's doubled role and in the film's narrative. The "ghost" has generative powers, but the film's mystery is unresolved by the discovery of origins. It is the film's temporality that "fleshes" out the ghosts. The *tableau vivant* is a suspension-event, rendering obsolete the privileged relation between figure and ground that simply places characters in the world, releasing elements such as form and shape to enter into new compositions of space and time. The color green thus moves through several temporal registers in the film, especially in the form of a light that is both the "medium" of pastness and the banal insistence of material presence (much like Lynch's suspended projector beam in the opening of *Inland Empire*). The greenish tint infusing Scottie's spiral in Judy's room is not just a poor copy of a cherished memory (the artificial neon against the leaf-infused sunlight), but the suspended medium of a set of relational elements released via the suspended body's obsolescence.

Animation through the Body

The productive problem of Novak's body forms a key part of the figural analysis of suspense in *Vertigo*. This problem is announced "narratographically," to borrow Garrett Stewart's term, from the film's first frames, in Saul Bass's remarkable credit. Reading the credits narratographically, as outside the narrative proper, this "sponsoring first image" intimately links seeing and nonhuman animation. It sets up the question of animation's liveliness in this film both as the puppet master's absolute control (with animation "infecting" live action, repeated later during Scottie's dream sequence) and as the uncanny direct sensuous experience of nonhuman materiality. Narratography for Stewart requires close attention to cinema's material conditions, "the reading of an image *and its transitions* for their own plot charge."[137] Attending to the intensive inbetween (of material substrate and onscreen image, as well as images' transitions) refocuses our attention not on the narrative drive of "what is there to see in the next image?" but "what is there to see in this image itself?" Bass's credits introduce the animatic into the film's body as a whole, strikingly condensing key themes, including the foregrounding of special effects. In highlighting the film's materiality as a composition of colors and shapes that ambiguously resolve into or double recognizable forms, the central (unresolved) question of *Vertigo* is raised from the start.

When Scottie pressures Judy to become Madeleine, he tells her, from the fixed axis of obsession, "It can't matter to you." But the film hinges on the difference made in the mattering itself, for everyone involved. This is the film's ethico-aesthetical force, frequently reduced to a moral question of Scottie's treatment of Judy, ignoring the "real" woman behind the image. But the credit sequence stages recognition as a problem, what Comolli might call the "ghosting" of the actor-medium in favor of the role. Credits are often treated as peripheral to the film: expressive or functional adjunct. In *Vertigo*, though, this poetic sequence not only sets the tone for the film, but is repeatedly echoed throughout. It visually conveys the film's refrain of vertiginous spiral movements, and associates these explicitly with questions of identity, the inner self, and the act of looking. Credits are both explicit *lectosigns* (asking us to look with a double vision—to see or to read?) and disavowed; the opening's graphics put reading into suspense. We read the actors' names even as we are enjoined to forget them as they body forth characters. That we are made to *feel* the labor of this forgetting around the recognition of "Novak," rather than simply take it as habitual, is one of the ways that *Vertigo* reopens the body's anotherness.

The credits stretch and condense the time of the film like a musical overture.[138] Combined with Bernard Hermann's melancholy and romantic score, they plunge us into a dislocated and unsettled frame of mind via their fragmented vision of a woman's face and eye, and abstract forms and sharp colors. They demonstrate the technical flourishes that Hitchcock cunningly deploys to pull against the lure of character, interiority, and identity. The eye is the window to the soul, but the descent into Novak's eye is neither an interior journey nor a demystifying special effect, but an ambiguous embodiment articulating human body and machine/effect. The single eye both highlights the conventional understanding of the camera as an anthropomorphized extension of human vision, and reanimates the strangeness of this conjunction of the binocular and monocular. To see with a single eye is to be decentered, eccentric: a vertiginous effect. This tension illuminates how the camera's eye simultaneously produces effects of disembodiment and intimate embodiment when used in an extreme manner, as in *Lady in the Lake* and *Suzhou River*. This is the first of several sequences in which highly artificial, comprehensible though unconventional means are used supposedly to figure inner states or consciousness, including Scottie's dream, the vertigo shot and the 360-degree shot. In each case, however, we do not get a subjective perspective but an "emergent alterfication" of anotherness. These are shared states, indistinctions of character and a POV technique that signals a "metamorphosis of the true."[139] A narratographic approach attends to time precisely because it attends to the specificity of the image *as it happens,* in an immanent evaluation.

The credits begin with a tracking shot, punctuated by pauses, of an immobile woman's face: attentive, nervous, with furrowed brow and shifting eyes. From the bottom-left half of the face, the camera moves to the lips, the eyes, and then into the right eye. The image turns red with the name credits, a graphic wash of color that is repeated later in the film, notably in Scottie's dream sequence and in flashbacks. Abstract forms emerge from the eye; as the camera tracks into the pupil, the eye disappears, leaving the figures spinning toward the viewer. The subjective perspective suggested by this interior movement is undercut by the analytical detachment of the camera and the abstract nature of the images themselves. Bass used Lissajous figures, graphic figures used to determine the frequencies of sound or radio signals, to create a hypnotic state in the viewer. As Pat Kirkham writes:

> These figures seemed startlingly modern in their abstraction and were read by many contemporary viewers as modern art in motion. Like Bass's own work, they are both minimalist and complex, representing the rational and known world of science, and the uncharted worlds of outer space and the human mind. They seem to float free in an enormous dark universe in an ever-changing array of colours—but any feeling of liberation is held in tension by the fact that the forms have emerged from (and will return to) a human eye.[140]

What Kirkham does not explicitly note, though, is that the human eye is not left untouched by this experience. Lissajous figures are graphic representations of the invisible—sound waves—but here they figure visually emotions and mental states. That this functions via inducing sensation in the viewer is not coincidental; their spiral form nonsensuously evokes the suspensive movement later used to sensational effect in the "vertigo" shot. Their regular patterns convey inevitability and repetition that (alongside the score's quiet motif) prefigures the intimate, isolated world that the film will build. It is unclear if the images emanate from the woman, or if she is caught up in them: indetermination of cause and effect.

The credits strikingly combine live action footage and animation. Lissajous figures are indexical in nature, the visible trace of sound wave that bear no iconic resemblance to its source. The credits encapsulate the indexical's double pull: the verifiable (in Novak's recognizable figure) and an attenuated relation to source (the sound waves). The index is usually described as the trace, the evidence of a thing "having been there": a registration mark that persists in time. Phil Rosen notes that the indexical as trace is frequently incomplete; the spectator actively "fills in" the reference in order to stabilize its meaning.[141] However, the constant "becoming" of the present offers the spectator an impossible position from which to proceed. Narrative assists in the transformation, as indexicality transfers from profilmic trace to diegesis. Thus subjective investment is as crucial to the index's referentiality as its objective standing as an existing referent. Through Bazin, Rosen identifies atemporality as all representation's desire to avoid death, but argues for recognizing the subject's temporality as the indexical's *contingency* in engagement. When and how reference becomes a productive problem prompts a double vision of *Vertigo*'s genre, from detective film to "sci-phi" of suspense. It also asks, What does it feel like to be animated? The film's answer takes us from the film's ambiguous criminality of action to an emergent sense of "the crime of time" itself.

The opening credits animate a tension between intellectual and affective modes of knowing that remains active throughout the film, echoing Deleuze's distinction between communication and resistance. For Hitchcock, suspense worked most effectively on the affective, not intellectual, level. While Hitchcock speaks of creating particular emotional responses in his viewers, it is at the level of a powerful, affective response unqualifiable as emotion that his films are most effective. Theorists of suspense endlessly puzzle over the seemingly contradictory emotions of pleasure and fear that suspense generates; is it not in their uncertain modulation that we find affect instead? As Hitchcock notes, "There is a great confusion between the words 'mystery' and 'suspense.' The two things are absolutely miles apart. Mystery is an intellectual process, like in a whodunit. But suspense is essentially an emotional process. You can only get the suspense element by giving the audience information."[142] Thus in *Vertigo*, the intellectual instigation of suspense only magnifies that which has unsettled the audience throughout the film via the use of repetition.

The spiral's repeated motif—in the opening sequence, in the picturing of vertigo, the curl of a hairstyle, the path of a car—already tells the audience what is going on and attentively attunes them to the something happening of the film's anotherness as felt rather than explained. The suspense generated by the key revelation (the letter-writing scene) is in fact a MacGuffin.

That suspense exceeds narrative function is illustrated by the fact that it is never "made right in the end," evident in the abrupt ending to a film that is characterized by romantic lingering and a languorous, immersive tone. The final sequence begins once Scottie recognizes Madeleine's necklace. His discovery is conveyed through flashbacks; he delays informing Judy. The following scenes are excruciating as audience knowledge fails to align with characters' known relations. Atop the tower, Judy confesses. After a long buildup of tension as (repeated) durational movement through space, from the drive to the mission to the painful ascent and Judy's admission of complicity, the film seems to be moving toward merging Judy and Madeleine in one body: visually perfect as Madeleine reincarnated, Judy modulates between the two characters' distinct voices. Creeping toward Scottie, "Judy" seems to be winning him over, and they kiss. This time, Scottie *is* lost in the moment, but now Judy opens her eyes: frightened by what she sees, she repeats Madeleine's fall. Scottie, too, catches and repeats this: poised on the tower's edge, his position mimics the outstretched arms of the falling body in his dream. The camera tracks backward out the tower's window, and ends by briefly framing Scottie in the open space. It hangs suspended in the air in an "impossible objective shot" whose position mimics that of Scottie at the beginning of the film, suspended over the void; the ending topologically folds these temporally distinct images of Scottie against each other. This shot barely registers before the end title appears. Hitchcock said that suspense must always be cathartically accompanied by humor to "relieve the audience": "When [the film] is over, when the criminal is properly trapped and you are returned to your private worries, you find that your little excursion has made your mind clearer, your nerves calmer, your problems somehow easier to attack."[143] Suspense clears the way for active efficiency. This fails in *Vertigo*, where the criminality is not properly trapped; repeatedly voted greatest film of all time, we forget that contemporary viewers of *Vertigo* stayed away, disappointed by the film's flat ending providing neither resolution nor catharsis.

In *Vertigo*, the key question of suspense as spectatorial involvement concerns time, with form as duration, with repetition, and with the role of audience in the making of a film. More than a certain knowledge on the spectator's part, suspense provokes the question "What am I *supposed* to know?" and the impossibility of answer except through repetition as affective sensation. In *Vertigo*, the spectator is immediated, thrown back on his or her own knowledge of the viewing situation, but not through a Brechtian alienation: not distancing, but stretching. Visually represented by the stretching of perspective in Hitchcock's famous vertigo shot, the spectator *experiences* the same sense of movement and stasis all at once, a visceral sensation of the passing of time, the event's semblance. Immediation is the time of the film's eventness (which is not simply coincident with its projection). The suggestion that cinema is always in a perpetual present has often led to a conflict between the film and the spectator—even critics who seek to reintroduce the spectator's experience often do so at the expense of the film's temporal flow. Even Scottie, to an extent, seeks to do away with "flow," striving toward the frozen perfection of stasis.

The vertiginous spiral is one of the film's most spectacular special effects. But Novak's doubled body is no less vertiginous, a special effect as special affect. It is perhaps in feminist readings of *Vertigo* that this duality has been most carefully scrutinized. What difference does a consideration of anotherness make to the legacy of feminist analyses of *Vertigo*?

Traveling the Dead Ends

Hitchcock has remained a crucial figure for feminist film theory since Mulvey's "Visual Pleasure and Narrative Cinema," though it was in the 1980s that his films were seen as central, even foundational, to the feminist critique of classical Hollywood cinema.[144] Explicitly thematizing voyeurism, fetishism, and questionable sexual politics, Hitchcock seemed "cut to the measure of the film theorist's desire" in readings as much about a conflicted love for the cinema as a critique.[145] His films reflexively provoked self-examination on the part of many of his female fans and critics.[146] Why is (or perhaps, was) *Vertigo* such an important film for feminist film theory? Has the film outlived its usefulness? As Patricia Mellencamp claims, "Feminist film theory begins with Judy/Madeleine, luminous and revolutionary work, but a blind alley, perhaps a dead end": "What is critical is that women's history and identity, and maybe scholarly answers, mean absolutely nothing to the story. The trick is to make us believe women are significant while the only thing that matters is obsessive male desire. . . . Male obsession drives the film; female sexuality is only a screen, neither cause nor effect."[147] Frustrated with the gossamer quality of Madeleine/Judy's identity, Mellencamp suggests looking at questions of money and power—"real" issues with real-life consequences—in the place of the illusion of femininity. Mellencamp's claims here brings to mind Mulvey's contention that the female body as *spectacle* effectively suspends the progress of the narrative. Recall Branigan's claim that narrative, with its structures of cause and effect, involves "knowing and *thus being able to tell*."[148] Mellencamp's critique of *Vertigo* as a "dead end" implies that as a feminist film critic, one should only be interested in films that can "go somewhere," that is, to produce knowledge.[149]

Mellencamp's analytical strategy seeks out traces of Judy's past, what the photos in her room might mean. The photo's lure points to the ambiguous embodiments of the cinematic body itself, staged via the unsatisfying contrast between appearance and "reality," between ghosts and all-too-incarnated bodies, between ethereal fantasy and the dull thud of reality. In the doubled body of Judy/Madeleine, refracted through Novak's indexical pull, the female body becomes a special effect. In her essay "Allegory and Referentiality: *Vertigo* and Feminist Criticism," Susan White identifies as the key problem of much critical work on gender in *Vertigo* "a nostalgia for an empirically-based history, the essence of which is an unproblematized set of references, upon which the "truth" of the film or the ultimate reading of that film would rely." For White, critics repeatedly try to locate the "truth" of *Vertigo* in the feminine and in the woman's body: "The recovery of the feminine abject, cast-off, waste-product—the very honorable project of Marxist and feminist scholars—

is nonetheless a problematic one. The bedrock of critical thinking is the notion . . . that somewhere here the real woman, a victim, is speaking."[150] As the profoundly unsatisfying ending of *Vertigo* (both for the spectators and for Scottie, not to mention Judy!) suggests, the issue of Madeleine/Judy's real identity is a McGuffin: her death does little to release anyone, including the spectator, from the vertiginous spiral. Mellencamp's "blind alley" is less a dead end, perhaps, than an experience demanding a different conception of time from that which a focus on representation traditionally enables. In the time-image, the undecidable exchange between the virtual and the actual also creates a condition of exchange between subject and object. The excess here is a direct bodily relation effectuated through the creativity of point of view, which recomposes both subject and object in "mutation."

How might this "spatial" proximity read as "too much body," the vertigo of a critical distance, be productively retheorized as a type of temporal relation to the body, opening up a space for feminist reconceptualizations of the relation between the virtual and the actual, and the anotherness of a body in time? Lesley Stern argues that the double force of film is both to "transmit something that is red hot" but also to "deaden and embalm." Stern rethinks this contradiction, arguing not that film "kills" reality but *"participates in the genesis of the bodily"* through sensation. This intensity is the threat "of enacting a death drive."[151] The ecstatically sensible effects of cinematic doubling, becoming beside oneself, are both transcendent rapture, and an intense, physical sensation. *Vertigo*, with its sustained ecstasy echoed in Hermann's score, also presents a curiously chaste version of desire, where Scottie longs to see Judy's inverted striptease, "all dressed up and ready for love," as Hitchcock says. The film spectator likewise experiences this duplicity relative to the film body—to be caught up in maximum sensation is also to be taken outside of oneself, experiencing self-enjoyment as a re-worlding.

Hitchcock has often been valorized as a practitioner of "pure cinema," inventing purely cinematic techniques—editing, camera movement—to make his points. This does not imply that the technological elements of Hitchcock's films are not socially and culturally determined; technique is distinct from technological determinism. Rather, pure cinema as technique addresses the complicated relation among human, machine, and material. Tomlinson argues that in *Vertigo*, Hitchcock never trusted the actors to be able to convey meaning, emotion, and state of mind strictly through performance, but choreographed meaning cinematically. For instance, he ascribes the greatest significance in the opening scenes, when Scottie is hanging from a rooftop, not to the information conveyed by the close-up on Stewart's face but to the technique of the simultaneous track/zoom shot repeated throughout the film.

In looking at questions of suspense, I noted that the three most significant cataphors in the film were three looks "offscreen," looks that unhinge the closed narrative world of a movement-image onto the potential of the time-image. The first is Madeleine in the stable, when Scottie thinks he has "broken her dream" by bringing her to the real mission. They kiss, but Madeleine opens her eyes and looks off to the side, claiming "It's too late." A moment later, she runs toward the tower (as Marker notes, this matte image was the only thing Hitchcock added to a set where he "invents nothing") and plunges to her death. The second is Scottie's open-eyed registration of the change in scene during the 360-degree shot; repeating Madeleine's earlier look, he now sees the surroundings his closed eyes failed to register in the stable. The last is Judy and Scottie in the bell tower; as they kiss in a final reconciliation, she again opens her eyes, repeating the scene in the stable, and frightened by her vision, plunges to her death. In "Object Relations in the Cinema," Raul Ruiz writes, "The image of two lovers looking into each other's eyes has no off-screen space."[152] Two lovers swept up in each other make a world. What happens when one looks away, not into off-screen space, but into time?

In the first look, one *could* argue, retrospectively, that Madeleine is looking at the tower, knowing Elster awaits. But when she says "It's too late" (which Scottie will repeat in the bell tower), her look into time is vertiginous. It launches a relay of looks—hers, then Scottie's, then hers again—that don't match, that don't close the space. Nor is the off-screen simply maintained; in each case, the lover who opens his or her eyes sees something untimely. What they see cannot be simply resolved through inclusion in the narrative thread later on. As Deleuze writes, "The out-of-field testifies to a more disturbing presence, one which cannot even be said to exist, but rather to 'insist' or 'subsist,' a more radical Elsewhere, outside homogeneous time and space."[153] In the 360-degree shot, it is Scottie who opens his eyes and looks, but Judy doesn't. Scottie records but does not register the scene, and is swept up in the multiple layers of time. Judy, we presume, remains "in the moment"; finally completely compliant with Scottie's demands, the tension between Judy and Madeleine seems dissolved, subsumed. These looks are cataphors in the sense that they are artifacts of time, not just of the past but of the future as well. In the repetition of the gazes, across three moments and into time, cataphors don't simply point to the future anterior, but maintain suspense as a special case of movement, a violent spasm that figures death, but something else as well.

Flaxman, in his "sci-phi" philosophy, describes the concept of the "other person" in Deleuze and Guattari's work through a description at the beginning of *What Is Philosophy?* of a frightened face that "looms up and looks at something out of field":

> The face constitutes a relay between the Outside, which it wears as an "affect-image," and a possible world, which it projects. The face does not represent the real but unfolds an image of the affected, which is no less real, and thereby furnishes a source of imminent concern and conjecture. In other words, because it is not (yet) realized, the possible is inscribed as a *virtual reality*.[154]

These looks offscreen, these frightened faces that decenter the couple form, rendering character relations asymmetrical through the look into time, inscribe such a virtual reality. As cataphors, they are the advance referent not of the puzzle falling into place, but anotherness' excess, the virtual reality of the body in time. When Scottie stares down from the edge of the bell tower, he also looks (back) at himself, in an incompossible displacement of mirror-vision by movement-vision; the camera hangs in space in a position Scottie has been in since the start of the film: suspended. Scottie's own doubling is itself doubled and exceeded by a camera consciousness as the really apparitional of time. This is why *Vertigo* can only be repeated in its remakes.

The affective suspense of vertigo, its indetermination, is not resolved by the film's end, nor is it simply anomalous suspense that is activated upon repeat viewing. For Marker, the perfect crime is reversibility itself; the ambiguous criminality of *Vertigo* rather enacts Deleuze's contention that "there is no crime but time itself." It is affect as excess that characterizes the film, the extended presence of a cinematic body that is not so much lived, as repeatedly relived. I turn now to remakes of *Vertigo* in works by David Lynch and Lou Ye, to examine their affective reanimations of the ending's suspense.

CHAPTER TWO

Into the Folds

David Lynch's Hollywood Trilogy

> Existence, as a process of deterritorialisation, is a specific inter-machinic
> operation which superimposes itself on the promotion of singularized
> existential intensities. And, I repeat, there is no generalized syntax for
> these deterritorialisations. Existence is not dialectical, not representable.
> It is hardly liveable!
>
> —Félix Guattari, *Chaosmosis*

At *Vertigo*'s end, Judy's confession seems poised to release her from her deadly suspense as a puppet, helplessly animating Madeleine's form at Scottie's insistence. Playing out the dramatic judgment within the folds of a cinematic architecture (the bell tower matte painting Hitchcock's only addition to his found set), Scottie seems already released, no longer suspended by acrophobia and effectively resuming his role of detective. When Judy confesses, Scottie closes his eyes and kisses her, no longer needing to witness an emergent possible world. But his gesture leaps across bodies, as with the first spiral vision of Madeleine at Ernie's: Judy catches it and opens her eyes. A nun's shadowy figure looms up; frightened by her double vision out of the past, Judy falls to her death. "I heard voices," the nun remarks, voicing our dreadful suspicion that the film's second half is but Scottie's mad dream.[1] Judy's guilt returns to haunt her, her attempt to restore and reveal her full embodied presence an invitation to the ghost. As I argued before, however, Scottie's final pose, reactivating a figure of self-referential doubling, fringes this actuality with a brief glimpse of the scene's continuing virtual potential. How might we read this scene non-dialectically, rearranging the dualisms of life/death, true/false to think instead in terms of an experiential event? How have remakes of *Vertigo* rediscovered this remaining vitality affect through the pedagogical imperative of a double vision that exceeds demasking?

In the cinema of the time-image, redemption arrives too late, evacuated by the force of a suspense productive, not relevatory. In a free replay of *Vertigo*, we do not "wish for a different outcome," a domestic resolution for Scottie and Judy via a willful anomalous suspense. Bodies are not *saved* by redemption; Deleuze concludes that

> redemption, art beyond knowledge, is also creation beyond information. Redemption arrives too late. . . . It appears when information has already gained control of speech-acts. . . . But the too-late is not only negative; it is the sign of the time-image in the place where time makes visible the stratigraphy of space and audible the story-telling of the speech act.

Art beyond knowledge "forces us to think" as the work of an emergent "will to art" "defined in relation to the speech-act, and no longer . . . in terms of a motor action."[2] This is the *spiritual automaton,* drawing on Schefer's cinematic encounter with the "unknown center of ourselves"; "anterior to all motivity," its aberrant or eccentric movement of force results from the vertiginous pull of this unknown center: the spiral's eye.

Deleuze's automaton emerges from the "debris" of a shattered world, where the human body as stable orientation has been lost in the face of a screen filled only with information, a readable image. The automaton is the "pure informed person capable of . . . receiving into his visible body the pure act of speech." When information de-ranges orientation, relations are no longer those of causality, but are directly productive. The aim here is to "go beyond information via the question: What is the source and what is the addressee?"[3] In this way, the creative fabulation of a speech-act beyond information, directly registering in a receptive and plastic body, is the direct time-image of semblance, the elements of time that do not appear.

Speculating on the potential of an emergent electronic image, Deleuze traces an aesthetic that *precedes* any technology, characterized by asymmetrical doubling. Critically, sound/image, speaking/saying are disjunct;

puppet and reciter, body and voice together constitute "not a whole nor an individual, but an automaton." This is the regime of the "tear," a rip in the fabric of the world, "where the division into body and voice forms a genesis of the image as 'non-representable by a single individual', 'appearance divided in itself and in a non-psychological way.'"[4] This nonpsychological divided appearance invites anotherness as the body's own creative capacity, as with the pure speech-act's receptivity. Deleuze elaborates on this via Michel Chion on lip-syncing, which no longer has the function of "making believe" (as successful illusion), but heightening disjunction:

> So what is the purpose of synchronization? Ask Michel Chion. It becomes part of the creative function of myth. It makes the visible body, not now something imitating the utterance of the voice, but something constituting an absolute receiver or addressee. "Through it the image says to the sound: stop floating everywhere and come and live in me; the body opens to welcome the voice."[5]

This staging of doubling, the really apparitional of giving a body to a phantom, is precisely *not* an incorporation or merging. When information is overcome by asking after the sender and addressee, it does not fix positionality to relativize knowledge. It attends to the specific becoming or *arc of the event* as the direct perception of relation itself. The pure informed person is one who is maximally open to connection, to affect. This receptivity is necessarily figured through the double, not an individual split psychologically, but through the body's own power of anotherness. Here audiovision is "occurrent," a "relational effect" (Massumi): Deleuze's creative function of myth.[6]

When Deleuze qualifies time-images as a "cinema of the seer, not the actor," he evokes suspense as a doubling in intuition's abyss, a return to the fundamental movement of matter itself. Divested of the power to act, the seer lives and unlives a fracture in the "I." Spiritual automaton, this seer experiences the paradox of being suspended in duration itself. "That we are in time looks like a commonplace, yet it is the highest paradox. Time is not the interior in us, but just the opposite, the interiority in which we are, in which we move, live and change."[7] This fracture in the I is felt as the sensational intuition of durations other than ours, and the modification of our own duration in affective relation. Deleuze offers "the affection of self by self" as the definition of time.[8]

As with the disjunctive synthesis, "the audio-visual image is not a whole, it is a fusion of the tear."[9] Deleuze echoes *What Is Philosophy?*'s citation of D. H. Lawrence's sense of art as a "tear in the parasol" that we use for protection; we draw a firmament on the underside and think it the sky.[10] In this *fusion* of the tear, we do not simply look into another world, we *feel the immediate re-worlding* of this one in anotherness: creative re-composition *through* the body, and not through the intermediary of the body.[11] In *Vertigo,* the modulation of Judy's and Madeleine's voices, fighting for one body, is a moment of fabulation, a lived disjunction of that film's repeated rip in the parasol as the felt presence of what does not actually appear: the past and the future. The will to art in this scene is not the triumph of artifice over reality; it is the direct expression of the creativity of the real itself as re-composition at the very edge of unlivable existence. The nun, transcendent figure of a redemptive elsewhere, cuts this "metamorphosis of the true" and brings things down to earth. For Judy and Scottie, untimely redemption comes too late; but though individual bodies are not saved, the persistent force of fabulation is. The direct time-image insists as the mark of immanent evaluation, a double vision asking us to look again.

In this chapter, I pick up on redemption's too-late, to consider the folds of Hitchcock's *Vertigo* in David Lynch's films. For Lynch, Hitchcock is a mediator, and the pedagogy of perception he models is a double-vision. If in *Vertigo,* Hitchcock "unhinges" a time-image from the movement-image, Lynch picks up on this nonpsychological "profoundly divided essence of the psyche," reanimating the double folds of characters, film form and world. Lynch repeats Hitchcock's mirroring of Judy/ Madeleine's doubling in Scottie's mental break, as well as the spectatorial split in identification, in a scene from *Lost Highway,* where Pete's hallucination clearly references Scottie's dream in *Vertigo.* Swamped by dizziness, Pete sees Alice's floating, disembodied head (displacing Scottie's "castrated head" from the animated dream in *Vertigo*) while the room behind her spins. Her face glows a cold blue. The overhead light jumps in and out of focus, emitting a buzzing noise as dying bugs fly again and again into the bulb. Interior emotions and states of mind are rerouted through electricity and "special effects" of temporal and spatial dislocations. Pete is living two lives at once, and this unlivable existence tears him and the surrounding space-time apart. Theresa Brennan, noting that "we are peculiarly resistant to the idea that our emotions are not entirely our own," tracks this distribution of affect through their "energetic dimension."[12] Affect's contagious energetics are felt explicitly in the world crossings of Lynchian doublings.

Funny How Secrets Travel

Lynch's work has long been haunted by *Vertigo*, his Hollywood trilogy an intensive replay of Hitchcock and of himself, in a transversal and vertiginous auto-affection. From *Lost Highway*, a film explicitly foregrounding its fever-dream reimagining of *Vertigo*, I read the trilogy as a resonance chamber, a molecular remaking of *Vertigo* in which that film's major narrative break around *"les deux morts"* and rebeginnings are replayed as intensive micro-repetitions. 2001's *Mulholland Drive* and 2006's *Inland Empire* remake Lynch's own work, with a consistent emphasis on the major narrative break (which *folds* the film's structure), the doubled body/role of the female lead(s) (which asymmetrically spreads to double the worlds), and a meditation on our lived relation to media technologies *via* the figure of the unfaithful woman.

The Hollywood trilogy maps an increasingly depersonalizing decomposition of the female lead, always an actress, through an intensification of the incorporeal dimension of the body. The affective suspension of knowledge these films produce asks us to feel the body's own indeterminacy, or to experience art "beyond knowledge." Although these films' complex temporal structures have led some to categorize them within the emergent twenty-first-century genre of "puzzle films," the minor change of the remake as repetition offers a model more relevant to the work of temporal critique. Warren Buckland's cognitive reading of *Lost Highway*, for example, walks the viewer through the film, noting at every point the revisions and recursive reevaluations. Beginning with

Bordwellian linearity, he then turns to an approach drawn from Edward Branigan, opening to the horizontal (paradigmatic) axis. The Mystery Man, for instance, both provokes contingent stabilizations along the narrative line (for example, seeing him with the video camera at the beach house, "we have conclusive evidence that the Mystery Man made the video tapes"), and undercuts this certainty by the possibility that he is just a figment of Fred's imagination. These horizontal permutations shift into "levels of narration," to more accurately assess "how ambiguities are produced and what effect they achieve," but though this doubled analysis offers multiple ways to reassemble the puzzle, it does little to account for the work of the film beyond questions of knowledge and character. Buckland's undeveloped contention that the film is "governed by a non-rational but meaningful energy" tells us little about the double vision that film requires, where we move between the discontinuity of discrete episodes and characters to the work of this energy itself.[13] This puzzle film logic re-sorts the film's layers, but cannot effectively account for the *lived effects* of the competing temporalities and the redistributed points of view traveling *across* media images and focalizing characters.

Thomas Elsaesser proposes the "mind-game" film as a revision of the puzzle film genre, to better account for complex narratives and also cinema as emergent life form, both a "reality and a way of thinking."[14] These films are "new forms of spectator-engagement and new forms of audience-address" prompted by a crisis of spectatorship, where traditional concepts like suspension of disbelief or cinematic techniques like point of view are no longer adequate to the feeling of today's cinematic and media experiences.[15] Lynch's Hollywood trilogy films are canonical examples for him of this *tendency* (in Truffaut's sense, rather than genre) characterized by moments when "a specific scene draws attention to the fact that there might exist *another level of reflexivity,* less in the sense of the mirror or a *mise-en-abyme* construction and more as pure brain activity, as a 'virtuality' in Deleuze's sense." These films are "ghostly or spiritual" in the felt sense that "cinema itself has a mind 'outside' or in excess of (the narration or the characters, the auteur or the spectator) that eludes fixed positionality."[16]

Elsaesser defines mind-game films through the "productive patholo-gies" they engage, "the somatic or pathologized body as an advanced 'neural' or 'biological' medium, in its mental instability and volatility potentially more efficient than the current." But where Guattari argued for schizoanalysis's productive multiplications, Elsaesser more cautiously attempts to feel out the "rules of the game," arguing that 'bona fide' mind-game films "maintain a basic consistency and self-consistency or they enact the very condition their hero suffers from, in the structure of the film itself" as with his example of *Memento*. These films reflexively refer to their "rules of the game." Elsaesser ambivalently assesses the "social use" of mind-game films in terms of "performative agency," where "we cannot be sure if contemporary cinema is 'part of the problem' (Fou-cault, Deleuze) or already 'part of the solution' (Johnson, Gladwell) in the reorientation of the body and senses, as we learn to live symbiotically with machines and 'things,' as well as with hybrid forms of intelligence embedded in our many automated systems."[17] Deleuze's automaton opens onto this complex question of agency in a way that exceeds the individualized subject and *requires* an ambiguous embodiment. Both the puzzle film and the mind-game film seek to efface ambiguity in order to restore film to action, something "useful." For this reason, I briefly distinguish the movement-image as a spatialization of time (what hap-pens in the linear and horizontal decompositions of the puzzle film approach) and the time-image as a shift toward a falsifying narrative in Lynch. This distinction also clarifies Deleuze's rejection of the dream as a time-image, especially relevant for Lynch's films where narrative devi-ations are often explained away as dreams or madness.

Narrative resolution differentiates the movement-image from the time-image. Where the movement-image is organic, kinetic, and indexi-cal (meaning that as a description, it assumes the independence of its object), the time-image is crystalline, chronic, and a description that *constitutes* its object. Rodowick parses the organic regime as measuring the real in terms of continuity, where "descriptions are assumed to be haptic or continuous with the objects they represent. . . . The imaginary is presented as a deviation from the real, the better to *restore* belief in it."[18] *Haptic* refers to the eye or the visual functioning as an "advance guard for the eye," organizing the visual field and distinguishing objects to prepare for touch's incipient action.[19] In *Inland Empire*, an iconic scene that condenses Lynch's oeuvre shows the deviation from this haptic, organic regime.

When Dern's character stumbles off of Hollywood Boulevard into Carolina's nightclub, we see a long hallway lined with red velvet curtains; a disembodied forearm waves slowly in the air leading the camera, less indicating a definitive direction than calling attention to the space of the passage itself, in a curious re-articulation of mechanical eye and human hand. Like velvet's sensual texture, this hand both points and delays via its strange embodiment. Where Dern is going is into time and sensation, not an organic (organized) space. Even as a puzzle film approach allows irresolution to persist, its analytical impulse shelves irresolution's force by organizing the film according to a spatial logic that cannot fully account for the minor way difference is made qualitatively.

It is not that narrative disappears in the time-image; initially, "the cinema is always narrative, more and more narrative, but it is dysnarrative in so far as narration is affected by repetitions, permutations and transformations which are explicable in detail by the new structure": the crystal image displacing the organic regime.[20] Dysnarratives, however,

Disarticulated gesture in *Inland Empire*.

retain the organizational force of the shift from the syntagmatic to the paradigmatic drawn from semiotics; for this reason, Deleuze makes a further turn toward the *productive* effect of falsifying narrative. Falsifying narration's dysfunctionality cannot simply be broken down and reassembled; the effect is affective, not informational or intellectual in nature:

> Each sheet of past, each age *calls up all the mental functions simultaneously:* recollection, but equally forgetting, false recollection, imagination, planning, judgment. . . . What is loaded with all these functions, each time, is feeling. . . . It is feeling which stretches out on a sheet and is modified according to its fragmentation . . . and feeling is that which is in continual exchange, circulating from one sheet to another according to what transformations occur. But when transformations themselves form a sheet which crosses all the others it is as if *feelings set free the consciousness or thought with which they were loaded:* a becoming conscious according to which shadows are the living realities of a mental theatre and feelings the true figures in a cerebral game which is very concrete.[21]

Effectively, this is what it means to give a body to a phantom, when virtuality effectuates a sheet of transformation via a becoming conscious. The brain then becomes the set of "non-localizable" relations between feelings or affects, a continuity of folding that "rolls them up and unrolls them like so many lobes, preventing them from halting and becoming fixed in a death position."[22] The effect, a direct image of time, is not *in* the image, but happening *"around the image, behind the image, and even inside the image,"* and this blurring is the experience of double vision.[23]

Around, beside and inside the image: the *really apparitional* of the virtual, or semblance. Dreams or hallucinations are not virtual, as temporarily delayed actualities: those are images that fail to get lost. The oneiric quality of Lynch's film produces a shared dream for which there is no recourse to reality testing, no return; Elena Del Rio notes that "even a cursory look into the activity of dreaming in [*Mulholland Drive*] alerts us to the idea that such creative powers are not owned by any of its characters, but are rather the film's to select, combine and express."[24] Schefer calls cinema an "experimental night where something stirs, comes alive and speaks in front of us"; this is how Lynch's film is like a dream.[25] The virtual image simultaneous with the actual image, around, beside, and inside; this is the *mutual image*. This productive haziness is the world-glue of affect, made evident when the virtual begins to become valid for itself. World-glue involves getting lost in the medium, the felt fusion of the tear.

Bodies become abstract here in the sense of feeling relation outside of its terms, echoed throughout the Hollywood trilogy in the indiscretion of doubled bodies; Pearson describes the goals of Deleuze's notion of a superior empiricism as the recognition of a continuity between things, prior to their selective delineation by a perception bent on action.[26] The seer has "gained in an ability to see what he has lost in action"; this doubling of the spectator makes the viewer's problem "What is there to see in the image?" and not "What are we going to see in the next image?": another figure of the suspense of the time-image.[27] Pearson claims that in Deleuze's work, *hearing* is usually understood as a better register of the continuity between things than sight, as more qualitative in nature.[28] In Lynch's films, "auto-audition," the aural equivalent of "movement-vision," functions similarly to suspend action. Overemphasizing the visual "seer" of the time-image may cause us to underestimate the importance of recorded music and ambient sound in the trilogy as commentary on the difference inherent in repetition, or the discontinuity of continuity.

Chion describes Lynch's films as enveloped in a "sound bath" of environmental sounds—humming light fixtures, rumbling of pipes, buzzing TV screens, scratchy record players—that usually escape our conscious attention, sounds we "rediscover."[29] Lynch amplifies these noises (Chion calls them "dronings") not to draw our attention to them in terms of their recognizable function, nor as indexed to the image, but to heighten their uncanny effect of not quite subjectivity, but no longer objectness as well.[30] Objects in Lynch are *impressionable*, even vulnerable, in their liveliness. Like radiation, memory and action are continually rearranging the molecules of time and space, not with fluidity, but with the potential of violence. As Chion describes the relation of continuity and discontinuity in Lynch's sound work:

Given its fundamentally temporal nature, sound, far more than image, is ordinarily likened to a continuum, a flow, and used in that way. However, in Lynch's work, the pulsation of sound environments does not give rise to a flow which overrides the cuts. The pulsation is perpetually stopped and started by scissors which at once separate and join, often in synch with the visual cuts. . . . The result is a paradoxical style of sound editing which . . . reaffirms continuity through interruption.[31]

The effect for Chion creates renewed life, more "monstrous" than ever, the monstrousness of becoming itself.[32] In Lynch's films, scenes of great violence (not only physical, but violence done to sense) are accompanied by recorded music: think of the joyfully deranged "*loco*motion" or "crazy" motion scene in *Inland Empire*, or the fatal and transforming shock waves in Club Silencio. Lynch saturates found sound with new suggestiveness, reanimating pop clichés to rediscover an essential singularity.

Chion notes Lynch's affinity for suspense as a special case of aberrant movement, where an inhuman simultaneity of immobility and mobility captures the "unlivability" of suspense as the direct experience of anotherness in time:

Beyond his visible eccentricities and his cabinet of monsters, the force of this director lies in his knowing better than anyone how to film immobility, which is supposed to be the opposite of cinema. In a country which most identifies cinema with movement, only a David Lynch could invent men who become potted plants or flowers in a garden bed. Frame by frame analysis confirms that beneath the apparent non-movement of the plant world, the most awful and violent things are brewing: heart rending torsions, horrible intertwinings, endless growth. For Lynch, such is man. No moment is ever as intense as when there is no more outward bodily agitation to hide the infinitesimal speed of an inner movement animating him, which makes him grow or take root. This static quality contains a great deal of violence, and Lynch's films seem able to capture it.[33]

In the trilogy, the undecidability of narrative events, the indiscernibility of dream and reality, the bleed between what is objective and what is subjective are the source of *both* the movement and stasis of the film. When our knowledge is put on hold, our participation in eventness is felt. Lynch activates this disorienting sense of disproportion character-istic of aberrant movement through *false* drama—both vividly (as in the simultaneity of a banal visual image and a dramatic sound image) and at a subtle, chilling level, in which the disproportionately long gaze of the camera on an everyday object invests it with uncanny life.

What happens when the trilogy tries to inhabit the unlivable passage of affect? Eric Rhodes summarizes the critical reaction to *Lost Highway's* narrative permutations: "interesting but impenetrably chaotic at best . . . unconcerned with narrative logic . . . either his picture is obscure by accident or that he is engaged in some frivolous form of cinematic gamesmanship."[34] This summary of critical responses has been echoed and amplified in relation to *Mulholland Drive* and *Inland Empire*. Rhodes himself argues that the lack of classical narrative structure does not simply render the film an inchoate mess. Rather, Lynch adheres to a "disciplined aesthetic formality," a "theme and variation" narrative (bor-rowing the concept from Susan Sontag), to develop a language of mad-ness, pursuing his theme of "mirroring" via several variations: "devices of duplication, opposition, repetition, deviation and inversion."[35] Despite arguing that Lynch's work offers few cues to signal differences between objective reality and a subjective perception ("one man's bad dream"), Rhodes remains committed to understanding *Lost Highway* as the repre-sentation of a coherent interior consciousness, spectacularly rendered; the theme is varied but retains an original priority.[36] However, I under-stand Lynch's repetition of the narrative break of *Vertigo* as neither anti-narrative nor an aesthetic tour-de-force that excuses it from sense, nor the warped perspective of a singular consciousness ("all in Fred/Diane/Nikki's head"). Massumi argues that in understanding affect, the real distinction is not between subjective/objective, but between continuities/discontinuities. Deleuze's discussion of narrative in *Cinema 2* arrives at a similar conclusion. The crack-ups of the subjects of the film, frequently rendered in Lynch via blurs in the image, a shaking camera, in-camera effects of double exposure and dramatic shifts in lighting (what I have elsewhere analyzed as "phase shifts") formally express the "fracture" in the I.[37] How does Lynch relaunch the "too-late" of redemption in his works to trade, as Del Rio puts it, "subjectivity for intensity"?[38]

This chapter reads the Hollywood trilogy *transversally*, for the positivity of a "too-late" as audible-visibility of medium as "event" of re-worlding. Deleuze describes two models of time-image narrative structures, "peaks of the present" and "sheets of the past," but notes that art can also generate a "sheet of transformation" or a "transverse continuity" of nonchronological time:

> We draw out a sheet which, across all the rest, catches and extends the trajectory of points, the evolution of regions. This is evidently a task which runs the risk of failure: sometimes we only produce an incoherent dust made out of juxtaposed borrowings; sometimes we form only generalities which retain mere resemblances . . . but it is possible for the work of art to succeed in inventing those paradoxical hypnotic and hallucinatory sheets *whose property is to be at once a past and always to come.*[39]

This transverse continuity works both within and across *Vertigo* and the Hollywood trilogy. With this property—"to be at once a past and always to come"—Deleuze signals the characteristic function of the artwork as a fold in time. In *Lost Highway,* the attempt to pinpoint a lost moment in time as "that night" (for Fred, the night of the supposed murder of his wife Renée; for Pete, the night he mysteriously appears in Fred's jail cell, for both men a night they can't or won't recall) is continually missed. Instead, it opens up a gap in time as a sheet of transformation "paradoxically hypnotic and hallucinatory" (one review of *Lost Highway* redubs it "Voodoo Road") that generates entire worlds in its wake.[40] The film topologically folds the past against the "yet-to-come," suspending the present, brings its beginning and end ("Dick Laurent is dead") into contact to elide the immediacy of transmission. In *Mulholland Drive,* Rita lives her amnesia as a material force that initiates the desire to know, which is then displaced and deranged by the intensity of feeling itself. In *Inland Empire,* as the cuts become increasingly irrational and we cling to the continuity of "Laura Dern" as a ship who is a fold of the sea. Dern doubles our derangement, frequently making a slight gesture of bemusement or reorientation (such as taking an extra beat before delivering a line), as if she were living the film's temporal displacements in real time, each cut a new fusion of the tear.

I focus on three concepts here. I begin with Nicole Brenez's contention that figural analysis, as a technique for thinking the eventness of cinema, requires the recognition that "in cinema, the image is not an object but an architecture."[41] On the one hand, this emphasizes the image as an assemblage, as visibly unnatural or constructed. On the other hand, it foregrounds the "experiential" side of the figure that one passes through as we pass through a building or space, its plasticity as being "unfinished," as its "morphology" is between the material and immaterial. How might we read the permutations of these films as an architecture, transforming the 2-D of a puzzle film logic, bent on the restorative and organizing force of after-the-fact knowing, to a 3-D walk-in as art's "fusion of the tear"? I return to the idea of the figural as "getting lost in the medium," reading across bodies and recording technologies in the trilogy for emergent speech-acts of fabulation. Last, I explore the femme fatale as conceptual persona in the Hollywood trilogy, the figure who transduces generic clichés into tendencies of intensive force, the actress-medium as a Lynchian figure of a suspended (re)animation. The femme fatale ambiguously embodies death in the films; if her existence is "unlivable," it is because we see her form not as object but as the mutual contagion of body and image, redeemed too late but making visible a direct image of time as anotherness.

Pete and Re-Pete

Figural Architectures

In *Inland Empire*, Lynch repeatedly revisits a type of shot from *Vertigo*. There, a contrast between two worlds mimics the cinematic environment of darkened theatre and bright screen: an interior shot containing a framed passage to a bright exterior, where the framed world becomes an impossible or unlivable environment, as if one were trying to step into the screen. Though this type of shot is repeatedly staged as Scottie's scopophilic desire, as when he spies on Madeleine at the florist, the most delirious example is after they kiss at the stable and Madeleine flees the dark interior "into the screen" where Scottie cannot follow. Elsaesser identifies the passages of Hitchcock's "female assistants" through such frames as "walk-ins," a 3-D lure to the spectator.[42]

In Lynch, these images manifest the machinic force of desire as the experience of living two worlds at once. In this topological architecture,

Walk-ins in *Vertigo*.

Walk-ins in *Inland Empire*.

this mode of passage means that the cinematic environment into which Madeleine flees (the bell tower as composite image, special effect and bright screen) becomes the anotherness of the world opening up before Dern, where she learns to live and move otherwise. Lynch redoubles Hitchcock, when Dern heads down a studio passageway only to find herself in a cinema, seeing her own "work" onscreen. Behind the screen is the passage onto the set. Passage isn't into another world in Lynch so much as *more* world, anotherness itself, as when a reanimated Nikki, arising from her death scene, stumbles along in a trance out from the studio into the banal Los Angeles sunshine. She turns back into the red velvet passage of Lynchland, which appears as a result of her choice to turn, and does not preexist as an actualized space. In Lynch's film, cinema as a new *multi-plex*—a form of folding that generates multiplicity— emerges from his reworking of Hitchcock.

When Scottie attempts to follow Madeleine "through the looking glass" into the tower, his body fails him. The indeterminate liveliness of the image as site of mutation is figured by the interplay between environment and character in Lynch's films, where unlivability is signaled by uncanny homes. Freud remarks that *heimlich,* homely or familiar, also comes to mean its opposite: secret, hidden. *Unheimlich* is not a state, but specifically a quality in motion that *develops*: "all that should have remained hidden, but has come to light."[43] This development is signaled by aberrant movement within the home space, as in the "disembodied" tracking shot through Betty's apartment in *Mulholland Drive.*

In *Lost Highway,* the interior of the Madison home folds the threat of the outside within itself; in this contact, stable relations become "non-localized" as "direct presentations of time."[44] Passage is decomposed throughout the film's first third, immediately undermining a clear sense of intrusion from outside. Fred and Renée receive strange videotapes: first grainy, black and white exterior shots of their home, and then tapes that progressively penetrate inside through the living room, down the hallway, and ultimately their bedroom where they lie sleeping. As they watch, they are confused rather than enlightened by recognition of their home. Its extremely closed space, with few windows, reads like a blank face from outside. Interiors feel half-finished because of the indistinction of wall colors and furnishings, both in the use of a homogeneous color palette, and in the lighting design, which suppresses a three-dimensional sense of space. It is not precisely flat, although there is frequent use of compression to create effects; rather space is broken and dimensionality fragmented within the shot through framing, composition, and cinematography. The home is the scene of multiple displacements in time: in the repetition of the videotapes, in Fred's position as both sender and receiver of the intercom message, and in the Mystery Man's simultaneous presence at Andy's party and in Fred's home. In all three instances, recording and communication technologies are the impetus, though not the explanation, for the way in which direct presentations of time give us "access to that Proustian dimension where people and things occupy a place in time which is incommensurable with the one they have in space."[45] When this happens, the home becomes a nonplace (*non-lieu*); divested of its functionality, it becomes invested with the senses in a decentering suspension of perception.

In the Madison home, hallways are treated as either dead spaces, lit as black gaps between rooms with no sense of transition, or singular spaces that are disconnected from the rest of the house. Rather than functioning as sensory-motor linkages, they start to function in a manner homologous to the "lost time" of recording and communication devices, or the between-the-frames of the film strip. Fred dissolves into the space of the hallway off his bedroom so repeatedly that we can only say that the space is suspended in and by lost time. These are passages into a paramnesiac time in which his double emerges from the mirror to take his place. But it is through the awareness of the splitting of time, registered via the repetition of the hallway sequence as narrated dream, lived experience, and videotaped memory that the exchange between the virtual and the actual manages to suspend the hallway's architectural function as "passing through."

The incremental journey through Fred's house is both interrupted and prefigured when Fred describes a dream to Renée that traces the same spatial progression as the videos. Fred and Renée are making love; she is acquiescent but disinterested. The scene is in slow motion, and we hear a tinny, distant version of the same song (This Mortal Coil's

"Song to a Siren") that later plays in full non-diegetic splendor when Pete and Alice make love on the sand. Afterward, Renée is remote, and Fred is uncomfortable. Each is isolated, filmed lying in bed in close-up, with the camera suspended over them. They seem to float in space on the black satin sheets; this technique of using blackness to undercut a three-dimensional sense of space and to suspend the bodies to allow them to travel through time is a hallmark of the film's figural architectures. Fred describes a dream in which Renée was in their house, calling his name, but he couldn't find her. He voices over seeming images of the dream: Fred enters the frame in a medium shot from screen right, the background is shadowy and indistinct as he approaches. There is a cut to a roaring fire, followed by a close-up of Fred's face. He seems to be looking at something; there is a cut to the half-wall dividing the living room from the entryway, and a puff of smoke slowly materializes in the air from behind it. The smoke's sensuous mystery doesn't lie in its indexical pointing (it is already disjoined from the fire); instead its slow suspended movements call attention to the invisible medium of air with an unnervingly ectoplasmic quality. Again, there is a close-up on Fred, and then a high angle shot that tracks along the floor of the hallway, across the bedroom curtain and towards the bed, where Renée is sleeping, hands folded over her chest like a corpse. Fred voice, "It wasn't you. It looked like you, but it wasn't you." As he says this, Renée wakes up and screams, throwing her hands up to protect her face as the camera drives towards her. We cut back to Fred in bed with Renée; he sees the Mystery Man's face superimposed over her own. Fred appears gripped here by Capgras syndrome, claiming Renée is not who she seems; but in this contagious architecture, Fred also is not who he seems.

This dream progression repeats when Fred and Renée come home from Andy's party, where they meet the Mystery Man. Renée is in the bathroom, Fred in the bedroom when he seems to sense something and turns around. A shot of the hallway reveals only darkness. Fred enters the frame from screen left and walks down the hallway, literally dissolving into a darkness (aided by his black shirt) that suppresses all sense of the hallway's length.[46] It is as if he is swallowed, a sensation intensified by the lighting of the hallway, with just two crescents of light clinging to either side like a vertical mouth. Renée, uneasy, calls Fred's name. We see a medium close-up of Fred standing uncertainly; suddenly he enters the frame from screen right (as in his dream), and we become aware that the initial image of Fred was a mirror reflection. Renée, peering down the hall, sees only blackness and calls again (the sound of her voice echoing the dream) and goes back into the bedroom. A slow pan sweeps the dim living room, and two shadows, vaguely human but not clearly delineated, pass across the wall, as if Fred and his double, freed from the mirror, were creeping across the room. In this way, a force escapes from the relation of indiscernible exchange of paramnesia. We return to the initial shot down the hallway; Fred materializes out of the blackness and walks straight into the camera. A cut reveals a black void framed by two gleaming metallic strips, echoing the framing of the hallway. Later this is revealed as the television set; the strange framing links passage and technology as spaces where Fred gets lost.

There is a bleed between Fred's interior experience and the objective externality of the recorded image. In making Fred's dream external, the videotaped images merely highlight the oneiric quality of all film images.[47] The doubled movement through the house begs the question "which is actual and which is virtual," but *neither* holds the place of the virtual image. The undecidability of these images in terms of originality or even relationality (the sense that Fred and Renée have become spectators to their own lives) generates the real virtual image. The images hold open the space of Fred's wanderings from himself. The virtual image is that which is *unexperienced* in these actual images, the intimation by which the repetitions differ from themselves immediately as the intuition of duration. In this mutual image, relationality itself is made visible, in the form of the force of the outside.

The hallway sequence replays one final time, repeating the delayed mirroring with Pete who, like Fred, visually enacts the sensation of déjà vu, as an awareness of doubling. The two matched and resonant scenes of mirror images suggest a disconnect between self and image, like the shadow as an incorporeal dimension of the body, or the body that invites in the voice, that becomes explicitly connected to electricity in the film. Although on the surface, *Lost Highway* is set as a Manichean structure, light and dark, *this* mirror-image, infected with movement-vision, suggests that duality is an insufficient concept for understanding the film. Bergson's work of intuition as a rearrangement of dualism is more apt. By placing the mirror scenes in a hallway, the representational stability is undermined by a logic of the event. Massumi explicitly links this to suspense as "viscerality":

> Viscerality . . . is a rupture in the stimulus response paths, a leap in place in a space outside action-reaction circuits. Viscerality is the perception of suspense. The space into which it jolts the flesh is one of an inability to act or reflect, a spasmodic passivity, so taut a receptivity that the body is paralyzed until it is jolted back into action-reaction by recognition.[48]

Pete and Fred may not share an actor's body, but they repeatedly share the same experiences: the mirror scene, a conversation with the Mystery Man, and a visit to the Lost Highway Hotel. Their relationship emphasizes the "exchange" of the virtual and the actual, the indiscernibility of the smallest circuit (as closely coupled as an actor and his role) as a "short circuit": a loss of power or extension, but also the spark of (re)animation. Although Pete and Fred do not appear together in the way that Alice and Renée are simultaneously doubled by Arquette's presence, this quality of the double spreads through each of their scenes and "infects" the film as a whole. In each instance of doubling, Pete and Fred meet in lost time since they cannot meet in space.

Recording and communications devices can unfold spaces to activate the impossible time of simultaneity, as with Fred's first with the Mystery Man during a party at Andy's house. Lynch describes him as "a hair of an abstraction"; this description is shorthand for the film, encapsulating its mystery while still insisting on its material status, as incarnated.[49] In the same way a single hair provides all sorts of *information* about the perpetrator of a crime, enough evidence to convict without ever revealing the entire story or motivation in certainty, *Lost Highway* contains a mystery that is felt rather than revealed, saturating characters, settings, and spectators without ever being fully actualized. The Mystery Man, his face made up like a mask—with a film of white make-up, kohl-rimmed eyes, and a garish, lipsticked mouth—is a figure of crossing in the film, appearing in both realities absolutely unchanged (one of the few characters to do so). He incarnates the delay of lost time, a figure of terror and uncertainty at once.

As he approaches Fred, the sounds of the party fall away, a vacuum of silence creating an aural intimacy while the party continues, as if he and Fred were now moving at a different rate of time from their surroundings. In a bizarre conversation, the Mystery Man claims that they have met before at Fred's house, telling him "I'm there right now." When Fred blurts out "That's absurd," the Mystery Man pulls out a cell phone and invites Fred to "call me. Dial your number." Fred dials and hears the Mystery Man's voice on the other end: "I told you I was there." As Fred demands an explanation, the Mystery Man claims to have been invited. We hear a doubled dissonant laughter, at the party and over the line, before the Mystery Man demands, "Give me back my phone." This scene recalls Betty's and Rita's call to Diane Selwyn in *Mulholland Drive,* where Betty whispers, as she and Rita share the earpiece, "It's so strange to be calling yourself." She addresses Rita here, but of course it is her own voice on the answering machine. She's not wrong to not recognize it, however. If in movement-vision the single axis of recognition is deranged by a multiplicity of points of view, auto-audition is already an intensive doubling. When we hear ourselves speak, we hear double: the external voice in the surrounding environment, and the internal voice modulated by the resonance of the cranial cavities. The voice, an incorporeal dimension of the body, produces a doubled body, one externalized and deboned. The answering message amplifies this existing internal split: auto-audition as the fracture in the I.

The Mystery Man, with his exaggeratedly pale complexion, dark suit, and red lips, and through his line "It is not my habit to go where I am not wanted" evokes the vampire, a Figure in Deleuze's sense for the fold in time that suspends the present. Between the past (as the preservation of the age and body before death), and the achronic eternal of the everafter, the vampire's lack of breath and heartbeat mark his temporality as aberrant and ametrical. The vampire, of course, has no reflection; in the game of doubles of *Lost Highway,* the Mystery Man is one of the few characters who travel unchanged between the various scenarios. However, he doesn't *retain* his identity because he doesn't have one to begin with. He repeatedly ripples the continuity of space and time; here, he is in two places at once, present and telepresent.

As images of each other, Fred and Pete are suspended in a folded architecture, on display during Fred's initial transformation itself. Typically for Lynch, the film insists on the literal nature of its most bizarre elements. An imprisoned Fred suffers from headaches and insomnia, subject to brief flashes of lurid, colored images of Renée's dismembered body. The night he "changes," Fred sits in his cell alone, suffering, invisible to the guards outside. Suddenly, the physical space of his cell begins to change. The scene alternates between shots of this transformation and Fred's dumbfounded reaction. Against the door of his cell an image is revealed, the wall peeling away like the opening of two curtains. A house, isolated on a beach, is burning in reverse, unexploding and coming together again. With a little Lynchian *whoosh,* the house is reassembled, grey and silent in the night. Even the burning beach house is the image as architecture, a strip of film running in reverse. There is no trace of the cell visible save in the reaction shots of Fred, who cannot believe his eyes. We cut to the door of the house, from which the Mystery Man emerges to look calmly at Fred, then steps back inside. Immediately, blue light flares around the cell. Fred looks up to the light fixture; it is not the source of the flare. Suddenly the image of the lost highway appears, filling the screen, and the car pulls over in front of a stranger by the side of the road. Behind the young man, a double exposure reveals a young woman and an older couple calling "Pete" and running toward the man, but they pass through the scene entirely. Back in Fred's cell, a figure (presumably Fred, though it is uncertain) writhes on the bed, clutching a bloodied head and screaming, amid flashes as the scene fades out.

The lost highway is another architecture of passage in this film, a site of bodily exchange and metamorphosis. There is no better image for the affective quality of Lynch's film than the opening scene and credits, plunging the audience immediately into a state of intensive uncertainty based on the relation between spectator and the film body. Rather than Sobchack's non-contaminative double occupancy, the spectator and film body are here in a relationship of participatory anamorphosis. There is no fade in: immediately, flashing yellow lines slice the screen in half. The lost highway itself opens before us, the yellow lines the only color in the dark night. This visceral image, saturated with danger as if something is about to happen, is devoid of context as to what it could be. The road implies destination and orientation, but the headlights illuminate only a limited field. The flashing yellow lines flicker discontinuously, like the frames of a film, but their repetition evokes a powerful sense of continuity. This scene exemplifies what Melissa McMahon describes as "the long take as repetition": a repeated return to the object beyond the length of time needed for recognition, destabilizing its initial determination.[50] In *Lost Highway* we repeatedly see this extended focus on everyday objects, exceeding their own representation as the selective perception of their utility bleeds away; also evident with the repeated body of Arquette as two characters, where repetition "brings the thing to an essential singularity," endlessly referring to other descriptions. McMahon calls this a "literal image" both clear and opaque:

> The image and the body is uncertain because it maintains itself in a space outside its determination in action, a space of infinite possibility, of the forces of grace or chance. This is not the secrecy of a dark interior, hidden so that it can all the better be inferred or perceived, the secret of a content within form, but a sort of unfolding or unraveling of the opposition between interior and exterior across a surface plane, across time, defying the depths of secrecy to create an impenetrability of the surface.[51]

McMahon distinguishes between representation, requiring a (hierarchical) distinction between original and copy and producing only a false movement where difference is understood in terms of the same, and a Deleuzian repetition that does away with this distinction and thus allows for a real movement of differential repetition. This destabilizing effect is of looking not as the perception of an incipient action, but as the delay of sense(s) in sensation. The opposition of interior and exterior becomes a topological continuity of affect.

Paralleling the opening's sense of urgency and rush, of anxiety before a cause (enacting William James's contention that we do not run because we are afraid, but we are afraid because we run) is a sense of slackening, of overfamiliarity. The road races beneath the car, but the landscape never changes. The soundtrack is hard and pulsating, fast and rhythmic, but the beat is suddenly overcome as the languid voice of David Bowie floats in the air, singing "funny how secrets travel." The urgency remains, underpinning the scene but inaccessible under the hypnotic voice. *Lost Highway* is about the way secrets travel between the audience and the film without being revealed or resolved. It locates secrets not in a depth to be plumbed or "brought to light," but in the topological modulations of the surface, like the rippled folds of a curtain in Fred's bedroom obsessively detailed by the camera's gaze, shot so that what is behind the curtain (the secret, the hidden) is less interesting than the way in which the curtain itself sensuously embodies mystery and concealment. This opening scene illustrates this sense: though we can identify elements that contribute to this feeling, the experience of the scene exceeds any cause. We have no object as cause for our emotion, but similarly we do not properly have a subject either.

The street or road as an image architecture travels across Lynch's Hollywood trilogy, both picking up on the uncanny spiral of Scottie's pursuit of Madeleine, where his intensive spectatorship is nothing more than the return to a home he doesn't recognize (the "point of view" that belongs to the object of the gaze) and the later drive to the mission, where everyone's knowledge (spectator and characters) hangs suspended in the air. Lynch has already replayed Hitchcock's melancholy vision of Scottie's melancholia, the changing streetlight on an abandoned San Francisco corner, in the lonely traffic light of *Twin Peaks*. Lynch reimagines LA's car culture, where cars are mobile homes, portable foldings of the inside, and in *Lost Highway* and *Mulholland Drive* makes the car a place for recomposing bodies and identities in intensity. Throughout the Hollywood trilogy, the actual geographies of LA streets and roads are refracted through a double vision of hazy cinematic memories to explicitly reroute the ambiguous embodiments of criminal intentions.

In *Lost Highway*, Pete is held hostage during Mr. Eddy's terrifying high-speed pursuit through the canyon roads of LA; this scene, rather than simply concentrating the "criminality" of the film in Mr. Eddy, distributes it across bodies, machines, and forces, drawing in Pete's ambiguous embodiment as well. The scene explicitly cites Nicholas Ray's *In a Lonely Place*, where Gloria Graham, one of noir's most sympathetic "femme fatales," is likewise helpless when her lover, Humphrey Bogart, ends a tense and reckless drive, after he cuts off another driver, by brutally beating that man before Graham's horrified eyes. Ray's film, also a drama of confused criminality, here recomposes the bodily and gendered relation of Pete to Mr. Eddy, putting Pete in Graham's place in a redirection of erotic and criminal trajectories.

Mulholland Drive also reinscribes the actual geography of Los Angeles through the refracted gaze of cinema rerouting the "dead ends" of certain bodies, opening them up to other embodiments through the multiplicity of time. The car, a habitual embodiment of motivity, thus *regains* its strange force to accentuate the immobility of bodies moving through space, as they move through time instead. Lynch transduces the credits of *Sunset Boulevard* and redistributes it in two scenes. In Billy Wilder's film, the opening voice-over, suspending relation of voice and body, is itself doubled by a phantom body in the long and sensationally embodied tracking sequence that opens the film, an impossible objective shot that effectuates a double disjunction not wholly resolved by the eventual meet-up of drowned corpse and voice-over. In *Mulholland Drive*, Lynch repeats Wilder, first in the "death drive" of the opening credit sequence, starting with the street sign and trailing the car toward the accident that will unhinge Rita from knowledge, and then through a suspended POV in Betty's apartment, where a sense of camera consciousness is intensely manifested by the empty space. In *Sunset Boulevard*, from the beginning we are in an untimely Hollywood, where the corpse time of the screenwriter and the "vampiric" lingering of Swanson are the unhinged side effects of the Dream Factory. In *Sunset Boulevard*, Norma Desmond's car eventually rolls onto the set as the substitute for her own, undesirable body. In *Mulholland Drive,* Diane's own dreams are snuffed out when the director runs a make-out scene with Camilla in a car, pulling her close and calling out "kill the lights."

Bliss Cua Lim has reimagined a "modal" theory of the genre of fantastic films through the terms of temporal critique, rejecting the exclusions of a modern time consciousness as "disenchanted (the supernatural has no historical agency); empty (a single universal history includes all events, irrespective of cultural disparity); and homogeneous (history transcends the "singularity' of events, because it exists prior to them)."[52] Fantastic narratives, marked by *immiscible* time or traces of untranslated otherness, instead allow the supernatural to regain an agency, that of "making the present waver."[53] Immiscibility names a state of suspense, in which a homogeneous mixture is not formed: "This wavering is precisely the inscription of fantastic scandal at the limits of modern temporality's field of vision—time is out of joint."[54] Although Lim's major emphasis is on postcolonial cinema, she suggests that temporal critique can be productively enacted to evoke the immiscible trace as an "ethics of time." Lynch's LA turns up the volume on the ambiguous relation between California's Spanish past and its whitewashed present in his films, where the ghosts haunting Hollywood don't rely on a simple distinction between movies and real life, but themselves deploy fantastic figures of alternative temporalities, and include "what-if" scenarios and the persistence of other identities. In *Mulholland Drive,* for instance, Hollywood's modern time consciousness serves to eliminate the history of re-composed bodies like that of Rita Hayworth, and her notoriously torturous electrolysis sessions to raise her Hispanic hairline, floating around the body of Laura Haring. "This is the girl," the now of identification, transfers ambiguously between Haring and Melissa George, the blonde and blue-eyed woman we first see lip-syncing, who both share the name of "Camilla Rhodes" (Roads?). Roads, streets, and highways are all figural architectures of force and exchange.

In *Inland Empire,* the haunted streets and back alleys of LA are likewise sites of impossible alterations, folds in space and time. Lynch's whores are literally streetwalkers here, traveling between the found streets of

Hollywood and Hollyłódź (a popular nickname for this film-centric town) in Poland. Stumbling through time, Dern dead ends on the streets of LA until she awakens from her death scene in the studio space; we repeatedly get an indistinction between inside and out in these terms. The streetscapes in *Inland Empire* are the figural architectures of a found set, reanimating the *tableau vivant* of Hitchcock's San Francisco through Dern's spiritual automaton as actor-medium. Dern watches, but does not participate in, the lip-syncing that pervades the film, but her body repeatedly hosts other incorporeal forces. Hollywood Boulevard becomes the lost highway of this film, where wounded bodies live out the intensive transformations of their own anotherness, in a way that exceeds (just as Dern's "death scene" exceeds its own boundaries), any *restoration* of voice to body. In the audio-visual image as an architecture, we instead get the repeated "fusion" of the tear in the parasol, as in the final skyscape vision of Rita and Betty over the city, larger than life.

Lost in the Medium

Thinking of time as an incorporeal dimension of the body asks us to reanimate questions of media form. Lynch's Hollywood trilogy may not be the scene of the spectacular special effects typically associated with the digital turn. However, whether on celluloid with a commitment to the production of in-camera effects (*Lost Highway*) or shot with a prosumer digital camera and self-distributed (*Inland Empire*), Lynch's films have, as with the rediscovery of Hitchcock in the 1990s in the new multiplex of the museum, in a similarly untimely fashion embodied the post-cinematic affect of "what it feels like to live in the twenty-first century."[55] *Mulholland Drive* has fared better than both *Lost Highway* (though that film's critical appraisal has improved considerably) and the spectacular excesses of *Inland Empire*, frequently assessed as for true believers only. At the end of the century's first decade, *Mulholland Drive* was on many lists for best films of the first ten years, read as a successful integration of a new digital cinephilia of intensive reviewing. This is made possible by the ubiquity of home media, the increasing importance of the computer as a vehicle for spectatorship and the Internet as a twenty-first-century cine-club of analysis, speculation, and re-assemblage. Its

convoluted narrative seemed to speak to the figural force and recombi-
natory potential of digital editing and spectatorship.[56] In the Hollywood
trilogy, a falsifying narration deranges the sense of discrete episodes in
favor of the intensity of passage itself; although bodies and identities are
discontinuous, time's difference is continuous. A Lynchian spectatorship is both an engagement with suspense films as "films that do things
to bodies" (and brains, as per Elsaesser), but also provoke the feeling
of re-worlding. If direct images of time embody contagious mutations of
form, especially via a "point of view that belongs so much to the thing
that the thing is constantly being transformed in a becoming identical to
point of view" or a direct perception of relation beyond its terms, Lynch
provocatively enacts this through falsifying narratives in which characters get "lost in the medium," in the delay of lost time.

Mediums are not passed through but participate in immediation; they
are repeated fusions of the tear, as in the opening composite image of
Inland Empire, drawing on Germaine Dulac's work of "pure cinema,"
Disque 957. That image, repeated and re-composed later in the film under
the lost girl's evocative question, "Do you want to see?," is an image of
the folds of media. It remixes record needles and ephemeral airwaves,
Dern's character and the Lost Girl, and the strange, amorphous blot that
repeats throughout the film as the wound in the gut of Dern and Julia
Ormond's character, and the ketchup stain on a T-shirt, a playful evocation of Godard's reminder that it's not blood, it's red. Though all of
Lynch's films have, to some extent, thematized recording and other technologies and their forceful mutations of human forms, the Hollywood
trilogy binds this thematic to the dream machine of Hollywood images
themselves. In his work, we see the emergence of a Deleuzian automaton, which, rather than the insistent spectatorial interrogation of a
Hitchcockian camera consciousness (Do you see?), provokes an affective contagion of art beyond knowledge. When the Lost Girl asks Dern,
"Do you want to see?," Dern builds a time machine in response, from a
piece of folded silk, a cigarette, and a watch. Burning through one layer
of the silk, she looks into the fold; what there is to see is the mobile force
of the medium itself as a "voyage in place," remade from the combination of duration (burning cigarette), folding and the unhinged time of

the watch running backward. What she sees is the movement of becoming itself.[57]

In Lynch's films, technologies have an *ana*morphic effect on human bodies; that is to say, they do not *meta*morphize the body into a new, completed form, but serve to *de-figure* it—visibly and aurally. This disfiguring is both the insistent difference of anotherness itself, and the making visible of forces, the body as a composition of speeds and slownesses. Like the double, the effect is not simply an other form, but the making visible of the forces shivering any misleadingly stable form. As Francois-Xavier Gleyzon describes this in Lynch's work: "The formless does not arise in any way from the categorical refusal of form. . . . It is more about the setting into motion of forms . . . which . . . commits itself to the work of forms all the better to defile them."[58] Everyday technologies of electricity or telephones are rendered to highlight their "dirtiness," amplifying their echo focus, making sensible what we usually ignore. Lynch amplifies noise to the point that it interferes with "information," where materiality, for example, is "received" by the body as the productive effect of a speech-act: a self-affection, or auto-audition. If for Deleuze, Hitchcock's innovation was to turn characters into spectators, Lynch is one of the great thinkers of the relationship between recording media and the human form, turning characters and spectators into receivers. As early as *The Alphabet* (1968), Lynch calls attention to the sensational materiality doubling sense, through a refusal of the blank place-holding of letters. The alphabet song is blithely sung by children and juxtaposed with the image of a young girl writhing on a bed.[59] This cheerful recitation has a direct effect: pain. "Please remember you are dealing with the human form," a narrator blandly intones: an ambivalent reminder infusing all of Lynch's films.

In *The Machinic Unconscious*, Félix Guattari describes *strong resonance* as the mark of molecular becomings, intensive relations that render "fuzzy" the discrete boundaries of the components that make up an assemblage.[60] This strong resonance characterizes the doublings of *Lost Highway*, picking up on the cross-gender doublings of Hitchcock's *Vertigo*. Molecular materiality resonates across the Hollywood trilogy when an image on a TV competes for significance with the static, through the fatal effects of lip-syncing or the insistent impossible embodiment of a mobile point of view unattached to character. Like a skipping record stuttering information, these failures of technology are not mere annoyances, but the sign of "something happening" (the repeated lyric at the end of *Inland Empire*), an emergent anotherness, all the more critically in forms of recording and repetitive media.[61] Also like a skipping record, they generate a field of doubles and differential repetitions, requiring a rethinking of medium, a stretching of the frequently overlooked transition and change that these media entail. Repetition thus highlights the temporal element of medium usually ignored, making it the agent of a repetition with a difference. Like the blue key in *Mulholland Drive*, turning the key does not solve the mystery, but releases energy to re-fold space and time.

Lost Highway puts the observer into the scene via a movement of affect, in a vertigo of suspense that is not simply epistemological in nature. Inspired by Hitchcock's spiral form of time, *Lost Highway* evokes Bergsonian *paramnesia*, a doubled derangement of self-reflectivity by the moving-mirror of self-referentiality. *Lost Highway* takes to an extreme Deleuze's contention that the character of the time-image "records rather than reacts."[62] The transformations of memory, experience, and paramnesia provoke a violent stretching of time. Deleuze describes this as being "prey to a vision," when seeing renders the viewer passive, rather than being an exercise of power and knowledge.[63] Intensifying the Hitchcockian suspension of character, Lynch's characters are prey to their own image in an awareness of the splitting of time. Bergson's paramnesiac exchange (of actor and role, body and mirror image) reinscribes doubling precisely along *molecular* lines; it is not simply a case of the doubled subject, but an intensive resonance between two worlds. The "moving mirror" flattens ecological distinctions; the exchange prompted by the conscious perception of mirroring is not a misrecognition of the subject, but a mode of recomposing ecological relations: the entry into anotherness.

Across the trilogy, the operation of technology manifests in two main ways: first, through temporal delay, such as *Lost Highway*'s delayed intercom message that impossibly answers the question "Who is the sender and who is the addressee?," and second, through attention to the "molecular" materiality or fringes of mediums themselves, as with *Inland Empire*'s opening projector beam. In *Lost Highway,* delay is launched immediately after the credits: Fred Madison (Bill Pullman) nervously smokes a cigarette in his living room when the intercom buzzes. He responds by pressing only the listen button and hears "Dick Laurent is dead."[64] Looking out the window, he sees no one outside; he is puzzled by the message about a man he doesn't know. At the end of the film, we see Fred is (impossibly) the one who sends this message to himself. The opening message initiates a series of events that *culminate* in Laurent's murder, an impossible trajectory, and so the murder itself is suspended in time, evoking Deleuze's contention that in fact there is no crime other than time itself. Rather than a closed loop, we have a spiral of suspense, the two Freds vertiginously making contact at the point where the spiral loops back around.

The immediacy of the intercom relay is undermined in the gap between them; the "beyond" of information through the question of addressee and sender doesn't stabilize position or relativize perspective, but through the suspense of participating in the event provokes the creativity of thought beyond information. The experiential event means getting lost in the medium rather than getting the whole picture. At the ending of *Lost Highway,* repetition takes the form of a loop that marks the *indeterminate* quality of change; the making of difference, and not its measure. As spectators, we cannot simply follow the events of Lynch's film in a linear unfolding, not even retrospectively; instead, like Fred sending a message to himself through that intercom, we pass anew through the film in a free replay. These distributed doubles are not defined by resemblance or the same, but anotherness as an affect of time.

The two main doubles in *Lost Highway* spark a tale of madness, uncertainty, and the refraction of subjectivity in the camera's gaze, but it is not a psychological double. Renée/Alice are both played by Patricia Arquette; rather than facilitating recognition, the actress's doubled body engenders a confusion that exceeds the narrative suspense over her identity. Pete (Balthazar Getty) and Fred share memories and experiences but inhabit different bodies; Pete's recognizability as Fred relies on the dream logic of the double, where nonsensuous similarity is evoked through repetition and a familiarity that is felt but not understood (as when Fred tells Renée "It was you, but not you" in his dream). In this "twenty-first century film noir," the mystery lies less in distinguishing original from bad copy than in the generative effects of repetition necessary to any discussion of the increasing importance of the "body" in recent film theory. Lynch's film provokes an intuitive participation by the spectator, rearranging the duality of material body and spectralization of film, video, and other reproductive technologies. As Elsaesser and Hagener put it: "Cinema is a reality *and* a way of thinking" if we do not begin from a representational perspective.[65]

When the relay of technology is highlighted, when it becomes de-lay and we linger in sensation, then the virtual appears "in the cracks." Relay as arc of eventness is doubled by delay as self-referentiality, the doubled temporality that Massumi calls semblance and event. This is in *Lost Highway* activated primarily through a thickness of mood. Slow motion, a commonplace shorthand for memory, is evoked in distortions of image and sound, even when it is not used. Recording devices can function as moving mirrors, displacing the single axis of mirror-vision via the emergent alterity of movement-vision as a multiplicity of temporal perspectives. When characters become witnesses to their own existence, Deleuze says, "Everything remains real, but between the reality of setting and that of motor action there is no longer a motor extension established, but rather a dreamlike connection through the intermediary of the sense organs," as if "the action floats in the situation," suspended in its utility.[66] In this suspension, the virtual becomes important *for itself*, not only as a future actuality. The actual is not replaced by the virtual, but in their indiscernibility their mutual image becomes a "purely optical and sound situation, in which the seer [*voyant*] has replaced the agent [*actant*]: a *description*."[67]

The displacement of figuration by the figural puts the emphasis on passage itself. Flaxman calls the image a sensible aggregate or a sign

> that we can't simply re-cognize and that we encounter as such at the very limit of the sensible. Sensations possess the capacity to derange

the everyday, to short-circuit the mechanism of common sense, and thus to catalyze a different way of thinking; indeed, sensations are encountered at a threshold we might call the thinkable.[68]

To become lost in the medium is to fail to recognize; the productive force of the virtual becoming valid "for itself." In terms of sense, the provocative hesitation of recognition of the figural provokes *aberrant movement.* Rather than the smooth passing through of the medium of representation, the figural interposes the doubled delay of immediation, displacing the opposition between a material real and a mediated unreal (where images exist on the side of the unreal), with a mutual image. This doubled delay is the duplicity of the occurrent arts, radically reorienting conventional thinking around questions of media, mediation, and reflexivity.

Lost in the medium, we solicit the "delay of lost time," as what Keith Ansell Pearson describes as "giving time a positive reality":

> If we take seriously the *delay of duration at instantaneity* we allow for a creative evolution and not simply a mechanical one in which time would simply be given and things would exist as preformed possibles awaiting realization. With this "delay" or reserves of duration we are able to conceive of a "hesitation" and an "indetermination" which, *while vague and nebulous,* are wholly positive aspects of time and becoming.[69]

Here, delay is itself *productive,* not simply *revelatory.* This echoes the difference between suspense as narrative withholding, where an affective experience of delay is merely a front for a properly intellectual experience (suspense grips you in the mind, not the guts), and my definition of suspense as a special case of movement. Barthes's suspense more closely relates to Deleuze's movement-image, where temporal and intellectual deviations of plot and story are like the stretching of an elastic, snapping back into place by the end of the film. Likewise, Mulvey's "cinema of delay" is what she terms "elongating the road."[70] The form never changes, it simply returns to or reveals its original state. Deviations or perversions of that form are ultimately "made right in the end"; in narrative, this takes the form of an explanatory resolution, even if it only occurs retroactively (that is, when the film is done, you can go back over it and give each element a logical place). At the end of *Inland Empire,* the film's images rewind until Dern returns to her first split from herself. But no narrative explanation can simply reverse, and thus erase, the difference made in the intervening 2+ hours, and that difference is explicitly signaled as self-referentiality, a look across the space of the room and the aberrant time of the encounter with the self.

Please Remember That You Are Dealing with the Human Form

Bergson writes, "In reality the body is changing form at every moment; or rather there is no form, since form is immobile and the reality is movement. What is real is the continual change of form; form is only a snapshot view of transition."[71] Lynch's films interrogate the effects of electricity, recording, and communication devices on our own beings and bodies to show that we don't yet understand the effects that we already live: participation precedes recognition. The human body is repeatedly rendered obsolete by the changes this new world imposes on us.[72] His work destabilizes the opposition between film as an industrial art form and video as electronic, precisely through the notion of electricity and its anamorphic effects on the human form. Although the Industrial Age is often described as a crisis of boundaries, where human and machine are increasingly blurred because of changes in work and the development of new technologies, in the Electronic Age the crisis has shifted to a fluid disintegration of boundaries, as in the cliché of the "loss" of the body. Lynch's films question this fluid loss without denying the transformative effects of electricity and electronic devices; his work explores the suspense of obsolescence. Deleuze's idea of the spiritual automaton, the pure receiver, closely resembles Lynch's approach.

Electricity, as that which renders space refigurable through illumination and shadow, marks corporeal transformation. A red lamp seems to travel across the trilogy, showing up at key moments of anotherness, as in the room where Nikki/Sue and Billy/Devon make love for the first time. Later, amid the play of multiple beams of light, Dern looks into her own face in *Inland Empire.* In *Lost Highway,* when Pete transforms into Fred, electricity shocks the image into transformation. Alice and Pete make love on the sand, illuminated by car headlights. However, their bodies also seem lit from within; the white bodies of Alice and Pete are overexposed, so that they glow "hot" and the outlines are blurred.[73] The scene continually highlights a disintegrative movement: wind gusts throughout, blowing around the glowing blonde hair of Alice; the car's headlights highlight the sand caught in the wind, texturizing the air, Pete and Alice initially seem connected but this begins to fray and they lose sync. All this recalls Schefer's contention that cinematic bodies are made of grains of time, of luminous dust. Shots of Pete occur in "real time," while shots of Alice are in slow motion. Pete repeatedly tells Alice, "I want you"; her eventual reply, as she leaves him on the beach, walks into the cabin, and disappears from the film, is "You'll never have me." With this, Fred reappears; the headlights fade and the music on the car radio disappears, as though Fred has stabilized that dimension. The time out of sync, the lost time of these devices, the field of doubles and repetitions generated by them have been absorbed in his body.

Fred hears a voice behind him; it is the Mystery Man in the car. He looks at the cabin, when he looks back the Mystery Man is gone. "Here I am"; he has reappeared at the cabin door and disappears inside. Fred follows; there is no sign of Alice, only the Mystery Man holding a bulky video camera that suggests a surveillance camera. "Where's Alice?" Fred asks; there is some kind of continuity here. Like Pete after his appearance in Fred's cell, Fred is not initially panicked or disoriented. "Alice who?" asks the Mystery Man, filming Fred. "Her name is Renée. If she told you her name was Alice, she's lying. And your name, what the fuck is your name?" Fred flees; the Mystery Man follows as the scene shifts to his camera POV, the grainy black-and-white image like that of the tapes Fred and Renée received. Just before the Mystery Man reaches Fred, Fred speeds off into the desert. The effect of the taping is uniquely terrifying. Although POV is a standard feature of many horror films, often used to play around with the uncertain identity of the killer, in this instance the tension between the clichéd use of POV in suspense with the subject of the image (Fred, whose identity is radically uncertain) is doubly uncanny and again displaces and makes criminality contagiously vague.

Fred's difference (familiar and strange at once, at least as different as last is to next) begins to come to the surface. Unlike in *Vertigo*, where the oscillation of identity is ostensibly narratively resolved, at the end of *Lost Highway* the storyline reels towards resolution but never achieves reintegration of character. Things are being forced back toward the beginning, toward our original questions. We never see Alice again in the film; are we to think it has been Renée all along, that Alice was nothing more than a mask for Fred's psychosis? Retracing Pete's steps, Fred spies on Renée and Mr. Eddy at the Lost Highway hotel; when she leaves, he kidnaps him at gunpoint.

Back at Andy's, who was killed during Pete and Alice's robbery, the police have arrived. They pick up the photo of Alice and Renée with Andy and Mr. Eddy, only now Alice is gone. Things seem to be snapping back into place. However, the cops note that they've got "Pete Dayton's prints all over the place," the indexical trace of what? A ghost? A figment of the imagination? At the same moment, Fred is out in the desert, struggling with Mr. Eddy. Fred reaches out his hand and out of nowhere a knife appears. Fred slashes Mr. Eddy's throat; we see it was the Mystery Man who handed over the knife. The Mystery Man hands Mr. Eddy a Watchman; he sees grainy images of himself at Andy's, watching pornographic films of Alice while making out with Renée. "You may hand that back to me now," the Mystery Man says, and he shoots Mr. Eddy in the head. Only in the next scene, we are left with only Fred, gun in hand. He drives home to send himself the message, too late, that "Dick Laurent is dead." Not a vicious circle, but a spiral of suspense; Fred flees the house and once more heads down the lost highway. Has the film ended where it began, or are we still lost in the space of the message in the intercom that lets Fred be in two places at once, never coinciding with himself? In his car, he shakes so violently that his flesh seems to explode, echoing Dave in *2001*.

If Fred comes "unhinged" in *Lost Highway*, such that "time itself is out of joint," it would seem that it is the suspicion of sexual infidelity that is the cause. Female infidelity has a close association with two-facedness, made bluntly literal in Lynch's film. But the double woman is herself doubled by the split of the male lead between Pete and Fred. The notions of causality and originality are put in suspense by *Lost Highway*'s looping narratives, which suggest that despite the fear of sexual straying, the real crime in *Lost Highway* is that of time. In its violence and horror, Lynch seems to share in the sense that this *is* a crime.

A Love Letter, Straight from My Heart

If media anamorphize human forms, Lynch's Hollywood trilogy plays this out through a corpse time. Taylor's tacky joke, calling *Vertigo* "To Lay a Corpse" effectively hits on the animating desire for the nocturnal Eurydice, and Lynch's reanimation of Hitchcock picks up on the cross-contagion of of necro- and cinephilic urges. In *Blue Velvet*, Frank (Dennis Hopper) threatens Jeffrey (Kyle McLachlan): "Do me a favor. Don't be a good neighbor to her anymore. Or I'll send you a love letter straight from my heart, fucker! Do you know what a love letter is? It's a bullet from a fucking gun, fucker! You receive a love letter from me, and you're fucked forever! You understand, fuck? I'll send you straight to hell, fucker!" Frank's circuitous threat conflates love and death, the delay of postal transmission and the immediacy of bullet time. *Lost Highway* and *Mulholland Drive* both stretch out along this affective elasticity of becoming-corpse; while in *Inland Empire,* death as the name of every intensity is the intensity of getting lost in the medium of repetition itself. The spiral of suspense in *Lost Highway* makes the last image of Fred deeply ambiguous; is he frying in the electric chair, a reality bleeding through at last, or are we witnessing the lived abstraction of becoming itself? Through the theme of the condemned man on death row, *Lost Highway* evokes the short film *An Occurrence at Owl Creek Bridge* (1962), in which the moment between the drop of the prisoner from the scaffolding until the crack of the neck stretches into a long flight of escape from the noose and an imagined life, revealed only retrospectively as fantasy by the brutal snap of the neck at the very end of the film.[74] Only here, the crack of the neck never unambiguously comes. Unlike *An Occurrence* and *Vertigo*, the "truth" is never revealed, there is never the dull thud of Judy's fallen body that breaks the spell and seems to demarcate life from death. In *Lost Highway,* there is only the nauseating feeling of adrenaline stretched beyond the moment of flight, the threat disseminated and suspended. An excised scene in the original script, taking

place immediately after Fred's trial and conviction, also suggests a connection with *An Occurrence*. Two beautiful young women discuss the
case while shopping for lingerie. They debate the relative merits of hanging versus the firing squad as a way for a convicted killer to die.

> MARIAN: So you'd rather be hung, huh? (They both giggle at the obvious
> joke.)
> RAQUEL: Absolutely. . . . Soon as your neck snaps, you black out. It might
> take a while for the body to die, but you wouldn't feel it.[75]

Fred's break with reality has often been interpreted as a flight from his
impending doom; the scenes cut in the original script would have made
Fred's situation clearer and more obvious to the viewer. Lynch makes
indiscernible the last gasps of a dying brain and the delayed message of
the intercom.

But if this doesn't yet quite read as love, *Inland Empire* makes the
case for a kind of grace in the suspended (re)animations of the femme
fatale. In this way, Lynch makes obsolete the tired cliché of the femme
fatale through the crime of time. Elsaesser and Hagener identify "post-
mortem" films as a category of mind-game films, part of a new cinema
of the brain, where the body is not saved but the brain carries on sending
signals and making connections, in a "ghostly, but also banal" embodiment.[76] Lynch's emphasis on the suspensions of mediums, however,
binds this much more closely to the body's own anotherness as its creative power. For this reason, it is insufficient to simply read the splitting of Lynch's characters and worlds as the result of trauma. Rather, we
see the really apparitional of "appearance divided in itself and in a non-
psychological way."

A 2009 retrospective at the British Film Institute, "Screen Seductresses: Vamps, Vixens & Femmes Fatales," asked, "Whatever happened
to the femme fatale?," noting a dearth of this iconic character in contemporary cinema.[77] The retrospective celebrated "transgressive women
in film, strong and complex seductresses, with razor-sharp wit and un-
restrained sexuality."[78] This description is one side of femme fatale cliché
of American film noirs of the 1940s and '50s, which reads noir's deadly

women as subversive portrayals of sexuality and power. The other side
sees the femme fatale as misogynistic projection of male fear and long-
ing. Iconic performances like Barbara Stanwyck's Phyllis Dietrichson
in *Double Indemnity* helped establish her defining characteristics: rarely
directly criminal, she instead *incites* criminality via sexual power, manip-
ulating men like puppets. In classic noir, the femme fatale is punished
for her transgressions: murdered (*Double Indemnity*), more rarely jailed
(*The Maltese Falcon*) or domesticated (*Laura*). In her study of the femme
fatale, Julie Grossman convincingly argues that such a traditional conception is frequently at odds with the affective tones of noir films, where
femme fatales are more nuanced, sympathetic, and whose extreme actions
and dazzling attraction can be understood as a desperate response to an
unlivable set of conditions that oppress her. Grossman suggests that the
time has come to put the femme fatale in her place.

Lynch's Hollywood trilogy provocatively reimagines what the femme
fatale is and what she might do. Though Lynch has explicitly tackled this
iconic figure in his vivid reimagining of the noirs at least since 1987's
Blue Velvet (or even with the Girl across the Hallway in *Eraserhead*), a film
that retained the classic noir distinction between good girl Sandy (Dern)
and the femme fatale Dorothy (Isabella Rossellini in her first major
role), already the femme fatale had begun to display a Lynchian twist.[79]
Although Dorothy's sexual allure leads amateur detective Jeffrey into a
criminal underworld, her actions are those of a glitchy automaton. Her
excessive "acting out," particularly in their disturbing sexual encounters when she begs Jeffrey to hit her, does not signal the *typical* duplicity
that incites criminality (Jeffrey's violence and self-disgust) via sexuality;
instead, performance renders her vulnerable. Like a human record, she
is forced to replay not only her nightly performances of *Blue Velvet*, but
also her grotesque sexual encounters with Hopper, an endless audition
for a role she needs but that is killing her. Discussing her role, Rossellini
remarked that "we don't know why we read the details of murder stories
in newspapers with a certain gluttony"; her performance elicited both a
ravenous craving and queasiness in equal measure.[80]

Ever since *Blue Velvet*, the demarcation between good girl and femme
fatale has become indistinct; one need only think of Laura Palmer, one

of Lynch's most tenderly rendered characters, simultaneously small-town sweetheart and a dark, desperate, and often cruel figure. In the Hollywood trilogy, the femme fatale is always the actress, endlessly auditioning at a crime scene where she herself may be the criminal. She has become the key figure through which his increasingly scathing critique of Hollywood's murderous criminality has developed, but who also provokes a specifically cinematic re-enchantment of mystery and creativity. This critique does not operate via a logic of exposure, in the way that some critics have read the Club Silencio scene in *Mulholland Drive* ("no hay banda!"), but rather intensifies the femme fatale's affective force of the femme fatale, quite literally. Her duplicity is transformed into the "powers of the false," a creative power of metamorphosis, rather than revelation, of the true.[81]

By amplifying her metamorphic power, one constrained in her iconic incarnations as simple duplicity or manipulation, Lynch's films re-animate the femme fatale as a "conceptual persona." Deleuze and Guattari describe conceptual personae as "thinkers, solely thinkers, and their personalized features are closely linked to the diagrammatic features of thought and the intensive features of concepts."[82] These "diagrammatic" features indicate that conceptual personae do not simply map the possible, but open onto the thought of potential. Conceptual personae, analyzed by David Rodowick relative to "unthinkable sex," "express qualities or perspectives that want to become-other."[83] Critically, conceptual personae are "situated between multiple points of enunciation," divided from within by the irrational interval; this "expresses a power of falsification in which difference is no longer subsumed by identity."[84] The femme fatale is such a conceptual persona for Lynch as a cine-philosopher. "She" (and here I signal how this figure, even within each film, never holds to a single name) is situated between multiple points of enunciation: author and character, present portrayal and audiovisual archive, actress's body and character; different genders; roles, and (most critically as a means of differentiating her from an aesthetic figure) human form and emergent camera consciousness, this last distinction for Deleuze the mark of the free indirect discourse that is the conceptual persona's prerogative. The femme fatale names the emergent alterfication of a subjective multiplicity in these works, the very figure of anotherness as the creation of new modes of existence. Rodowick specifically binds the ethical, creative force of desire of the conceptual persona—the desire for difference—to the question of how to liberate "unthinkable" sexual positionalities.[85] How might the femme fatale as conceptual persona rearrange the binaries of sexual difference, where difference starts to function "in the interval" of becoming other to oneself? Through the figure (not simply character) of the femme fatale, Lynch's films open up the interval; "she" embodies the productive problem of anotherness as the body's becoming in time.

This (re)animation occurs both via her return from the margins of contemporary cinema and her link to technological (re)animations like lip-syncing and recording devices, and the (re)animation of dead bodies. We see this in the rotting corpse of *Mulholland Drive*'s Diane Selwyn dreaming a different life as a bullet "makes a leisurely journey through her brain," Nikki Grace arising as a zombie from the corpse of Susan Blue in *Inland Empire,* or the temporal dislocations that make our last image of Renée in *Lost Highway,* previously glimpsed as a grotesque restaging of the Black Dahlia's corpse at the hands of her husband, her flight into the night.[86] In this way, Lynch continually (re)animates the murdered woman whose death initiates so many noirs and who is quickly forgotten and displaced by the femme fatale (*Laura, The Lady in the Lake, Vertigo*), by folding them into his femme fatales and having this (re)animation infect the film's temporality. Lynch's dream noirs become topological sites for the femme fatale's expanded affective power; her duplicity mutates into a doubling that engulfs all elements of the film. Refigured as performance, this duplicity is no longer a threat, or measured against the standard of a preexisting truth, but a truly creative act.

Critical to the reanimation are several factors. The first explicitly figures the femme fatale as a creation (and victim) of the Hollywood system (his main female characters are all actresses), highlighting the femme fatale as not only represented in the Hollywood system but as a specifically cinematic mode of embodiment. Lynch reimagines the moral and criminal place of performance and automatism in the femme fatale, turning these signs of her guilt into that which deflects death and guilt, resituating her criminality against Hollywood. Although this displaces questions of criminal actions at the level of narrative in a way that could be seen as glorifying violence against women and refusing the proper assignation of culpability, it opens up myriad possibilities at other levels that can lead to a renewed sense of what the power of the femme fatale might actually be, as well as to radically refocus the question of crime in these films. As Elena del Rio notes of *Mulholland Drive*:

> Lynch's implicit attacks on Hollywood's manufacturing of creatively exhausted, dead images is undoubtedly at the centre of the ideological ramifications spun by the film. The film embodies this extinction of vital creativity through the image of Diane's fetid, decomposing body, which like the monstrous, disintegrating body of Hollywood, lies beyond any capacity for action or transformation.[87]

It is crucial to remember, however, that this is not the final scene of the film, which concludes with the invitation to witness reanimation and the vital force of staged performance at Club Silencio. As we are shushed ("Silencio!") by the blue-haired figure, as if the show were about to start, we are invited to "listen again," in an interactive auto-audition where we hear becoming itself. Those who would read such scenes and reenactments as only condemnations of Hollywood's dream factory should remember that tenderness and horror are two sides of the same topological coin in Lynch's universe. Lynch's deployment of the femme fatale is not a generic condemnation of unrealizable ideals of feminine iconicity; rather, Lynch deploys the femme fatale as a specifically cinematic creative force that exceeds and can renew its institutionalized form. Redemption comes too late, but also makes visible the working of becoming itself.

Second, Lynch disrupts the femme fatale's iconicity through the violence and vulnerability of iconic bodies *as* signs; again, rather than emphasizing the subjectivity of the femmes fatales as unique and fleshed-out individuals, he amplifies their reproducibility. In doing so, he attunes us to the difference that emerges in repetition, through his redoubled narratives, multiple characters played by the same actress (Renée/Alice in *Lost Highway*, Rita/Camilla, Diane/Betty in *Mulholland Drive*, Susan/

Nikki in *Inland Empire*), and undecidable indistinctions between roles. One way Lynch reroutes the femme fatale's criminality into creativity is to make apparent the violence of the stillness and stasis of iconic signs. He thus takes up the frequency with which the femme fatale is played "as image"; through cliché, he suspends a certain body toward obsolescence.

Last, Lynch's Hollywood trilogy, while featuring graphic representations of violence and murder, displaces questions of culpability and guilt at the level of representations and condemnation. Both *Lost Highway* and *Mulholland Drive* can be read as the mad fantasy of a murderer fleeing responsibility, but the films themselves are less interested in a moral condemnation than in asking what else the body of the femme fatale can do.

In Lynch's film, the performer is the figure of creation, increasingly the double of Lynch himself, who might, in a Flaubertian gesture, pronounce that, in *Inland Empire*, "Nikki Grace, *c'est moi.*" Lynch's emphasis on the femme fatale parallels an increasing, though still timid, critical claim that his recent films are in fact deeply feminist, in a way that speaks to the insufficiency of the divided reception of the femme fatale herself as either misogynist creation or subversive liberation. For critics like Martha Nochimson, Laura Dern in *Inland Empire* represents the liberation of a feminist creative energy, a figure in full control of her creative powers who takes up arms to defeat the forces that would keep her down.[88] Julie Grossman suggests that Lynch is the future of the femme fatale, arguing that *Mulholland Drive*'s femme fatale is a force of feminine vitality as "a deeply feminist reworking of gender typography in order to endorse an imaginative openness with regard to experience," in part because of how the femme fatale remains a mobile signifier in the film fluctuating between Rita and Betty.[89] Lynch reroutes questions of affective engagement into uncertainty and hesitation specifically around the recognition of the actress's body, highlighting themes of death and challenging identification to disrupt understandings of criminality.

Grossman suggests that if we reimagine the femme fatale, "the woman labeled as dissembler has a story *of her own* to tell."[90] But I argue that in Lynch, she has precisely an-other's story to tell, that the force, and indeed, the crime of the femme fatale is simply "the crime of time," the films' violence the felt force of becoming other than what we have been. If in classic noir, this has meant specific dreams of becoming another (changing class position, escaping a dead-end marriage, and so on), in Lynch's films the reanimated femme fatale must always be read alongside her corpse, her double, auto-auditioning herself to make uncertain space for someone else to emerge, provoking the crisis of recognition and learning to produce new subjectivities from frozen clichés.

In classic noir, the femme fatale is instantly legible as the incitement to criminality. She uses her sexuality (or whose sexuality is passively provocative, as in *In a Lonely Place*) to essentially turn a man into a puppet, to act out her transgressive desires. Classically, and cruelly, the body that incites crime is also ultimately the victimized body. Her excessive force, characterized by affective potency, is inevitably dimmed. Her duplicity or "performance" is both her power and her weakness, what justifies her violent end. To illustrate Lynch's reimaging, I consider scenes of performance and audition in the Hollywood trilogy as privileged moments of reanimation, both announcing her presence and generating an affective uncertainty around identification. In this pause is the potential for her to become other than she was, for a certain automatism of performance and response to signal the emergence of the new. In these scenes, she becomes a topological figure, amplifying the traditional femme fatale's surface effect to a literal dimension written on the body, generating a hesitation of recognition around these bodies and codes that don't simply reverse expectation but develop a critical sense. Valorizing her performance, Lynch reimagines criminality as the powers of the false. Thus, the apparently central questions of these films: "Who are these women, really?" and "Are they really dead?"—go unanswered. We need to understand this question of rerouted criminality in Lynch's film not in ethical terms, assessed via their representational status, but in ethico-aesthetical terms, accounting for the femme fatale's affective force. These scenes are "magic moments," re-enchantments of the world through the felt force of becoming to reactivate the agency, not of individual characters, but a "will to art."

The second act of *Lost Highway* is steeped in a combination of film noir and 1950s stereotypes, offering the viewer the pleasures of recognition;

however, why this world is evoked is unclear, and its easy familiarity, after this abrupt shift in the film's focus, serves to unsettle. As with the videotapes Renée and Fred receive, the pleasure of recognition is quickly undermined by excess. Typically for Lynch, this setting is difficult to place in time because of the proliferation of generic codes and a layering of material artifacts (for example, the mobster drives a 1950s convertible, the detectives drive a brown sedan from the '70s); yet it is not a period piece. These fragments are loosened from their historical, generic, or conventional references; they refer forward instead of backward. Exceeding bare repetition, they open up a space of possibility. Deleuze describes clichés as a "sensory motor image of a thing"; habitual in nature, we know how to respond, to put it into action. After the unspeakable and unrepresentable murder of Renée, known and yet continually undercut, that occupied the film's opening section, the film restarts by proliferating clichés, characters that we as an audience seem to know how to react to but that are quickly cut off from their sensory motor extension.

Despite the sharp narrative break, as an audience we cannot help but refer the events, actions, and characters of the second act back to the first. We look continually for the play of doubles to try to reorient our sense of what has happened. When we are finally given our first "concrete" evidence of some sort of significant continuity between the two worlds, in the person of Patricia Arquette's first appearance as Alice, things begin to come together; however, the body's "concrete" evidence is hazed by the virtuality of the actor. What is normally closely coupled (the present and past, the actor and role) is enlarged by a suspended perception. Before Alice's first appearance (as silent image), a connection has already been aurally established between Pete and Fred. At the garage, Pete works on a car as another mechanic listens to the radio. Its tinny sound can't disguise that it is Fred's sax performance from earlier in the film coming over the waves. The radio as medium plays with our expectations of liveness and referentiality (as with *Inland Empire*'s opening juxtaposition of record and radio announcer). A jazz performer, Fred is associated with immediacy and the "hot" live moment. When his music's delay comes skipping over the radio waves, Fred's earlier claim to prefer his own memories over recordings is reactivated. Pete and the

audience experience the same dislocation as earlier when Fred transforms: the scene goes in and out of focus, Pete grabs his head. He turns
off the radio, but in some ways, this eddy from the film's past is what
attracts Alice's appearance.

Arquette's dual performance sparks multiple doublings throughout
the film, initiating a contagion of duplicity that repeatedly twists and
folds characters, narrative progressions and repetitions against each
other. Deleuze's reassessment of the powers of the false as perhaps not
crime can be understood relative to the confused criminality and culpability of *Lost Highway*. Criminal acts of murder and violence are rampant,
and yet culpability and the crimes themselves are undecidable, ambiguous in their reality, even to the point of asking, Did this really happen?
This confusion stems from the uncertainty over whether an act of violence has been committed externally (Did Fred kill Renée?) or whether
the real 'crime' is the violence that ensues when "I is an other." Crime
becomes suspended precisely *in time* in this film.

Alice's first appearance at the garage creates a "ripple" effect in the
film. The clichéd use of slow motion to highlight Pete's first glimpse
of her figurally echoes the slowness and weightiness of her actions, linking to the first half of the film, where time could be seen developing in
the characters. As she steps out of the car, the soundtrack resonates with
a sense of familiarity and disquiet. Lou Reed performs a tight, minimal-
ist cover of the Drifters' hit "This Magic Moment." The song is immediately recognizable, but also unfamiliar and newly inflected. In the
film, it is literally a magic moment, "so different and so new," but "like
any other": "at least as different as last is from next." In the same way,
Arquette's body (un)grounds the film's second part as the eccentric, vertiginous point around which all other elements revolve. The mystery of
her identity plays second fiddle to the generative effects of her "masked
difference." What is the relation between Alice and Renée?

Even their names complicate the question. Renée, the original, is
named "reborn"; belonging to the section of the film with narrative primacy, she is always affiliated with repetition and cliché. Likewise, Alice
inverts the rabbit hole of the second half; rather than traveling to a world
of nonsense, she becomes the figure of sense (by focalizing questions of

understanding) in a world turned upside down. A figure of surfaces, though, she also resists notions of sense and of identity. Her identity is refracted by fantasy, photos, films, and Arquette's sly performance. Her duplicity is evident; she always slips away. The fetishization of her body and her affiliation with clichés of womanhood might lead one to analyze Alice/Renée as yet another "immaterial" male fantasy: not "woman as woman," without depth but trapped by the body. However, the very slipperiness of this character and the entire structure of the film belie this. Renée/Alice has no "genuine" depth because identity itself is an effect throughout the film, one already created and recreated. In *Vertigo*, the late split in viewer identification between Scottie and Judy/Madeleine, the ghostliness of Madeleine as figure of the past has been rethought by Tania Modleski in gendered terms as being evident from the start of the film. The narrative split merely brings to a crisis the epistemological split and uncertainty of the viewer. In *Lost Highway*, however, Lynch further intensifies that splitting, playing out the duplicity of the spectator's participation before the screen.

This is evident during a later scene between Alice and Pete meeting illicitly in a hotel, a classic narrative incitement to criminality. This scene cuts back and forth between the present and Alice's narration of a past event, doubling the story of her past audition for Mr. Eddy (though what she is auditioning for is still ambiguous) with a present "performance" for Pete, who needs to know if she can successfully perform the role of his fantasy woman as helpless victim. The lovers meet in a motel room; Alice is upset and tells Pete she thinks Mr. Eddy knows about them. Like Fred, Pete becomes increasingly obsessed with uncovering Alice's secrets; unlike Fred's obsessive jealousy, however, Pete's position as lover, not husband, means that his intentions toward Alice involve rescuing her from the brutal and imperious Mr. Eddy. Although Mr. Eddy never directly mistreats Alice, it is clear that she is under his thumb and a sort of possession. Pete longs to escape with Alice and equally longs to hear that she is Mr. Eddy's victim. Alice tells Pete that they can leave together, change their identities and begin anew. In order for this to happen, though, Pete needs to uncover Alice's secret—the story of how she met Mr. Eddy, to make space for a new identity via a grounding in truth. As

Alice tells her story, there are clear parallels with Renée's story of how she met Andy. Both begin at a place called Moke's, both involve meeting Andy, who tells them about a job. Alice's job offer leads to her meeting with Mr. Eddy. The scene cuts to Mr. Eddy's house, where Alice waits nervously in a hallway, guarded by a man. Her voiceover describes the scene, doubling its temporal location; it is unclear whether these are her memories, Pete's imagination filling in the images or whether the images are the visual manifestation of Alice's fabulation, which may or may not be true. Ultimately, there is no way to know. Description continuously replaces its object. There is a curious, motivating literality to the voiceover. "It got dark," Alice says, and the scene turns black, but it was only a close-up of the back of her black dress, and sound and image continually come together only to expose the void between them in this scene. Description is never what it seems; the images motivated by the words fail to line up. When she finally meets Mr. Eddy, he is seated in a chair, accompanied by his thugs. He looks at her and gestures, and when she hesitates, one of his henchmen holds a gun to her head. As in her earlier introduction to Pete, the soundtrack once again plays a new copy of an old song, this time Jay Hawkins's "I Put a Spell on You" as performed by Marilyn Manson. Again, the lyrics suggest a distorted temporality: "I put a spell on you because you're mine," and the circular nature of desire: "You're mine"; "I don't care if you want me, cause I'm yours yours yours. . . ." As she strips in this audition, Alice fluctuates between being a victim of Mr. Eddy's command and a seductress taking control of the scene; in the same way, the images that unroll tell a familiar story both appealing and appalling to Pete. He is simultaneously disgusted and turned on by what he sees/imagines/is told. When Alice is left only in her panties, she walks over to Mr. Eddy, and kneels in front of him. She reaches out her hand to caress his cheek, and the scene cuts to her hand touching Pete's face. At the cut, the music, which had been building hypnotically in the scene, cuts abruptly with the picture (the shock of contact will later reappear when Alice points to herself in the picture at Andy's). This containment of the non-diegetic music is often repeated throughout the film. The cut of the sound juxtaposed with the continuity of the gesture between scenes inverts the usual sound–image relation both highlighting the transition and not bridging the cut, but making the trespass shocking and powerful. Non-diegetic music is used to undermine the "referentiality" of the images, their primacy in the film, which is also associated with the play between imagination and reality throughout. In this audition scene, the femme fatale is revealed, and she's revealed in her power to create images, to produce a magical effect that literally reaches out to touch the spectator. This audition in *Lost Highway* not only performs the powers of the false in the femme fatale's ability to manipulate her male prey, but more importantly illustrates the effect that this mutability has on the logic of narration, cause and effect, and normative temporality.

In *Mulholland Drive*, an audition scene condenses these two impulses, both replaying that uncertain identification of actress/part beyond the narrative boundaries of the film, and testifying to the way that cinema's magic works not through an illusion, a glossy surface hiding a dirty truth, but in an affective transmutation right before our eyes, disrupting the revelatory logic the classical duplicity of the femme fatale seems to promise. Betty's audition is the first moment when the clear distinction between the femme fatale (as Rita) and the good girl (as perky Betty), starts to take a topological twist, and Betty is revealed as a femme fatale whose control emerges via an automatism of performance. George Toles has offered a brilliant reading of this scene, in which he claims that the effect of seeing Betty, up until this point a rather shallow and clichéd character, suddenly transmute into a brilliant performer leaves the audience scrambling to recognize the woman in front of them. Betty becomes "possessed" as it were, by this actress. He writes, "We behold Betty crossing over, in so many ways at once that the effect is breathtaking, from guileless pretending to majestic double-dealing," concluding that "the viewer is virtually commandeered (ie. we are made automatons) into thinking about 'Naomi Watts' herself."[91] Toles makes the link between femme fatale and performance explicit when he argues that the audition scene is where "Watts/Betty effectively steals the sense of danger and darkness that her friend Rita had previously embodied . . . and *theft* is exactly the right word for it, calling to mind the old acting phrases, 'scene stealing' and 'stealing the show.'"[92] He concludes that

Betty is Lynch's Eurydice (even as she is also, in his description, Orpheus, though he fails to name her as such); "she attempts to revoke her alter ego's death," coming back through death via performance as resurrection).[93] Toles's description suggests that our "recognition" of Watts is *untimely*, and a problem for the viewer's agency: "Nevertheless, we need more time than we are given to register the fact that the woman who intuits under pressure what her role might include to enrich itself (moving well beyond the cramping straightforwardness of the script writer) is not—cannot be—Betty as we have known her."[94] The opening of this untimeliness, however, is not explored in Toles's analysis, which restores creativity to Watts as actress, but also to Lynch as unmentioned Orphic bard.

If this scene throws the audience into a crisis of identification (Are we seeing Betty or Naomi Watts, and why is this a problem?), the uncertainty resonates and is echoed by the very next scene, in which Betty is taken to a film set where actresses audition for a part via lip-syncing. The hesitation of Betty as femme fatale set against this backdrop of the uncertain possession of lip-syncing, is a making space for an-other's performance within the body. Lip-syncing, of course, offers the possibility of a perfect repetition; the invitation to the voice is thus also the invitation to an untimely and nonhuman temporality. As the performances unfold, the director of the film does a double take of Betty in slow motion, again suggesting an uncertain recognition that asks us to look again. Del Rio reads this as the work of the sheets of the past that call up all the mental functions simultaneously, an intuition of what might have been. However, we should also recall that this includes Camilla's own doubling by Laura Haring and Melissa George, whose automatic performance here opens the gap in time. Betty's fatal indistinction as dreaming corpse and vengeful lover who causes Rita's death are condensed in the double play of the femme fatale's power of reanimation.

In *Inland Empire*, auditions and performance shift yet again, and increasingly become the sites of auto-audition, where Dern's characters feel their anotherness. Nikki's first reading for the film *On High in Blue Tomorrows* is interrupted by a mysterious figure, who turns out to be herself stumbling onto the film set from another time and place. In that film, criminality is incited by the mysterious cursed film itself, and it is never certain whether the murders and violence we continually witness are contained by the fiction of the script, or topologically fold studio and set into lived realities. The entire finale of the film is a drawn-out experience of resurrection in which Nikki Grace reemerges as a kind of zombie or automaton from the corpse of Susan Blue on the floor when the camera pulls back to reveal the set.

The final sequence, which unfolds when Nikki enters the Rabbits set, is bookended by two double encounters with the self. The first is when Nikki shoots the Phantom (*the* figure of deathly terror in the film), only to be confronted with her own distorted and maniacally grinning visage. Jennifer Pranolo has read this scene as the eruption of the *unheimlich*, Dern "discovering herself within the Phantom that she must kill"; claiming that in the end, Dern is returned safely back home:

> She remains pristinely untouched, poised for the whole apparatus of torture to begin again. Through this circular non-ending, Lynch substantiates Sontag's claim that "camp taste transcends the nausea of the replica." Dern returns anew as Lynch's digitally remastered woman in trouble, wound tight into the reels of her timeless execution.[95]

For Pranolo, this film is an exercise in torture and undeath, where the film's star never dies, where there is no difference made by these reanimations, merely a "punched out cliché from the factory of dreams."[96] Pranolo notes that neither film nor woman is "redeemed."[97] But in Lynch's films of the time-image, concerned fundamentally with *how difference is made,* the untimeliness of redemption means that even a rewind is an eccentric movement, just as slow motion is not simply a revelatory slowing of something that simply stretches, but a different nature revealed in the fusion of the audiovisual image. The final rewind, alongside the "long take" of Dern's spotlit stare, is another instance of Dern's speeds and slownesses felt as an indistinct assemblage of body and image. The final image of Dern on the couch is not a mirror-image, despite the impossible perspective of Dern's shot-reverse-shot POV from the beginning of the film; it is a movement-vision of eccentric doubling,

a movement we perceive because of the effect of the film as a whole, that
we do not simply rewind into place.

I briefly look at two scenes of Dern's encounter with the self, to show
how we might think of this not as a discovery of an "interior" horror,
but rather the recognition that "we are in time." The first is Pranolo's
example, when Dern shoots the Phantom. This is a scene composed of
multiple speeds, and he undergoes several transformations. The bullets
that pierce him are simply beams of light; lighting changes throughout
the film have signaled phase shifts or moments of collective becoming.
Dern sees her own face in a composite image (the composite image, as
we see from the start of the film, is also a "fusional" image of the time
machine of becoming), a reminder of an earlier scene in which Dern
approaches the camera slowly up a forest path, only to speed up dramatically as she reaches the camera (in aberrant movement).

Dern's "recognition" of her own face is followed by a second composite image as the Phantom dies, a distorted and soggy head, like a face
decomposing underwater, suggestive of the fluid immersion of the environment previously signaled through the use of lighting.

Here, the composite image renders the surface of the image an entire
world, mutable and connected, a body in de- and re-composition. Although
it is horrifying, it also sparks a movement on Dern's part: she stumbles

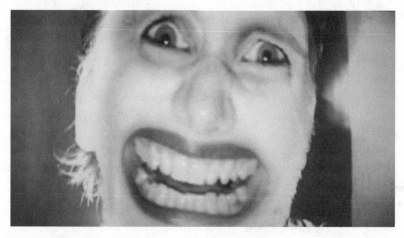

Laura Dern's face superimposed on the Phantom's body in *Inland Empire*.

backward into the *Rabbits* room, and from there, we see her encounter with the Lost Girl, now dressed and ready to leave, as the live and the recorded enter into the vibratory image of figural anamorphosis—the doubling of the two girls racing by in the hallway, Dern's appearance on the television screen and in the room simultaneously, and the persistence of the composite image as a means of legitimate contact—the reality of connection via the medium in the tender kiss and exchange of tears.

The Lost Girl's story ends in a conventional "happily ever after," one which in some ways rewrites the suspense of *Blue Velvet*. Dern's performance, and the dark-haired and European Lost Girl who reunites with her husband and small son, call to mind another way to end *Blue Velvet* in which the femme fatale is not the figure of horror who intrudes on suburban domesticity, and who can only be a mother when adult males no longer have any claim to her. From Dorothy's horrible automatism to Sandy's imperiled purity, Dern's performance in *Inland Empire,* her presence on stage, is precisely what releases the Lost Girl, who leaves the room after hearing the breathless laughter of the two women who race down the hallway, the doubled spirit guides for Dern's character throughout. Redemption comes too late for Dorothy Vallens, and is likewise untimely for Dern, whose "end" is ambiguous. Dern looks out into an

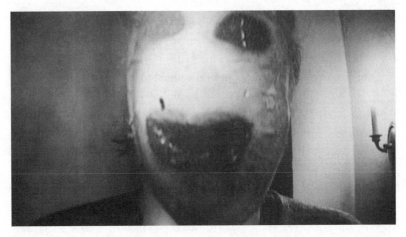

Just after Dern shoots the Phantom in *Inland Empire.*

empty theatre space, the single eye of a spotlight her only witness. As she cries, the image of a slow-motion ballerina bleeds through in a final composite image. It can be read as melancholic, in that the live performer will know a contact and approbation from their audience that Nikki, performing as femme fatale, will never know. Constantly, Nikki is her only audience, and her perception is of her othered self. But it is crucial to recall that the ballerina moves in slow motion—she performs a dance that can only exist on the screen. This final composite image of Nikki and the ballerina not only signals a cliché of grace, beauty, and bodily control, but immediately frames the dancing body and Nikki's sense of the self's intimate otherness as a response to the challenge of living the deformations of iconicity. This performance made possible through the "illusion" of cinema takes us back to the very ending of *Mulholland Drive*, where a spectator waits in the balcony for the show to begin again. The affective potential of the ending of *Inland Empire* is Lynch's final and graceful gesture of the double movement of creative re-composition. That this is immediately followed by the lip-syncing credit sequence, featuring, among others, Laura Harring from *Mulholland Drive*, in a joyful indistinction between characters and actresses, is strong evidence for Lynch's project of (re)animating the femme fatale to a different end.

The second encounter revisits Dern's first scene in the film, with Visitor #1 (Grace Zabriski), where once again Dern looks over to where she will be and sees herself on the couch opposite, this time alone and looking back at where she would have been. This final face-to-face encounter of Dern's personas is not about a simple recognition, or stabilization of a copy/model distinction. These encounters are consistently asymmetrical; here, the first Nikki is shot in extreme, fish-eye close-up, while the second is in an undistorted long shot. This asymmetry is critical to the way that Lynch reimagines the femme fatale as a figure of becoming-other, which is why although I do agree with Grossman that Lynch's films might be the future of the femme fatale, I can't agree that dissemblance is about simply telling her own story. As Deleuze argues in *Difference and Repetition*, "lack of symmetry" is "positivity itself."[98] "Something is happening" (the refrain of the song that accompanies these images) between these two shots (in the interval opened by the conceptual persona) that escapes a closed circuit of mirror reflection and opens onto the movement-vision of "the point of view of the other in me."[99] Nikki experiences a self-referentiality, amplified by the juxtaposition of two types of aberrant movement: the ballet dancer and the rewinding images, two modes of automatism. Between these instances, Nikki/Laura Dern enters the *Rabbits* set; like them she too is living herself as a medium, what Deleuze might term an "actor-medium" or automaton.[100]

Traitors to the Cause

When Deleuze draws on Chion's contention that the purpose of lip-syncing is not to make us believe in an illusion of wholeness but to witness a re-worlding in the fusion of audiovision, he reimagines an entire sense of performance that undoes a distinction between self and mask, and undoes a revelatory logic behind the "actor-medium" of the time-image. What is revealed here is not the medium, but a doubling of event and semblance, what Massumi terms "amodal perception."[101] This "art beyond knowledge" is intimately linked to the untimely redemption of concepts that are frequently conceived in negative terms. The crime of time is ultimately the force of becoming itself: like the ambiguous incitements of the femme fatale, the criminal feeling of becoming-other and the betrayal at the heart of the femme fatale becomes linked in Lynch and in Deleuze, to a poetics of the event in which we *participate* in agency, rather than simply wield it; this is the "unthinkable sex" of the femme fatale as conceptual persona.

An "aesthetics of betrayal" is what Mary Brydon identifies in Deleuze's thought through the work of the artist, displacing an idea of the artist as source with that of style as an activity that writes the author, style as an "assemblage" *(agencement)*.[102] Here, writing is a minoritarian gesture, an "encounter with what is not given"; Deleuze rejects the homely advice "Write what you know" in favor of the imperative to "be a traitor to one's own (proper) regime. . . . What other reason is there to write?"[103] Such an act stutters into productivity, defined as an openness to plasticity: "This aesthetic does not dispense with form, but subjects it to pressures and intensities which may fracture or re-align it."[104] The re-composition of form is a reminder that "seeing and hearing occur through and between words, rather than being enclosed within them."[105] This figural hesitation, the stallings and startings doubling the flow of creative production, is the movement in stasis that shifts from regimes of recognition and representation to those of fabulation, the speech-act and the automaton as the unknown centre of ourselves. *Vertigo*'s mad love deranges norms of fidelity, realigning spectatorial identifications and making characters live a doubled experience of fixed form and the relentless positivity of betrayal. In Lynch's films, infidelity becomes the motor of desire—a desire for anotherness that treads the line of unlivable existence.

It Had Something to Do with the Telling of Time

In recent years, the scene of crime has been reanimated by a dynamic forensics, thanks to digital imaging technologies that turn speculation into photorealistic moving images *representing* thought in motion. Such images are at once speculative and authoritative; they make evidence appear. Errol Morris's *The Thin Blue Line* is a non-digital precursor, but the dynamics also echo the evidentiary status of other medical imaging technologies, which at once must be interpreted and stand in for an indexical image of reality itself. Voiceover narration is one such tool that underpins the alluring yet ambiguous status of such images and guarantees their ability to make sense of motive, disparate temporalities (like a rewind function of crime time), and decomposed bodies and crime scenes. Such positivist faith in media has been noted particularly in television shows. Such images also reroute and sanitize the affective force of extremely graphic imagery through a scientific lens. Little is off limits, it seems, if it is shown as dispassionate altered motion, channeling aesthetic pleasure into fact. The forensic approach marries intellect, science, and the spectacular nature of visual culture, and in fact argues that crime *demands* an audience, and more specifically, the audience of popular media.

When David Lynch takes up the tender corpse of the femme fatale in his Hollywood trilogy, he does so with a specifically antiforensic gaze. Against a disembodied authority that effortlessly traverses the boundaries of flesh, bone, and environment to rein in the messiness of the past,

Lynch offers a resistant and spectacular materiality in the figure of the femme fatale both as corpse and automatic performer. The body that arises in the time-image, the absolute receiver, takes off in Lynch's films from the interval opened up in the delay of a human body to receive the voiceover of *Sunset Boulevard*. When Lynch reanimates that gap through the corpse time of the Hollywood trilogy, he makes the gap of the medium itself that fracture in the I, linking cinematic repetition with anotherness as the creative fabulation of the body.

CHAPTER THREE

Suzhou River and the Movement-Vision of Love

> The in-itself of the past and the repetition in reminiscence constitute a kind of "effect," like an optical effect, or rather the erotic effect of memory itself.
>
> —Gilles Deleuze, *Difference and Repetition*

Lou Ye's dreamy portrait of millennial malaise, *Suzhou River* (2000), is littered with characters lacking self-actualization. The second feature film from Sixth Generation[1] Chinese filmmaker Lou shares many of the movement's signature characteristics: contemporary urban settings, a rejection of the sophisticated aesthetics of Fifth Generation filmmakers for a rougher realism (for example, handheld camerawork),[2] and a broad range of cinematic references. Originally two short films for German television reworked into a feature after Lou received additional funding, this restitching leaves evident fault lines of relation between the numerous doubles and ambiguous embodiments that populate the film. Characters are always engaged in a process of self-virtualization, or auto-affection. At character level, this translates into death, apathy, immobility; at another level, this translates to immanence and the rejection of *promise behavior*. Infidelity again drives this film, staging the affective force of the body in time as an opening to anotherness.

In the previous chapter, the femme fatale as performer served to develop a critique of self-actualization as a reassertion of subjectivity. How might *self-virtualization*, as an intensity of affect opening onto an experience of time as anotherness, be understood as the "affection of self by self"? Rather than an externally oriented acting upon the world, the affection of self by self is an experience of re-worlding, the intimacy of anotherness. Deleuze describes this in terms that make explicit this alter-intimacy:

> Subjectivity is never ours, it is time, that is the soul or the spirit, the virtual. The actual is always objective, but the virtual is subjective: it was initially the affect, that which we experience in time; then time itself, pure virtuality which divides itself in two as affector and affected, "the affection of self by self" as definition of time.[3]

From this perspective, we are not alienated from subjectivity, which is *never* ours; that preservation of a preconceived wholeness is refused in favor of a suspended time that is movement and stasis at once. Subjectivity is reconceived as anotherness. Imagine a topographical memory as an extreme of infolding that leads to an outfolding: memory not as our most personal possession, but that which dispossesses us.

In the crystal of the time-image, Deleuze argues we see time in its pure, *formal* state: Aion, of the straight line. Time is formal when not subordinated to content.[4] Pearson glosses this as "the form of change that does not itself change: the straight line becomes a labyrinth and the time of the self can be shown to be a vertiginous one . . . a virtual self (a self that is never actual to itself 'in' time)."[5] Here, repetition breaks with any idea of origin: "It is repetition itself which is repeated."[6] *Suzhou River* takes up the vertiginous pedagogy of double vision from inside this pure form of time as the form of interiority, not within us as subjective measure, but in that we are interior to time as the mode of self-affection. This occurs at a moment of thinking the outside as the time we are interior to: a direct perception of affect, or op-son images. As Flaxman puts it:

> When perception encounters pure optical images, images it cannot recognize or explain, the heterogeneity of affect refuses the conversion into action; the continuity from perception to action is disrupted as in an irrational cut, and suddenly we find ourselves thinking the affect itself—thinking the virtual, the outside. The transformation is tantamount, as Alliez suggests, to the shift from delimited affection to

self-affection, the latter of which is, not incidentally, Kant's formula for the subject.[7]

Op-son images spark *double visions* and *auto-auditions* as receptions rather than incipient actions. If the seer is the primary figure of the time-image, she sees not a perception of a world "out there," but what Bergson calls an intuition of tendencies, an affective receptivity. "Do you see?," Judy asks Scottie in a crucial moment in *Vertigo* as she dons Madeleine's necklace; in choosing the active quality of the recollection-image (as opposed to his passive affection by hallucinatory vision during the 360-degree shot, undoing his active influence on Judy's transformation through his powerlessness before this "affection of self by self"), he regains his power to act, but only in the most limited fashion through what he already knows will happen. Action-vision restored, he recovers his detective self, in a "bare repetition."[8] But the pedagogical force of *Vertigo* lingers in the doubling of Scottie's vision by the affective force of the virtual; in the déjà vu of his self-puppetry, we intuit the differential that ultimately leaves him (and us) in suspense. The pure form of time reopens as a spiral form of suspense, rather than a closed circle: intensive labyrinth rather than a mapped route.

Auto-affection directly intuits time as difference, as Bergsonian *élan vital*; in this impersonal form of life we sense our duration inbetween others "above and below." This inbetween is not a space, but a force, the vertigo of time. The space of the interstice in *Cinema 2*, for instance, opens up a gap for Deleuze that is not primarily spatial (between the physical frames of celluloid) but temporal, a minimal delay that is the condition of change unsubordinated to movement as spatialized time. Though this gap in Deleuze's work has often been theorized as the incommensurable, or images that don't match up or rhyme, repetition has not received the same attention. But there is no less a gap opened up by this immediacy of difference in repetition, and it is perhaps closest in form to auto-affection—a minimal distance felt as the abyss. Deleuze's hesitation over the figure of the double in *Cinema 2* addresses the paradox of restoring temporal indeterminacy—anotherness—to a double too often conceived of in spatialized terms. Self-affection is time as resonance; formal time thus de-forms as well.

In *Difference and Repetition*, Deleuze describes the impact of thinking this form of time in relation to the subject, or the "I." The "affection of self by self" is explicitly linked to Rimbaud's claim (crucial in the cinema books) that "I is another." Deleuze outlines the shift from Descartes's "I think therefore I am" to Kantian notions of the self, where it is impossible for the determined (I think) to bear directly on the undetermined (being—I am). Kant seeks a form via which this determination can take place, namely time:

> Here begins a long and inexhaustible story: I is an other, or *the paradox of inner sense*. The activity of thought applies to a receptive being, to a passive subject that represents that activity to itself rather than enacts it, which experiences its effects rather than initiates it, and which lives it like an other within itself. To "I think" and "I am" must be added the self—that is, the passive position (what Kant calls the receptivity of intuition); to the determination and the undetermined must be added the form of a determinable, namely time. Nor is "add" entirely the right word here, since it is rather a matter of establishing the difference and interiorizing it within being and thought. It is as though the I were fractured from one end to the other: fractured by the pure and empty form of time. In this form it is the correlate of the passive self which appears in time.[9]

This description of the fractured I corresponds to the passive figure of the seer in *Cinema 2*. The seer's loss of action refigures the body not as tool, but as the perceptual feeling of the self in time.

Deleuze outlines three syntheses of time: the first synthesis of habit, where repetition takes the form of the circular and cyclical; the second synthesis of memory, time regained as a selective reanimation of the past; and the third synthesis of the Aion as the empty form of time, or Nietzsche's eternal return (which denounces representation in its insistence that only difference repeats). In the third synthesis, what returns is difference, operating selectively. In the empty form of time: "The synthesis is necessarily static, since time is no longer subordinated to movement; time is the most radical form of change, but the form of change does not change. The caesura, along with the before and after which it ordains once and for all, constitutes the fracture in the I (the caesura is exactly the point at which the fracture appears)." As such, "repetition is never a historical fact, but the historical condition under which something new is effectively produced."[10]

Repetition and difference are yoked by understanding repetition's productivity. This is how I define the remake as a mode of repetition, the doubled figure of the actress across Hitchcock's and Lynch's films repeating difference, not identity. Despite their popularity, the film remake is notoriously difficult to define, beyond new treatments of previously existing material. In *Play It Again, Sam: Retakes on Remakes,* Andrew Horton and Stuart McDougal define the remake as a special case of narrative: "a special pattern which re-represents and explains at a different time and through varying perceptions, previous narratives and experiences."[11] Remakes add an extra productively problematic dimension to the organization of experience through narration. With the remake we don't know whether to watch the film or to read it. The remake injects a frequently unresolved tension into the viewing experience—a suspended reference. In remakes of *Vertigo,* the doubled body of the actress provokes this same question—to see or to read?

This question animates Deleuze's critique of a representational understanding of film. He proposes the "lectosign," a visual image that must be read as much as seen. "Here again all reference of the image of description to an object assumed to be independent does not disappear, but is now subordinated to the internal elements and relations which tend to replace the object and to delete it where it does appear, continually displacing it."[12] Reading is opposed to an action-oriented perception, delaying the perception's selectivity to allow non-habitual elements to emerge. Nowhere is this more strongly felt than via repetition or the double. As Bergson describes this, "We must strive to see in order to see, and not in order to act" to experience the force of becoming itself.[13] To *see in order to see* is the condition of double vision. A lectosign is a "crystalline description" of the indiscernible exchange of the virtual and the actual—a description that replaces the object. This does not disappear the real: as Rodowick describes this, "It is not reference that disappears as much as a description based on the discernibility of the real and the imaginary, original and copy."[14] The lectosign is a visible marker of the suspense generated by repetition and remaking.

Horton and McDougal draw on Gérard Genette's category of the "hypertext" to determine the relationship between a remake and its source, in which a new text, the hypertext, transforms an anterior text—the hypotext. However, they extend Genette's definition to acknowledge what they call the criminalized "pleasure of the pirated text" that problematizes originality.[15] As with the questions of infidelity and culpability in *Vertigo* and Lynch's Hollywood trilogy, I reorient the criminalized pleasures of the remake through the crime of time, as the intimacy of anotherness. The remake is a *productive* problem of time; as Leo Braudy remarks in his essay "Rethinking Remakes": "The remake is intriguing because it intensifies basic critical conflicts between the intertextuality of film meaning and its contextuality, between the uses of taxonomy in grouping films and the renewed look at the individual text, between artistic intention as a gesture of originality and artistic intention as a gesture of mediation." In particular, the question of interpretive precedence between a *then*—the hypotext—and the *now*—the hypertext—is also a key problem in the remakes as repetitions under consideration here, especially as the films rework themselves repeatedly. As Braudy notes, "The remake exists at the intersection of genetic and generic codes."[16] This problem of time, however, exists equally for viewers not only when watching a remake, but also in the experience of repetition that film allows as a time-based medium: both through the film's narrative time, which can include repeated episodes, and in repeated reviewings of the whole.

The remake asks us to consider repetition's potential beyond subversion of the original. As Sven Lutticken notes:

Much as the current practice of remakes and other forms of repetition seem to warrant opposition, mere rejection not only misses what is most problematic of them but fails to notice the potential dormant of the remake, the promise inherent in repetition. For if repetition could be perverted from within, exacerbating the newness that disguises sameness until it changed its sign, might there not be a kind of remake in which repetition served difference, rather than enforcing mythic identity?[17]

Here, remakes are bad or faithless copies, thematically reiterated as infidelity in *Vertigo* and its remakes. Copies are faithless to their origin; this infidelity is precisely the perverted potential dormant in the remake.[18] Lynch's lost highway literalizes this perversion: it is a road going nowhere. Similarly, in *Suzhou River,* the ever-flowing river fluctuates continually between change and identity as a mode of minor change.

This chapter considers "double vision" as the solicitation of the virtual in repetition. "Double vision" in *Suzhou River* resembles the "magic moment" of *Lost Highway,* where the different and new are found in a moment "like any other," indeterminately charged by the sensational awareness of time's splitting. Double vision focuses the "fracture in the I" through problems of embodiment, memory, and selfhood. A remake as repetition of *Vertigo,* this film occupies this abyssal fracture as an undecidable suspenseful topology of infolding and outfolding. Although Lou repeats Hitchcock's splitting of the lead actress into two roles (Zhou Xun plays both teenage Mudan and Meimei, a young woman), and Lynch's redistributed corporealizations of Scottie's split into two male characters, he takes this in a new direction via what Vivian Sobchack terms the "film's body": one main character, a videographer, narrates the film but is never seen (except in fragments). We spend much of the film seeing through his (camera's) eyes. Thus Lou (re)animates the experiment of Robert Montgomery's *Lady in the Lake,* a popular failure in which the "special effect" of having the audience see exclusively through Phillip Marlowe's eyes made for a leaden experience, despite its perceptual disorientations. Lou's version, however, taps into the "special affect" behind the effect. The indistinction of the videographer's gaze, its propensity to go with the flow, is linked to the suspensive force of the river and to the irreversibility of time.

Film's Body

In classical movement-image films, the film's body (Sobchack's term) is *disguised* by how vision's sense-making intentionality shifts between characters. For this reason, Branigan attributes a destabilizing force to "impossible objective shots," unaligned with any character's perspective. For Sobchack, this shifting is usually unproblematic; it does not call attention to embodiment (much as humans don't notice their own heartbeat) and is habitually "recognized" by viewers as a human form of cognition. Human bodies on screen refract the film body, muting echo focus and "deferring" responsibility for perception. A (hermeneutic) problem only emerges for Sobchack when a film body attempts to pass as human; the paradigm for such passing is *Lady in the Lake.*

Concurring with the critical assessment that this is a failed film, Sobchack is skeptical that its relentless reflexivity offers any valuable insight into our mode of "being in the world." Quoting Merleau-Ponty's shuddering aside concerning the "inhuman secret of our bodily mechanism" (the functions of our anatomy and physiology) she claims, "The 'inhuman secret' of the *partial inhumanity* of the film's body in its material substantiality and clockwork physiology is not a secret that is necessarily revealed by the film." Other theories of cinematic bodies propose a different perspective on cinema's automatic nature: rather than a banal and submissive clockwork function, the alter-timing of the "spiritual automaton" in Deleuze, for example, is a site of potential rather than threat. But for Sobchack, a film's "partial inhumanity" threatens both film as subject and spectator: "We discover the film's body as *inhuman* much as we discover our own: when it troubles us or when we look at its parts upon a dissecting table" (my italics).[19] Like Shaviro's cinematic body as rotting corpse, Sobchack's film body is a dead body. Is there a creative counterpart to this deadened image, as with Lynch's reanimated femmes fatales? Can we machinically reroute this "inhuman secret" not only through the body's clockwork functions, but through the "autonomy of affect" as anotherness?

In *Lady in the Lake,* the film is entirely shot from Philip Marlowe's POV, after an opening pedagogical scene explaining the novel conceit to train viewers. A notorious flop, critics attributed its failure to the lack of identification between Marlowe and viewers. Despite the film's ad campaign proclaiming that "you" walk in the shoes of Marlowe, contemporary audiences failed to buy it. Sobchack focuses instead on the discomforting incongruence between the film's technological embodiment and the character's human embodiment: the bodily disparity *within* the film, in the "impossible bodily identicality claimed between the film and the character/actor."[20] The film's annoying corporeal preoccupations disengage viewers; the film is incoherent *because* of its evident disguise. Increasingly, the film is revealed as a *bad copy*. Its explicit claim (via advertising but also within the film itself) to isomorphic identicality is thus problematic because it is based on *existential* not narrational appropriation—the disguise becomes more uncomfortable over time.

Sobchack locates the key problem in *Lady in the Lake* at the level of intentional attention; Marlowe throughout seems excessively interested in "trying out" his body, showily attentive to what should be background habits, such as lighting a cigarette, and failing to achieve the selective perception characteristic of human vision, everything in the frame equally in focus. Even greater technical competence—one could more effectively simulate human embodiment, as in Gaspar Noe's *Enter the Void*—would not for Sobchack disguise a fundamental difference: "As the film pretends to a human character's intentionality, it exposes its own difference from the material form in which that intentionality is embodied in existence."[21]

What difference precisely does the material form of embodiment make? Sobchack's film body is primarily in its imitation of functional human intentionality. She teleologically parallels the development of cinematic technologies and the human lived body achievement of increasing bodily competence:

> The instrumental history of the cinema is a record of a medium striving to realize its perceptive and expressive intentions—first by consciously recognizing the possibilities of its body for action, then by refining its initially crude and clumsy activities, adapting its "body" to contingent situations and broadening its repertoire of *possible* responses to the world that it inhabits and expresses.[22] (my italics)

For Sobchack, the lived body is the competent and action-oriented body. Such competence aims to *avoid* delimitation of what a body can do, but it ironically serves the same purpose. Her second main criticism of the "disguised" body in *Lady in the Lake* is that it is so worried about sustaining its disguise (as human) that it isn't free to transcendently live its body: "It becomes a slave to that body, *afraid* to leave it for fear that it will lose its already tenuous hold on its disguise." The film body's perversion of action, its uncanny fascination with itself and its desedimented habits, raises the question: Is the source of this fear found within the film, or within the viewer?[23] I argue that it is Sobchack who sees this "distraction" as a source of fear and disgust. The film's body in *Lady in the Lake* is overwhelmingly immanent, and primarily an instrumental object; Sobchack ends up arguing that this makes the film body like a woman (!), prescribed in its possibility by this role.[24]

I return to the corporeal turn via Sobchack's notion of the film's body in part to re-inflect it with the autonomy of affect: against intentionality and through the body's anotherness. Sobchack underestimates the potential of the ambiguous embodiments of *Lady in the Lake* as a question of a "body too much"—a mask of the human body when the film body suffices to give an analogue of human perception. For me, what makes *Lady in the Lake* a failure in terms of sustaining the interest of an audience is that the productive suspense of Marlowe's suspended POV is immediately defused by the introductory scenes in which Marlowe, visibly played by Robert Montgomery, explains the trick of the film. Thus any disquieting affective suspense of the suspended POV shot short circuits into an affection of annoyance, complacency, or recognition: the mystery has already been resolved. Ultimately, not so much a bad copy, *Lady in the Lake* embodies the deep boredom of the good copy.

The "echo focus" of *Lady in the Lake*'s good copy disrupts our immediate appreciation of what is unrolling onscreen by interposing a delay in reaction that is at best irritating. Attempting to show that embodiment is not reducible to the sum of its parts, Sobchack repeatedly dismisses any intimation of strangeness in cinematic perception, arguing for the recognition of intentionality at work as its primary characteristic. There is never, except negatively, the interposition of the hesitation of "to see or to read" in this vision. The double mediation between (filmmaker–camera)—world—(projector–spectator) is "enigmatically charged." Sobchack argues that this ambiguity becomes hermeneutic; it is in the dialectic between the embodiment and hermeneutic relation that the film experience exists. However, persistently prioritizing the embodiment relation means that the hermeneutic element is rejected in favor of an "enhanced embodiment" that is fundamentally unchanged. All visible mediations are secondary to the primary perceptual correlation that film allows: enabling, not mediating. A reflexive and reflective turn is always predicated on the first experience as directed *toward* the world. The film has a body, then, in the sense of a "substantial if invisible embodiment as significance and bias." The film body functions to animate perception via movement—i.e. to convey the sense of a centre that can perceive. This is the special importance of moving pictures, the only other version of which is the "moving pictures accomplished and projected without reel changes by our own lived body."[25]

Lady in the Lake's reflexivity turns the spectator toward their own body, and we don't necessarily, according to Sobchack, like what we see. She sums up this danger by quoting Stan Brakhage: "I am not when I see." A bad copy, the film body threatens the spectator's self-assured embodiment; turning inwards, our relation to the world becomes "disabling and dysfunctional," overly "hermeneutic," and lived from without, only useful when "we should want to present and represent the bodily comportment, motility and style of someone who is neurotic, ill or elderly to some specific purpose."[26] Sobchack predicts the effect of any inward turn, one that already knows what it will find.

Sobchack's take on the corporeal turn illustrates some of the potential limitations of her approach, specifically around temporality conveyed via aberrant movement, and the transformative, decentering value of such experiences. Although the "delay" of the film body of *Lady in the Lake* is annoying and artificial, for her merely a "bad copy" with no potential for inciting a positive reconfiguration of the body, Sobchack sees precisely that in her essay "Nostalgia for a Digital Object: Regrets on the Quickening of QuickTime." There, the choppy animation of QuickTime films, a form of "half-life" like "wooden puppets with chipped paint, forsaken dolls with gaping head wounds or missing limbs, Muybridge-like figures in old flip books hovering with bravado and uncertainty between photograph and cinema" are valorized for the way they reflexively foreground the 'labor' of becoming embodied, intensifying "our corporeal sense of the intensive molecular labor and matter of human and worldly 'becoming.'"[27]

This approbation relies on a cut-and-dried distinction between animation and live-action cinema, in which the two regimes never contaminate each other. Sobchack maintains an affective encapsulation of its effects via her solicitation of nostalgia in relation to the fleetingness of the "failed technology" of QuickTime, sure to be swept away in the tide of progress. Here memory as nostalgia recaptures the disturbing affect of the double vision of *Lady in the Lake*'s echo focus, its continuous reminder of "this and what else." Nostalgia, always belonging to a subject, is predicated on a tamed past, not the ungrounding force of a Bergsonian past, and thus the "threat" but also the possibility of the QuickTime films remains contained as an amusement for the nostalgic spectator, where their "laboriously animated life" is at most a memory-image, not a genuine time-image.

To become animated is to experience the machinic in ourselves, an intensive sense of auto-affection. Movement-vision's self-referentiality names the rerouted potential of auto-affection, an alternative to the mirror-vision we usually associate with reflexive films. As with the transversal movements of animation in *Vertigo*, from credits to dreams to puppeteered characters—all sights of the ambiguous embodiment of auto-alterfication of the subject—*Lady in the Lake* presents and recaptures affect into emotions of annoyance. When Lou's film takes up Marlowe's relentlessly awkward POV in *Suzhou River*, how does he reanimate suspense's potential, drawing out rather than delimiting the potential of ambiguous embodiments, to make them move between bodies? How then does the film open onto aberrant experiences of time activated by this spiral form of decentering, rerouting questions of intention and action into a suspended ecology of a desubjectifed past, rather than nostalgia's treasure box? In *Vertigo*, Judy opens a box and puts on Madeleine's necklace; this reframes everything that has happened and puts it back into place through the slow torture of an action image that ends in death.

Remaking *Vertigo*, how might a filmmaker like Lou reprise the jewel into a crystal that refracts time, reanimating its splitting into vectors of potential? How might a consideration of the body in time refract the corporeal turn, with its concern for spectatorial agency and embodiment toward Guattari's mutant enunciations? How can we turn from the commodified emotion of nostalgia, that which we can possess, to the erotic effects of memory itself?

A crystal image figures the workings of time itself as the circuit or exchange of the virtual and the actual. Deleuze continually asks throughout *Cinema 2* what takes the place of the virtual image in relation with the actual, noting that "Bergson constantly posed the question and sought the reply in time's abyss." Rejecting such alternatives as the dream or recollection-images (with their delimited play of memory), he suggests that the answer lies in time's affective "ungrounding," its immediation, the aberrant movement of suspense. This "indivisible unity of an actual image and 'its' virtual image" is a *mutual image*, intimately linked to a double without origin—"the putting into abyss (*mise en abyme*) does not redouble the unit, as an external reflection might do; in so far as it is an internal mirroring, it can only ever split it in two"—subjecting "it to the infinite relaunch of endlessly new splitting."[28] Deleuze draws on Gilbert Simondon's notion of *individuation* to illustrate the affective and generative dimension of this doubling:

> Individuation is mobile, strangely supple, fortuitous and endowed with fringes and margins; all because the intensities that contribute to it communicate with each other, envelop other intensities and are in turn enveloped. The individual is far from indivisible, never ceasing to divide and change its nature. . . . The fringe of indetermination which surrounds individuals and the relative, floating and free character of individuality itself has often been commented on. . . . The error, however, is to believe that this indetermination or this relativity indicates something incomplete in individuality or something interrupted in individuation. *On the contrary, they express the full, positive power of the individual as such, and the manner in which it is distinguished in nature from both an I and a self.*[29]

This individuation is neither a subject nor an object, but anotherness as power: indetermination as a fluidification of the actual within the abyss of the fractured I. "For it is not the Other that is another I, but the I which is an other, the fractured I."[30] Here, anotherness is the mode of subjectivation that Guattari describes as "emergent alterfication." In *Vertigo* or *Lost Highway,* suspense functioned largely in relation to questions of identity: "Who is Madeleine/Judy?" or "Who is Alice/Renée?" These externalized questions emerge from a fracture within the self. Scottie's dementia, splitting mind from body when he watches his own actions like a sleepwalker, internalizes the seemingly external split of Judy/Madeleine. Lynch externalizes this split between Pete and Fred, turning the private, isolated drama of Judy/Madeleine and Scottie within the found set of San Francisco into a rip in the larger fabric of reality itself, generating a wave of doubles and confusions that turns the entire world of *Lost Highway* into a resonance chamber. In *Inland Empire,* a figural architecture comes to occupy the entire world, ambiguously embodied between character and set, Hollywood as a perversion of reality that Lynch renders as wholly real.

What is different about *Suzhou River* is the explicit way the fractured I is tied to questions of love *as* infidelity. In Lou's film, as in *Inland Empire,* love can be understood as an aberrant movement: a passional suspense that is at heart an in-fidelity to the self. This is the "full positive power of the individual." This infidelity is not a crime; although the theme of sexual infidelity runs throughout all of these films, it is a mask or bare repetition of a deeper infidelity at work. Infidelity is a necessary openness to sensation, affect, and intensity. Here, my concept of infidelity develops Deleuze's argument that cinematic perception is essentially *de-*centered, drawing out the vertiginous delirium of love itself. Although our habits of viewing and producing cinema are often akin to our own centered mode of perception, cinema itself does not begin from this center. The indetermination of the individual, potentially amplified by cinema's nonhuman perspective, is exemplified in impossible objective shots when the camera wanders away from characters, such as that which ends *Vertigo.* As Flaxman describes, "This cleavage of camera and character (center) suggests the way the cinema surpasses human perception:

what we discover is not perception, but rather a means to 'rid ourselves of ourselves.'"[31] This acentered perspective is an attenuation that amplifies the otherness of a cinematic body. However, an *intensification* of the relation between camera and character can produce an even stronger effect in the attempt to "rid ourselves of ourselves." This dramatizes the fractured I, much in the way that staring in a mirror for too long has the uncanny effect of defamiliarization by generating a "mutual image" or an intensified self-resonance. This intensification can take the form of a repetition suspended between the imperatives: to see or to read? Merely opposing human and nonhuman perception is insufficient; the nonhuman is always part of perception.

In *Vertigo*, a crucial moment comes when, for a second, the camera detaches itself from Scottie as he leaves Judy's apartment; though it quickly attaches itself to Judy via focalization, the disquieting presence opened by this gap persists in the film, and comes back in full force at the end in the final impossible objective shot of Scottie. Deleuze claims that time is out of joint when a beginning and end no longer "rhyme"; this is made evident in *Vertigo*, when the closed circle "rhyme" of Judy's fallen body, repeating the thud of the policeman's fall from the beginning, is undone by the dissonant doubled rhyme of the final shot. If the opening scene ends by looking down at Scottie suspended over the void, the film ends with the (impossible) reverse shot, looking up at Scottie gazing down into the abyss. Shot-reverse-shot: How is this not harmony? By Scottie's proximity to himself: a closeness that creates the dissonance of playing two adjacent keys on the piano, a minor difference of the fracture in the I. Recall that the real (animated) opening of *Vertigo* is the spiral in the eye, an abyssal image of subjectivity. Throughout *Vertigo*, Scottie continually asks "Who is Madeleine?" and repeatedly tries to bring her in line with herself—first purging her of Carlotta, then refashioning Judy as Madeleine, "all dressed up and ready for love." His actions bear the taint of infidelity centered on the woman, and the film tricks us into forgetting that Scottie is "the other man." But the infidelity in himself is the real threat for Scottie, his own anotherness; its potential as the powers of the false is what both Lynch's and Lou's remakes pick up on.

In *Lost Highway*, Fred's metamorphosis into Pete ripples through the world, rendering all elements of the landscape into a lectosign. But the irresolution of the self is already evident in the matched mirror scenes—the mystery lies not only in "Is Pete Fred?" or vice versa, but simply, "Who is Pete?" and "Who is Fred?" and the continual immanent evaluation of when and how these questions come to matter. Lynch taps into acentered perception via his long takes of marginal objects like curtains, but acentered perception is as much a function of the characters as of an independent camera consciousness. In *Inland Empire*, Laura Dern's performance reanimates Kim Novak's tremulous vocal inability to crisply distinguish Madeleine and Judy and embodies this oscillating force, playing Nikki/Sue as a resonance chamber continually rippled with the indiscernible exchanges between the virtual and actual. The sensational quality of her performance exceeds any narrative resolution and can only be experienced as an event. In a different register, *Suzhou River* also renders the infidelity of the self *as* event: not as an *active* attempt to "rid ourselves of ourselves" but through the emergent sensation of the body in time. The narrator remains suspended throughout the film (save in one shot), doubled by the split between voice/body and sound/sight, at the mercy of a minimal distance from the self that is a Bergsonian déjà vu ("as tightly coupled as an actor to his part"). In this intimate circuit lies the skip of the fractured I. The irresolvable tension between the human perception of the narrator in Lou's film and the mechanical perception of the camera is a case of double vision—a blur in perception giving a body to a phantom.

The New Vague

In *Suzhou River*, which combines the fog-filtered dreaminess of *Vertigo* with a *nouvelle vague* immediacy, the double is encountered in the flesh. Circuits of love, obsession, memory, and infidelity that characterize the relationships between characters extend to the spectator. Just as infidelity continually undoes and reconnects various couples in this film, so too is the dyadic relation between spectator/screen, human body/film body, made indeterminate, in a rearrangement of the dualism of ordinary experience. Far from subjective perspective understood as limited, personal, or untrustworthy by dint of having only a piece of the puzzle, the cinematic body of *Suzhou River* activates the pressing field of potential, where a bare repetition of a (coded) human perspective destabilizes subjectivity through the force of time. Memory makes us "live time," rather than retrospectively ordering events, giving us access to the incorporeal but fully real dimension of the body. Too often, the body in cinema has been understood as a fixity of position, both materially and temporally. Sensation and affect unmoor the body through anotherness. Like the use of electricity in Lynch and the thickened dampness of *Vertigo*, *Suzhou River* uses both electricity, in the form of the dangling buzz of a light bulb, and water to serve as visual and aural counterparts to the affective passional dimension of the body in time.

Often understood as a time-based medium, cinema is not so much based *on* time as immersed in it; the distinction is between an understanding of time as mechanical, reversible, and segmented and the pure form of an irreversible time, including intensive repetitions. One reason Deleuze's time-image is exemplified by discontinuity is that it relies on an understanding of time as the moment of an irreversible break—time in the form of a straight line. If the present is a continuous splitting between a present that passes and a past that is preserved, the straight line of time implies that a past that returns is not so much remembered as (re)lived. This is why Scottie's revelatory flashback (of the necklace) in *Vertigo* is not a time-image; Scottie forecloses the fragile potential of his happiness with Judy for the limited certainty of what a body must do, trading the processual falling of love for the fall of death. The terrible repetition of the final act is also its greatest chance for escape: as the space between past and present is gripped ever closer by the repetition, the intensity of the vibration becomes ever more violent in the attempt to break through. In Lynch's films, we get something different, a minimum of belief in the world of the image to play again. When Dern stands drenched in light on stage at the end of the film, before her final look across time back to herself, we are reminded of artist James Turrell's words about light as an activator of auto-affection:

> We eat light, drink it in through our skins. With a little more exposure
> to light, you feel part of things physically. . . . Seeing yourself seeing is

a very sensuous act—there's a sweet deliciousness to feeling yourself see something.[32]

Light fringes the contours of the self such that auto-affection is the nourishing experience of becoming other than what we were. In a definition of affect echoing Deleuze's in *Cinema 2,* Massumi claims that affect is "precisely this two-sidedness, the simultaneous participation of the virtual in the actual and the actual in the virtual."[33] In crystalline description, cinema no longer refers, but *describes.* Crucially, the spectating subject no longer recognizes what is onscreen, but is caught up in relation itself (the inbetween). Massumi terms this the *transindividuality* of affective attunement,[34] where "relationality pertains to the openness of the interaction rather than to the interaction per se or to its discrete ingredients."[35]

In *Suzhou River,* intensity takes the figural form of vagueness: through a narrative uncertainty, the repeated use of a blur in the image, a soundtrack characterized by suggestion rather than determination, and a disjunction among the said, the seen, and the seer. This vagueness stems equally from a restlessness of the wandering camera. Last, the vagueness is the blurred sentiment evoked by the double, the double of the film body, the doubles within the film (once again with the dual role of the lead actress), and the repetition of sequences, shots, and snippets of sound. Vagueness is the virtual fringing the actual, the "difference in the process of repetition" that is "what relation looks like in action—not just a simple lack of information."[36]

Described by Jerome Silbergeld as a Hitchcock "with a Chinese face," the question of *Suzhou River'*s relation to *Vertigo* is downplayed by Lou. Lou claimed, "I haven't seen *Vertigo* since film school. The mistaken identity in *Suzhou River* was something I never really wanted to resolve— it took me a while to decide if I would have one actress playing two parts or two actresses playing the same part."[37] In activating the comparison, I am less interested in judging Lou's debt to Hitchcock than thinking the remake as repetition via its differential: not "How does Lou draw on Hitchcock as intertext?," but "How does Lou reanimate the problems of repetition, remaking, and relation that we have considered in relation to *Vertigo* and Lynch's films?"

Throughout *Vertigo*, a sensation of witnessing pervades the film, through Scottie's paramnesiac relation to his own experiences, the foregrounding of mirrors that manifest the splitting of time, and in impossible objective shots. In particular, the final impossible objective shot of Scottie suspended over the void is doubled by the evocation of camera as an embodied presence. *Suzhou River* literalizes this, making the camera into a character, repeating the experiment of *Lady in the Lake*. For Sobchack, the presentational aspect of that film's body (exemplified in her analysis of Montgomery's film), reflexively spectacularizes the fact that this *is* a film, and needs to be muted in order for film to succeed. But in *Suzhou River*, the problem of the film body refuses such delineated boundaries, and the spectator of the film is in a connection not of recognition, but of *relation*, and thus transformation. It is a film filled with liminal figures, not the least of which is the mermaid, and the sensation of water as an affect of flow and ungrounding.[38]

Often compared to Wong Kar Wai's *Chungking Express* (because of the use of voiceover narration, the green and pink rain-drenched neon tones of the film, the parallel storylines and their blonde, bewigged femmes fatales), Lou's film shares a sense of a narrative that changes direction almost at whim. It has an improvised feel, not in the sense of a cinema verité, documentary liveness, but in the continuous invocation of the invitation to chance. An unresolved tension between chance and repetition conveys the sense that what is repeated is difference, even in the minor sense of "as least as different as last is from next."[39] This invests the seemingly subjective perspective of the narrator with an authority that cannot be called objective either, but is rather the power of the author as fabulator. The film draws on an affective reserve that exceeds the personal and leads to a "breakthrough of the real." This breakthrough is figured in the film by the doubled body of the actress, but as in *Vertigo*, this is a MacGuffin, a bare repetition that solicits the real repetition of difference. Instead, what breaks through is "affection of self by self" that the double produces. This is true both for the male narrator, and ultimately for Meimei. If Judy's duplicity in *Vertigo* is knowing but guilty, if Alice/Renée openly scorns the attempt to pin down her identity, Meimei in *Suzhou River*, like Dern's actress, manages to be more of a person than merely the figure of an enigma, but not because she is "fleshed out." If Meimei is more "real," it is in her own experience of the infidelity of the self. At the end, Meimei disappears into the mirror as an open line of flight.

Suzhou River takes the realism of affect in *Vertigo* without translating into *Lost Highway*'s psychogenic fugue, which amplified *Vertigo*'s oneiric quality into nightmare. Instead, both everyday reality *and* the blatantly artificial (the dyadic essence of cinema) share in a hallucinatory quality. As Massumi describes "the reality" of anotherness:

> The ultimate fact is the certainty of a "really next effect" whose nature cannot entirely be foreseen: an indefinite ever "more" that "fringes" every determinate context with a timeless margin of chance and newness. Reality is not fundamentally objective. Before and after it becomes an object, it is an inexhaustible reserve of surprise. The real is the snowballing *process* that makes a certainty of *change*. To be expected: the arrival of the new, the uninvited ingress of the singular.[40]

Determination's fringe is never more evident than in the repetition of the seeming same; *Suzhou River* plays off of this paradox through repetition that retains the freshness and vitality of movement in suspense. If in *Lost Highway* this movement was violent, in *Suzhou River* it is watery—a heavy-limbed languidity of drunkenness. Delay expands the circuits of connections. In short, *Suzhou River* is the story of two love relationships (Meimei and the unnamed videographer, and Mudan and Mada) and their intersections, where their affective attunements, connections, and passages between characters, film body, and audience *are* the story.

On the Surface of Things

Reviewing *Suzhou River*, Damion Searls sees the film as organized around the fundamentally opposite demands of love and narrative:

> Love is a story you tell yourself—about yourself, about the one you love, and about your lives together. But we want love never to end, while a story, a narrative, must come to an end, or else it is not a story.

Does that make love a special kind of story, or is love the arena where we can see storytelling working against itself, undercutting its own narratives?

Searls associates love with repetition as fixity, as "immune from the narrative drive toward an ending." Narrative relinquishes love: "That is just where the narrator ends up in the movie's haunting conclusion: on the Suzhou River, drunk, stranded at the end of one love story and waiting for the next to begin."[41] Tracing the dysnarratives of *Suzhou River* via comparisons with *Vertigo* and *Chungking Express*, Searls claims that the differences outweigh the similarities, making the film less a "remake" than a revitalization or a "riff." Scavenging for signs of chronological orientation, he continually weighs these elements in terms of their truth-value. Something murkier is at work, however: the opposition between an unending static love and narrative (closure) underestimates the force of repetition as difference. This repetition figures as an *infidelity to the self* at the heart of love. Rather than an *opposition* between stasis and movement, *Suzhou River*'s affective motor is the aberrant movement of love, an acinematic perversion of intensity.

Suzhou River isn't simply anti-narrative, despite the undecidability in reconstructing the narrative, categorizing events definitively as "real" or "imagined," or reconstituting a definitive chronology. This will be evident in my description of the film, littered with necessary permutations.[42] As remake, *Suzhou River* problematizes origins and truth in favor of storytelling or fabulation, not identical with narrative. Instead, this film moves from the dysnarrative (a term Deleuze adapts from Alain Robbe-Grillet) that signals narrative breakdown in the time-image toward falsifying narrative. This breakdown prioritizes the paradigmatic over the syntagmatic:

The cinema is always narrative, more and more narrative, but it is dysnarrative in so far as narration is affected by repetitions, permutations and transformations which are explicable in detail by the new structure. However, a pure semiotics is unable to follow in the tracks of this semiology, because there is no narration (nor description) which is as

"given" of images. . . . Perceptible types cannot be replaced by the processes of language.[43]

In falsifying narrative, there is no recourse to structure; as in *Inland
Empire*'s figural architecture, the structure is the event of re-worlding
itself. As Andres Kovacs puts it, the break between classical and modern
cinema does not map onto narrative/non-narrative but onto: "different
modalities of narrative. . . . The narrative principles of modern cinema
consist in making possible the realization of *virtually existing suprasensi-
ble worlds*. The aim of modern cinema as such is the creation of *mental
images* that are independent of the logic of practical sensory experience."[44]
One might term this figural narrative: a productive disfiguring of classical narrative via time's felt forkings. Recall Barthes's association of
narrative distortion via suspense with a privileging of the paradigmatic,
the thrill intensified because "all is made right in the end."

What happens when all is not made right in the end, films of the
spiral of time? How is difference made by how we get there from here?
Here, the dysnarrative emphasis on the paradigmatic tips into falsifying narrative, where description replaces its objects. Barthes claims that
suspense is intellect merely *disguised* as affective intensity: "Suspense
grips you in the mind, not in the guts,"[45] but this intellectual unmasking
only occurs when all is resolved. Searls's review of *Suzhou River* ends on
this very problem:

> Love is the real story, as always—our emotional investment in love
> stories, at least my emotional investment in love stories, simply out-
> weighs epistemological considerations. *Suzhou River*'s true accom-
> plishment is to do two synonymous things at once: to undercut its
> own intellectual paradoxes and force us to this conclusion, and to cre-
> ate a beautiful and moving film which speaks this truth for itself even
> if all the epistemological trickery goes unnoticed.[46]

There is a tension in Searls's piece between his affective engagement
with the film (hedged by his bracketing of it as "merely'" personal), and
his attempts to reconstruct and sort the narrative's "epistemological

trickery." This opposition between feeling and thinking/knowing was part of what both Shaviro and Sobchack attempted to dismantle in their theories of cinematic embodiment. How might we rearrange this dualism through attentiveness to the body in time? It is *via* the narrative paradoxes, exceeding rational knowledge and unresolved identities, that sensation is *affirmed* as difference. Although I agree that "love is the real story here," I argue this doesn't bracket the personal as "merely" subjective, but understands it via Deleuze's claim that "subjectivity was never ours."[47]

Falsifying narration displaces the transcendent form of the true through immanent evaluation, an ethics of time.[48] We might then read "beauty" in *Suzhou River* as an aesthetic feeling immediately doubling our felt engagement with the world. "Disinterest" names this mode of immanent evaluation, the vertigo of a critical distance. Massumi describes beauty's ethico-aesthetical work this way:

> Beauty, like the sublime, enfolds the dimensions of linear time. But it does so in banality, not in anxiety, and immanently rather than transcendentally. It is this immanence that affectively translates as "disinterest" or nonchalance, manners of being easily confused for lack of encounter and subjective estrangement: not a here and now, but an ubiquitous nowhere of whatever. If this is lack, it is only the lack of a supplemental dimension from which to judge or desire: the absolute (superficial) proximity of access to excess. "Disinterest" is the impossibility, in encounter, of separating the object from the subject—because the course of things follows. In other words, *object and subject, in their mutual difference and reciprocal trajectories, are consequent to the encounter. It is they that are new, already and all over again.*[49]

In Lou's film, beauty is such a banal lure of this double generative distinction, a slightly tatty immanence to clichés of spectacular beauty.

Immanent evaluation's aesthetic feeling is a lure to thought; in the time-image's suspension of action/reaction, we are at best made aware that we are not yet thinking. Affective intensity mustn't be unmasked, but rather intensified to the point of no return, producing the unlived-as-yet.

As Peter Canning writes, "It is by the current of immanence that Deleuze defines affect as transition from affection to affection, from sensation to sensation or image to image. Affect is the movement of immanence, a virtual movement or becoming time." This movement is the "libido of time": "Libido is an affect through which one life becomes another."[50] Remaking is itself a mode of immanent evaluation, like cinephilia's gestural outlet of repetition. When the judgment of truth becomes impossible, as with aberrant movements of falsifying narratives, "it is a matter of evaluating every being, every action and passion, even every value, in relation to the life which they involve."[51] This is what it means to "give a body"; when truth is lost

> there remain bodies, which are forces, nothing but forces. But force no longer refers to a centre, any more than it confronts a setting or obstacles. It only confronts other forces, it refers to other forces, that it affects or that affect it. Power (what Nietzsche calls "will to power" and Welles "character") is this power to affect and be affected, this relation between one force and another.[52]

Here, the body is not a ground or center, but an ungrounding zone of affect. To give a body to a phantom is to give the body in *all* its dimensions. Hence, Searls's opposition of love as stasis versus narrative as terminal movement overlooks the generative possibilities of the affective intensity of love as aberrant movement.

The River Will Show You Everything

The first section of the film, set in Shanghai, is viewed through the lens of a videographer who never seems to put his work aside. What is onscreen reads as his perspective (nameless and seen only once in silhouette); there are no clear distinctions among embodied eyes, mind's eye (as when we get the story of Mudan and Mada), and camera's lens. It would often be awkward for him to be filming, such as while drinking and smoking; at other points, it might be more likely that he is filming (as in scenes of his girlfriend where he mentions he loves to film her), but there are few determinate clues. Even when he couldn't be holding the camera, there is a persistent slight distance from the action at hand (which I discuss later via the disjunction between sound and image). In short, the narrative voiceover, even when describing what is at hand in the image, creates a duplicitous distance via redundancy.

Unlike Fred's distaste in *Lost Highway* for video cameras because "he prefers to remember things (his) way," here, subjective memory and recording's impersonal objective status are not opposed. Exceeding a handheld perspective, videography *is* his way of seeing the world. The images evoke *Lady in the Lake*: camera mounted on the body, lens homologous to the eye. But where *Lady in the Lake* was stiff and awkward, with scenes in real time with no cuts, *Suzhou River*'s camera doesn't restrain the body in the same way and cuts are frequent: all aspects of cinema become embodied. Post-handheld cameras, this positioning lacks the novelty aspect marketed in *Lady in the Lake*. However, though conventionally we understand this POV as goal oriented and directed, the look of a human subject, it is still unusual for us to experience the camera *as* a body.

A low-budget film, the handheld camera work of *Suzhou River* evokes a New Wave style, and its "evidentiary" charge, a sensation of documentary and of "being there" that has been co-opted into a cliché. In *Suzhou River*, though, the camerawork and the narrative voice-off serve less as guarantees of presence and of a body than a way of *making* space, an unsettling and a potentializing within the camera's gaze. The first-person perspective, as well as the actress's doubled body as Mudan/Meimei, continually *insists* on the film body's presentational aspect, effectuating a radical singularity. "Presentational" devices—unusual sound effects, double exposures and strange dissolves, use of fades, and the actress's doubled role—highlight the audience's relation to both character and film body as an experience of the body in time.

The film opens with a black screen and a man and woman speaking. As in *Lost Highway*, these opening words will return with a difference (matched with the image of the woman speaking) at the end. The woman asks, "If I left you someday, would you pursue me, like Mada?" A man replies "Yes."

WOMAN: "Would you pursue me forever?"
MAN: "Yes."
WOMAN: "Your whole life?"
MAN: "Yes."
WOMAN: "You're lying."

As it turns out, he's not, not exactly. The nature of such a promise is the subject of the film, a meditation on the search. Against the futility of active repetition, the film lingers in the delay evoked in this promise, one repeated by postponing the visual match until the end.

The suspension of this promise both evokes and rejects the happiness promised by cinematic love stories. In "Happy Objects," Sara Ahmed analyzes the "genealogy of expectation" via the promise of happiness, an anticipatory causality that is the "sticky" end point of the pursuit of happiness: "To think the genealogy of expectation is to think about promises and how they point us somewhere, which is the where from which we expect so much." Happy objects temporally orient us; those who resist have an aberrant relation to time. Affect aliens are melancholics pointing to the unhappy effects of injustice or presumptions of what counts as happy objects. Ahmed's critical suspicion of happiness argues for the value of a melancholic return to the past, to "histories that hurt" not as reactionary or a "backwards orientation,"[53] but precisely via affect's ability to loosen the bond between object and feeling, as an infidelity to the promise of happiness as the already written, already known.

In *On the Genealogy of Morals,* Nietzsche asks, "To breed an animal with the right to make promises—is this not the paradoxical task that nature has set itself in the case of man? Is it not the real problem regarding man?" The right makes humans temporal creatures able to imagine a future, but in this process they become "calculable, regular, necessary." The paradox of promise behavior lies in the roots of "bad conscience,"[54] as an internalization of the will to power, manifesting particularly in the form of guilt and a sick sense of criminality. Nietzsche describes bad conscience as an illness, as pregnancy is also an illness. A promise means rigidifying memory (memory as a *techné*), a concerted effort to stem the tide of forgetfulness; this is not merely a passive loss, but an active suppression necessary for healthy functioning to avoid being swept away in becomings. For Nietzsche, both memory and forgetting are active forces; the past, even what is not actively remembered, does not simply pass away, but persists and returns both willfully and as unexpected visitor. The latter is memory's threat.

Nietzsche asks, How can we actively live our promises without simply predetermining the future? How can we avoid being sickened by the past, mistaking the force of becoming for the bad conscience of a debt? In other words, how can we relive memory as an affirmation? In *Vertigo*, Scottie and Judy are both poisoned by the past, made sick by guilt that binds them in a perpetual exchange, stunting the possibility of affective encounter. The rigidity of these terms leads continually to death, but as I have argued, the ethico-aesthetical potential of that film, its continued imperative to *look again,* is a double vision of anotherness, repetition in itself as the film's indeterminate potential. How to repeat with a difference?

A promise for Deleuze negotiates the forking of time into the present that passes and the past that is preserved: "It is in the present that we make a memory, in order to make use of it in the future when the present will be past." He associates this aspect of memory with Janet's "story behavior" or Nietzsche's "promise behavior."[55] However, these remarks arise during Deleuze's discussion of the *insufficiency* of the recollection image to act as a virtual image, because the recollection image is always actualized. Thus the paradox of promise behavior for Nietzsche: a promise as placeholder for the future is the ability to preserve the self against time's vicissitudes, but at the cost of rigidity and "bad conscience." What if the alternative was not so much a future-oriented preservation of the self, but instead the affirmation of the past, even (or especially) that past that is not consciously recalled, but steals up on us unawares? At the end of *Suzhou River,* we have two alternatives to the problem of the promise, both of which reject the immersion in guilt and the reactive vengeance that is Scottie's response to his failed promise to keep Madeleine safe. The black screen that accompanies these words at the beginning of the film is an op-sign of delay, an opening in time against a precalculated future. One response will be a passive immersion in the stories, in the becoming of the world, a refusal of action. The other will be a flight into the mirror as a response to an affective encounter, a self-reflection displaced by an impossible imperative: "Find me if you love me." It will remain unclear to whom those words are addressed. A promise is an actualization of the future in the present, but a failed promise intuits the virtual as the infidelity at the heart of the self.

After the opening blackness, the film fades in to images of Shanghai's notoriously polluted Suzhou River, this film's lost highway, panning across its glistening surface, revealing only floating garbage. Bits of a larger narrative picture surface disjointedly; a series of jump cuts of riverside sights—barges, fishermen, shabby houseboats, and so on—is at odds with the continuous flow of the river itself: movement and stasis at once. The flighty shots feel spontaneous; zooms, quick pans, and odd, unpracticed angles evoke an unfocused searching. As the voiceover begins, we tie this elliptical attention to the unnamed narrator (Hua Zhongkai), who identifies himself as a videographer. He addresses us directly: "Look, you can see them," as passers-by on the bridge point and wave at the camera. He tells us, "If you watch it long enough, the river will show you everything." The camera repeatedly seizes on images, mostly faces and bodies, that briefly hold the camera's attention even as they float away. The space filmed is charged with a thickness, the air invested with the sensation of passing through water. He says, "Once a girl jumped to her death from a bridge outside my window. I saw the bodies of two lovers being dragged out of the water by the police." The visual "match" for these words arrives at the end, but fails to fix this restless attention. Suspense as a special case of movement emerges between the fixed perspective of the narration and the random quality of the images, where jump cuts create temporal gaps. The uncertainty of his words is summed up when he says, "As for love, I could tell you that I saw a mermaid once, sitting on the muddy banks, combing her golden hair, but I'd be lying." "Pay me and I'll shoot it," he says, "but don't complain if you don't like what you see. The camera doesn't lie." The disavowed responsibility is at odds with his highly subjective perspective: he self-identifies as a neutral observer, occupying the place of the detective in film noir.

He is hired to shoot a mermaid act in a large tank of water in a bar; his employer speaks directly into the camera, trying to describe what he wants. "What I want is" (jump cut), "the feeling is hard to describe" (jump cut); unlike *Lady in the Lake*, little temporal continuity undergirds the disguise of the human body. "I don't believe in mermaids," he scoffs, but at first glance of the performer, Meimei, he is won over.[56] His first view recalls Scottie spying on Madeleine, clarified in a later repetition of this shot featuring Mada: Scottie's doubling in the mirror is here split between the two characters. Peering through a crack in the doorway, he sees Meimei at her vanity, bathed in the neon glow of the sign outside.

He falls in love, and we see Meimei continually through his lens. Meimei meets him on the street and playfully dances around him. A pop song plays in the background with the full, crisp sound typical of non-diegetic music, but the music quickly morphs (a characteristic sonic gesture of the film) and becomes hollow and distant, like sound filtered through memory or heard over the phone. From the start, their relationship is marked by this odd simultaneity of distance and contact.

Contact's intensity repeatedly produces a ghosting effect, part of the film's figural force. During their first sequence together, marked by indistinction between shots he films and those simply from his perspective, Meimei poses for him in a medium long shot. There is a quick cross-fade to a close-up of Meimei's face looking directly into the camera. This type of cross-fade is used repeatedly in this sequence, so quickly that it seems more a blur in the image than a transition. His hand reaches out to caress Meimei's face; as he touches her, another quick cross-fade on contact to a different close-up. She leans into the camera as if for a kiss; the image blurs as two Meimeis overlap, and finally there is a jump cut to a brief shot of Meimei's closed eyes. The sequence conveys Meimei's flightiness, pointing toward the doubled identity she later assumes. However, it is less the end points than the passage inbetween that characterizes these cross-fades; the blur in the image is the source of the uncanny double here. Likewise, the blur emerges as the indiscernibility of recorded image *or* live experience, but also memory as the past that is preserved *or* the present that passes.

The videographer's obsessive recording of Meimei stems from her mysterious allure; he knows little about her past, and she is subject to sudden disappearances and inexplicable sadness. He is passive in the wake of her comings and goings. In one scene, we see Meimei getting ready to leave from his seated perspective: changing, fixing her hair, putting on a coat. She blows him a kiss; exiting, she strikes a dangling light bulb and sets it swaying, and the next shot opens on a swaying light bulb in his room—the aberrant movement of false continuity that characterizes cuts in this film. "Every time she closed the door behind her, I felt my life had stopped," he says. He stands on his balcony to watch Meimei returning, the time between departure and return evaporating like a puff of smoke. "If she had too many [drinks], she would ask me, 'if she left one day, would I look for her, like Mada?' 'Who's Mada?'" he asks, and the second sequence of the film begins.

In the casual evocation of a solicited promise ("Would I look for her?"), we see promise behavior transformed into fabulation. Here, the reported recollection of Meimei's question is answered by an evident act of creation and storytelling, and the attention in the film shifts to the story of Mudan and Mada. Throughout this sequence, it will remain indeterminate whether this is a "real" story, a truthful accounting of independent facts, or a story made up by the narrator. In this falsified narrative, truth is suspended in favor of becoming. However, this is not a free for all: the powers of the false have real effects, and the narrator is not so much in control of his creation as becoming with them, beside himself.

Suspended on his balcony while Meimei is gone, the narrator's story of Meimei's story of Mada is told over images of the flow of people below. The camera begins picking people out at random with abrupt cuts and zooms that briefly cause a ripple around individuals in the moving crowds below. It has the effect of tracing a line, through the repeated attention of even a briefly longer shot on these individuals—a thickening of the virtual accruing around them. Mada, it seems, was a bike courier who spent his whole life searching for his lost love. "I could make up a story like that," the narrator voices, as the camera lingers on a couple arguing on a balcony, and then starts looking again, dismissing the potential subjects with only a fleeting glance, until a bike courier is spotted. A flicker of focus is granted, and then a fast pan tightens in on a schoolgirl with pigtails and a line is traced from her back to the courier. This random quality is dismissed by a cut to black, and then a fade in on the face of the same courier. The refresh of the black screen has a dual effect. It makes a break between the "activity before the action" of the story we're about to be told, marking a discontinuity between prep work and story proper. At the same time, however, it serves as a gap in itself, the *écart* that activates affect. Although the subsequent story is more developed than the disaffected searching of the first part of the film, it is equally a story of the suspense of relation. What links these characters (Mudan and Mada) to the characters we already know?

The videographer begins to tell us Mada's story. For the first time, music with a driving beat is heard, a rare instance of sonic tonal complementarity. As well, the camera is no longer tied to the body of the videographer. However, the fabulation of this story could still be tied to him, taking place "inside his head." This is evidenced throughout by his pause as he asks "And then what happened?" as though he didn't yet know, or couldn't remember. This section of the film also differs from the opening in its closer harmony between sound and image and more stable images. Shots are clearly linked to unfolding narrative and are often illustrative (of the voiceover) in nature. As well, they now focus on identified and recognizable characters, not the random pedestrians of the first sequence. Takes are longer, with fewer cuts, mostly reaction shots, such as close-ups. Time is compressed, with few establishing shots, and the lack of varied costumes makes each encounter largely indistinguishable from the last. The conventional nature of this sequence is undermined by the questionable status of the narrator.

Who is Mada? The narrator muses over this question while we see shots that flesh him out: "His past could be . . ." as we are shown in a particularly illustrative manner Mada acquiring his first bike. This illustrative fidelity strives to lend credence to the narrator's account. Mada's favorite pastime is watching pirated movies, linking him to the narrator who also spends all his time with a copy—videos of Meimei. In several scenes, a light bulb figures prominently in the shot, a pun on the idea of inspiration, as the narrator seems to be making up the story as he goes along. However, repeatedly the pulsating filament of the light bulb adds a spark to the static quality of the scenes: a figure of suspense. It also conveys the incorporeal charge of electricity and chance fringing the unfolding of this story. The light bulb allows us to see, but its electricity (as in Lynch) is also what is continually escaping the space. The question throughout this sequence is less "Did this story really happen, and in the way we are being told?" than "What is the effect of this connection, of this eddy in the current?"

The story of Mada and Mudan, a teenage schoolgirl, is a fairly conventional story of doomed young love. Mudan is played by Zhou Xun (who also plays Meimei), although the two performances and characters are so strikingly different that it is not evident right away. Where Meimei is a young woman, Mudan is still childlike in her demeanor, given to joyful, open and emotional excesses. Unlike Novak's "failed performance" with its slippage between voices, Xun's dual roles don't slide into indistinction in the performance, but rather as a thematic.

Mada, a mob courier, is hired by Mudan's "legitimate businessman" of a father to act as her chauffeur/babysitter. He kidnaps Mudan for ransom, impassive to Mudan's despair and disillusionment. A ransomed Mudan flees Mada and threatens to throw herself in the river, swearing she will return as a mermaid to find him. She jumps; we see her falling. Her fall and (presumed) death are delayed, postponed and deferred from this moment on. As in *Vertigo*, there is a slip in the moment of finality. As Mudan hits the water, the scene cuts to an underwater perspective, and Meimei in mermaid costume swims through the shot in slow motion, dressed as an exact replica of Mudan's mermaid doll, a gift from Mada. This is a very short shot, followed by a dissolve into another underwater shot with a school of fish swimming through the frame. As Meimei floats in the water, as Mudan disappears from the film, we have the very figure of a suspended (re)animation.

What is the effect of this cut? Is it a signal to the viewer that Mudan and Meimei are the same? Mudan leaps clutching her doll; the cut to Meimei implies a sort of fusion between girl and doll in the translation from one environment and one action (air/falling) into another (water/swimming). Is Meimei, like Judy, a sort of living doll? There is a confusion of time and place in this sequence; we see Meimei and presume that she is not in the river, but in her tank at the bar, putting on an act.

The dissolve to the fish superposes the tank and the river, however; the water becomes the medium of suspended animation. Meimei and Mudan are linked through the affective force of becoming itself. The mermaid doll/costume as figures of artifice, living doll, or mask, is less the artifice of an external resemblance than bare repetition plunged into the real repetition of difference. The preservative force of the river, saving everything, is also the space of the *plunge into time* that Mudan takes, and the ripple effect undoes the narration of her story.

Mada's reaction to Mudan's leap is delayed by the narrator, who intervenes to mention his recollection of reading this story in the paper. Her body was never found, but for weeks there were mermaid sightings (we see one such encounter between a fisherman and the "mermaid" on the banks of the river). In a strange temporal mix, these reports in the weeks after Mudan's death play out before we return to the immediate moment after she jumps. Mada makes a futile leap after her. Until now, the narrator has claimed only secondhand knowledge of these events, but as a drenched Mada is held by the police, the camera pulls away from him and travels along the crowd of onlookers on the bridge, like a shot from the videographer's perspective—the camera acts like a human jostling for position, and finds a space in the crowd to get a view of the river. A diver splashes into the water, and for the third time in this sequence, the splash engenders a change in time, cutting to several years later.

Released from prison, Mada searches the city for Mudan. Fragments reminiscent of Hermann's score for *Vertigo* fade in and out on the soundtrack; it is "Madeleine's theme" and Hermann's haunting style that Jorg Lemburg's score echoes. Rather than that score's immersive feel, however, Lemburg's music is more like a memory "on the tip of one's tongue," never fully resolving into a piece of music, but hovering in the background.

At the barber, Mada asks for news of his former associates. A cut from a shot of Mada in the barber's chair, reflected in the mirror, to a medium close-up that eliminates the mirror's frame, signals a bifurcation point. From now on, the narrator's fabulation of Mada's story comes back to haunt him. "And that's the end, I suppose," he narrates, as a close-up of Mada's enigmatic face begins to fade out. "I don't know how to finish the story, unless Mada can finish it for himself," he says, and the image and sound fade back in, as he disappears into the mirror. Is it the same image, or does the fade make a break between them? Is it less a break than a modulation? Though Mada does not begin narrating the events, in what way can what follows be said to be "Mada's" story?

The narrator's coyness, if intentional, becomes problematic for him almost immediately. Mada poses on his bike beneath the spray-painted ad for the videographer and begins to haunt his footsteps. We are reminded of Scottie's perplexed pursuit of Madeleine after she has jumped into the bay, where he tracks her across the city until he finds himself simply back at his own home. At Mada's old hangout, he literally runs into Meimei; shocked to "recognize" Mudan, he is disconcerted by her cool dismissal and "failure" of recognition.

Later, he follows her to the Happy Tavern, walking in the videographer's footsteps up the stairs to the bar, lit in a shimmering blue light that gives the impression of being underwater, the delay of Mudan's dive resurfacing. In a repeated shot, Mada peeks through the curtain at Meimei putting up her hair in the mirror. The mirrored door of the flower shop in *Vertigo* has been displaced in time, and a different type of mirroring occurs; the referentiality of this scene is not simply reflexive, but evokes in the audience a doubled sensation. We have been here before, and now the ambiguous embodiment across characters (Mada doubling the videographer doubling Scottie) stretches across time as well. Typically for this sequence of the film, however, the shots here linger in longer takes: Meimei's transformation into a mermaid is drawn out. Bits and pieces of disparate music fade in and out, like memories coming to the surface: a solo guitar piece, a trip-hop piece with a lazy beat, and the Hermann-influenced bits of *Vertigo*'s strings score. These pieces fold each other in continual modulation, changing not only the pieces but the resonance of the sound—sometimes full and beautiful, sometimes tinny and distant. When Meimei leaves for her act, Mada enters the room, and at the instigation of his glance, the camera pans around until it reaches the mirror. Mada follows her into the bar and witnesses her act; the music shifts from a solo version of the *Vertigo* theme to a swelling orchestral sound that emotionally conveys Mada's mounting conviction that he has found Mudan. In her dressing room, Meimei again rejects him and denies knowing him. He follows her home bent on recognition. When he leaves, rejected yet again, the camera stays with her (for the first time we are "alone" with Meimei) as in *Vertigo*, except there is no confession, only lingering close ups of Meimei's face. Throughout the film, close-ups are less revelations of an emotional sense than moments of affective uncertainty, underscoring the virtual fringing the actual. Potential accrues to this portrait and reanimates it. The snatches of music underscore a refrain function of the face, asking us to attend to the in-consistency of the face we see.

It is simple duration, a rarity in this film's pacing, that creates the opening, but also the mystery of the characters, an effect Melissa McMahon calls the "long take as repetition."[57] This sense of the long take is complemented by a different type of repetition. We start to see seemingly identical shots from earlier in the film. Meimei is seen once again from the window of the videographer, crossing the street with her arms folded to her chest. Upon her arrival, she becomes the hinge for the perspectives of Mada and the narrator. We initially get two shots of Meimei from the videographer's, first a long shot from his balcony of Meimei crossing the street, and then a medium shot of her, head bowed, from his front door out into the hallway. The third shot cuts to a medium close-up frontal shot of Meimei as she turns to screen left and speaks to the videographer, and then a head-on close-up of her from the videographer's perspective as she says she has to leave. His hand reaches out to caress her face. Once again, we cut back to the third shot, the medium close-up, only this time immediately there is a pan from Meimei to the videographer, silhouetted behind a stained glass window with only his arm reaching out. There is no camera silhouetted, only a man's face. Meimei begins to leave. The final shot cuts back to the videographer's point of view, which pans up from the departing Meimei to reveal Mada on the stairs, retrospectively coding shots three and five as Mada's point of view.

The triangulation of perspectives here hinges around the doubled woman, only more clearly than in *Vertigo* or *Lost Highway* the male perspective is immediately doubled. In the next scene, Mada sits in a café with the videographer, looking directly into the camera. Before he speaks, the narrator tells us what he is going to say. Mada then speaks, and tells the videographer about Mudan, and that Meimei is her double. When the videographer responds ("That's impossible, I've known Meimei a long time. Meimei is my girl"), it is one of the only times he speaks "in the present" and not in voiceover in the film.

It may seem that the question of Meimei's merely coincidental resemblance to Mudan is now resolved. But after Mada leaves, his words cause a ripple effect in the past, an act of "pure science fiction" within the time machine of the film's ambiguous embodiments. Again, we see a repeated sequence from earlier in the film, of Meimei leaving the houseboat. However, the images, initially shown in a long take, are now broken up by jump cuts. Upon review, the images are not the same; Meimei now appears less carefree and more tense; she does not blow him a kiss good-bye; there is a puff of smoke from the videographer not there in the first version. The actions seem identical, but the tone has changed. The sound of rain dominates the second version, utterly lacking in voiceover. Is this a reshaping (or affective reliving) of memory in light of Mada's story and the videographer's growing jealousy? Does he now see a distance that was always there? Is this Mada's story (suggested by the silencing of the voiceover)? It is impossible to assign a priority of truth to either sequence. Note too that the order has been changed; in the first part of the film, Meimei's departure precedes her return as seen from the balcony; in the second part, it follows.

The videographer voices that he knows Mada has been going to see Meimei every night, repeatedly telling her the same story of him and Mudan. We see them together in Meimei's dressing room, alternating close ups with two shots as Mada speaks. There is no way to know whether this is the first time he has come, or the fiftieth; there is no original to this scene. Mada tells Meimei that Mudan always wore a flower tattoo on her leg. Meimei denies having one, and then undoes her costume to show the tattoo's twin. During a close up of her face, she asks, "Am I the girl you're looking for?" The close-up is not revelatory, but affective; she is moved by her connection to Mada, but it is not clear how. Mada's solicitation of Meimei is not a straightforward externally imposed transformation as in *Vertigo* ("Judy, your hair . . . it can't matter to you"), nor is his persistence sadistic. The scene is a fabulative description, in which the virtual and the actual are indiscernibly mutual. Is Meimei Mudan? In this scene this possibility remains open, uncertain, but what is more suggestive is the potential the scene solicits. The possible: Meimei is or is not Mudan. The potential: Meimei is becoming other. . . . From the close-up of her face, there is a cut to a medium close-up of Meimei lying in bed underneath a man; they have clearly made love. We see only the back of his head; it could be Mada, but we can't know, especially given that we have no idea what the videographer looks like. Meimei's face is lit from outside the room, as from the headlights of a car. As it passes, her face shades into darkness, and her question repeats: "Am I the girl you're looking for?" With her face in shadows, we cannot tell if she speaks this out loud, or if this is a remembered echo from a previous scene.

Meimei breaks up with the videographer. As Mada persistently lingers at the edges of Meimei's life, it becomes increasingly difficult for Meimei to resist putting herself in Mudan's place. Her mermaid costume is an exact replica of Mudan's doll, but of course it has a retroactive meaning; she was a mermaid before she met Mada. When Mada tells her that Mudan liked to wear stick-on flower tattoos, we see Meimei carefully licking and applying the same kind of tattoo. The images in this sequence are part of a story still being told, and as such have no logical narrative arrangement. As with our version of Mada's nightly visits to Meimei, there is no way to know how many times these gestures have been repeated, or if they are "live" or recorded.

Increasingly jealous of Mada, the videographer has him beaten up (in a prosthetic action, by the owner of Meimei's club); Mada comes to see him and has a conversation in which he directly addresses the camera/videographer. But even as we hear Mada speaking, the videographer renarrates Mada's words in a superposition of sonic temporalities. Finally Mada offers a compromise: "If I would let him go on looking for Mudan, he would give me back Meimei." The narrator says, "And suddenly it was like none of this had ever happened." The uncomfortable relation between the videographer and Mada, hinged by Meimei, is resolved through their gentlemen's agreement. The intensive bifurca-tion points of suspended questions impossibly actualize: Mada traces Mudan through a clue that the videographer gives him, as they share a drink of buffalo grass vodka like the kind Mudan's father distributed. The vodka leads him to a twenty-four-hour convenience store, where the clerk turns out to be Mudan. Her welcoming smile and a shot of them drinking together on the banks of the river are all we see of their reunion.

The police show up at the videographer's door with the news that two people have drowned in the river; the man had his business card. The bodies are Mada and Mudan. Hearing the news, Meimei runs to see for herself. Pulling back the sheet covering the dead lovers in the rain, she is shocked to see her double, and struggles to process the sight as the rain pours down her face. Says Meimei, "I thought it was just a story, I didn't think she existed." We can only ask, Did Mudan exist before the "compromise" between the videographer and Mada?

The videographer is temporarily happy: "That night we were together like old times." Meimei faces the camera and asks the film's opening question: "If I leave you someday, would you look for me, like Mada?" Mada's search for Mudan is seemingly resolved, but Meimei's repeated question fails to tie up the loose ends. In their agreement, the men have forgotten Meimei. He leaves her and goes home to watch videos of her. In the morning, Meimei is gone, leaving a note taped to her mirror: "Find me if you love me." Meimei's room dissolves to a shot from the back of her boathouse, looking down the river. The videographer lifts a glass before the camera and drinks. "It reminds me of days with Meimei," he says. "Nothing lasts forever, I'll take another drink and close my eyes, waiting for another story to begin." Thematically, drunkenness is linked repeatedly to the river, an affective unmooring or flow, change and pres-ervation from which anything could surface. From these unmoored ele-ments, he fabulates a story as a means of loving Meimei, requiring a postponement, a relation of the missive. It is a radical passivity of giving oneself over to sensation. In the act of seeking, what is sought changes: his impossible promise to look for Meimei forever is the paradox of the promise undone by time. His passivity is a different way of looking, his reliance on old videos and mediation not a rejection of the real for the abstract or already known, but a different unmooring. What type of gesture is it that Meimei leaves and isn't followed? "Find me if you love me," the note says, but the videographer looks to the fabulating cinema in his head, outward flight and inward turn.

Is that note really for him? Repeatedly, when both Mada and the videographer see Meimei, it is in shots where she is doubled by her reflection. Mada's every perception of her is a double vision of his memory of Mudan. The videographer's every look is a doubled vision of camera and live experience, literalizing the past that is preserved and the present that passes. Is Meimei immune from double vision? In *Vertigo*, Judy's complicity prevents her from speaking her own doubleness; it silently animates the bare repetition that will lead to her death. Meimei's doubleness seems to be a fantasy of the men around her; fear of her sexual infidelity leads the men to strike a bargain to divide her to manage this doubleness.

Meimei's note: "Find me if you love me." Is she seeking a bare repetition of Mada's obsessive devotion? In *Vertigo*, Judy's letter is never sent, her secret festering inside her. What if Meimei's letter, taped to her own mirror, is for herself? Where did Meimei go if not into the mirror, plunging into its reflective surface? Meimei is profoundly shaken by auto-affection when she sees Mudan's body, face to face with her uncanny double. Seeing Mudan with her own eyes is not truth, revelation, or finality. It is autopsy or self-survey. This is why Mudan's stilled stasis on the sidewalk, plucked out of the river into which she has been falling throughout the film, its *montage interdit* resolution of suspense (Is Meimei really Mudan?), is doubled by Meimei's open-mouthed, drenched shock. In that mutual image, Meimei is ripped open by the encounter, not reassured of the boundaries of her self; and the shattering of the water of the river as continuous flow into the multiple brutalities of the raindrops hitting the scene is the shatter of incompossible worlds, briefly held in suspense. Meimei's certainty ("I'm not the girl you're looking for") has become a question ("Am I the girl you're looking for?"). She questions her own identity, like Dern's actress in *Inland Empire*. Meimei's seduction by Mada's story is via openness to affect, the erotic effect of memory itself beyond a nostalgic capture in possession; the foreclosure of their possible relationship persistently opens to becoming something other than the self, through the "libido of time." While she tries out the guise of Mudan, something else is going on. With actualization fringed by the virtual, Meimei must find a different route to explore her affective openness. The note, Meimei's auto-address, does not coyly solicit a fairy-tale pursuit, but follows a line of flight, reanimating the dead end of Judy's disguise. Connecting with Mada, she began to forget herself, but not to become Mudan. For Meimei, there is no going back. Leaving, Meimei exposes the infidelity at the heart of love—as much about forgetting as it is about promises. Her real infidelity is to herself, an auto-affection of time.

"Duration," Deleuze says, lecturing on Spinoza, "always happens behind our backs," speaking to duration's illicit quality, the crime of time.[58] He connects Bergson's and Spinoza's concepts of duration as lived and irreducible transitions from one state to another: a transversal movement. This becomes a definition of affect (*affectus* in Spinoza) as duration, the lived passage, which is enveloped by an affection (*affectio*). Although there is no definitive sexual infidelity in *Suzhou River,* the film is moodily infused with this theme. The jealous narrator's attack on Mada is the only clichéd (and ineffectual) response to infidelity's threat. Here, infidelity is the duration that folds time. Duration is the lived passage, the transition (or affect/*affectus*) that differs from the end states that are only ever the result of decomposition, the affections that envelop the affect. Infidelity continually slips away and stretches out, virtuality's intimation. The impossible nature of promises points to this.

Crystalline Description

The Center as Point of View

The videographer's promise appears broken when he fails to pursue Meimei, choosing instead a drunken reverie on the river. Throughout, he is a figure of failed or indirect actions, a passive "developer" of images and stories. This passivity is sensationally figured by his embodiment: its affiliation with the camera puts the body into suspense, such that direct actions (for example, smoking) remain purely habitual, subcontracted (the assault on Mada), or glazed by memory's uncertain patina such that distinguishing lived from relived moments is impossible, the everyday double vision of those who record events while living them. It would be inaccurate to describe the experience of watching this film as simply mediated. The undecidable attribution of so many images is imme-diated as relived or unlived body. Immediation turns the body into a resonance chamber; the indistinction of interior/exterior hollowing out concrete embodiment and opening it to the play of forces as heterogene-ous assemblage of speeds and slownesses. To give a body to a phantom neither concretizes or situates, but to give all the body's dimensions, corporeal and incorporeal, as a zone of intensity and a site of free replay. The passive ending and the videographer's passion for Meimei, so intense his life is "suspended" in her absence, so removed that we see little of this except as he tells it, are difficult to pin down as emotion. Why does he abandon their story so easily for a semblance's suspended reanima-tion where the body is capacitated, but with nowhere for capacity to go? Its intensity exceeds "a narrative or functional line" in favor of a line of flight.[59] Meimei and the videographer's relationship is ghosted from the start by Mudan and Mada. Meimei's departure does not simply repeat Mudan's leap, however. The ambiguous affections between them are not actual infidelities, but the force of duration's existential infidelity. Though Mada and the videographer's "deal" seemingly halts the fluctua-tions around identities and relationships ("Give me back Mudan and I will give you back Meimei"), their promise is impossible.

Love is an act of infidelity to the self: connect, and forget yourself in the process. The videographer recognizes this, choosing not to chase Meimei along the already-trodden path of that story, but to sink into the depths of the stories in his head (the sheets of the past). This passivity seemingly contradicts his status as narrator, fabulator, and master of what we see and hear. He continually speaks over the film's diegetic voices, repeating and interpreting others' speech for us as an aural blur in the soundtrack. His voice turns the body into a resonance chamber and divides image and sound, rendering sound a description. I briefly revisit Deleuze's discussion of description in the time-image before con-sidering the videographer's voice in *Suzhou River*, connecting it to the "delayed or suspended POV shot" as not immediately (or ever) attributed to a particular character. Recall that these shots undo the logic of linear narrative: "Unusual evocations of time permanently suspend the parts that might otherwise form a causal unity of beginnings, middles and ends in favour of surveying a field of possibilities: a multiplicity of partially realized narratives and nonnarratives competing equally."[60] Although we might argue that this is not the case in *Suzhou River*, because the camera is frequently tied to the (invisible) body of the videographer, I claim that voice serves the same function here. Voice undermines the unity of sound and picture, undoing the narrative's linear logic and producing affect logic as a "temporal sink," the "passion" of activity before action.

For Deleuze, when the sensory motor schema fails, a passing through into action is not extended, generating instead an image of thought. The actual enters into a circuit with its own virtual image. In the movement-image, the camera view is the free indirect subjective: not the subject's mental view but the imposition of another view. He claims that the "most subjective vision approaches the most objective position: that of free-flowing matter."[61] The "forking" of time into past and present continually divides us from ourselves—thus free indirect discourse is the only way for a direct time-image to appear. The camera, or the image as objective and the character's point of view as subjective, mutually "contaminate" so there is no definitively truthful point of view.

The biggest change from movement-image to time-image is from identity to undecidability (not the same thing as indifference). The lectosign (to see or to read?) and the double are problems of this nature. Deleuze refigures Alain Robbe-Grillet's concept of description, to express this: "[Description] once claimed to reproduce a pre-existing reality; it now asserts its creative function."[62] In Robbe-Grillet, the function of description, now the chief preoccupation of the new novel, is deframing. Previously, description ornamentally framed the "image of man," in essence the story's action. In the new novel, description changes from an ornamental appendage of human sensory-motor action to creative activity; skip the frame, which was previously redundant, and the content (now synonymous with expression) will have escaped the reader completely: "Imagining he has been dealing hitherto with nothing but the frame, he will still be looking for the picture." In *Mulholland Drive*, Betty's first views of Rita are continually posed against a Japanese painting where the signature is written on the frame. There is no outside to the dream world, no framing not fully part of content itself. In the movement-image, description was organic, reflecting the unity between human and world via the object's independence. In the movement of the real, description adds nothing to the object, and nothing is lost. Cinema doubles reality as mirror. By contrast, crystalline description occurs when the sensory-motor link is broken, when the unity between human and the world is gone. Frequently in *Suzhou River*, shots of a character looking in the mirror are immediately followed by a shot that loses the mirror's frame, or where only the reflection is visible. Although action now stutters or fails entirely, this is still life as the "unlived as yet" body, the puppet without strings, or semblance. Deleuze terms this impersonal or "*a* life," the subjective as becoming other to ourselves in time. A crystalline description of anotherness.

This description is not representation but a "double movement" of erasure and creation, lending a vagueness or blur to experience. Deleuze cites Godard: "To describe is to observe mutation."[63] This has a dual sense. On the one hand, the time-image as the cinema of the seer not actor is highlighted: description as observation. On the other hand, what is observed is not an independent object but *the undecidable space of the body* doubled by the virtual. "Do you see?," Judy's question to Scottie, "To see or to read?" is misleading when it is clearly both, double movement of destruction and creation. In my act of seeing with my own eyes, I *am* no longer—I is an other. The object does not have an independent existence; description is not then an act of representational fixity, but is itself a process through which the observation of mutation takes the form of the circuit.

In crystalline description, the center becomes point of view via a false movement of decentering. Point of view, especially in cinema, is often associated with subjectivity, mastery, and character expression. Deleuze's discussion of point of view is in the chapter "The Powers of the False," in which the shift in understanding of the true is linked to a shift in vision: the rise of perspectivism, linked to the question "Is there a center or not at all?" Deleuze writes:

On the one hand, the centre becomes purely optical; the point becomes point of view. This perspectivism was not defined by variation of external points of view on a supposedly invariable object (the ideal of the true would be preserved). Here, on the contrary, the point of view was constant, but always internal to the different objects which were henceforth presented as the metamorphosis of one and the same thing in the process of becoming.[64]

Description in the time-image is subject to a double movement. Firstly, crystalline description involves the circuit of the actual and the virtual, one of indiscernibility, although not confusion, and not the disappearance of the poles. At the same time, there is a movement toward an outside, the crack of the "unthought," which is not the relation of a circuit. This is also the case in the relation of description to its objects. On the one hand, there is obsessive repetition and return to the object, not as the same, but in a process of displacement. This same process likewise acknowledges a *radical singularity*. In the time-image, description involves the picking out of a few things, a "thinness" or "singularity" of the object. In this way, objects are "typical" or "rich" in that description endlessly refers to other descriptions that "displace" each description in turn. This is a result of the forking double movement of time. Unlike the movement-image, in which there is continual modulation of the part in reference to a whole, the dual pressures of the time-image retain this notion of a singularity which is generative and ungraspable. *Suzhou River* is a film where the pressure of the past continually drives the force of the present, not as unbearable weight or as determination, but as radical uncertainty. More than anywhere else, this is played out in the "thinness" of the narrative voice, divested of a narrator's typical omnipotence: "I don't know how to finish the story; perhaps Mada can finish it for himself."

Deleuze's lesser attention to sound in *Cinema 2* still serves as a powerful opening in his theory, drawing heavily on Michel Chion's innovative work. Chion describes sound as temporalizing, because it attunes us to tiny qualitative shifts, temporal vectors, and directionality. I explore Chion's idea of "phantom audio-vision" to analyze the function of the voiceover narration in *Suzhou River*.[65] How does this fabulating voice fail to simply shore up the "film body" of the videographer?

Chion locates phantom sounds in the "afterlife of the image," when nothing in the image itself is identifiable as the sound's source. He borrows the idea of the ghost from Merleau-Ponty, as a "kind of perception made by only one sense,"[66] but also affiliates it with a memory of experience never *actually* experienced: engraved, but not *consciously* registered.[67] This effectively "hollows out" the image, neither adding to it, nor complementing it as counterpoint: this disjunction produces a "vibration."[68] In *Suzhou River*, the first time the narrative voiceover is "divorced" from the camera mounted on the body (with the first turn to Mada's story), we get for the first time a "complementary" soundtrack in the form of music that is in explicit, additive harmony with the image. To phantom audio-vision Chion ascribes a particular mode of giving a "body to a phantom," which he dubs the *acousmêtre*, a neologism conflating *être*, or being, with acousmatic, a type of sound in which the source is not seen.[69] The *acousmêtre* has an ambiguous relation to image, neither inside nor outside: for Chion it produces an oscillation. Like the suspense of the impossible objective shot, this cinematic figure produces an aberrant movement of suspense, the vibration of the "activity before action." In fact, this is exactly how Chion characterizes the *acousmêtre*, always implicated in and about to be part of the action, differentiated from a "master of ceremonies" or a "witness."

Typically, the *acousmêtre* has three powers: it is all seeing, all knowing, and all powerful. However, Chion is equally fascinated by the special case of "paradoxical *acousmêtres*," those deprived of at least one of these powers. This usually happens when an *acousmêtre* becomes embodied and particular, reduced to a human existence. However, in his analysis of *The Invisible Man*, Chion identifies the horrifying suspension of partial embodiment, what we might call a *body effect*, when the camera repeatedly traces the trail of the invisible man even when he is not to be seen, and where the body as an invisible emitter of force (as when he covers himself with a blanket and we see the outline of his form underneath) serves as a dreadful special effect: "We are frightened to see that the blanket marries the contour of a nothingness, but this nothingness—which speaks—is a form that makes us feel cold."[70] Although lacking a visible body, this paradoxical *acousmêtre* remains capable of affecting and of being affected; in fact, this fundamental ability of the body is *intensified* by his lack of a visible, delimited body. The failure of full objectification serves to remind us that "where objects are, there has also been their becoming,"[71] and that such becoming-body is ongoing.

The *acousmêtre* puts into question without doing away with the offscreen/onscreen distinction, which generally remains in play until the *acousmêtre* is demasked and exposed as a human body. What happens when that moment never arrives, as in *Suzhou River*? The *acousmêtre* renders the space of the body undecidable and ambiguous; its offscreen/onscreen oscillation opens an irrational cut between sound and image. Sound is released from its dependence on the image, acquiring an autonomy allowing it to relink with the image not through adequacy or resemblance, but as a mode of suspense.

In Chion's idea of phantom audio-vision, this phantom is the breakdown of the lived body. The body in Deleuze's time-image is in a similar state of breakdown, caught up in the undecidable space of the circuit between virtual and actual. Chion's translator notes that phantom is a translation of *en creux*: "negative space—the shape of the space in a sculptor's mold, defined by the mold." In this chapter, Chion is negotiating the territory of transference from one sensory channel to another, which sometimes produces physiological "presences" in the face of perceptual "absences."[72] The importance of Chion's phrase "audio vision" is the attempt not to simply prioritize sound, but to re-mark the transition between the two senses addressed directly in cinema. Sobchack analyzes as synesthesia an enabling function of the film's body: "What my fingers knew." Chion, though, suggests something different via the phantom, in which physiological presences function like "phantom pain," intensive sensations that defy rational explanation and extend the body beyond its material limits. Phantom engages those elements of the body that are "incorporeal, yet real," signaling an impersonal force of vitality, "a form of life in-person."[73]

In *Suzhou River,* this really apparitional quality of audiovision appears as a blur in both the image and the soundtrack, or not precisely *in,* but *between.* At times this is evident: in the aforementioned shots of Meimei when brief superpositions create a blur; in the soundtrack's modulation, so that music seems to change "source" (for example, from the "full-ness" of non-diegetic music to a tinny quality as if the sound were local-ized within or just outside of the image). At other times, it is more ambiguous. For instance, the blur in the shots of Meimei can be seen as the result of the superposed images, but this technique fails to explain the blur's effect. This becomes especially obvious when the blur results from the narrator reaching out to touch Meimei's face; in the solicitation of touch via the visible hand, the visual image is briefly undone, intensi-fied. This could be understood as haptic; Laura Marks, for example, has analyzed "intercultural cinema" as characterized by a haptic visuality, in which images work via touch, to trigger memory in an embodied spec-tator.[74] However, this appeal to the spectator's embodied recognition misses the *undoing* of recognition by the virtual's fleeting presence; this blur is an intensification of sensation that undoes synthetic experience to highlight the "real irrational cut" between the senses.

Taking another example: Searls theorizes that Mada is not "real," but a fictional character made up by the narrator who "comes to life" in his imagination. He justifies this idea, seemingly challenged by two scenes in which Mada directly confronts the narrator, by claiming these scenes have a quality that renders them unreal, despite the face-to-face encoun-ter in the flesh: "They are slightly out of focus, or opaque, as if shot through a pane of glass; most affectingly, Mada looks directly into the camera, with an open expression on his face that is the exact opposite of his usual dour scowl."[75]

Looking at these scenes, I don't *see* this unreal quality, the slight lack of focus. It *is* there, however, in the soundtrack, which superposes the narrator's voiced version of Mada's words over Mada's dialogue. I don't *actually* see it, but it infects the visual field, sensationally—that is to say, virtually. If this is synesthesia, it is a nonsynthetic synesthesia, with a dysfunctional quality that comes not from the recognizable similarity of the film body's way of being in the world, but from its nonsynthetic embodiment, the hallucinatory gap in experience opened up. Equally, the narrative uncertainty prompted by such scenes (the encounters disturb the hermeticism of the Mudan/Mada, Meimei/Mada, and Meimei/narrator relations) must not be simply dismissed as "epistemological trickery" beside the scene's affective sensation. If it is trickery, it is as special effect becoming special affect. To separate "epistemological trickery" from affect, too quickly defined for Searls as an object-oriented "love" (*of* beauty, *of* storytelling), is to miss the copresence of the virtual and the actual, their exchange that is the point of Deleuze's claim that the time-image gives a body to a phantom. To heed sensation should not necessitate a bracketing off of knowledge, which preserves that knowledge as a preformed ideal. To give a body to a phantom reinvests the phantom with its ability to affect and to be affected. This is difficult to express as experience because the virtual only appears "in the gap" as a new vagueness subsisting and insisting. Even to claim that the "real story" is love forecloses these effects of what love can do beyond the romantic dyad of the couple.

What does attentiveness to the virtual's vagueness do to the film body? This is "semblance," the charging of the body with potential when the most immediately available actions are suspended. It is the (un)experience of the virtual: "The semblance is the form in which what does not appear effectively expresses itself, in a way that must be counted as real."[76] Massumi describes experiments that attempted to achieve a physical and physiological reduction of senses to their constituent element to uncover their essence (for example, Ganzfeld's experiments where vision was reduced to the condition of the full spectrum of light striking the entire retina equally). What was persistently discovered at the most "elementary" level of perception was not simplicity but chaos, an inability by participants to articulate their experience in terms of the relevant sense:

Pure visual experience resulted in a "complete absence of seeing." Researchers concluded that the "total field of vision" was not a "phenomenal field." In other words, it was not a field of experience. What was produced by the experimental setup was less a building block of experience than an anomalous event befalling experience. The anomaly obviously pertained to experience, but couldn't be said to be experienced per se: of it, but not in it.[77]

Other effects included fatigue, a loss of motor coordination, dizziness, a failed sense of time, and depersonalization. "Activate the most simplest and fullest physical and physiological conditions of vision, the most straightforward objective condition of vision, and you not only extinguish seeing, you make people float out of their bodies and lose themselves, literally lose their selves." He concludes that what the experimental subjects were "unexperiencing" was an "always accompanying" chaos that is the virtual. Critically, the body's immobility in laboratory experiments, or in comparable situations like dreaming, allows for the "unexperience of the 'total field,'" or the virtual limit of the sense. Movement is what allows for "self-referencing," a mode of containing the "circuits" of reference of emergent experience. In describing the continuum, not separation, of experiences of natural perception, dreams, experimentally induced hallucinations, and pathological hallucination, Massumi argues that a distinction of degree but *not* kind can be made based on the richness or impoverishment of conditions for "feedback-enabled cross referencing": "The danger is that, through insufficient cross referencing, experience might overreach its own lifeboat."[78] When this happens, the body does not disappear, but becomes, in my terms, the "unlived-as-yet." There is no pure unlived body; the closest approximation might be Bergson's disturbing description of matter without consciousness: "Matter thus resolves itself into numberless vibrations, all linked together in uninterrupted continuity, all bound up with each other, and traveling in each direction like shivers through an enormous body."[79] Perception immobilizes this movement into a bounded body and discrete objects, but affective sensation intuits this chaos, a suspense that is not immobility but movement and stasis all at once.

One might ask, given the anti-representational nature of time-images for Deleuze, why his examples are not drawn primarily from experimental films. One explanation lies in his repeated but hesitant use of the double throughout *Cinema 2*. In the chapter "Cinema, Body and Brain,

Thought," Deleuze notes the importance of the black or white screen as a "genetic element" of time-images, explicitly connected to a bodily "genesis." Of Phillip Garrel's work, for example, he writes, "Over-exposed and under-exposed, white and black, cold and hot . . . they are the categories which 'give' a body,"[80] in a "cinema of constitution." Cinema cannot give a presence of bodies as theatre can, but has the potential, in its "experimental night" (the suspension of natural perception) to "carry out a primordial genesis of bodies in terms of a white, or a black or a grey (or even in terms of colors), in terms of a beginning of visible that is not yet a figure, that is not yet an action."[81] This occurs in immediation, the spiral form of time that exceeds mere immediacy of presence as the vibrating, oscillating suspense of the virtual's fleetingness. No special effect can stand for or be the virtual; only the special affect of the time-image can generate an (un)experience of virtuality:

> The virtual, as such, is inaccessible to the senses. This does not, however, preclude figuring it, in the sense of constructing images of it. To the contrary, it requires a multiplication of images. The virtual that cannot be felt also cannot but be felt, in its effects. When expressions of its effects are multiplied, the virtual fleetingly appears. Its fleeting is in the cracks between and the surfaces around images. . . . The virtual can perhaps best be imaged by superposing these deformational moments of repetition rather than sampling differences in form and content. Think of each image receding into its deformation, as into a vanishing point, as into a vanishing point of its own twisted versioning.[82]

In considering *Suzhou River* as a remake of *Vertigo*, I have not assigned Hitchcock's film an original priority, as if mapping its influences, we could uncover meaning or truth. As a free replay, Lou's film takes up elements in Hitchcock's film that resisted actualization: the pressing insistence of Scottie's suspension in the final shot that unravels the finality of his actions; the problem of Judy/Madeleine around the question "To see or to read?" as the free fall of identity; the delay of action that does not preclude the passion's affective vitality, or the "activity before action" as the intimation of the virtual. Special effects become special affects around the question of what a body can do. The film body that *Suzhou River* gives to *Vertigo*'s intimated witness in the form of the narrator shows the limitations of thinking love in both films solely in terms of romantic love. In romance's resonance chamber, as in the spectral intimacy between spectator and screen, the violent affection of bodies is also a productive violence to the self, the infidelity to the self at the heart of love. "All stories are love stories," Searls writes, but he misses the connection between stasis and movement that characterizes love.

Romances and action films as genres are usually diametrically opposed, but they share predictable outcomes. Romances are action films in the limited sense of the possible, foreseen from the start, the ultimate in stasis (Who cares what happens after the couple finally gets together?) and the triumphant power to act which saves the day ("I do!"). In both cases: a closed circle, a completed action. In *Suzhou River,* the suspense of the love stories, their expansion of circuits, and the ambiguous but productive connections they enable suggest that the film body is less an analogue of human experience than about an-other body, or rather, the anotherness of the body itself. The narrator, just like the doubled body of Zhou Xun, both of which refuse the screen as simple mediation of or reference to an original world, renders the film body a *machinic mode of delay* whose generative vagueness may allow for something else.

If the cinema of the time-image is that of the seer, not the actor, we must put into suspense the doubled meaning of seer (*voyant*)—the seer as *clair-voyant*; not merely as a perceptual act, but a perception generatively clouded by its double, affect, or "felt futurity." At the end of *Cinema 2,* Deleuze writes:

> The sensory motor break makes man a seer who finds himself struck by something unthinkable in thought. Between the two, thought undergoes a strange fossilization, which is as it were its powerlessness to function, to be, its dispossession of itself and the world. For it is not in the name of a better or truer world that thought captures the intolerable in the world, but, on the contrary, it is because this world is intolerable that it can no longer think a world or think itself. The intolerable

is no longer a serious injustice, but the permanent state of a daily banality. Man is not himself in a world other than the one in which he experiences the intolerable and feels himself trapped. The spiritual automaton is in the psychic situation of the seer, who sees better and farther than he can react, that is, think. Which, then, is the subtle way out? To believe, not in a different world, but in a link between man and the world, in love or life, to believe in this as in the impossible, the unthinkable, which nonetheless cannot but be thought: "something possible, otherwise I will suffocate."[83]

CHAPTER FOUR

Time Takings

Suspended Reanimations and the Pulse of Postdigital Cinema

> As much the color of the human soul as of animal becomings and cosmic magics, affect remains fuzzy, atmospheric, and yet is perfectly apprehendable, in so far as it is characterized by the existence of thresholds of passage and of reversals of polarity. The difficulty here resides in the delimitation not being discursive, that is to say, not being founded in systems of distinctive oppositions that are set out in linear sequences of intelligibility or capitalized in informatic memories that are compatible with one another. Assimilable in this respect to Bergsonian duration, affect does not arise from categories that are extensional, susceptible of being numbered, but from intensive and intentional categories, corresponding to an existential auto-positioning. . . . Affect is the process of existential appropriation by the continuous creation of heterogeneous durations of being. For this reason, we would certainly be well advised to give up treating it under the aegis of scientific paradigms so as to turn deliberately toward ethico-aesthetic paradigms.
>
> —Félix Guattari, *Schizoanalytic Cartographies*

Oblivions Founded in Being

Forgetting the Bomb under the Table

Definitively opposing suspense versus surprise, Hitchcock, like Barthes, notes that suspense relies on affect's warping of clock time, in a parallel intensive attention to time passing (immediation). Suspense doubles time into a heterogeneous duration sparking with sensations unresolved into emotional categories, and a relentless, homogeneous metricality. Between the two is a double movement of intensive extension, impossibly expanding in an eccentric, assaultive rhythm. Without the countdown of the bomb under the table, we feel only surprise and postfactual inevitability, not the frantic bifurcations immediately doubling every tick of the clock, first into possibilities and then into pure affective potential itself. Hitchcock, of course, was himself partly responsible for the domineering metricality of on-time moviegoing. Linda Williams has described Hitchcock's marketing strategy for *Psycho,* forcing moviegoers to be inhabitually prompt. Propping his cardboard doppelgänger outside theatres, pointing to his watch, Hitchcock measured out affect by refusing admission to latecomers in order to remain faithful to the film's big, and unusually early, reveal.[1] The untimeliness of suspense lifts off from the timeliness of habit, just as a regular heartbeat can immediately double itself into an inhuman and secret bodily mechanism. This untimeliness is the close coupling of anotherness, a body and its own becoming.

In the previous citation from Guattari, affect exists precisely as an experience of becoming, akin to the work of suspense, testifying to the "existence of thresholds of passage and of reversals of polarity."[2] Like Bergsonian duration, affect is a rediscovery of oneself, an "experience of auto-positioning," or what we considered in the previous chapter as "auto-affection" through the rediscovery of other durations. Affect is excorporative, an "existential appropriation by the continuous creation of heterogeneous durations of being."[3] In other words, we are continuously appropriated by life itself through the creative heterogeneity of duration: this is the experience, through intuition, of our own anotherness. Auto-positioning is nonlinear, non-numbered; suspense is such an experience of becoming beside ourselves, appropriated for purposes that are not simply our own. If Hitchcock understood such appropriation as objectifying the audience, an organ to be played upon, the reanimations of his work and body tell us something different.

If, as Bergson says, we continually rediscover heterogeneous being through the untimely intuitive experience of durations "above and below" our own, timeliness can function as a recuperative recollection of the self. It is practically an anachronistic motion these days to check a watch, though new smart watches may bring this habit back from the movement archive. That old gesture of lifting wrist to eye line figurally recalls the body to itself, gathering in abstract forces such as indifferent metricality through a movement that is part automatic habit and part intentional control. Relinking hand to eye as a precursor to action, this move re-claims the alienated rhythms of abstract time as one's own. Prompted usually by a state of bodily disquiet or disorientation (I have lost all track of time!), this time-taking gesture dampens the disquieting effects of sus-pended moments of waiting, syncing us up with other schedules and bod-ies not our own—metros, buses, coworkers, movies, and so on—through a performance of control. This gesture is the contemporary corporeal equivalent of sampling the skip of a vinyl record in electronic music. But in the crack of this movement made newly legible, and no longer simply informational, by the obsolescence of clockwork mechanisms, we might ask, when does a clock or a watch become a time machine?

In "Backwards to the Future: Outline for an Investigation for Think-ing Cinema as a Time Machine," Siegfried Zielinski traces the intermit-tent, propulsive mechanism of automatic chronometers as articulating both mechanical and machinic relations of cinema and time. Their stop-and-start movement makes regularized time legible by connecting them to reading instruments, such as a clock face. Mechanical clockworks thus form the "foundation for all machines or media artifacts in which movements or processes need to be regulated."[4] A nineteenth-century cinematograph is "nothing more" than an adapted clock, the cinema screen simply a clock face on which we witness time in action. He traces temporal relations between spectator and cinematic bodies at the inter-section of labor, experience and corporeality. Early cinemagoers were witnesses to a "re-experienced" time, one distinct from their daily expe-rience. They could only "rent" this strange temporality, one that had been stolen from them. Cinema expands through spectatorial bodies, taking up more and more time as the cinematic moves into the territories of TV, electronic images, and gaming, where touch and time work together. Ultimately, though, a future cinema for Zielinski is an incorporated cin-ema, "a machine that not only enables us to travel through time using our imagination but also using our bodies," presumably a machine that no longer needed a legible surface.[5] An incorporated cinematic time machine (such as the brain as the screen?) requires a different legibility. Faced with the (un)coordinates of existential auto-positions shearing off madly in heterogeneous disjunctions, we hesitate: To see or to read? How do we learn to read a cinematic time screen without a clock face? What would a time machine look like that resisted being numbered?

Time machines are well known to be deadly, making embodiment ambiguous precisely in relation to unlivable rhythms and compositions across speeds and slownesses. Checking the time often re-places and reorients us in space and time when we start to drift, an alarm that breaks the dream. However, in all of the films explored so far, checking the time instead invites anotherness, actualizing the difference of "as last is to next." The first instance of self-aware temporal and spatial displacement in *Inland Empire* occurs when Susan (Dern) slouches against a wall during her first encounter with a posse of jilted young women and hears their prediction: "In the future, you'll be dreaming, in a kind of sleep; when you open your eyes, someone familiar will be there."[6] She responds by covering her eyes like a child. She pulls her hands away and appears shocked to find herself in a completely different place, a wintry Polish street, accompanied by two women. Her gesture actively incorporates the cinematic cut (the black frame) of temporal and spatial displacement, making the transition surprising, not smooth. She has a bumpy return as well to her starting point, seated against the wall; this displacement is redoubled when she watches as the camera tracks away from her and over to the window, now opening onto the same snowy Polish street below, as if the camera had gone to look on her behalf. The camera doesn't step in to occupy her subjective perspective; instead this spatial and temporal displacement is lived transversally across character and cinematic bodies. These are two modes of negotiating this relation: in a kind of internal edit, Susan makes the cut herself through a relation between hands and eyes, a direct action on her body inserting a black frame between two worlds, and then she allows the camera to take responsibility for her own displacement, to move on her behalf. Two tools of cinematic transition—the edit and the camera movement—are deployed, and they result in the first instance of *reaction* to seeing herself in that film, as if the goal of such encounters was to discover that otherness of the self, in an "auto-affection."

Susan lives this sequence as if from within a movie, where irrational cuts are not accepted examples of a cinematic shorthand but experienced, as for early spectators, in their shocking and disruptive immediacy. When she returns from the Polish street, the sequence ends with her seeing herself from above and below, in a shot/reverse-shot/shot sequence. She experiences the heterogeneity of her own multiple durations catching up with her. This moment is not the familiar face-to-face frontality of the mirror-image; instead, a seated Dern looks up in a distorted close up at the impassive Susan gazing down from above, dropping a plumb line of temporal distortion through the center of their eye line match. A movement-image of the body in time.

Although Nikki's psychogenic fugue into Susan's world can be read through an actress's immersion in character, this doesn't account for how this fugue is presented less as the play of multiple subjectivities and more as the stuttering of a certain mode of cinematic expression. In other words, the tools deployed to render Dern's personae incommensurable and indiscernible with certainty are all tools of the image itself. Suspended in this chaotic state, Susan/Nikki receives a message from the Lost Girl via the interface of the record player from the film's opening. "Do you want to see?" she asks, and gives Nikki/Susan instructions to build a time machine: Wear the watch, burn a hole in a piece of silk, fold it over and look through. Typically for the film, a time machine does not make legible regularized and instrumentalized time; rather it activates an anotherness equally composed of body and imaging.

If time machines require a legible surface, what does it mean to "see" here? With the time machine, the interface becomes the encounter in itself. When Susan looks through the hole, she sees more silk: another screen. Her eye is inside the fold. Next image: the watch racing backward at an accelerated rate; time is literally rendered "out of joint" here. A hole is burned in the silk that functions like an optical device to frame space, while duration (the smouldering cigarette as an alternative to metrical clock time) literally burns a passage through rationalized time. However, this frame fails to hold as a window onto the world. Instead, the silk is folded over so that what is framed and highlighted is the texture of the silk itself, a doubling of perception that screens passage in a literal image of Zielinski's clock face that is suspended between seeing and reading. The screen itself, rather than any projective content, is made visible, as a cinematic time machine that doesn't look out onto a represented world as through a window, nor reflects a world as in a mirror, but instead shows us a secret coherence and connectivity of texture. What Susan seeks to see in those instants is what cannot be represented directly, but which comes to us through the figure of the interface— the figural quality of audiovisual media. In this way, the silk is part of a time machinics that stretches across *Inland Empire* to repeatedly stage the passage into anotherness (from the opening shot where the beam of light doesn't land to Dern's encounter with her own image on screen in the theatre). The folds in *Inland Empire* don't simply press the past of *On High in Blue Tomorrows* against the present; they are the ambiguous embodiments of a time machine when the brain is the screen.

Mulholland Drive timestamps the duplicity of the time machine. Rita, dreaming after the first time she makes love with Betty, cries out in her sleep "Silencio! No hay banda!" Betty shakes her awake and Rita, half dreaming, immediately asks Betty to go somewhere with her. Betty's first reaction is to check the clock: "It's 2 AM," she demurs, sensibly. Rita, like an automaton, repeats "Go somewhere with me," replaying the moment in a proximate disjunction that will start to shake apart Betty's and Rita's double occupancy of Watts's and Haring's bodies. The repetition of Rita's request launches the long arc of aberrant movement to Club Silencio, where the time machine of sound recording and playback proves unlivable for human bodies. Sobbing and seizuring in affective response, they time-travel on a trajectory of violent affects and spatial displacements that only stabilize (momentarily) with the cowboy's injunction to Diane: "Time to wake up." The machine is distributed in this film between recording and playback mechanisms and the mysterious blue box, and the atmospheric thresholdings of Hollywood life.

In *Lost Highway*, Alice and Pete plan to steal money from Andy so that they can run away together; this entire scene is bathed in the blue light of Alice's porn films, a relentless archive of her past. Between the doubled pulsing of the 16mm images and the porn's long thrusting, and Alice's vulgar embodied thievery (she sucks Andy's finger to remove his ring), Pete's headaches ripple the scene as distortions of the image. We are caught up in a bad film of sex and violence. Pete goes upstairs to the bathroom, but instead encounters yet another Alice, mocking his desire to make sense of the scene while she fucks another man. He comes down the stairs and the camera tracks downward from onscreen Alice and her headless partner still thrusting away, to live Alice putting on a stolen watch, before pulling out a gun and playfully threatening Pete. Her vulgar pragmatism is at odds not simply with the murderous scenario, but also with Pete's melodramatic reaction to the image archives that surround and redouble her body. Alice's watch arms her with the tools not to reintegrate her fragmented selves, but to escape and rewrite the image archive: she will only repeatedly disappear from view and from photos alike from this point on. In this scene, there is no crime but time itself, and the police will be able to do nothing with it.

In *Vertigo*, the clock tower/crime scene that allows for a substitution of bodies is only a repeated appointment with death, deferred: the very space of a suspended existence. As with Lynch's untimely machines, animating affective duration in parallel to clock time, Hitchcock's tower is only a composite image of imagination and index. And in *Suzhou River*, videos serve as a timestamp that paradoxically unleashes imprecision; against the measure of recording capacity and perpetual playback, the whole swell of affective memory returns. In these films, time machines are intensive rather than extensive, a time machinics of anotherness. They spark impulsive, eccentric movements, which cannot simply be put right.

These time machinics ask how to negotiate the differential of excess as the remainder of anotherness. Machines here are black boxes of relation, serving to derange. But the ethico-aesthetical question across these films is, How to live in the intensity of becoming's heterogeneity, without falling into exhaustion or death? What kinds of time machinics open to anotherness as a felt futurity? Across *Vertigo* and its affective remakes, this differential might fail at the level of character body, but is made felt, across spectatorial and cinematic bodies, as the sign of the more-to-life, or the productiveness of bodies in time.

At least since Georges Méliès's *Le voyage dans la lune* (1902), the history of cinema is a long archive of images of the future, beautiful and dreadful visions of how the future might look and sound. Cinema today is in what we might call, borrowing from Steven Shaviro, a "postcine-matic" moment, affected, though not caused, by the technologies of the digital turn in cinema. The postcinematic marks a moment when cin-ema has lost its cultural dominance, and enters into an experimentation with new "powers of expression"; in a sense, the anachronistic persistence of the cinematic is precisely a productive eccentricity. An *anarchival* impulse characterizes the postcinematic moment, as we feel new poten-tial emerging from cinema's pastness: a "suspended re-animation" of post-cinematic time machines.[7] Cinematic time machines are reinvented through the production of what I call "anarchival bodies." Suspended between memory and emergent novelty, this anarchival impulse figures suspense itself as a mode of ambiguous embodiment, characterized by the double. This chapter reimagines the question of suspense through two recent examples of anarchival bodies in time-travel cinema: *Looper* (Rian Johnson, 2012) and *The Clock* (Christian Marclay, 2010). These films do not simply represent what the future could look like, but act as machines for felt futurity, sending back affects and sensations as anar-chic artifacts of future potential. The potential of these postcinematic bodies is not as a representational mirror, nor as a prosthetic enhance-ment of our own bodies, nor as a means of experiencing the alterity of others' bodies. These are bodies *as* time machines: our primary mode for rediscovering the heterogeneity of our own existence in time.

Looper

The Face, the Watch, and the Image-Repertoire

These men are Seth. On the right, a young Seth, right on time, stands ready to kill. On the left, Old Seth has just popped out of thin air, having traveled back in time from 2074 to 2044 (the "present" of Johnson's film), the very image of a *décalage*. In the frantic visual collage of an aban-doned and undone structure, their life hangs in the balance. In 2074, time travel is possible but highly illegal, controlled by powerful elites who regulate time in order to maximally extract life from the human bodies under their control. In this dystopian future, people are biotagged and relentlessly surveilled in a society of control via a promise, familiar even to those of us today, of a life without crime. An expanded panopticism

Old and New Seth in *Looper*

renders ambiguous distinct criminal embodiments, preempting any body into a becoming-criminal by the presumption of future guilt. Murder is thus nearly impossible, because a body can always be found.

A futuristic mafia has thus outsourced crime not in space, but in time: by creating a team of assassins thirty years in the past. These "loopers" are recruited by Abe (Jeff Daniels), a seen-it-all type sent back from 2074. When they receive their assignments, the loopers wait in abandoned non-spaces (back alleys, fields and factories: sites of now-defunct labor). They create a tidy and delimited order zone, immediately containing the chaotic potential of time travel by wiping out its effects before they can even take hold. A laughably small square of plastic is spread over the ground, exactly the right size to capture the gory effects of execution. The weapon of choice is a blunderbuss, so named because of its incredibly delimited range. Everything is about precision and compression here: reining in the past and the future.

The loopers patiently wait for their victims to pop up into their crosshairs: springing out of thin air just in time to die. Instantly upon arrival, a brutal and proximate shotgun blast violently thrusts them backward as they are killed. Their disruptive, time-traveling corporeality is thus contained in the characteristic gesture of an automatic chronometer: propulsion and pause, reregulating time. They are one tick of a second hand that goes no further. This image of spatial displacement neatly condenses the tidiness of their temporal displacement and atemporal

murder, archived in the past. Affectively, these murders are both shock-
ingly violent and yet equally bland and predictable, utterly lacking in gore.
Time travel's notorious unruliness is recaptured by this movement-
image of violence, keeping everything in its place. Nothing to see here.
The looper collects his payment—bars of silver strapped to the back of
the victim—banks it with his boss, and goes about his day.

Every now and then, a looper is sent back from the future when his
time is up. These are the past assassins, who wait to contain the temporal disruptions of time-traveling bodies by putting them in their place.
They get to retire and stop killing when their future selves are sent back
for disposal, at which point they know they have only thirty years to live.
Simply a cog in a tightly wound machine, loopers act without thinking.
Only after the fact can it be seen whether the body he has just disposed
of is his future self, signaled across the intervening years by a payload
of gold bars, rather than silver, strapped to the body. In this evaluative
extraction of a life's time, self-murder is paid for by the knowability of a
predictable lifespan. Talk about a retirement plan!

Hooded, bound, and bundled into a time machine in 2074, the (old)
looper named Seth knew his fate, having already lived it via a murderous
gesture thirty years before. Frantically toggling between the long arc of
the past catching up with him and the short circuit of his urgent desire
to live, he lands in the past with a weapon of his own: the refrain of a
childhood song evoking deep memories of a mother's care. He turns on
the playback machine of his body, and hums a few lines as he travels
through time to a past he already knows. Gun at the ready, his younger
self was startled into recognition. Describing this after the fact to his
friend Joe, young Seth remarks in amazement: "He was singing."

The song evoked the memory of a mother's touch in a darkened
room. Guattari describes refrains as "option machines," as a way of putting on hold to perceive the bifurcations of potential springing up at any
moment; that is what is enacted here.[8] Upon hearing that lost refrain,
young Seth lost action's blunt grip on the present, and that brief pause
triggered by the song's affective contagion jammed the machine. Young
Seth removes Old Seth's hood to look into his own face; in the searching
suspension of recognition, he unties Old Seth and "lets his loop run."

Old Seth flees into the city, running off not just into space but into time: a renewed futurity, to be precise, where all bets are off. His refrain functioned to buy enough time to find a different line of flight.

What binds these two Seths? In the shared economy of a single life-span, a doubled life is more than anyone can afford. Young Seth is turned over to his bosses; fearing the temporal disruption that could ensue, they send Old Seth a message to get time running back on track. This communication happens through the medium of a postdigital cinema, intensively rewriting on and through bodies that are simultaneously medium and message, information and materiality. As Old Seth makes his way toward the outskirts of Kansas City, he tries to scale a fence when suddenly a message manifests in the flesh. Whatever happens to Young Seth's body in the present moment manifests as pastness on Old Seth's form. Suddenly scars on his arm reveal an address and time, his flesh becoming the legible clock face of suspense. He hesitates but decides to keep going when his grip fails as his fingers start to disappear. Young Seth is being re-edited, carved up bit by bit, and Old Seth can only try to race back to sync up with his younger self before everything is gone. This scene plays out classic narrative suspense—Will he make it back to Young Seth "on time"?—while also staging a postcinematic fascination with mutable form.

This scene demonstrates two critical points about cinematic time travel. First: it is barely livable: it warps and rearranges the body, it leaves a mark. If our bodies are already composed of speeds and slownesses working at radically different rates, time travel simply amplifies this condition to a noisiness we can no longer ignore. For Old Seth, the present is unbearably intensified by the immediacy of a future manifesting itself as a pastness he hasn't even lived through: scars, amputations, and a body reduced to a vegetative state, kept for the next thirty years in suspense to hold in place the events of the past. His past thus appears so fast that he can't even see it move. At least since *La Jetée*, the bodies of time travelers have been explicitly depicted as physically damaged by the experience, drained of a vital force, and needing machines to keep them alive. In that film, still images double the stutter of the protagonist's wasted body, brutally contrasting the violence of change and the exhaustion of a body that cannot even get up. In other time-travel films, even if the bodies stay visibly intact on the outside, they are disrupted in other ways, often expressed through the warping of cinematic form as well. No one comes through unscathed. Consider the dangerous force of attraction released by Marty McFly's temporal dislocation in *Back to the Future* (1985); when he travels back in time to the bifurcation point that makes his own existence possible—the moment where his parents fall in love—he introduces through his smooth embodiment a crack in the past when his mother falls in love not with his father, but with him. Her hot desire for Marty threatens to retroactively erase his own birth, and the film figures this through the fading in and out of his body, as if he is being overexposed by the glare of lust. His visible body ghosts as it waxes and wanes between futures. These threats figure how bodies do not simply move through time, but that time as a key element of their makeup is as vulnerable to existential mutation as DNA.

Second, time travel in a postdigital cinema plays out on two bodies at once: in the flesh, and in the image. Cinema today has stutteringly incorporated, through the ubiquity of digital effects, a wholehearted shift to digital shooting, editing, and distribution platforms. At the same time, cinema is itself *ex-corporated* and re-embodied by digital technologies. This doubling, an intension of extension, extends to our own corporealities via new potentials for embodiment and through new kinds of intensity. In considering time travel today in postdigital cinema, the urgent question is, How do we live our media archives? Hagener and Elsaesser have suggested that cinema today is shifting from a way of seeing the world to a way of being in the world—a new life form. But this claim's potential exceeds a shift from digital to analogue, also speaking to the saturation of our existential territories with media images and experiences that we ambiguously possess and are possessed by. Suspended across memory, replay, and remixing, these images are not of a world, but are wholly what the world we live in feels like, traveling across subjective, social, and media ecologies. Time travel, here understood as something other than a displacement along a predetermined continuum, a spatialized image of time, is a practice of anotherness. The violence toward bodies, the generic affiliation of time-travel cinema with the motivational spur of death or apocalypse, can be understood here through the crime of time precisely as the making-apparent of anotherness in the act.

Surrounded by the moving mirror of media that continually duplicate our actual existence, what do we do with an archive of media pastness? How and when does this allow us to experience futurity not as a utopian image of "the future," but as an immanent, *anarchival* sensation of futurity itself, a re-worlding? My term *anarchive* doesn't simply invert the archive as the uncaptured, like the ephemerality of the living body in performance. Instead, and in proximity to the derangements and destruction of time traveling bodies, the anarchive releases an anarchic impulse geared toward disorder, chaos, or the virtual dimension of existence—What else could happen?—and the ethical question that accompanies it—How else can the future be?

Time travel's link to futurity is often figured through a visible engagement with extensive technologies of expanded action. The trick often seems to involve reining in the unlivable quality of the expanded possibilities of these technologies, to give the unthinkable potential a human dimension. One could see, for instance, the desperate gesture of a re-mixed, dinosaur-riding Adam and Eve as response to the secularizing imperative of geological time measured against a granular scale of human action. Promptness—the need to be right on time—as in *Back to the Future,* or the Sisyphean labor of repeated murder in *Timecrimes* (2007), is another response. Marshall McLuhan described media as an extension of human beings necessarily counterbalanced by a preservative "auto-amputation": "Such amplification is bearable by the nervous system only through numbness or blocking of perception."[9] But to think media archives otherwise, through the intensions of extensions, is to become attentive to their anarchival effects. Not a numbness or blocking of perception, this expanded perception includes what does not directly appear: the linear form of time, or suspense in its double action. To think in these terms, we need to be attentive to how difference is made: repetition as a free replay. If cinema is a time machine for communicating with the future, that communication works through intensity and the body. How are time machines sites for auto-affection, means of directly experiencing the fracture in the I?

During the *in extremis* of time travel, the nature of this intensity stems from the sensational awareness of other durations, emergent when one's own habitual rhythm is suspended. Our engagements with media allow us to experience our corporeality via an intensive extension. By this, I mean an extension of the body that is not simply spatial, but one that works via the resonance of affective encounter on the incorporeal dimension of the body, which includes memory, habit, gestures as well as an interstitial glue holding together materiality over time. Bodies are sites of the duplicity of the informational and material that makes up our contemporary media ecologies. This is a feeling of futurity that allows us to sense the body's ongoing becoming in time, how we endure futurity itself. This intensive extension doubles our sense of immediate perception, introducing a perceptible delay into experience, a minor gap. No longer a question of a perceiving subject and a perceived object, this intensive extension makes relation felt as a resonant reserve of potential. In a reconsideration of how we live our media archives, and what kind of experience this gives us, we must ask, is cinema—ambiguously embodied in both our memories and the actual archives of media forms—more than a set of secondhand memories? How can we see cinema as an archive of the future, beyond just the picture postcards it seems to send back? In Chris Marker's *Sans Soleil,* this sense of the postcard is animated in the *Vertigo* sequence. Frames from *Vertigo* are presented alongside a narrated recall of this film. But each still shot (formally suspended between Hitchcock's film and Marker's own time-travel photo-essay *La Jetée*) is presented and then immediately animated through a gesture of blur and refocusing. This is not just a reintroduction of movement, but a foregrounding of the act of perception itself as a double vision. In this way, reanimation activates the vitality affect of the thing *and* its perception.

Anna Munster describes intensity as an extension that is not itself corporeal (as with, for instance, prosthetics) but "comprising an intensive capacity for being affected by the diverse speeds, rhythms and flows of information."[10] The effect of this is an "extensive vector that draws embodiment away from its historical capture within a notion that the body is a bounded interiority."[11] This requires thinking ecologically, rather than environmentally, as bodies are displaced in time. A requisite side effect, I suggest, is a reconsideration of subjectivity in Guattari's terms of emergent alterfication, of a "play" of intensity that is not for the self, but for the whole cosmos. In the Stargate sequence in *2001,* we can no longer discern not only the difference between cyborg Dave's intensive corporeal experience and the external form of outer space, ultimately resulting in a body time traveling through a constant lag with itself, triggered through not an amputated perception but a movement-image in which the double is released from the mirror. This play of the self for the cosmos is an impulse muted and modulated in *Looper,* where the key conflicts of the film are played out in a sugarcane field. Although sugar is not a crop currently grown in Kansas, where the film is set (though it is found in Louisiana, where it was shot), the everyday-apocalypse feel of the film suggests that climate change has simply edged the warmth needed for sugarcane ever further north.

Looper embodies a number of the potentials of a postcinematic moment, where the "post" is an ambivalent marker of what else cinema might be. On the surface, the film is well within the generic tradition of time-travel movies, a specific genre that in some ways is becoming a generalized condition of a postdigital cinema. Looper *is* about time travel, but it also gives us the feeling of time travel as a way of feeling futurity itself, precisely through a suspended reanimation of the media archive. In other words, form and content indiscernibly duplicate each other to produce a heterochronic encounter, the feeling of multiple times coexisting at once. The main characters of the film are a pair of Joes: Young Joe (Joseph Gordon-Levitt), a callow young looper with Mommy issues working in 2044, and his future self, Old Joe (Bruce Willis), who successfully survives his outsourced assassination and who seeks to find and murder the child in 2044 who grows into 2074's Rainmaker, a mysterious figure responsible for the order to suddenly "close all the loops" and murder the loopers en masse. Unlike Old Seth, who hits pause by activating memory, Old Joe manages to fight back when he is captured in the future. During his struggle, his wife is accidentally shot and killed; though he manages to escape his captors, he still decides to return to the past in the hopes of rewriting her death. He appropriates the time machine for his own purposes, and spins around to emerge in the past with his back to Young Joe. The blast hits him right in the gold bars; though stunned, he gets up and punches out Young Joe before he can recover from the shock, and then escapes. Replaying the earlier scene with Seth, Young Joe reaches out to Old Joe by carving a message into his own flesh. Old Joe's scars direct him, via a woman's name, to an old diner he used to frequent.

The two Joes meeting in the diner is a key scene: the potential of this encounter inspired the whole film. Here, *Looper* both evokes and dismisses the impossible narrative of time travel in favor of an extended showing of an intensive prosthetics. Like Winkie's diner in *Mulholland Drive*, *Looper*'s diner serves as a cinematic non-place anchoring time travel in the body and simultaneously exposing the artificial rhythms linking bodily urges and ecological surrounds (Breakfast all day! Open 24 hours!). Both films exploit the diner's indifferent and homogeneous space-time, drawing from its clichéd repetition what Foucault would call the heterochronic quality of this heterotopic space.[12] In *Mulholland Drive*, during the first diner scene, one man (Patrick Fischler) tells another (Michael Cooke) that his real motivation for their meeting was to replay a terrifying dream. Their conversation begins as banal and conventional shot-reverse-shot, but within this conventional choreography, the camera repeatedly moves restlessly in an eccentric fashion. The scene continually animates the replay on every level, building the repetition to horrific

Old and New Joe meet for the first time at the diner in *Looper*.

effect. The first man recounts his dream in a long take only interrupted when the camera follows his look when he says to his companion, "Of all people, you are standing right over there, by that counter," and the camera, shooting the dreamer's face from the point of view of the second man, floats its gaze across the room. The second man starts to live the dream as it makes its way into his flesh and movements: we witness the virtual actualizing. After he describes the dream, everything plays out helplessly in the most literal fashion that does nothing to undercut the absolute terror of the scene. The second man takes action; standing up and walking to the counter to pay, he says, "Let's go out back and find the source of the dream terror." The first man turns his head and the camera repeats the pan across to the counter, only now, as in the dream, the second man stands there.

Here, the replays don't supplement (with other subjective perspectives or more information) our knowledge of the scene. They redistribute embodiment across camera and character, dream and waking, original and repetition. This scene is the LA version of Scottie's first glimpse of Madeleine in Ernie's restaurant, with a gesture that arcs across bodies. There, the impossible objective shots float away from character perspectives, but here, the impossible objective activates a time lag through the replay of the gesture of turning one's head. The second man's gaze is first traced by the camera, and then repeated to allow him to see himself, impossibly, across two moments in time, and between dream and action. Winkie's, of course, is replayed twice in *Mulholland Drive,* and those subsequent scenes, first with Betty and Rita and then with Diane and the hit man, continually try to recenter our attention and calm us down, as with the close-ups of the waitress's name badge that seem to help put things in place. But the diner conversations are also haunted by a movement-vision of that most restrictive of character-based cinematic techniques: shot-reverse-shot. In a thoroughly eccentric gesturality, the camera gives us the feeling of anotherness through the floating away from a stable, centering shot. It is an incredibly eerie effect, replicated later in the floating tracking shot through Betty's apartment with no body attached after Rita opens the blue box. Double vision here is suspended formally between character focalization and a suspended POV that floats around the body, and narratively between the dream account that becomes description replacing its object, a terrifying enactment of the powers of the false.

Differently, *Looper* also plays with the formal and figural problem of double occupancy. Old Joe enters the diner warily, attuned to the danger of the present moment and caught up in a past he both recalls and works against. The Joes sit face to face, and the film lingers over profile two-shots and close-ups that both mirror how they search each other for signs of themselves, and how we as audience members assess the persuasive value of their likeness. If in *Vertigo* and its remakes, the actress's body kept rippling our surface reading of character, in an uncertainty that traveled across diegetic and non-diegetic forms, here, the actors' bodies put their labor-of-likeness on display, the work of time itself held up for us to see as the narrative cover of the physical gap. The Joes examine each other skeptically. Young Joe asks for an explanation, and Old Joe blows him (and us) off, mocking the explanatory cliché: "I'm not here to talk about time travel shit, because if we start talking about it then we're going to be here all day and making diagrams with straws. It doesn't matter." But Young Joe picks up on the figural problem of the body in time when he takes Old Joe's rejection of sense making—"It doesn't matter"—and immediately makes it into a lived experience of corporeal/incorporeal change: "If I hurt myself it changes your body; this what I do now, change your memory." The scene stages time as a problem that can't simply be elliptically ignored.

What fascinates in this face-to-face encounter with another self is the helpless obviousness that they aren't the same person. Cinematic time travel involves not a displacement from place to place, but travel as intensity of staying in place—the production of heterochronic fissures. In this encounter, the body's anotherness is both externally present, as both Joes search each other to refocus the movement-vision jet lag of time travel, into a mirror-vision that will allow (one of) them to act in a determinate way. But it is also intensively present, in an image that won't settle down, in the searching of the audience to refocalize these multiple identities to make sense out of sensation. In *Looper*, the gamble of the diner scene is also a delicate negotiation of convention, expectation, and fragile belief; in this scene, if not in the film as a whole, double vision continually pulls away from self-reflexivity to self-referentiality, a coming-to-believe. This move includes the audience as well, and the gamble on self-referentiality, the movement-vision of auto-affection, is what makes the film itself into a time machine. Three forms of the anarchival impulse are manifested through the bodies in *Looper,* which suggest that futurity is communicated through bodies, that our bodies *are* the way that we live the media archives of cinema as an anarchival time machine.

The first is the use of prosthetics, most notably used to make Gordon-Levitt's face more closely resemble that of Willis. These prosthetics were created by Jamie Kelman and Kazu Tsuji, and took three hours to apply each day of shooting; no digital effects were used. We have previously considered films in which the doubled body of the actress produces a prosthetic effect of a body too much, where performance itself becomes a prosthetic. In *Looper,* prosthetics are a mode of ambiguous embodiment distributed between Levitt's and Willis's bodies, holding open the relation between them as the very image of suspended potential. The exaggerated visibility of the prosthetic devices in *Looper* is frequently remarked in reviews of the film; they don't smooth the gap between the two actors, but produce an uncanny valley of just-noticeable difference. In a film with a careful attentiveness to setting and art direction as the signs of a heterochronicity (at one point a world-weary crime boss remarks to Joe that the trendy styles he wears are based upon movies that are just themselves copies of older movies), the actor's face functions as another platform of heterochronic instability, signaling the film's commitment to the messiness of time travel when time is not longer a spatialized linearity. This is explicitly illustrated in a flash-forward sequence that is actually a flashback. Young Joe falls out of his apartment window while trying to escape his bosses, seeking to make him pay for letting his loop run. He smashes into a car on the way down and is knocked unconscious. Suddenly, the film cuts and he is back in the field waiting for Old Joe to arrive to be murdered. In the exaggeratedly blue sky, a strange cloud, a long scrawled form more like a signature, signals figurally the clock face of an as-yet illegible time. Is this a dream? A fantasy of another life? Old Joe arrives, and this time Young Joe successfully murders him, and retires. We witness his prescribed future unfold: he squanders his fortune in China, and eventually becomes a gun for hire. The years leap ahead at the rhythm of his degeneracy, and there is suddenly a gap of thirteen years. This gap is the opportune space to cover the difference between Willis and Levitt, but instead we are offered one shot, before the leap forward, of a ridiculously bewigged Willis before the film settles into his future Joe. What we witnessed is a flashback on Old Joe's part; this was his life, and we accompany him right up to the moment when the future comes for him to send him back to the past. But it is equally an unrealized future for Young Joe, and in staging a double occupancy of Old Joe as his younger self, the film once again dramatizes the problem of a body in time.

In a similar suspense, Levitt's face never quite belongs to him. He plays the role with an exaggerated facial mobility, like he is constantly practicing actions in front of a mirror. His face is immediately relational in its plasticity in a way that isn't simply a self-reflexive commentary. Like Novak's insufficiently delineated performance as Madeleine and Judy, Levitt never quite disappears into a younger version of Willis, but remains a formal image of the body in time. As such, the performance of Levitt stages the problem too of the "proper name," as described by Deleuze and Guattari. For them, "the proper name does not designate an individual: it is on the contrary when the individual opens up to multiplicities pervading him or her, at the outcome of the most severe operation of depersonalization, that he or she acquires his or her true proper name."[13] Although Levitt's performance lacks the tour de force quality of Laura Dern's in *Inland Empire,* there remains a productive ambiguity in his performance that confuses character body, actor body (both his and Willis's) and cinematic body (the resolutely nondigital prosthetic).

The second form of the anarchival impulse in *Looper* is in the suspended referentiality of casting. If Levitt is indistinctly himself and a mobile semblance of becoming-Bruce-Willis, both actors and both Joes are themselves duplicated through the persistent tickle at the back of memory of their other time-traveling roles. For Levitt, this is most notably for *Inception,* in which time travel is both a fight for the future and a kind of transversal surfing across different speeds and slownesses of dream strata. He also played as a child in the time-travel TV drama *Quantum Leap.* In a flickering suspension between diegetic and non-diegetic, a different kind of time travel played out in the long arc of his growing into adulthood from child-star fame on the television series *Third Rock from the Sun.* There, the fact that his character's human teenage body housed a much older alien consciousness meant his character continually lived two lives at once, a gap played for laughs. In *Looper,* there is a curious gesture Levitt makes with his mouth and his thumb, a kind of grimace and wipe, that cinephically invokes not Willis but Robert De Niro (himself a notoriously mutable body and doubly incorporated as a time traveler between himself and Marlon Brando in his role as young Don Corleone in *The Godfather II*). Willis is of course most famously a time traveler in Terry Gilliam's remake of *La Jetée: 12 Monkeys.* There, he reprises Davos Hanich's role as "The Man," in an elastic take on the part that stretches into a whole other storyline but snaps back into replay at the moment of his airport death, a moving mirroring of Hanich's suspended fall in *La Jetée.*

But beyond the tight circuit of the two Joes, *Looper* is littered with such recastings and reembodiments, provoking memories of a generic archive of time travel media. Sarah (played by Emily Blunt, star of the sinisterly bureaucratic time travel 2011 film *The Adjustment Bureau*) is the mother of the child that Old Joe has traveled back in time to kill, and Young Joe's lover. This character instantly recalls by name and function Sarah Connor, mother to John Connor in the *Terminator* series. That series is notable both as a set of time-travel movies and as a key reference in cinema history for the digital/analog bodily divide (between Schwarzenegger's machinic T-1 and the liquid fluidity of T-2, not to mention the fluidity of the endless remakes, which more than sequels are remakes as re-worldings). This reference is transmedially extended when the hit man who arrives at Sarah's door to kill Young Joe is played by Garret Dillahunt, from the TV series reboot of *The Terminator: The Sarah Connor Chronicles.* In that series, he plays Cromartie, a terminator sent back from the future to assassinate John Connor. Dillahunt also starred in *Damages,* a television series characterized by what Toni Pape calls "preemptive narrative," mobilized around figures of time, which exceed a simple and explanatory flashback structure.[14]

These ambiguous embodiments are what make *Looper* a suspense film in the expanded sense I have been exploring throughout this book, through the relations of affect, embodiment, and time. As with the corporeal turn, the work of the spectator's embodied relation to the image is central here. Unlike Barthes's suggestion that suspense grips you in the mind, not the guts, this isn't just a question of being "in the know" in a way that allows a spectator to play with the pleasures of recognition in a postmodern pastiche. The malleability of these ambiguous references don't just call up and re-sort the database of a media archive, they give us the *feeling of memory* itself in a sensation duplication of the film's narrative refoldings of time. However, beyond a "what my fingers knew" of corporeal recognition, the time travel unleashed by the film's play and punning on circuits of memory remain held in the productive ambiguity of what counts in our recognition. Bodies are problems here, and although the film literally enacts Comolli's wish, "May it disappear!," when Young Joe ultimately kills himself to unwind the crime of the boy's murder by Old Joe, this narrative capture of self-referential excess remains unsettled in our own memory archive. *Looper* doubles the film's time travel renarrativizing through reaching out to the archive of other media in a way that makes our knowledge a productive problem.

Finally, the film's third instance of anarchival impulses redistributes archives not in objects, but in movements and gestures, locating it in time itself as the site of an anarchival impulse. In *La Jetée*, a film composed of still images, time travel leaps into the past first into a museum as archive, and the Man and Woman tend their love in sites of memory. A key scene involves a repetition of the archival forest of *Vertigo*, when Madeleine touches the rings of a redwood tree trunk in a natural–cultural gesture across ghostly bodies. Between the tree's taxidermied remains and Madeleine's performed possession, spotted by Scottie's recording gaze, the green glow of the leafy canopy—equally borrowed from the media archive (Hitchcock's memory of tinted silent cinema)— serves as the medium of suspense. In *La Jetée* this happens again, only this time

The Man doubles and echoes The Woman's reach into the past in the face of a sectioned tree.

The gesture between lovers here is suspended in a repetition intensifying between still image and screen duration, opening onto the thirdness of spectatorial memory. Guattari writes, "Discursivity is not pure succession without memory. Memories themselves are not simple passive

Madeleine in the forest of time in *Vertigo*.

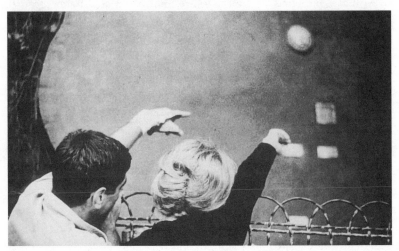

Double gestures of cinephilia and love in *La Jetée*.

The violence of cross-temporal touching from *Vertigo* to *Looper*.

recordings. All memories are machines. All machines are memories."[15] This machinic quality of heterogeneous production is evident in the work of memory itself. In the reversible loop of memory and machine, playback and recording are made felt as experiences of immediation. That is to say, something is added and made out of the work of memory.

In *Looper*, our first sight of Sarah is her chopping away at a stubborn tree trunk in the middle of a natural–cultural field surrounding her farm, evoking the tree rings in Marker's *La Jetée*, repurposed from Hitchcock's *Vertigo* as the archive of untimely love and reanimated by the gesture of tracing the arc of a life. The violence of her nonpreservative chopping situates her body against the violence of a time travel that will seek to undo her life. Like Madeleine, Sarah lives a life that is not entirely her own; pretending to be an aunt to the child she is raising, she is in fact his mother. The entire last half of *Looper* takes place, improbably, on her farm, miles away from the frenetic rhythms of urban life that so often make up the archive of the future as imaged by cinema, and that characterize the opening of *Looper* as well. The surrounding fields are themselves temporal archives of a future yet-to-come: as danger comes closer and closer to home, Sarah still doesn't want to burn them and clear a protective field of visibility despite the threat that they can hide, because they hold the promise of an income for next year in their seeds. Danger and debt conflict as competing temporal rhythms of urgent immediacy and projective stability. The fields become a stage of the appearance and disappearance of bodies in time. When she finishes with the tree, Sarah takes a seat on her porch and, miming the gestures, pulls out an imaginary cigarette, taps the tobacco and, draws in the memory of smoke as the mark of labor's pause. Suspended across memory, gesture, and cliché, the image speaks to the complicated embodiments of anarchival impulses.

These impulses are for me the key interest of *Looper* as a work of a postdigital moment, beyond any narrative of time travel itself. The film ends conventionally enough, recuperating many of its disruptive impulses via narrative smoothing. At the same time, though, the film as a time machine continually produces a series of suspended reanimations that self-referentially have no where to go except into the spectator's body as a site of intensity. The effect, the sign of suspense we have been tracing here, is a double vision of a suspended reanimation at work in postdigital cinema, which, as part of its repurposing of cinematic archives to anarchival ends, is concerned with making potential itself felt.

In the scene of the first encounter at the diner of Old and New Joe, the heterochronic potential is figured as "cloudy" or blurred, with images of the past coming only into an after-the-fact focus for Old Joe. For example, as he begins to rewrite the past, he struggles to hold onto the memories of the life he has led, and in particular those of his wife. As he speaks he clutches but does not look at a photo of her that he carries, an unstable index like that of Renée and Alice in Pete's home. We could easily think of this description as a lazy cop-out designed to elide the narrative problems of time travel cinema, a kind of sleight of hand that misdirects our gaze. But actually, this blur is not only a good description of what futurity feels like (not an image of or from the future, but the future as heterogeneous potential, or the virtual). It also shifts our attention in the scene to the strangeness of trying to resolve these two characters, a struggle they experience and that we do too: a shared and distributed problem. The multiplicity of points of view at play here are not simply an accumulation of relative perspectives, one that could be resolved by a question of which identity will win out, of reconciling competing claims to possession. Here, point of view "belongs so much to the thing that the thing is constantly being transformed in a becoming identical to point of view.

Metamorphosis of the true."[16] This metamorphosis of the true is anotherness is action: the feeling of futurity. The thing here is not simply an
object described, but precisely the ambiguous embodiment where it
is not clear what belongs: the event of the cinematic moment. We witness and participate in the making-sensible of the movement of change
itself through the blur of double vision. This is the effect of a cinematic
time machine, giving us not simply a representation of bodies, but a
direct, *self-referential* experience of the incorporeal dimension of the body,
a moving image of our own potential in relation. As a time machine,
cinema makes us feel the futurity of our own embodiment, communicating a reservoir of potential precisely through an embodiment much
like our own.

Staging the problem of resemblance in this scene, the suspense that
fails to simply resolve or disappear thus extends into semblance. Bodies
are supercharged with a potential that does not, or cannot, immediately
extend into action. What is at stake is the potential of different modes of
suspense. Early in the film, Young Joe, orphaned at an early age, revisits
his mommy issues during a bought session with his favorite stripper/
sex worker, Suzie (Piper Perabo). He seeks to trade money for affection;
though she does what she is paid for, she refuses his offer of more money
to help her raise her child. Images of a clock open and close that scene,
bookending a period of paid time. Although he asks her to activate an
altered state for him, first through her applying a drug to his eyes, and
then through her reenactment of his mother's touch by running her
fingers through his hair, the film reminds us that this affect is *quantifi-
able* as simply memory-images or altered states, limited by the exchange
of money for time. Our first view of Sarah, who will be part of a love
relation that travels across and between bodies in time, is bookended by
the tree trunk and the imagined cigarette, ambiguous archives of a time
that hesitates between seeing and reading. This tension between clock
time and affective time hinges on the notion that the time of affect cannot be bought and paid for. It creates an alternative form of suspense.

For an action film, *Looper* engages in a lot of waiting, as the cane field
setting of much of the second half of the film turns characters into plant
men, living slow rhythms of change rather than explosions. Semblance

is felt as intensity itself, unlivable to the point of auto-destruction, deadly to the body's integrity, and triggered by love. At the diner, Old Joe tells the story of how after he retired, he became an addict and a criminal, squandering his life and money. Finally, he met a woman (in a tired cliché, a smiling, silent, and helpful Asian woman), fell in love, and thus came back to a life ticking away in a predetermined finitude. As he tells the story, he clutches a locket, resembling his old-fashioned pocket watch, with her photo inside. Young Joe, negotiating their twining lives and looking for the double way out, says, Show me the picture, when I see her I'll walk away and she will be safe for never having loved me. But Old Joe cannot accept this infidelity of his former self to his image of love, needing to remain wholly faithful to his own experience, even at the cost of his lover's life. He just grips the image tighter, unwilling to let the (re)semblance go, needing to keep the charge of its capacitation for himself to deploy in a future he has already mapped. In time travel cinema, the derangements of linear causality and narrative produce conditions that are *actually* unlivable, hence the continual association with death. Old Joe clings to this archive of the future as fixed, because he wants to live. When he looks into time, a fixed image of the loved one's face fails to open onto another world; a seeing through to himself is his only response to the intensity of double vision. Semblance describes the sensational temporality of the event itself, the form of what does not appear, the felt presence of both past and future. This double vision, a blurred gaze, sees form with and through potential, undoing the sharp point of the single axis of vision.

A feeling of futurity does not emerge from a traditional distinction of the live and the recorded, but speaks to the liveliness of the media archive itself today. Semblance, despite the connotation of a second-order reality, or irreality, is not the ghostly trace of a past event, defined by resemblance. In *Looper*, the suspension of knowledge and the refusal to identify a "knower" is consistently delayed as the affective motor of the film, and is part of the eventful openness of the work; it matters beyond the narrative resolution. In fact, this resolution—Young Joe kills himself to prevent Old Joe from killing the child who will become the Rainmaker—still produces an excess of impossible and ambiguous knowledge. The final scene of the film shows Sarah running her fingers through the hair of Young Joe as he lies dead (after taking his watch), carrying forward a gesture of care from Joe's memory archive of his mother, reanimating through touch an immediate past that should be wiped out by the paradox of time travel (How can she remember Old Joe when New Joe's suicide has eliminated him?). That which should (no longer) appear still lingers through a borrowed corporeality, layering the image of the mother and the lover in a nod to Tarkovsky's *The Mirror*, another time travel film where the same actress doubly embodies both mother and lover as well.

Semblance provocatively foregrounds the powers of the false, the creative force of artifice not to represent but to generate "more world" and reroutes them away from their negative and even criminal orientation; this generative falseness is the name for creative recomposition. It doesn't just produce a near-miss that we should gloss over; semblance is there to be felt as one of the ways that *Looper* gives us a feeling of futurity through a cinematic time machine. As Barbara Flisser points out, "There is no reanimating the past without a fabulation of the future."[17] Semblance is felt when things are sundered from their utility; Massumi makes this argument in the context of redefining "interactivity" not as the ability of a subject to act upon an object, but as the sensation of a re-worlding, the event's unfolding and the self-enjoyment of the event in an affective attunement. This charging of capacity does not reflexively reconfirm what we already know, but activates the powers of the false as the emergence of the new. The self-referentiality of experiencing eventness is felt as "duplicity," yet another term laden with criminal intent. Semblance and duplicity displace the connotation of a second-order of representation or copying with the directly expressive powers of the false.

Cinematic suspense gives us the image of how we are in time, the double experience of the consistency of the self in its becoming (an) other. This suspendedness is neither displacement nor alienation, but a felt infidelity to the self in *Looper* dramatically evidenced by Young Joe's suicide, understood here as the "crime of time." "Suspense" films subject us to "the crime of time" as the felt force of becoming, producing a disorienting "double vision." Young Joe announces in voiceover his intention to suicide by saying "I saw it" (a future that loops through his own past as abandoned and traumatized child); his clarity of action cuts through all the suspended potentials of the scene. In *Looper*, character bodies become the legible instruments of the time machine, which produce an uncoordinated excess beyond the narrative erasures of the complicated problem of shared embodiment. I turn now to Christian Marclay's recent twenty-four-hour compilation film, *The Clock*, to explore a new mode of suspense film working its irresolutions.

Time Takings

Marclay's award-winning film could be seen as the high-art take on the same emerging postdigital genre that *Looper* engages, classified as database cinema, the puzzle film, complicated narratives, atemporal cinema or the mind-game film, those films that offer complex articulations of time. As a postdigital reactivation of the cinematic archive, *The Clock* is a suspended (re)animation. If *Looper* relies on the suspended reanimation of acting, characters' bodies, and embodied gestures to help give the feeling of futurity in a deviation of expectation, *The Clock* capacitates spectatorial bodies in a related but different mode, displacing the camera with the digital video editing system. Marclay's archival compilation film is an artifact from a postcinematic future that makes reading into a productive problem. Is his work just a nostalgic re-viewing, along the lines of something like the enormously popular compilation films, such as *That's Entertainment* (1974), a recut of the greatest hits of Hollywood musicals? Is it just an appropriation of the low cultural form of fan-produced supercut? Or does Marclay's film (itself wildly popular and made of popular media) intensify repetition through the work of the remake, in order to shake loose a new indetermination of cinema?

Describing a new virtuosic fascination with the exceptionally long take enabled by digital recording in films like *Russian Ark*, David Rodowick argues that "this conceit or folly of wanting to film uninterrupted duration is a way of showing that (real) time is neither homogeneous nor continuous."[18] How does Marclay's work also produce suspense, not in the traditional form of narrative suspense, but through an affective solicitation of our own habits of memory and recognition to reopen us to the intensive multiplicity of repetition? Like *Russian Ark* (also an example of cinema in the museum), the inhuman duration of *The Clock* not only speaks to the shifts in contemporary viewing practices, but is also a witty commentary on the increasing institutionalization of cinematic practices within the museum spaces. As a twenty-four-hour film, *The Clock* is impossibly suspended between object and lived experience, and as such, reorients questions of interactivity at the heart of contemporary debates around art in general and the specific fate of cinema as an old media. Marclay's film is a loop of microevents that go nowhere, alternating between seriality and sequence, staging movement events and mini-narratives across diverse films that continually fail to resolve. In the midnight hour, a woman hears a noise and crosses the room, passing through multiple years, across spaces that flicker between black and white and color, across homes grand and plebeian, to open a door into nothing. She is impersonally embodied across actors' forms in a shifting exchange of possession. The causality of her movement impulse dissolves into a virtual set of relations; narrative suspense is staged, "capacitated," but has nowhere to go, except into an intensified recirculation in the cinematic body. What difference does this experience make?

In *Looper*, the discomfort and destruction of blurred vision proves unlivable in a way that largely recuperates narrative sense, reinvesting futurity in the figure of the child via Young Joe's messianic gesture of self-erasure. A more interesting and even more ethical proposition of futurity might be not to stage the future in the image of the past. Instead, how can a film amplify a counter-effectuation that destroys and disorganizes a body to increase the potential for the anotherness of connection itself? Claire Colebrook identifies this potential as a specifically cinematic impulse, or what Deleuze might call "having an idea in cinema." She writes, "Cinema both extends the eye—as in forms of documentary or realism that expand the organism's range of possible action through greater knowledge and familiarity—and also destroys the eye as organ: this occurs when the potential for the eye is detached from an organic time of possibility, tending toward a *counter-actualizing* time of potentiality."[19] This time is the feeling of futurity. Colebrook's nonpreservative extension raises the question: Can we think media archives beyond a prosthetic model of memory? The prosthetic model tends to keep the body intact, minimizing the intensive side of these extensions. How might we think this intensity as a counteractualizing force, a destructive cut necessary for a relinkage?

Hitchcock was not known for his concern for the tender fallibility of the human body. His legendary cruelty, which included daring a technician to spend a night chained up in an allegedly haunted studio, only to secretly dose him with a laxative beforehand, made him a ruthless manipulator of his audiences, noting that they should be "played upon" like an organ, reimagining flesh as instrumentalized. But in a rare instance of concern for the human weakness of his audience, Hitchcock once thoughtfully mused that "the length of a film should be directly related to the endurance of the human bladder." Twenty-first-century posthuman fantasy, concerned with the extensions of humankind in many corporeal directions, has done little to extend this particular endurance, making the idea of a twenty-four-hour movie a seemingly sadistic joke. Only nostalgic masochists, yearning for the iron-fisted authenticity of a theatrical experience, too foolish to let the DVD remote serve the rhythms of the body and to let human agency reassert itself over the machine, could possibly think this was a good idea. Or is it rather the case that in a postcinematic moment, a twenty-four-hour film is the only possible response of cinema's exhausted body, stumbling through the dance marathon of the contemporary 24/7 audiovisual cycle we live in? Is even cinema exhausted by the homogeneity of modern time consciousness, where one moment is the same as the next, so that the entire world can synchronize its watches so that planes and trains run on time? If Bliss Cua Lim argues that the homogeneity of modern time consciousness is an attempt to eliminate the felt force of the fantastic as the trace of immisicible time, the magic hours of cinema, long read as a kind of emblem of modern time, now appear as the really apparitional of a special and rare experience of untimely duration.

It is a cold night in February 2011, and Ottawa is dark by the time we arrive at the National Art Gallery. Only a special, twenty-four-hour screening of *The Clock* is happening; the rest of the art sleeps out of sight, drowsy and invisible. Everything is appropriately dim and hushed as we enter a long black room graphically studded with white couches. It is already 11 PM, and people loiter at the edges of the room with one eye on the screen and the other on couching patrons, ready to dart over and claim a comfy spot when a seat is abandoned. Discouraged by museum staff from bringing in our sleeping bags and other small, sustaining comforts, we make do with the mass market IKEA couches cut to the measure of a mannequin's body. Too short to stretch out on or to accommodate a non-intimate threesome, with no support for neck and back, the couches are an unlikely choice for an endurance event. What kind of person has given serious thought to what it might take to sustain such a film? Marclay's work prompts the question: How would you curate such untimely art?

The conceit of the film is simple and clever at once, so much so that upon reading the description, you may already feel like you "get it," and maybe don't even need to see it with your own eyes. Over the course of three years, Marclay and his assistants trawled the depths of TV and cinema archives from more than one hundred years to assemble a vast database of material. Made up of remixed and extracted clips almost exclusively from feature-length films, at first *The Clock*'s central idea plugs easily into our contemporary attention economy of the forwarded video clip.

Marclay has a long history of working in this remix tradition, and was a pioneer in the potential of working with digital images. With *Telephone* (1995), he brought the present and the past into ambiguous communication, in a hilarious and horrifying compilation of actors answering telephone calls in the movies, a conversation without end or point that relays the replay of the audiovisual archive. With *Video Quartet* (2002), a four-channel DVD projection with sound, he redistributed the remix mode across four horizontal screens in an astonishing audiovisual symphony. Working with images of musical performance from seven hundred feature films, he created a fourteen-minute loop that dances rhythms of attention across the four screens. The images sync and desync repeatedly; sometimes all the screens share the same image, sometimes none. That work sparked admiration from critics for its display of the potential of digital technologies, a heroic effort that would have seemed dauntingly impossible just a few years before.

His remix films both pillage and re-sort a doubly distributed cinematic archive. First, he and his assistants dig through archives, inscribed in hundreds of films, in a long process of cataloguing, sorting, and editing: the very definition of a "database cinema." Second, and more ambiguously, however, his work also accesses an archive of recirculations, virtually distributed across spectatorial memories of cinema. He creates compilations that draw on and deviate from the source material in the search for something new, but where novelty is also an emergent property of the habitual experiences of cinephilic gestures. For *The Clock*, he searched for images that spoke of time—clocks, watches, references, bodily postures, hourglasses, and rhythms of life personal and collective.

This idea, the compilation remix, has already lived a thousand lives in YouTube videos, which extract a theme and replay them to humorous and/or exhausted effect. Again and again, a thousand rebellious police officers angrily surrender to a bureaucratic mandate to "turn in your badge and gun." These compilations dry up the source material quickly, gaining instead a movement across the impulse to share, in a digital gesture of forwarding. Marclay's films, repositioning the interactivity of a media termed "participatory" in the museum, instead "capacitate" the work, suspending this gesture in a forwarding without end. The effect is a detouring not only of narrative time, but equally of the circulatory time of digital media in the suspended body of his film. It creates a kind of force in the work, a whirlpool of vertiginous reference. How do audiences feel this force? There is no question that *The Clock* engenders an abstract admiration, for the sheer labor of collecting, sorting, and editing. At the same time, it can provoke a desire to engage or to take it on, much like that of an athlete faced with an especially challenging obstacle. Why watch a twenty-four-hour film? Because it is there. This is especially evident during twenty-four-hour screening events, when the temporal marker of midnight draws an especially large crowd, and audience members stubbornly refuse to circulate and surrender their seats.

In a banal way, this is the eventness of Marclay's cinema. *Video Quartet* opened onto this gamelike quality through the permutations of its four horizontal screens, a landscape that exceeded the scope of perceptible attention and stimulated one's peripheral perceptions. You could play at

combining the screens over and over again through different distribu-
tions of attention, and Marclay foregrounds this by repeatedly bringing
the screens into variable forms of synchronicity. At times all four screens
show different images, at others just two, three, or none. Or you could
let a more abstract experience take hold, letting the fringes of attention
do their work at a different level. It is not possible to simply exhaust the
potential of this database film and occupy every permutation of perspectives, adding up to a total knowledge. Instead, the work is constructed
to render the blur in perception, what works at the edge, fully part of the
experience precisely in its anexactitude.

Such an approach encourages oblique angles of attack, where the lack
of theatrical seats in a gallery space invites us to rearrange our corporeal
habits of cinematic perception. Today, multiscreen spectatorship is a simple fact of everyday life for most of us who watch movies on our laptops,
telephones, or other mobile devices. But reading across these screens in
the gallery is obviously a different experience than reading the windows
of multimedia, even as the latter experience folds into our attentive stance.
It is not only our bodily dispositions that are in flux here. This recomposition of the senses and sense making is made possible by more than
just the physical placement of the screens: attentiveness is continually
derailed by the incursion of other forms of virtual presence, most notably memory itself. In Marclay's installation films, something is always
opening up between form and content in the duplicity of the event itself.

Marclay's works make us live time, and the conceit of a twenty-four-
hour film and its attendant discomforts belies the more profound experience on offer. Far from the myth of total cinema, *The Clock* works the
eccentric gap opened up between the time running on screen and the
lived duration of the spectator, via a diagramming of potential. It's simply the longest suspense film ever made—still going, in fact. A diagram
does not only map existing actualized forms, what Deleuze terms "possibility," what we already know can occur based on what is already there
(via recognition). The diagram topologically transforms an actual social
field, engaging both with possibility and also with virtual potential, a reserve of newness and difference. Memory, though not the limited form
of a memory-image, is one name Deleuze gives this potential.

The first way that *The Clock* makes us live time is through the deep pleasure of cinephilic memory. The sheer fun of "Name that film" is alluring enough for an extended stay, and often the basis for excited whispers and sighs of contentment during the screening. These are the marks of disciplined gesturality that cinephilia demands: performed recognition. We might also ask if stillness can be understood as a cinephilic gesture of suspense. One thing that characterizes much audiovisual material in the museum is that it is often delinked from the regulatory time of theatrical presentation. A stillness before the image can often provoke a self-referential sense of performed passivity, as opposed to the sinking into habit we might feel in the plush seat of the cinema theatre. In an interview with Marclay in which they discussed improvisation in musical practice, experimental filmmaker Michael Snow remarked, "There really isn't any thought, in a sense, because you can't think fast enough. It's all about gesture. As soon as you hear something you recognize, but not in a conscious way, it's happening. Improvisation really is an art of living."[20] Although audiences may not be improvising in the sense of the invitation to remix, the narrative impulses that go nowhere activate, paradoxically, this improvisation of the art of living: the more to life. The intensity of the responses that Marclay's opening onto familiarity produces may vary, but recognition provokes the same set of responses, and Marclay's choices from the source material are frequently conventional enough that even the least cinephiliac spectator can find a spur of the known on which to stay afloat, even in the minor form of a familiar face. I don't know which Humphrey Bogart film that scene was from, but I had the feeling of knowing something. Somebody somewhere is writing a digital humanities PhD database thesis of "Name that film" about *The Clock*.

In this repetition of the familiar made (sort of) strange and newly available, character and actor become ambiguous. We are no longer sure what provides the consistency of a body in time. This heterochronic experience of recognition is normally backgrounded in narrative cinema, something *Looper* brought out as well. Marclay also draws extensively on the language of continuity editing, across the unlinked situations and characters with which we are confronted. Cuts on action and serial repetition highlight genre consistencies, while clichés of cinematic suspense play out over and over again. The film continually asks of its content, What are you doing? The effect is a film that frequently *feels* like it makes sense, even as storylines drop off and are ruthlessly left behind over and over again. The film forces you to continually abandon all hope of resolution, even as the anticipation of the "What's next" fails to finally wane, and then in the breathless uptake of familiarity, forget that you had left hope behind.

But if that was all that was happening, this would be a technical accomplishment, but little more, instead of a mysterious, joyful, and continually surprising experience. Reviews of Marclay's films are full not simply of admiration, but genuine pleasure and affect, and the long waits to get in to see his work, the repeat visitors and the stubborn refusal to leave even after hours of watching are all evidence of this. Marclay's film makes us live time, but *not* through its proximity to the real or "real time," tied as it is to the twenty-four-hour clock, accented by the redundant absurdity of each new person who sat down on the couch next to me, only to reflexively check their watch. Who even wears a watch these days, when time taking is tied not to temporal orientation but to our communication devices? What does it mean to think of time machines as communications technology? Why the need to double what is already always on screen?

The film's gamble is that its intensive structure can still produce something new out of the archive, a strategy of activating the unexpected through a suspension of the present. Much avant-garde cinema has exploited the manipulation of the qualities of the image, stretching duration, distorting sound, and so on, to alienate our perceptions and repurpose our affects. In his tactic of the remix, also rooted in avant-garde cinema traditions from Joseph Cornell to Bruce Connor and the Dadaist ecologies of collage, Marclay's manipulation of his source material is obvious. But its strongest effects are at the level of the persistent and the consistent rather than decontextualization and self-reflexivity; we feel the affective expropriation of durations above and below our own. While evoking our memories, he also derails them, existentially appropriating them and putting them in suspense with nowhere to go, capacitating the body. Stories fail to unfold; conventional suspense builds repeatedly, but characters, scenarios, and gestures rediscover an opacity or mystery to their actions and decisions. Our memories are not banished but regain an impersonality disjointed from nostalgia or simple recognition, rejoining the anonymous murmur that for Deleuze underpins the diagram.[21] Marclay's films are about the event of cinema as lived. This is its potential: to regain the anonymous, to tap into the otherness at the heart of the self, to free oneself from the accumulated habits of identity. The pleasures remain and are renewed. Forget, and maybe re-collect, then, is the message on the back of this postcard from the media anarchive.

In this way, Marclay's works and particularly *The Clock* are perhaps better thought of as examples of *chronic collage* rather than remixes.[22] Jean-Pierre Criqui has suggested that all of Marclay's work emerges from the concept of the "general 'replay' movement" as a sort of ghost story.[23] But the ambiguous embodiments of Marclay's work, I argue, "give a body to a phantom" in a way that moves beyond the elegiac or the haunted. His work with memory explicitly reanimates the body in both its material and incorporeal dimensions. Chronic collage are media forms that activate the incorporeal dimension of media forms alongside their foregrounding of material conditions of existence. Beyond context, chronic collages foreground duration and endurance, borrowing the machinic qualities of bodies, memories, and performance in their delicate recompositions. His works have frequently addressed this junction of performance and endurance. In *Guitar Drag* (2000), the drawn-out shatter of a guitar dragged behind a truck painfully holds open the memory of the murderous lynching of James Byrd Jr. The guitar is not simply a stand-in or metaphor for an unrepresentable horror, but a chronic collage of the long history of violence against black bodies and their recirculation in media forms, such as lynching postcards. The destructive drag is not representative; it affectively enacts the complicated ecologies of bodies, memory, medium, and media. As Marclay describes this, the film is simultaneously about the murder and stimulating people's imagination in contradictory ways. Chronic collages likewise emerge in other media forms, such as dance performance, that stage a tension between repetition and difference, including the performing bodies as recording machines. Chronic collages are themselves machines: time machines for producing, rather than representing, duration. They are obscurely appropriative in the capacitation of spectatorial bodies that they produce.

Hours pass at the screening. There are no comfortable positions to be had, only degrees of discomfort. Marclay's film partially works by putting the body in suspense, making it obsolete through discomforts that interrupt flow. This does not preclude the strange bliss of sleep. A film without end, Marclay's *The Clock* undoes the tyranny of a regularized eventness. This may explain his eccentric choice to include a handful of random television shows, a recuperation of what in the 1990s was called "appointment TV," even more constricted by the demands of good timing, scripted down to the second. *The Clock* is a free replay, a *cri de coeur* against the idea of database cinema exhausted by an archival impulse. *The Clock* performs forgetting as the will to more life.

One doesn't enter *The Clock* without giving some consideration to what it means to live time at the movies. For Jean-Louis Schefer, this was cinema's monstrous and monstrating effect: that we are made to endure the time of life through a parasitic appropriation of spectatorial memory. This parasitism is well documented, perhaps best exemplified in the astonished incredulity of spectators at the events of September 11, 2011, where live and mediatic spectators alike were convinced that what played out live was in fact a ghost from the media archives. In its endless repetitions, Marclay's film is such an amnesiac, and we have the sensation of memory passing through the body, recognition solicited and swept away. "Memory is our own recording device," Marclay reminds us.[24] We tune in and tune out to the flow on these terms. An inhuman temporality governs Marclay's film, and it self-referentially nods at this by repeatedly including scenes of temporal discomfort and disruption. At 2 AM, we enter a relentless series of rude interruptions of the quiet night's rest via the brutal ring of the telephone, continually jolting us from our helpless slumber. "Do you know what time it is?" characters persistently demand. Ugh, we sigh, unable to stretch out and nod off ourselves, of course we do.

The second way in which Marclay's film makes us duplicitously live the crime of time is via its ambiguous objectivity. If Hitchcock at the museum asked us to walk into a world of 3-D objects that ambiguously double the "walk-ins" of his own films, we have to ask what cinema thinks it is doing under these temporal conditions. This is a time machinics rather than a discrete mechanism. In this way, he returns the uncanny to the untimely. What kind of object or artifact is this work? What does (post) cinema think it is doing under these temporal conditions? What happens to all the hours of Marclay's film that fall outside of museum time, which will only rarely draw life from being watched? A twenty-four-hour film, an ouroboros biting its own tail, in *some way* approaches the condition of objectness generally demanded of museum-worthy artwork. An installation artist whose films are mainly shown in museum setting told me that his work was a headache for curators. "Do you know how long the average visitor spends in my museum?," a curator once asked him. One hour forty-five minutes; your ninety-minute film would take up too much of their time. When Andy Warhol's *Sleep* and *Empire* were shown at the Montreal Museum of Fine Arts as part of a retrospective of his work, a single, uncushioned bench occupied the space before them, both invitation to watch and imperative not to over-stay your welcome. The museum is indeed *unheimlich* for both cinema and the cinematic viewer. Keep moving: a strange imperative for the cinematic spectator out of place.

Marclay's *The Clock* simply *persists* in time, in a way that seems to scoff at the concerns of a time-based narrative cinema as a moment "out of time," extravagantly abandoning the charge of narrative suspense in favor of a more intensive affective force. The topological aesthetics of *The Clock* as a diagram of forces, giving a body to a phantom and fold-ing information into perception, evoke an art beyond knowledge that *exceeds* an archival impulse of preservation. Our perceptions are not *of* a world, but immediately part of it, in a space-time that changes as we move through it in an immanently relational configuration: the tear and its fusion as an ongoing process of rediscovering duration.

Despite its grounding in a database, Marclay's work doesn't fall into a superficial category of interactive art. Instead, both the film material and spectators are subject to a repeated singularization; again and again, existential appropriation results from "the continuous creation of hetero-geneous durations." *Existential appropriation* is another phrase for the crime of time, a reworking of excorporative theft (clips ripped and remixed from the media archive and protected by the label Art, bodies ripped and remixed from their habits of audiovisual consumption). In this way, Marclay's films rediscover cinema in a postcinematic moment as what Massumi terms an *occurrent art*, an intensive experience inviting contemplation and disjunction in equal measure. Massumi argues that if we take process seriously, we should understand objective and subjective positions not as discrete, but as "successive takings of each other." Deleuze describes a "point of view that belongs so much to the object" that it sparks a convulsive metamorphosis of the true, an affective cross contagion of audiovisions. To think subjective and objective in terms of takings is to think them in terms of time, specifically as multiplicity. We could then think of Marclay's postcinematic intervention as participating in the creation of a new kind of multiplex, folding the cinematic into the museum but also folding out via the flows of digital circulation and YouTube aesthetics. How might the duplicity of the occurrent art involve such practices of refolding space-times, creating new contact points that lift off from and exceed the potential of the cinematic cut?

Marclay's film stages the impossible passivity of the cinematic spectator at the museum; we are made to feel the histories and habits of our own participation even as they are staged as "obsolete." Shifting the debate so that the term up for valuation in 'interactive art' is art itself, Massumi argues for the uselessness of art as precisely that which allows potential to be felt, its "occurrent" quality. The contemporary moment demands that we "need right now to revisit the aesthetic in relation to interactive art," to understand what art does, what it makes appear. One such thing is that

> art brings back out the fact that all form is necessarily dynamic form. There is really no such thing as fixed form—which is another way of saying that the object of vision is virtual. Art is the technique for making that necessary but normally unperceived fact perceptible, in a qualitative perception that is as much about life itself as it is about the things we live by. Art is the technique of living life in—experiencing the virtuality of it more fully, living it more intensely.[25]

This "more intensely" is the effect of Marclay's rendering obsolete a body that can't simply submit to a twenty-four-hour screening. Although the challenges and excitement of new media art have led to a turning away in some quarters from the question of aesthetics, Massumi argues that questions of form become even more relevant in the light of these changing definitions of art:

> How do you speak of form when there is the kind of openness of outcome that you see in a lot of new media art, where participant response determines what exactly happens? When the artwork doesn't exist, because each time that it operates the interaction produces a variation, and the variations are in principle infinite? When the artwork proliferates? Or when it disseminates, as it does when the work is networked, so that the interaction is distributed in time and space and never ties back together in one particular form?[26]

It might seem like these are questions that don't apply to cinema, where anomalous suspense can be read as perversion because the objective ending will never change These are the kinds of questions that might make cinema seem obsolete, more than ready to close its loop and retire to the museum, its crumbling, traumatized form unable to sustain its time travel any longer. The ambiguous embodiments of Marclay's own film, with long stretches unseen when the museum's body is closed, or out of sync, make it a bad object, with an indistinct form. What does it take to actually see this film? Questions about what is occurrent in art return to the self-referentiality of semblance itself, the capacitating of a body with nowhere to go. Anomalous suspense names such a capacitating; where it goes is into the intimate recognition of the body's anotherness.

The Clock opens our new eyes to an abstract movement of the aesthetic event, one that requires a seeing with and through actual form in a productive double vision. Form is understood here, where futurity is felt, as the *apparition of potential in present experience*, a doubled vision of both the object and a lived relation (or interaction): "The potential we see in the object is a way our body has of being able to relate to the part of the world it happens to find itself in at this particular life's moment." To see in this way is not just to see an object but an event, which is fully real movement, in the sense that the virtual is fully real, because "something has happened: the body has been capacitated. It's been relationally activated."[27] Marclay's *The Clock* may not at first meet the definition of an interactive art; in fact, at first glance, the sheer endurance of a twenty-four-hour film, the physical discomfort of attempting to stay in the space for an extended period with nothing to do but watch, exaggerates the inert old media of cinema itself. But it is precisely as a staging of suspense that *The Clock* capacitates the body, where one mode of endurance tied to the homogeneity of clock time gives way or becomes obsolete to the experience of the body in time, the infidelity to the self. Existence, Guattari reminds us, is barely livable. We really live in those moments of intensity that Deleuze and Guattari identify as forms of death: when our habits of organized and action-oriented movement fail, when we see instead of acting, prey to the movement-vision of our own becoming. In these moments, we are traitors to our own regime, unfaithful to our most intimate stranger, to self. This infidelity is what Deleuze calls the experience of "a life."[28] Postcinematic time machines don't just displace us in a spatialized time, but are intensive movements in place.

So how do we live time at the movies? These are *anarchival* lives, a feeling of futurity in an excess that is not spent or redeemed: in other words, art beyond information. This gives the lie to the promise of a cinema called "database"; we might instead think in Raul Ruiz's evocation of a baroque "combinatory."[29] In the spiral of Marclay's suspense, there is no next image, only another. We enter into his film as into a flow, no proper beginning or ending, but just repetition itself; it is a mediator. When Deleuze says that the direct time-image forces us to ask not "What is there to see in the next image?," but "What is there to see in this image?," he articulates the suspense of a double vision, seeing and reading, semblance and event. At Marclay's film, we check our watches both to reorient ourselves, but also to sync up with our heterogeneity, to welcome the corporealizing phantom that doubles our own anotherness.

Affective Atmospherics and Living Time in Cinema

Our eyes are not ours to command; they roam where they will and then tell us they have only been where we have sent them. No matter how hard we look, we see very little of what we look at. If we imagine the eyes as navigational devices, we do so in order not to come to terms with what seeing really is. Seeing is like hunting and like dreaming, and even like falling in love. It is entangled in passions—jealousy, violence, possessiveness; and it is soaked in an affect—in pleasure and displeasure, and in pain. Ultimately, seeing alters the thing that is seen and transforms the seer. Seeing is metamorphosis, not mechanism.

—James Elkin, *The Object Stares Back*

In his introduction to *Sculpting in Time*, his influential reflections on time, art, and process in cinema, Andrei Tarkovsky credits the book as emerging partly from letters he received in response to his films, in particular *The Mirror* (1975), arguably his most personal and subjective film. *The Mirror* moves between three distinct time periods in a poet's life, layering personal histories and artifacts (such as Tarkovsky's father's poems) in the cracks of world historical events, as settings for the story and through found footage of war and conflict. Shuttling back and forth in time, the film's unique time machinics are activated throughout by impossible objective shots and incompossible embodiments, in a chronic collage of varied film stocks, color palettes, archival fragments, and dys-narrative lures. Again, the body in extremis, the dying moments of a poet initiates a time traveling.

In the letters Tarkovsky received, there are two main reactions from Soviet audiences: a failure of sense or an intuitive perception. These are not as distinct as they might seem. The first response—failure—is often

indignant, bristling with visceral complaints. Frustrated viewers identified a failure to *recognize and understand* in terms that express the shock
to mind and body they received. The bodily affects they describe Tarkovsky's film producing—"severe headaches," revulsion (one man describes
it as "unhealthy")—are perhaps surprising given that we so often see
films that "do things to bodies" as typical genre films, full of corporeal
excess of flesh and gore; Tarkovsky's slow cinema has little of this content.[1] Nonetheless, it is full of what he terms "time-pressure" as unlivable
intensity, echoing the broken-down bodies of the time-image. Indeed, as
time travel cinema, *The Mirror* conforms to genre clichés of the corrupted
embodiments of travelers. As in *Looper* and *The Clock, The Mirror*'s unlivable conditions are ambiguously embodied across character and spectator, in a time machinics experienced by some as deeply unpleasant.
Other letters echo this incomprehension, but with a more gentle wish
for supplemental guidance. Perhaps you could direct me to some extra
readings about the film, a woman inquires. "The episodes in themselves
are really good, but how can one find what holds them together?" another
man asks.[2] Tarkovsky admits that in this respect, he is of little help.

But another response, also typical for the affective working of the
film, testified to a radically different experience, an intuitive claiming
of the film's anotherness as their own. These responses came from people who *lived time,* writing to tell Tarkovsky with absolute certainty: "This
film is about me."[3] One factory worker wrote to say that *The Mirror* is a
"film I can't even talk about because I am living it."[4] Describing the
film's time-transporting affect, he continued: "If two people have been
able to experience the same thing even once, they will be able to understand each other. Even if one lived in the era of the mammoth and the
other in the age of electricity."[5] *The Mirror* activates the indiscretion of
such untimely affective contagion. The film is *not* a mirror-vision; the
letter writers did not "identify" and eliminate the differential. Instead,
they rediscovered their anotherness. A review from the Institute of Phys-
ics of the Academy of Sciences wrote, "It's a film about you, your father,
your grandfather, about someone who lives after you and is still 'you.'"[6]
This is not a list of potential identity positions, not the discrete identity
of a "particular man," and definitely something other than that cliché of

sentimental comfort that we live on in the memory of those who come after us. It is a time-traveling transversality across partial enunciators of subjectivation, a journey through anotherness that returns to a "you" at least as "different as last is from next."

People wrote to express their *surprise* at seeing themselves: a mark of intuition's methodological "rediscovery" of duration. "A woman wrote from Gorky: 'Thank you for *Mirror*. My childhood was like that. . . . Only how did you know about it?'"[7] A woman from Novosibirsk described the film's "walk-in" lure for her:

> I've seen your film four times in the last week. . . . Everything that tor-
> ments me, that I don't have and that I long for, everything that makes
> me indignant, or sick, or suffocates me, everything that gives me a
> feeling of light and warmth, and by which I live, and everything that
> destroys me—it's all there in your film, I see it as if in a mirror. For the
> first time ever a film has become real to me, and that's why I go to see
> it, I want to get right inside it, so that I can really be *alive*.[8]

Rather than a parasitism that offers only a second-order reality, the film generates for the viewer an affective atmosphere that lures and sustains a vitality affect. This woman describes the vertigo of a critical distance provoked by duplicity; rather than the assaultive crime of a failure of sense or the need for an explanatory supplement, she activates repetition as the will to anotherness. She experiences and names *as her own* the duplicity of the relational and qualitative process of becoming as "immanent evaluation," or "the powers of the false": "There is a point of view that belongs so much to the thing that the thing is constantly being transformed in a becoming identical to point of view. Metamorphosis of the true."[9] In the mirror of Tarkovsky's film, she sees a movement-vision, an exchange of the objective and subjective within the suspensive medium of Tarkovsky's time-pressure. Through these letters, one can trace a *movement-vision* of the multiple perspectives, the heterogeneity of points of view in exchange: seeing as metamorphosis, not mechanism.

The Mirror mixes three disjunct moments in a man's life and combines archival footage from World War II with a fictional and elliptical narrative, including Tarkovsky's own restagings of his childhood home, the voice of his father and the body of his mother, playing here an older version of poet Alexei's mother Maria. An anarchival impulse moves transversally across the film, compelling the aberrant movements of bodies. The memories are Tarkovsky's and immediately no longer his own, neither simply subjective nor rendered objective by the work of art. The media archive is reanimated through the intimacy of subjective experience, rather than an indexical and supportive referentiality, but retains the blur of this double vision as the film unfolds. A fidelity to personal memory underpins these efforts (such as the reconstruction of the family home), paradoxically opening onto the deeply impersonal, becoming unfaithful in the sense of falsifying, animated by the crime of time. In the suspense of this exchange something escapes and becomes indefinite. This is not to say simply confused, but *anexact*: charged with the potential of becoming something else. The work of memory in this film is machinic.

A key paradoxical consistency derives from the doubled role of Margarita Terekhova, playing both Alexei's mother Maria and his lover Natalia, a decision taken during the filming (in a further fold, the older Maria is played by Maria Vishnyakova, Tarkovsky's own mother). Across these incorporations, this duplicitous woman is a time traveler, like all the doubled women we have examined here. Her incompossible embodiments activate the depersonalizations of love itself, the affect/effect of love opening up the world in an existential appropriation. Terekhova's body repeatedly sparks aberrant movements of reversal, slow motion and the felt confusion of disjunctive sound-image relations; her performance is difficult to disentangle at times from the cinematic body, as in the celebrated dream sequence when Maria the mother rinses her hair in reverse slow motion in a crumbling house. Terekhova's doubled performance is part of the film's time machinics, playing out the suspense of a personal rippled by the impersonal in the indeterminacy of actor and roles. Tarkovsky's *Mirror* is Bergson's moving mirror of the past simultaneously unrolling alongside the present, as "closely coupled as an actor to his role." The effect of this is the qualitative experience of a body in time, that is to say, of "a life."

"A life" is what Deleuze describes as the transcendental field of a consciousness without a self.[10] Impersonal and indefinite, it names the relational work of existential appropriation, beyond belonging. In this way, art opens onto the virtual through what Tarkovsky terms "interaction": "And so there opens up before us the possibility of interaction with infinity, for the great function of the artistic image is to be a kind of detector of infinity."[11] A detector of infinity is the intuitive method, a crime-solving technique that uncovers only time via the rediscovery of durations "above and below our own," the creative suspense of the body in time. Affect signals this work; as Tarkovsky writes, "The true artistic image gives the beholder a simultaneous experience of the most complex, contradictory, sometimes even mutually exclusive feelings."[12]

"A life" is impersonal, abstract, and indefinite, both alongside and exceeding any individual expression or capture. It thus echoes the body's intimate otherness: "One is always the index of a multiplicity: an event, a singularity, a life. . . ."[13] "A life" is what seizes and exceeds the viewers moved to respond to Tarkovsky's film, even those for whom the encounter produces an unlivable affect such as headache or nausea. As Guattari reminds us, existence is barely livable. This "a life" is the barely livable as such—the virtual—which is paradoxically the very consistency of life itself, what the cinema's impossible embodiments make felt. "A life contains only virtuals. It is made up of virtualities, events, singularities. What we call virtual is not something that lacks reality but something that is engaged in a process of actualization following the plane that gives it its particular reality."[14] This quality of the virtual is precisely what I have traced here as the anotherness of suspense. It is via the duplicity of affect, a "two-sidedness, the simultaneous participation of the virtual in the actual and the actual in the virtual" that anotherness is made felt.[15]

For Tarkovsky's audience, whose letters encouraged him to document his reflections on time, watching *The Mirror* is such an experience of anotherness, a mirror-vision become movement-vision that is both "you," both "I": the arcing in time of a subjectivity that was "never ours." In this transindividuality of affective attunement, "relationality pertains to the openness of the interaction rather than to the interaction per se or to its discrete ingredients," exceeding a capture in either subject or object.[16] The doubleness is also that of a subject's experience of other durations "above and below" their own, Guattari's existential appropriation that is nothing more than the suspense of "a life."

The suspense of anotherness has been explored in this book as taking off from the suspense of the time-image through a reworking of the crime of time and what it means to give a body to a phantom. In the cinema of the "seer, not the actor," we suspended the doubled meaning of the seer as *clair-voyant*; acts of perception generatively clouded by its double affect. "A life" names the affective atmospherics produced by this double vision. In the aftermath of the "sensory-motor break" a suspension of action-oriented perception, Deleuze writes, "It is not in the name of a better or truer world that thought captures the intolerable in the world, but, on the contrary, it is because this world is intolerable that it can no longer think a world or think itself." This produces a "spiritual automaton" or the

> psychic situation of the seer, who sees better and farther than he can react, that is, think. Which, then, is the subtle way out? To believe, not in a different world, but in a link between man and the world, in love or life, to believe in this as in the impossible, the unthinkable, which nonetheless cannot but be thought: "something possible, otherwise I will suffocate."[17]

An affective atmosphere is the experience of relationality, freed from its terms, in the media ecology of the cinema. In exploring cinematic suspense not simply in terms of its standard generic coordinates, I have tried to articulate the differential of suspense that binds it, as a body genre, to the creativity and impersonal capacities of the body in time. In this way, suspense names the "something happening" of the virtual, the capacitation (semblance) that has nowhere to go but intensively into potential. What is experienced here is precisely double, something becoming something "engaged in a process of actualization following the plane that gives it its particular reality." A Deleuzian suspense of action is a suspension event that makes one body obsolete in order to solicit the new and unexpected. The contagion of this suspense is *self-referential*, asking the spectator to account for difference processually made. The corporeal turn attempted to bring the body into cinema theory to address the relation between spectator and screen. Through the untimely meditations of Deleuze's second cinema book, and considerations of affect and event in the work of Massumi, I proposed the notion of semblance to describe the cinematic body as a suspended body, focusing on the question of self-referentiality or the capacitation of the body prior to action. This intensive suspense, a "special case of movement" or "movement in stasis" is the temporal dimension of the body itself made sensational, or "really apparitional."

To conclude, I briefly revisit the facets of doubleness that characterize my affective theory of cinematic suspense. In thinking of the barely livable ways that cinema can make us "live time," I have contrasted an understanding of cinema as a second-order reality, or a mirror-vision that stabilizes relations between self and other, subject and object, to a movement-vision that expresses the sense that cinema is not a medium but a living reality in its own right. Thinking the body's anotherness has meant taking seriously what it means to think of the body not as object but as a process of living: to think anotherness as a way to tackle and make livable intensity (through expanding one's capacity to act) via a time machinics.

In *Mulholland Drive*, Rita emerges from anonymity through a movement-vision in a cinematic mirror. She gains a name only as an act of creative falsification that fuses the "tear in the parasol." When Betty arrives at her aunt's house, she stumbles across a strange woman in the shower. Mistaking her for a friend of her aunt's, she backs out of the bathroom, apologetically asking "What's your name," but gets no reply. The wounded woman sits at a vanity, looking at her own reflection in one mirror, while another smaller mirror reflects a poster of Rita Hayworth in *Gilda*. The camera tracks into the poster's reflection and the scene dissolves into the woman exiting the bathroom and announcing, "My name is Rita." This claiming of a name temporarily relieves a narrative suspense—will she be found out by Betty?—but, more important, relies on and intensifies the affective suspense of a body in time under the guise of a criminal falsification. She labels herself as actress, a figure of falseness, and the audience is reflexively reminded that she is simply playing a role; she is guilty of a lie that signals past and future duplicity that is the narrative arc of generic suspense, a time that eventually "catches up to you." But we seek "different metabolisms of past-future."[18] "Rita" is not simply a disguise to be revealed; it enacts the fragility of an order-word riddled with the crack of heterogeneous becomings. In this instant we see that to give a body to a phantom is to experience process itself as "incorporeal transformation." This is "recognized by its instantaneity, by its immediacy, by the simultaneity of the enunciation that expresses it and the effect it produces; this is why the *mots d'ordre* are strictly dated, hour, minute, and second, and take hold the moment they are dated," just as the bomb under the table doubles the chronic time of what we know must happen with the frantic proliferation of potential as affect.[19] This "simultaneity" is expressed in the dissolve or fusion as the recomposition of the world rather than the fixing of an identity. For Deleuze and Guattari, the proper name always emerges from the murmur of a collective assemblage, a sign of heterogeneity rather than conclusiveness. Rita names the generative power of relation itself that will tentatively hold together the existential territory of the film, a mirror-vision that becomes movement-vision, signaled by the blur of a double vision. Rita diagrams the anotherness of a body in time, the movement from crime to time itself, linking cinematic repetition with anotherness as the creative fabulation of the body.

"This is the girl" is the refrain function of unlivable embodiments in *Mulholland Drive*, a statement backed by the threat of murderous impulses and the suspense of recognition. When Deleuze reworks Schefer to conclude that "there is no crime but time itself," he articulates the shift I have traced from generic concepts of suspense affiliated with criminality and wrongdoing to the affective suspense of unlivable intensity. When Guattari writes that existence is "barely livable," he testifies to what it means to live in suspense, in the anotherness of becoming that is perceptually blunted by the habit of saying "I." The existential crisis of identity and embodiment explored in these films, their "vertigo effect" when "I is an other," is also a pedagogical practice of double vision. In the aberrant movement of love that I explored in chapter 3, the question turned from the suspicion and fear of infidelity to love's intensity as an infidelity to the self. Repeatedly, the films explored here ask an ethico-aesthetic question of how to live in intensity. Their lessons in anotherness, rather than resolutions or recuperations of the self, offer something other than loss as a way to think the intensity of *existential appropriation,* to imagine a commons of vitality. As an intimate archive, cinema gives us an ex-corporative experience of the "wholly positive aspects of time and becoming."[20]

Again and again, suspense turns on the double vision of anotherness, the hesitation of "to see or to read." In the epigraph to this chapter, James Elkin describes an affective autonomy of vision, one duplicitously traveling in time. The eyes wander autonomously and then report back to us. "You did this," Alice tells Pete after the murder of Andy. Eyes fail as quantitative time machines: "If we imagine the eyes as navigational devices, we do so in order not to come to terms with what seeing really is."[21] But they are producers of time machinics: "Ultimately, seeing alters the thing that is seen and transforms the seer. Seeing is metamorphosis not mechanism."[22] In this case, double vision is precisely the vision of relation itself, suspense in action. Like the beam of light that brackets *Inland Empire,* suspense generates double vision as a pedagogy of perception, the injunction to look again.

Cinema gives us not a representation of bodies, but a direct, *self-referential* experience of the incorporeal dimension of the body, a double-vision of our own "living in potential" as the "lived expression of the eternal matter of fact that is time's passing."[23] The double form of the cinematic body is the simultaneity of its relived and unlived-as-yet, the opening onto what Bergson terms absolute memory and an as-yet-undetermined future: in other words, the body's virtual dimension. The double was my focus throughout this book because it addresses the immediately relational quality of cinematic events, where the *givenness* of relations is directly perceived, registering first in the activity of the body before it registers in consciousness. This doubling, developed via Massumi's notion of duplicity as an "artifact of . . . immediacy,"[24] requires starting from a different place than a subject/object divide. It thinks the body in time as a suspended (re)animation: the felt experience of becoming other to ourselves, via the assemblages of cinematic bodies.

Through the concepts of affect and event, I asked, How can an attentiveness to time in the affective turn in media studies re-inflect the focus on sensation, which characterized the corporeal turn, from the spectator's body to the event of cinema itself? After the "death of cinema" debates initiated by the digital turn of the early 1990s, a "reanimated" cinema requires a different set of conceptual coordinates. If a certain mode of cinema was clarified by the sense of an ending provoked by the turn to the digital (or more ambiguously prolonged in the long parallelism of the electronic image), what new questions are emerging around cinematic becomings today? In the corporeal turn, an ongoing interrogation of the body in (the) cinema (as spectator or on screen), did not always translate into the same attention given to the body *of* cinema, and the obscure but suggestive potential of what such a body might do. Focused on the matter of sensation, less attention was paid to the question of what Massumi has termed the "incorporeal" aspects of the body; that is to say, the body in time. As Gregory Seigworth and Melissa Gregg have argued, "The capacity of a body is never defined by a body alone but is always aided and abetted by, and dovetails with, the field or context of its force relations"; simultaneously, this very capacity is the vertiginous "not-yet" of the body's indeterminacy.[25] *Bodies in Suspense* developed a theory of cinematic corporeality based on this affective capacity of the body in time, and the ethico-aesthetic potential of this body's "unlived as yet." Focused on suspense films that foreground aberrant experiences of time, and moving outward from a generic concept of suspense, I explored the pedagogical potential of the double vision of affect itself.

The potential of the cinematic body is not as a representational mirror, nor as a prosthetic enhancement of our own bodies, nor as a means of experiencing the alterity of other bodies. We might think of bodies as time machines; that is to say, our primary mode for rediscovering the heterogeneity of our own existence in time. This experience is that of suspended (re)animation, an ethico-aesthetical approach to thinking the body of cinema. Drawing on Deleuze's claim that "time has always put the notion of truth into crisis," David Rodowick argues that what we need at this contemporary moment is an ethics of time.[26] This crisis of truth is what Deleuze rearticulates as the "powers of the false." In bringing together and reorienting the corporeal and affective turns, *Bodies in Suspense* refocused central issues of agency, sensation, knowledge, and affect through the lens of time, tracing the arc of affect when "there is no crime but time itself."

Acknowledgments

Any work diagrams all the relations that hold it together and hold it up. The forces of friendship, thought, intensity, hope, and passion have marked every moment I have shared while writing *Bodies in Suspense*, and the pleasure of writing these thanks comes despite their inadequacy of expression. I am deeply fortunate to have had so many enriching encounters while working on this book; it has been a challenge and a thrill. This project began as my doctoral dissertation. At Duke University, the Program in Literature provided a home for thought that moved across the critical and the creative. At various stages my work benefited from the care and commentary of Michael Hardt, Tim Lenoir, Negar Mottahedah, Catherine Benamou, and Toril Moi. I thank Raul Ruiz and Fred Burns for the opportunity to bring research and creation together in ways that mark these pages. Jane Gaines was a generous reader and supportive chair throughout my dissertation; I was so glad to be part of the community of cinema and media studies that she founded at the Program in Film and Video. I thank her for her patience, her infectious enthusiasm, and for never hesitating to deliver a well-timed shove. Many dear friendships sustained me through grad school, including Desirée Martin, Laurie Bley, Greg Dobbins, Paul Husbands, Mendi Obadike, Kristin Bergen, Sallie Patrick, Jason Middelton, Courtney Baker, and Nayeli Garci-Crespo, comrades in work and play. Last, my deep thanks to Clay Taliaferro for his rich pedagogy of thinking the body and the keen care of his critical eye.

My postdoctoral fellowship at the Pembroke Center for Research and Teaching on Women at Brown University, where I began to transform a dissertation into this very different book, was an ideal initiation into the potential of institutional community, grounded in feminist principles. Elizabeth Weed's sharp intellect and wealth of experience created an atmosphere in which challenge and care came in equal measure. Lynne Joyrich modeled how to cultivate affective affinities and how to mentor new scholars through inclusion, support, and a genuine infectious delight; her wide-ranging brilliance across subjects high and low is a model for intellectual seriousness without pretension. I thank my fellow post-doc Eden Osucha for her precious friendship, her careful and cutting mind and ethical mode of thought, and for all the evenings out after a day at the office. To all the members of the Pembroke Seminar and the wider Brown community, including Rebecca Schneider, David Bering-Porter, Eugenie Brinkman, Julie Levin-Russo, Sarah Teasley, and more, I am deeply grateful for the chance to develop my work in your company and to present early versions of this book.

My home, Montreal, is a wonderful place to work in cinema and critical theory, a city where the edges of the institution flow easily into a rich and dynamic cultural life. This project has benefited enormously from my intellectual communities in Montreal and at McGill University. The Sense Lab provides a welcome like no other, where thought and life are linked by rigor and playful experimentation. The friends and encounters I have had over the years in that context are too many to name and are an ecology of good ideas in which I continue to thrive. I especially thank Erin Manning and Brian Massumi for making and sustaining this work for more than ten years, and for being so kind and inclusive with their time and ideas. I also thank Celine Pereira, Andrew Murphie, Lone Bertelson, Nadine Asswad, Ronald Rose-Antoinette, Nasrin Himada, Charlotte Farrell, Christoph Brunner, Troy Rhodes, Eric Bordeleau, Bianca Scliar, Mayra Morales, Leslie Plumb, Sean Smith, Stamatia Portanova, Diego Gil, Csenge Kolozsvari, Michael Goddard, Bodil Marie Stavning Thomsen, and Mike Hornblow for their precious collaborations over the years. And a special mention to my very cherished conspirators Toni Pape and Ilona Hongisto for their absolutely fabulous thoughts and enthusiasm for making work together. Across Montreal and elsewhere, I benefit every day from the conviviality and vitality of friends and colleagues who make this such an exciting place to be and who helped with this project with their thoughts, invitations to share, and support: thank you Mark Steinberg, Brian Bergstrom, Livia Monnet, Mario De Giglio-Bellemare, Viva Paci, Johanne Sloan, Kathy Casey, Francois Letourneux, Thierry Bardini, and Elsa Court.

At McGill University I have found a supportive and enriching environment full of colleagues across the university who share their passion for what they do without holding back. For making an institution into a home, I thank Jenny Burman, Stephen McAdams, Eric Lewis, Bronwen Low, Erin Hurley, Ned Schantz, Michael Jemtrud, Derek Nystrom, Nik Luka, Eugenio Bolongaro, Darin Barney, Karis Shearer, Lynn Kozak, Alain Farah, Lisa Stevenson, Charmaine Nelson, Michelle Cho, Brian Bergstrom, Eleanora Diamanti, Antony Paré, VK Preston, Noemie Solomon, and Thomas Pringle. Thanks to Diane Elam, David Hensley, and Karin Cope for being my wonderful profs back when I was an undergrad student. The Institute for Gender, Sexuality, and Feminist Studies and everyone who works there make coming to work a true pleasure. I especially thank Paul Yachnin, Jonathan Sterne, and Carrie Rentschler for the way that they use their own time and resources to generously make spaces for people to work together at McGill and for their humor, conviviality, and mentorship: they are models of how to hold open the door for others behind you. I deeply cherish Fiona Ritchie, Monica Popescu, Monique Morgan, Ara Osterweil, and Katie Zien for their encouragement and endless positivity while I was writing this book, and for labor-related karaoke.

I make special mention of people who provided key support and conversations around this work, and who are, each of them, role models of intellectual rigor, creative thought, and collegiality, not to mention dear friends: Masha Salazkina for her suggestions and commentary; Yuriko Furuhata for her sweetness, brilliance, and the deep pleasure of her company, and for all our future schemes; Thomas Lamarre and Michael Cowan, conspirators on projects too many to mention, fellow founders of the Moving Image Research Laboratory, and who despite their own extraordinary and brilliant output never said no to a chance to work together and make new thoughts; and finally to Will Straw, the first person to invite me to speak about my work at McGill and an indefatigable pillar of friendship, ideas, and mentorship for me, as he has been for seemingly every scholar who has ever crossed his path!

I thank my editor, Danielle Kasprzak, for her care in shepherding me through this process for the first time; I am delighted to work with her and with the University of Minnesota Press. Thank you to Anne Carter for her editorial assistance, to Mike Stoffel's copyediting, and to the readers at Minnesota for their feedback, which has contributed enormously to improving this book. I especially thank Todd McGowan, whose work is so influential to me. Special thanks to my research assistants for their help with this project and for the joy of working with them on theirs: Sara Yousefnejad, Kristin Li, Stefanie Miller, Julian Flavin, Sarah Manya, Carolyn Bailey, Cecelia Optaken-Ringdal, Ayanna Dozier, and Steph Berrington. I thank my students in ENGL 776 "Cinematic Time Machines" for their lively thoughts and discussions, and for coming to an overnight sleepover at Marclay's *The Clock* with me, and the students in my two classes on David Lynch for always meeting my enthusiasm with their own. I thank *all* of my wonderful students at McGill for their passion, commitment, creativity, intelligence, and willingness to risk—I know just how lucky I am to work with you. I acknowledge the funding support of an FQRSC Nouveau Chercheurs grant, a SSHRC Insight Grant, as well as research funding from McGill University, which allowed me to complete this project.

Other friends, many already named, have been patient and encouraging cheerleaders throughout this process and never failed to give me exactly what I needed when I needed it. I can mention only a few of those who have held my hand, poured me a glass of wine, taken me dancing, or listened to my ideas, complaints, worries, and excitement over the years. Thanks to Anne Marie Wheeler, Sherry Hergott, Shama Rangwala, Andrew Stoten, Katve-Kaisa Kontturi, Jen Spiegel, Ami Shulman, Veronic Morin, Amy Nyland, Joseph Rosen, Susana Vargas Cervantes, Marta Zarzycka, Selmin Kara, Jen Drouin, Neil McArthur, and Marie-Pier Boucher.

I have no better supporters than my family, and to them I dedicate this book and especially (or better—only!) all the moments of happiness that went into it. I thank my sisters Lauren and Sam for their dear compassion, fun, and optimism; my father and stepmother Alan Bristowe and Elizabeth Stein for the way they open my world to new experiences; my dear cousins Jessica, Tanya, Viki, and Meagan for company and laughs. My godmother Jane-Marie Carroll has fed and housed me at critical moments in this process, and her fierce pride has buoyed me on too many occasions to count. My uncle Gary lent me his sense of humor and endless zombie movies when I needed a break. My grandfather Jim Thain has always been my biggest backer in education, from report card bribes to his pleasure in my career. My grandmother Sheila Thain has always been a source of light, laughter, and strength; she taught me the restorative value of a good cup of tea. Many cats helped keep my lap warm during late-night writing and provided insistent stomping on the keyboard when it was time to take a break; my love to Cairo, Pix, Jaggy, Sailor, and Noki. No thanks for all the things they "accidentally" deleted! Michael Butler probably endured more drafts of this project than any living person; I thank him for his love, for retaining his sense of humor when I was an intolerable storm cloud of writing, and for his ability to make me laugh in any situation. This would not have been possible without him.

More than anyone, this book is for my mom, Linda. Anything is possible when you have a force like her rooting for you. She always pushed to make sure I had every opportunity in life, supported every decision I made, and has made me want to live up to the depth of her pride and love. I love her more than anyone in the world, and I dedicate this book to her.

Notes

Introduction

1. Michael Goddard and Jussi Parikka's excellent overview of media ecology theory focuses on the "messy ontologies" of a new kind of media "that is becoming less about apparatuses and solids, and more about waves, vibrations, streams, processes and movements," and attentive to new kinds of bodies. See *Fibreculture* 17, "Unnatural Ecologies," ed. Michael Goddard and Jussi Parikka. http://seventeen.fibreculturejournal.org/.

2. *Incompossible* refers to the impossible coexistence of two discrete possibilities under the logic of what Deleuze terms the regime of judgment (e.g., Dern cannot be in two places in the same room at the same time); such incompossibilities signal the emergence of a direct time-image in which the present includes a contemporaneous past not subordinated to a logic of spatial integrity or distribution. See Gilles Deleuze, *Cinema 2: The Time-Image* (Minneapolis: University of Minnesota Press, 1989), 130–31.

3. Ibid., 21.

4. Jean-Louis Comolli, "Historical Fiction: A Body Too Much," trans. Ben Brewster. *Screen* 19 (Summer 1978): 41–53.

5. David Rodowick, ed., "Unthinkable Sex," in *Afterimages of Gilles Deleuze's Film Philosophy* (Minneapolis: University of Minnesota Press, 2010), 177–90.

6. Gilles Deleuze and Félix Guattari, *A Thousand Plateaus* (Minneapolis: University of Minnesota Press, 1987), 40.

7. Deleuze, *Cinema 2*, 36.

8. Ibid., 80; Chris Marker, "A Free Replay: Notes sur *Vertigo*," *Positif* 400 (June 1994): 79–84, 80.

9. Félix Guattari, "Ritornellos and Existential Affects," in *The Guattari Reader,* ed. Gary Genosko (London: Blackwell, 1996), 156.

10. Rodowick, *Afterimages*, xiii.

11. Massumi, *Semblance and Event: Activist Philosophy and the Occurrent Arts* (Cambridge: MIT Press, 2011), 128.

12. Félix Guattari, *Chaosmosis: An Ethico-aesthetic Paradigm*, trans. Paul Bains and Julian Pefanis (Bloomington: Indiana University Press, 1995), 13.

13. Guattari, *Chaosmosis*, 53.

14. Ibid., 84.

15. Gilles Deleuze, *Difference and Repetition*, trans. Paul Patton (New York: Columbia University Press, 1994), 88.

16. Gilles Deleuze, "Having an Idea in Cinema [On the Cinema of Straub-Huillet]," in *Deleuze and Guattari: New Mappings in Politics, Philosophy and Culture*, ed. Eleanor Kaufman and Kevin Jon Heller (Minneapolis: University of Minnesota Press, 1998), 14–19, 17.

17. Massumi, *Semblance and Event*, 64. Massumi argues all relation is virtual (as in Deleuze's sense as not opposed to, but fully real); this virtuality or indetermination that is the source of its freedom. In *Inland Empire*, this freedom is precisely why Dern's encounter, via a double exposure, with the Lost Girl is immediately doubled by her impossible encounter with her self.

18. Cf. Massumi, *Semblance and Event*, 9.

19. Phase shifts in Lynch are characteristic moments of emergent embodiment in his films, where discrete bodies, objects, and subjects recompose collectively and enter into new relations. Frequently, phase shifts are both signaled by the intensified presence of light (especially as electricity or beams) and result in new powers, such as time travel or affective contagion. See Alanna Thain, "Rabbit Ears: Locomotion in Lynch's INLAND EMPIRE," in *David Lynch in Theory*, ed. François-Xavier Gleyzon (Prague: Litteraria Pragensia, 2010), 86–101, 87.

20. Ibid., 37.

21. Jean-Louis Schefer, *L'Homme Ordinaire du Cinema* (Paris: Gallimard, 1980), 128.

22. Jean-Louis Schefer, *The Enigmatic Body*, ed. and trans. Paul Smith (Cambridge: Cambridge University Press, 1995), 116.

23. Ibid., 128.

24. Paul Smith, "The Unknown Center of Ourselves: Schefer's Writing on the Cinema," *Enclitic* 6, no. 2 (Fall 1982): 33–34.

25. For a discussion of his original concept of monstration (derived from the monstrateur of early cinema) as exhibitionist showing, as opposed to narration as telling, see Andre Gaudreault, "Narration et monstration au cinéma," in *Hors Cadre* 2, "Cinénarrable" (Paris: Université de Paris VIII, April 1984).

26. Deleuze, *Cinema 2*, 37.

27. Amy Herzog's *Dreams of Difference, Songs of the Same: The Musical Moment in Cinema* (Minneapolis: University of Minnesota Press, 2009); Thomas Lamarre's *The Anime Machine: A Media Theory of Animation* (Minneapolis: University of Minnesota Press, 2009); Bliss Cua Lim's *Translating*

Time: Cinema, the Fantastic and Temporal Critique (Durham, N.C.: Duke University Press, 2009); Paul Gormley's *The New-Brutality Film: Race and Affect in Contemporary Hollywood Cinema* (London: Intellect, 2005); Elena del Rio's *Deleuze and the Cinemas of Performance: Powers of Affection* (Edinburgh: Edinburgh University Press, 2008).

28. Linda Williams, "Film Bodies: Gender, Genre, and Excess," *Film Quarterly* 44, no. 4 (1991): 2–12.

29. Roland Barthes, *Image-Music-Text*, trans. Stephen Heath (New York: Hill and Wang, 1977), 119.

30. Lim, *Translating Time*, 190.

31. Henri Bergson, *Creative Evolution*, trans. Arthur Mitchell (New York: Dover Publications, 1991), 301.

32. Massumi, *Semblance and Event*, 3.

33. Ibid., 8.

34. Deleuze, *Cinema 2*, 146.

35. Meaghan Morris, *Too Soon, Too Late: History in Popular Culture* (Bloomington: Indiana University Press, 1998), 151.

36. Melissa Gregg and Greg Seigworth take Barthes's idea of shimmer to describe the "registration of a form that is rarely taken into account: the stretching." Shimmer highlights the oscillation characteristic of affective engagement: a quality in motion is also the temporal anamorphosis of form itself. See Gregg and Seigworth, eds., *The Affect Theory Reader* (Durham, N.C.: Duke University Press, 2010), 10.

37. Thomas Elsaesser and Malte Hagener, *Film Theory: An Introduction through the Senses* (New York: Routledge, 2010), 12.

38. Deleuze and Guattari, *A Thousand Plateaus*, 28.

39. Gilbert Simondon, "The Genesis of the Individual," in *Incorporations*, ed. Jonathan Crary and Sanford Kwinter (New York: Zone, 1992), 223.

40. Vivian Sobchack, *The Address of the Eye: A Phenomenology of Film Experience* (Princeton: Princeton University Press, 1992); Steven Shaviro, *The Cinematic Body* (Minneapolis: University of Minnesota Press, 1993).

41. Sobchack, *Carnal Thoughts*, 55–56. As precursors to her theory of cinematic embodiment, Sobchack includes Sergei Eisenstein, Gilles Deleuze, and Siegfried Kracauer. Others might include Lesley Stern, Steven Shaviro, Linda Williams, Laura Marks, Elena del Rio, Anne Rutherford, Patricia Pisters, Mary Ann Doane, Amy Herzog, Jonathan Auerbach, Jennifer Barker, Thomas Elsaesser, and more. See Anne Rutherford, "Cinematic Embodiment and Affect," *Senses of Cinema* 25 (2003); Patricia Pisters, *The Neuro-Image: A Deleuzian Film-Philosophy of Digital Screen Culture* (Stanford, Calif.: Stanford University Press, 2012); Mary Ann Doane, *The Emergence of Cinematic Time: Modernity, Contingency, the Archive* (Cambridge, Mass.: Harvard University Press, 2002); Herzog 2009; Jonathan Auerbach, *Body Shots: Early Cinema's Incarnations* (Berkeley: University of California Press, 2007); Jennifer Barker, *The Tactile*

Eye: Touch and the Cinematic Experience (Berkeley: University of California Press, 2009); Elsaesser and Hagener, *Film Theory*.

42. Williams, "Film Bodies," 11, 4.

43. Amy Herzog's recent theory of the "musical moment" in cinema builds on this concept through careful analysis of the gendered spectacle of the musical genre, at once the "most conservative and irreverent filmic phenomena," showing how repetition can "generate patterns of representational repetition that are, simultaneously and uniquely, open to the interventions of difference." Amy Herzog, *Dreams of Difference*, 8.

44. Steven Shaviro, *The Cinematic Body*, 17, 256, 33.

45. Ibid., 32.

46. Massumi, *Parables for the Virtual: Movement, Affect, Sensation* (Durham, N.C.: Duke University Press, 2002), 23–45.

47. In 1989, *Camera Obscura* devoted a special issue ("The Spectatrix," 20, no. 1) edited by Janet Bergstrom and Mary Ann Doane to the multiple reconceptualizations of cinematic identification in feminist film theory.

48. Shaviro, *The Cinematic Body*, 53, 254, 256, 99, 258, 26.

49. Steven Shaviro, "*The Cinematic Body* REDUX," *Parallax* 14, no. 1 (2008): 53.

50. Steven Shaviro, *Post-Cinematic Affect* (Ropley, Hampshire, U.K.: O-Books, 2010), 2.

51. Shaviro, *The Cinematic Body*, 255.

52. Deleuze, *Cinema 2*, 133.

53. Ibid., 3.

54. From Merleau-Ponty, Sobchack takes the idea of the chiasmus, a reversibility between the lived body and the experienced world that is not synthesized.

55. Keep in mind the contrast between Husserl's phenomenological claim, shared by Merleau-Ponty, that all consciousness is consciousness of something, as opposed to Bergson's contention that all consciousness is something.

56. Sobchack, *Address of the Eye*, 10.

57. Ibid. (emphasis added).

58. Ibid., 143 (emphasis added).

59. Keith Ansell Pearson, *Germinal Life: The Difference and Repetition of Gilles Deleuze* (New York: Routledge, 1999), 72.

60. Sobchack, *Carnal Knowledge*, xviii.

61. For a discussion of an ethics of time see Rodowick, *The Virtual Life of Film* (Cambridge, Mass.: Harvard University Press, 2007), 73–88, and McGowan, *Out of Time: Desire in Atemporal Cinema* (Minneapolis: University of Minnesota Press, 2011).

62. Ibid., 231–32 (emphasis added).

63. Ibid., 231–32 (emphasis added).

64. Massumi, *Parables for the Virtual*, 5.

65. Deleuze and Guattari, *What Is Philosophy?*, 191.

66. Lone Bertelsen and Andrew Murphy, "An Ethics of Everyday Infinities and Powers," in *The Affect Theory Reader*, ed. Melissa Greg and Gregory J. Seigworth (Durham, N.C.: Duke University Press, 2010), 138–57, 145.

67. Jussi Parikka, *Insect Media* (Minneapolis: University of Minnesota Press, 2011), 82.

68. I take the concept of tendency from the work of Lamarre, *The Anime Machine* (2009), who suggests it as a way of thinking a Deleuzian reorientation of genre studies. A tendency both acknowledges the way in which genre film has been a critical site for interventions in demanding an account of cinematic bodies, and also shifts genre analysis from a structural to a temporal focus.

69. Deleuze and Guattari, *A Thousand Plateaus*, 482.

70. Massumi, *Parables for the Virtual*, 66.

71. See the chapter "The Evolutionary Alchemy of Reason" in *Parables for the Virtual*.

72. Massumi, *Parables for the Virtual*, 110, 101, 106, 107, 109.

73. Ibid., 109.

74. Penelope's weaving is a refrain function, creating the territory of the home but also generating the timing of a missed recognition.

75. Dave's violent shaking repeats at the end of Lynch's *Lost Highway*, when Fred Madison, fleeing down the highway, begins to transform into an as-yet-unactualized self, shaking so fiercely his entire body blurs.

76. See André Bazin, "The Virtues and Limitations of Montage," in *What Is Cinema?* (vol. 1) (Berkeley: University of California Press, 2005), 41–52.

77. Hartouni claims that the fetus is the "new humanist subject par excellence" (41). See her *Cultural Conceptions: On Reproductive Technologies and the Remaking of Life* (Minneapolis: University of Minnesota Press, 1997).

78. Massumi, *Parables for the Virtual*, 106.

79. Massumi, *Semblance and Event*, 23, 24, 42.

80. Deleuze and Guattari, *A Thousand Plateaus*, 20.

81. Deleuze, *Cinema 2*, 146.

82. Massumi, *Semblance and Event*, 9, 10, 8.

83. Ibid., 43.

84. Gregory Flaxman, *Gilles Deleuze and the Fabulation of Philosophy: Powers of the False* (Minneapolis: University of Minnesota Press, 2012), 313, 316.

85. Deleuze, *Cinema 2*, 130.

86. Guattari, *Chaosmosis*, 63–64.

87. Deleuze and Guattari, *What Is Philosophy?*, 213.

88. Ibid., 210, 212.

89. Deleuze, *Cinema 2*, 68, 293 (n. 8), 82, 295 (n. 25).

90. *Foucault* was published in French in 1986, one year after *Cinema 2*. Gilles Deleuze, *Foucault* (Minneapolis: University of Minnesota Press, 1988), 97–98.

91. Deleuze, *Foucault*, 107.

92. Massumi, *Parables for the Virtual*, 28.

93. Daniel Smith, "Deleuze on Bacon: Three Conceptual Trajectories in The Logic of Sensation," Introduction to *Francis Bacon: The Logic of Sensation*, ed. Gilles Deleuze (Minneapolis: University of Minnesota Press, 2002), xiii.

94. Tom Conley, afterword to Deleuze, *The Logic of Sensation*, 138.

95. Tom Conley, "The Film Event: From Interval to Interstice," in Flaxman, *The Brain Is the Screen*, 308.

96. Peter Canning, "The Imagination of Immanence: An Ethics of Cinema," in Flaxman, *The Brain Is the Screen*, 345.

97. Jean-Louis Schefer, *L'Homme Ordinaire du Cinema* (Paris: Gallimard, 1980), 116.

98. Deleuze, *Cinema 2*, 41, 262.

99. Ibid., 1.

100. Other recent reappraisals of Bazin, particularly in Anglo-American criticism concerning Bazin's commitment to realism and the concept of indexicality, include Phil Rosen's *Change Mummified: Cinema, Historicity, Theory* (Minneapolis: University of Minnesota Press, 2001) and Dudley Andrews's edited collection, *Opening Bazin: Postwar Film Theory and Its Afterlife* (New York: Oxford University Press, 2011).

101. Deleuze discusses Bergsonian intuition as a method in *Bergsonism* ("Intuition as Method," 13–35) and in the 1956 essay "Bergson: 1859–1941" in *Desert Islands and Other Texts* (New York: Semiotext(e), 2003), first published in *Les Philosophes Célèbres*, ed. Maurice Merleau-Ponty (Editions d'Art Lucien Mazenod), 292–99. Bergson develops his theory of intuition particularly in Matter and Memory, trans. Nancy Paul and W. Scott Palmer (New York: Zone, 1991), and Creative Evolution, trans. Arthur Mitchell (New York: Dover Publications, 1991).

102. Gilles Deleuze, *Bergsonism*, trans. Hugh Tomlinson and Barbara Habberjam (New York: Zone, 1991), 33.

103. Deleuze, *Desert Islands*, 22.

104. Deleuze, *Cinema 2*, 2, 80.

105. Ibid.

106. Ibid., 77, 25.

107. Deleuze, *Cinema 2*, 22.

108. Ibid.

109. Deleuze and Guattari, *What Is Philosophy?*, 167.

110. Deleuze, *Cinema 2*, 2, 80.

111. Deleuze, *Desert Islands*, 25.

112. Massumi, *Parables for the Virtual*, 141.

113. Deleuze, *Desert Islands*, 25.

114. Deleuze, *Bergsonism*, 27.

115. Ibid., 28. We can see here the roots of Deleuze's rejection of phenomenology as the starting point for an understanding of cinema. For a useful

discussion of Deleuze and the concepts of the inhuman/superhuman in his work, see Pearson, *Germinal Life*, 214–24.

116. Deleuze, *Bergsonism*, 33 (emphasis added).

117. I discuss the aspect of "recognition" in intuition in terms of anomalous suspense in chapter 1.

118. Massumi, *Parables for the Virtual*, 134.

119. Deleuze, *Cinema 2*, 189.

120. Massumi, *Parables for the Virtual*, 31.

121. Thomas Elsaesser, "Casting About: Hitchcock's Absence," in *Johan Grimonprez: Looking for Alfred*, ed. Steven Bode (Ostfildern: Hatje Cantz, 2007), 137–61, 146–47.

122. Barthes, *Image-Music-Text*, 119.

123. Alain François and Yvan Thomas, "The Critical Dimension of Gilles Deleuze: For a Pedagogy of Perception," in *Der Film bei Deleuze/Le cinéma selon Deleuze*, ed. Oliver Fahle and Lorenz Engell (Weimar/Paris: Verlag der Bauhaus-Universität/Presses de la Sorbonne Nouvelle, 1997), 198–217, 207.

124. Rodowick, *Gilles Deleuze's Time Machine* (Durham, N.C.: Duke University Press, 1997), 77.

125. *Mediators* is translated as "intercessors" in *Cinema 2*, 153; I use *mediators* here based on the better known translation in "Mediators," in Crary and Kwinter, eds., *Incorporations*, 285–86.

126. Deleuze, *Difference and Repetition*, 109.

127. Jean-François Lyotard, *The Inhuman: Reflections on Time* (Stanford, Calif.: Stanford University Press, 1992).

1. A Free Replay

1. Schefer, *The Enigmatic Body*, 119.

2. Ibid., 114.

3. Nicole Brenez, *De La Figure en Général et du Corps en Particulier* (Paris: De Boeck & Larcier, 1998), 11. "Comment l'oeuvre peut-elle retrouver son épaisseur, sa fecondité, sa fragilité, sa densité propre ou son opacité éventuelle, en un mot, ses vertus problématiques?" (my translation).

4. Massumi, *Semblance and Event*, 143.

5. See Anna Gibbs on mimesis and affective spectatorship: "Mimesis as a Mode of Knowing: Vision and Movement in the Aesthetic Practice of Jean Painlevé, *Angelaki* 20, no. 3 (2015): 43–54. See also Michael Taussig's *Mimesis and Alterity: A Particular History of the Senses* (New York: Routledge, 1993), where the mimetic faculty involves not only imitation, but a palpable connection between perceiver and perceived (21). Likewise, Schefer's understanding of spectatorship extends the plastic quality of anamorphosis to the viewer as well. See also Laura Mulvey's *Fetishism and Curiosity* (Bloomington: Indiana University Press, 1996), Shaviro's *The Cinematic Body*, Rachel Moore's *Savage Theory: Cinema as Modern Magic* (Durham, N.C.: Duke University Press, 1999),

and Elena Del Rio's *Deleuze and the Cinemas of Performance* (Edinburgh: Edinburgh University Press, 2008).

6. See, for example, Anna Powell, *Deleuze and Horror Film* (Edinburgh: Edinburgh University Press, 2005), and *Deleuze, Altered States and Film* (Edinburgh: Edinburgh University Press, 2007).

7. For Brenez, figural analysis has characterized French film theory since 1979. David Rodowick's *Reading the Figural, or, Philosophy after the New Media* (Durham, N.C.: Duke University Press, 2001) is another work linking Deleuze and the figural. Where Brenez's work is more formalist and aesthetic, Rodowick's concerns the historical and social necessity of reconceiving how power works between linguistic and plastic codes. He argues that the figural is the audiovisual, marking the shift from a linguistic to an image-based regime (49).

8. Brenez, *De la Figure*.

9. Chris Marker, *Sans Soleil*, 35mm, 100 mins. (France: Argos Films, 1983).

10. William James, quoted in Massumi, *Semblance and Event*, 32, 33.

11. Deleuze, *Cinema 2*, 79 (emphasis added).

12. Henri Bergson, *Mind-Energy*, trans. H. Wildon Carr (London: MacMillan, 1920), 165.

13. Bergson, quoted in Deleuze, *Cinema 2*, 79.

14. Schefer, *The Enigmatic Body*, 189, 110, 111.

15. Deleuze, *Cinema 2*, 168.

16. This parallels Deleuze's work in *Nietzsche and Philosophy* (New York: Columbia University Press, 2006) to rescue becoming from criminal condemnation and "restore" innocence to existence itself.

17. Deleuze, *Cinema 2*, 37.

18. Ibid., 36.

19. Massumi, *Parables for the Virtual*, 28.

20. Rodowick, *Gilles Deleuze's Time Machine*, 64.

21. Massumi, *Parables for the Virtual*, 101.

22. Massumi, *Semblance and Event*, 50.

23. Massumi, *Parables for the Virtual*, 217.

24. Massumi, *Semblance and Event*, 115.

25. Sam Ishii-Gonzales, "Hitchcock with Deleuze," in *Hitchcock: Past and Future*, ed. Richard Allen (New York: Routledge, 2004), 141.

26. Robert Kapsis, *Hitchcock: The Making of a Reputation* (Chicago: University of Chicago Press, 1992), 24.

27. François Truffaut, *Hitchock/Truffaut*, trans. Helen Scott (New York: Simon and Schuster, 1985), 9, 11.

28. Hitchcock, quoted in Kapsis, *The Making of Reputation*, 14.

29. Christian Metz, *Film Language: A Semiotics of the Cinema*, trans. Michael Taylor (New York: Oxford University Press, 1964), 94.

30. For a discussion of suspense in early cinema, see André Gaudreault, "Temporality and Narrative in Early Cinema," in John Fell, ed., *Film before Griffith* (Berkeley: University of California Press, 1983), 311–29.

31. Mary Ann Doane, *The Emergence of Cinematic Time* (Cambridge, Mass.: Harvard University Press, 2002), 195.

32. Ibid., 170. See Laura Mulvey, "Visual Pleasure and Narrative Cinema," in *Visual and Other Pleasures* (Bloomington: Indiana University Press, 1989), 19. Note that for Mulvey, this spectacle raises its own danger as well.

33. Barthes, *Image-Music-Text*, 119 (emphasis added), 120, 77.

34. Ibid.

35. Edward Branigan, *Narrative Comprehension and Film* (New York: Routledge, 1992), 75, 76.

36. Ibid., 69.

37. Ibid., 109, 87, 113.

38. Branigan, *Narrative Comprehension and Film*, 75, 190, 191 (emphasis added).

39. Ibid., 198.

40. Ibid., 194 (emphasis added).

41. For a discussion of the many permutations of "star presence," see Christine Geraghty, "Re-examining Star Studies: Questions of Texts, Bodies and Performance," in *Reinventing Film Studies*, ed. Christine Gledhill and Linda Williams (New York: Oxford University Press, 2000), 183–201.

42. Jean Louis Comolli, "Historical Fiction: A Body Too Much," trans. Ben Brewster, *Screen* 19, no. 2 (1978): 43 (emphasis added), 45–46, 51, 50, 45.

43. Ibid.

44. Ibid., 52.

45. Branigan, *Narrative Comprehension and Film*, 200.

46. Ibid., 215 (emphasis added). Branigan's comment is in reference to Chris Marker's *Sans Soleil*, a film that includes a partial reworking of *Vertigo*.

47. Noël Carroll, "The Paradox of Suspense," in *Suspense: Conceptualisations, Theoretical Analyses, and Empirical Explorations*, ed. Mike Friedrichson, Peter Vorderer, and Hans Wulff (Mahwah, N.J.: Erlbaum, 1996), 71.

48. This term is usually attributed to Richard Gerrig. See, for example, his *Experiencing Narrative Worlds: On the Psychological Activities of Reading* (New Haven, Conn.: Yale University Press, 1993).

49. Richard Gerrig, "The Resiliency of Suspense," in *Suspense: Conceptualisations, Theoretical Analyses, and Empirical Explorations*, ed. Mike Friedrichson, Peter Vorderer, and Hans Wulff (Mahwah, N.J.: Erlbaum, 1996), 93–105.

50. William Brewer, "The Nature of Narrative Suspense and the Problem of Rereading," in Friedrichson et al., *Suspense*, 107–28.

51. Susan Smith, *Hitchcock: Suspense, Humour and Tone* (London: British Film Institute, 2000), vii, ix.

52. Ibid., 22, 25.

53. Branigan, *Narrative Comprehension and Film*, 109.

54. Smith, *Hitchcock*, 35.

55. Ibid., 44.

56. Massumi, *Semblance and Event*, 35.

57. Ibid.

58. Deleuze and Guattari, *What Is Philosophy?*, 163.

59. Doane, *Cinematic Time*, 208, 213, 214, 229.

60. Paul Willemen, "Through a Glass Darkly: Cinephilia Reconsidered," in *Looks and Frictions: Essays in Cultural Studies and Film Theory* (London: British Film Institute, 1994), 227.

61. Ibid., 223, 235, 237, 239.

62. Paul Willemen, "On Reading Epstein on *Photogénie*," *Afterimage* 10 (1981): 40–47.

63. Willemen credits Delluc not as originator of *photogénie* but the first to make it relevant to the "cinematic impressionists."

64. Willemen, "On *Photogénie*," 42.

65. Ibid., 44.

66. Jean Epstein, *Ecrits sur le cinéma, 1921–1953: edition chronologie en deux volumes* (Paris: Seghers, 1974–75), 92.

67. Lesley Stern, "I Think, Sebastian, Therefore . . . I Somersault: Film and the Uncanny," *Australian Humanities Review* 8 (November 1997). http://www.australianhumanitiesreview.org/archive/Issue-November-1997/stern2.html.

68. Massumi, *Parables for the Virtual*, 231 (emphasis added).

69. Alain Bergala, "Les Deux Mortes," in *Cahiers Du Cinema*, special issue "Monstresses," ed. Pascal Bonitzer (1980), 30–31.

70. Bergala, "Les Deux Mortes," 30. At the "Fatal Coincidences: Hitchcock and Art" (Paris: Centre George Pompidou, Paris and Montreal Museum of Fine Art, 1999) exhibit on the centenary of Hitchcock's birth, one of the first to bring cinema into the museum and curated by Dominique Paini and Guy Cogeval, Hitchcock's repeated themes and influences were situated historically in the context of other artists and subjects (e.g., Madeleine's ghostly figure compared to John Everett Millais's "Study for Ophelia" (1852)).

71. Ibid. "Par son entêtement à s'abstraire de tout vraisemblable photographique, cette image réussit à produire une certaine vérité du film, quelque chose come une vérité chimique. Il y a dans l'apparition des figures sur cette photographie un décalage constitutive qui semble impossible à réabsorber: alors que l'image de l'homme est parvenue à son développement optimum, à cette gamme nuance de gris qui est repute produire le meilleur effet de réel en photographie, l'image de la femme blonde, avec ses larges plages blanches sans nuances, apparaît comme encore partiellement latente, insuffisement révélée, pendant que l'image de la brune, inversement, semble déjà trop <dure>, trop contrastée" (my translation).

72. Andre Habib, "L'Épreuve de la mort au cinéma," *Hors Champ* (August 2002). "Mutants, revenants, monstres, figures affaissées, mécaniques sournoises. Images mortifères, *a priori*, les images du film sont rendues vivantes

par le mouvement ou le flux du récit. Le récit n'est alors que la cosmétique, la parure qui tente de voiler ce temps rendu visible" (my translation).

73. Doane, *Emergence of Cinematic Time*, 214.

74. Massumi, *Semblance and Event*, 122.

75. The Borges story is "August 25, 1983," in which Borges writes of meeting his own anachronistic double. In *Johan Grimonprez: Looking for Alfred*, 54–59.

76. For a definition of open versus closed worlds drawing on Leo Braudy, and with Hitchcock as an example of a closed world, see Elsaesser and Hagener, *Film Theory through the Senses*, 16.

77. Johan Grimonprez and Chris Darke, "Hitchcock Is Not Himself Today," in *Johan Grimonprez: Looking for Alfred*, 77–99, 83.

78. Thomas Elsaesser, "Casting About: Hitchcock's Absence," in Grimonprez and Darke, *Johan Grimonprez: Looking for Alfred*, 137–61, 146–47, 148, 147, 161.

79. W. J. T. Mitchell, *What Do Pictures Want? The Lives and Loves of Images* (Chicago: University of Chicago Press, 2006), 30, 124.

80. Grimonprez and Darke, "Hitchcock Is Not Himself Today," 84.

81. Elsaesser, "Casting About," 142.

82. Slavoj Žižek, "Is There a Proper Way to Remake a Hitchcock Film?" In *Hitchcock: Past and Future*, ed. Richard Allen and Sam Ishii-Gonzales (London: Routledge, 2004), 262.

83. Patricia Pisters, *The Matrix of Visual Culture: Working with Deleuze in Film Theory* (Stanford, Calif.: Stanford University Press, 2003), 14–44.

84. Rodowick, *Afterimages*, xiii.

85. Elsaesser, "Casting About," 143.

86. Laura Mulvey, *Death 24x a Second: Stillness and the Moving Image* (London: Reaktion, 2006), 146.

87. Ibid., 101.

88. Mulvey, *Death 24x a Second*, 102.

89. Though conventionalizing projection time was key to consolidating the hegemony of feature narratives, the VCR remains undertheorized even as the fantasy of viewer intervention and control characterizes discussions of electronic media. The effects of "passive reworkings," such as pausing, are unclear.

90. In Mulvey, *Visual and Other Pleasures*.

91. Ibid., 24.

92. Many critics claim this as the only deviation from Scottie's perspective, but there are two others; both involve Midge. The first occurs as Scottie and Madeleine leave his apartment. Midge pulls up across the street and takes in the scene, unseen. The second is Midge's last appearance, when she leaves Scottie in the mental institution. Her perspective is always represented as wry and clear, hopelessly alien to Scottie's romantic tunnel vision. Her final appearance is a long-take, low-angle shot of Midge walking down a hallway

away from the camera, her shoes echoing like the metrical beat of the rational Mozart she played for Scottie in a failed attempt to "cure" him. The shot lingers; for Marker, Midge's disappearance is one of the strongest indicators that the second half of the film is, indeed, Scottie's dream.

93. Mulvey, *Visual and Other Pleasures*, 118.

94. Mulvey distinguishes between a "cinephilia that is more on the side of a fetishistic investment in the extraction of a fragment of cinema from its context," a possessive spectatorship, and a cinephilia that "extracts and then replaces a fragment with extra understanding back into its context" or a pensive spectator, the "descendent" of a "curious" spectator driven by a puzzle-solving desire. With this model of the puzzle the difference made by passage itself is obscured.

95. Mulvey, *Death 24x a Second*, 175.

96. Mulvey, *Fetishism and Curiosity*, 13.

97. Ibid., 135.

98. Ibid., 93.

99. Ibid., 184.

100. Maurice Blanchot, *The Space of Literature* (Lincoln: University of Nebraska Press), 172.

101. Gilles Deleuze and Félix Guattari, *Capitalism and Schizophrenia 1: Anti-Oedipus*, trans. Robert Hurley, Mark Seem, and Helen R. Lane (Minneapolis: University of Minnesota Press, 1983), 330.

102. Truffaut, *Hitchcock*, 48.

103. Marker, "A Free Replay," 81, my translation.

104. Donald Spoto, *The Dark Side of Genius: The Life of Alfred Hitchcock* (Boston: Little, Brown, 1983), 107.

105. Tania Modleski, *The Women Who Knew Too Much: Hitchcock and Feminist Theory* (New York: Routledge, 2005), 93.

106. Samuel Taylor, "A Talk by Samuel Taylor," in *Hitchcock's Rereleased Films: From* Rope *to* Vertigo, ed. Walter Raubicheck and Walter Srebnick (Detroit, Mich.: Wayne State University Press, 1991), 287–300.

107. In fact, just after the letter-writing scene, we see that Judy has also kept Madeleine's grey suit.

108. Taylor, "A Talk by Samuel Taylor," 292, my italics.

109. Ibid., 294–95.

110. Ibid., 295, my italics.

111. Lynch picks up on what we might see as a minor genre of the "lost woman" film; a woman is murdered but the real body is endlessly substituted for by doubles and mistaken identities. Lynch's preferred examples include Preminger's *Laura* and *Vertigo* (where the real Mrs. Elster garners little attention in critical response); we might also include *The Lady in the Lake* and even Antonioni's *L'Avventura*.

112. Tag Gallagher, "Hitchcock, Machines, and Us," *Senses of Cinema* 24 (January 2003): http://sensesofcinema.com/2003/24/alfred-hitchcock/hitch _machines/.

113. Quoted in Doug Tomlinson, "'They Should Be Treated Like Cattle': Hitchcock and the Question of Performance," in Raubicheck and Srebnick, *Hitchcock's Rereleased Films*, 105, 105–6.

114. By hinge, I mean that Hitchcock's films simultaneously embody both the movement-image and the time-image, not that Hitchcock is a historical marker of change. Although Deleuze does argue for a change in vision post–World War II, the cinema of the movement-image persists until today.

115. Ibid., 204.

116. Thomas Wall, "The Time-Image: Deleuze, Cinema, and Perhaps Language," *Film-Philosophy* 8, no. 23 (July 2004). http://www.film-philosophy.com /index.php/f-p/article/view/791/703

117. Truffaut, *Hitchcock*, 11.

118. Deleuze, *Cinema 1*, 205.

119. Deleuze, *The Time-Image*, 3, my italics.

120. Ibid., 7.

121. Jean-Louis Comolli, "Historical Fiction: A Body Too Much," trans. Ben Brewster, *Screen* 19 (Summer 1978): 46.

122. Deleuze, *The Time-Image*, 4.

123. Slavoj Žižek, *Organs without Bodies: Deleuze and Consequences* (New York: Routledge, 2004), 151.

124. Gilles Deleuze, "Mediators," in *Incorporations*, eds. Crary and Kwinter, 280–95.

125. See Girish Shambu's "Taken Up by Waves: The Experience of New Cinephilia" for a discussion of Internet cinephilia through Deleuze's concept of "mediators." In this piece, Shambu effectively pinpoints cinephilia's mode of subjectivation as neither simply personal nor generic, but as the "entering into existing waves" itself. http://projectcinephilia.mubi.com/2011/05/23 /taken-up-by-waves-the-experience-of-new-cinephilia/

126. Pisters, *The Matrix of Visual Culture*, 4, 16.

127. William Connolly. *A World of Becoming* (Durham, N.C.: Duke University Press, 2010), 24.

128. Ibid., 20–21.

129. Ibid., 38.

130. Chris Marker, "A Free Replay," *Positif* 400 (June 1994): 79, my translation.

131. In Allen and Ishii-Gonzales, eds., *Alfred Hitchcock*.

132. Pierre Boileau and Thomas Narcejac, *Les diaboliques: Celles qui n'était plus* (Paris: Denoël, 1952); Henri-Georges Clouzot, dir., *Les Diaboliques*, (France, 1955), 114 mins.

133. Spoto, *The Dark Side of Genius*, 413. The locations in *Vertigo*, showily deployed as landmarks, also emphasize how the "real as trace" fails in the film. They fail as mere background (or just ground), especially in the film's second half, where recognizable landmarks of San Francisco, and the film's remembered locations, are both subject to a searching that goes beyond recognition. Similarly, these scenes are intercut repeatedly with location shots that *only* function as searching: empty streets, traffic lights, a pan over the entire city that unsettles, rather than grounds. In *Sans Soleil*, the letter writer makes a pilgrimage to all the locations, to find them still there; it is less a verification or nostalgia that drives that film as the same, questioning, unsettled feeling as in *Vertigo*.

134. All quotes from Eleanor Kaufman, "Deleuze, Klossowski, Cinema, Immobility: A Response to Stephen Arnott," *Film-Philosophy* 5, no. 33, Deleuze Special Issue (November 2001). http://www.film-philosophy.com/index.php /f-p/article/view/654/567

135. Jean-François Lyotard, "Acinema." In *Narrative, Apparatus, Ideology: A Film Theory Reader*, ed. Phil Rosen (New York: Columbia University Press, 1986), 349–59, 350.

136. Herzog, *Dreams of Difference, Songs of the Same*, 141.

137. Garrett Stewart, *Framed Time: Toward a Postfilmic Cinema* (Chicago: University of Chicago Press, 2007), 17, 7.

138. Pat Kirkham, "The Jeweler's Eye," *Sight and Sound* 4 (April 1997) 18.

139. Deleuze, *The Time-Image*, 146.

140. Kirkham, "The Jeweler's Eye," 18.

141. Phil Rosen, *Change Mummified: Cinema, Historicity, Theory* (Minneapolis: University of Minnesota Press, 2001).

142. Hitchcock quoted in Spoto, *The Dark Side of Genius*, 535.

143. Robert Kapsis, *Hitchcock: The Making of a Reputation* (Chicago: University of Chicago Press, 1992), 37.

144. Modleski, *The Women Who Knew Too Much*, 1.

145. See, for example, the afterword to Modleski, *The Women Who Knew Too Much*, entitled "Hitchcock's Daughters," 115–21.

146. Robin Wood, one of the first English critics to write extensively on Hitchcock, states, "The central question that haunts contemporary Hitchcock criticism in article after article [is] 'Can Hitchcock be saved for feminism?'" Robin Wood, *Hitchcock's Films Revisited* (New York: Columbia University Press, 1989), 220.

147. Patricia Mellencamp, *A Fine Romance: Five Ages of Film Feminism* (Philadelphia: Temple University Press, 1995), 16, 15–16.

148. Branigan, *Narrative Comprehension and Film* (my italics).

149. Mellencamp, *A Fine Romance*, 16.

150. Susan White, "Allegory and Referentiality: *Vertigo* and Feminist Criticism," *MLN* 106, no. 5 (1991): 910–11, 923–24.

151. Lesley Stern, "Meditation on Violence," in *Kiss Me Deadly: Feminism and Cinema for the Moment*, ed. Laleen Jayamanne (Sydney: Power Publications, 1995), 254.

152. Raoul Ruiz, "Object Relations in the Cinema," *Afterimage* 10 (1981): 90.

153. Deleuze, *The Movement-Image*, 17

154. Flaxman, *Gilles Deleuze and the Fabulation of Philosophy*, 320–21.

2. Into the Folds

1. It is a popular myth about *Vertigo* that Novak dubbed the nun's line, but she denies it.

2. Deleuze, *Cinema 2*, 332, 270, 266.

3. Ibid.

4. Ibid., 268. What Hans-Jurgen Syberberg, one of Deleuze's key examples here, makes evident in films like *Our Hitler*, through techniques of front projection and lip-synced performance, is this immediate doubling of the Figure.

5. Ibid., 332.

6. Massumi, *Semblance and Event*, 81–82.

7. Deleuze, *Cinema 2*, 2, 82.

8. See the next chapter on *Suzhou River* for an extended consideration of the idea of the "affection of self by self."

9. Deleuze, *Cinema 2*, 268.

10. Deleuze and Guattari, *What Is Philosophy?*, 203.

11. In *Semblance and Event*, Massumi cites Chion's audiovision to get at a critique of the limited notion of medium, arguing for a shift (via Suzanne Langer) away from "analyzing art-forms not as 'media' but according to the type of experiential event they effect," 82–83.

12. Theresa Brennan, *The Transmission of Affect* (Ithaca, N.Y.: Cornell University Press, 2004), 6, 2.

13. Warren Buckland, "Making Sense of Lost Highway," in *Puzzle Films: Complex Storytelling in Contemporary Cinema*, ed. Warren Buckland (New York: Wiley, 2009), 42–62, 57, 54, 56.

14. Elsaesser and Hagener, *Film Theory through the Senses*, 158.

15. Thomas Elsaesser, "The Mind-Game Film," in Buckland, ed., *Puzzle Films*, 16.

16. Elsaesser and Hagener, *Film Theory through the Senses*, 154, 155.

17. Elsaesser, "The Mind-Game Film," 29, 20, 39.

18. Rodowick, *Gilles Deleuze's Time Machine*, 91.

19. Keith Ansell Pearson, *Philosophy and the Adventure of the Virtual: Bergson and the Time of Life* (New York: Routledge, 2001), 12.

20. Deleuze, *Cinema 2*, 137.

21. Ibid., 124–25.

22. Ibid., 125. Deleuze takes this topological image of the brain as a screen from Resnais, folding and refolding sheets of the past as affects, generating non-localizable and non-causal relations.

23. Ibid.

24. Del Rio, *Deleuze and the Cinemas of Performance*, 206.

25. Schefer, *The Enigmatic Body*, 111.

26. Pearson, *Philosophy and the Adventure of the Virtual*, 12.

27. Deleuze, *Cinema 2*, 271.

28. Pearson, *Philosophy and the Adventure of the Virtual*, 12.

29. Michel Chion, *David Lynch*, trans. Robert Julian (London: British Film Institute Publishing, 1995), 56.

30. In a sense, you could see this habit of Lynch's as amplifying what Vivian Sobchack calls "echo focus," which for her requires only a little adjustment. Lynch, however, intensifies echo focus not only in terms of technological enhancements of perception, but in a continual making strange of the "given body" itself; hence the proliferation of "different" bodies in Lynch's work—dwarves, amputees, mutants, the wheelchair bound (such as Richard Pryor in *Lost Highway*). This awareness extended to bodies not marked as "different," through excessive perfection and attention to details of clothing and hairstyles and an enraptured attention to the workings of the self.

31. Chion, *David Lynch*, 44.

32. Ibid., 45.

33. Ibid., 80–81.

34. Eric Rhodes, "Lost Highway," *Film Quarterly* 51, no. 3 (Spring 1998): 57–61, 57.

35. Ibid., 60.

36. Unlike, Rhodes argues, in Luis Buñuel's *Belle du Jour*, where the sound of tinkling bells on the soundtrack subtly alerts the viewer to the presence of fantasy.

37. For a discussion of phase shifts, see Thain, "Rabbit Ears," 86-101, 96.

38. Del Rio, *Deleuze and the Cinemas of Performance*, 181.

39. Deleuze, *Cinema 2*, 123.

40. Marina Warner, "Voodoo Road," *Sight and Sound* 7, no. 8 (August 1997): 6–10.

41. Ibid., 12. "au cinema, l'image n'est pas un objet mais une architecture" (my translation).

42. Elsaesser, "Casting About," 48.

43. Sigmund Freud, "The Uncanny," trans. Alix Strachey, in *Psychological Writings and Letters*, ed. Sander Gilman (New York: Continuum, 1995), 126.

44. Deleuze, *Cinema 2*, 129.

45. Ibid., 39.

46. Stephen Pizzello interviewed Peter Deming, *Lost Highway*'s cinematographer, about the techniques used to achieve the film's muddy and uncanny

blackness: "'David (Lynch) feels that a murky black darkness is scarier than a complete black darkness; he wanted this hallway to be a murky brown black that would swallow characters up.' . . . In one scene, Bill Pullman steps into a hallway so dark he seems to be walking through a wall. A single kino flo created a mere hint of depth along the sides of the hallway entrance" (1997, 37). Kino Flos are notable for their "soft" naturalistic lighting minimizing harsh outlines and shadows. Pizzello notes that the total effect recalls the paintings of Francis Bacon. Stephen Pizzello, "Highway to Hell," *American Cinematographer* 78 (March 1997): 34–38.

47. See Laura Rascaroli's "Like a Dream: A Critical History of the Oneiric Metaphor in Film Theory," *Kinema* (Fall 2002). http://www.kinema.uwaterloo .ca/rasco22.htm, for an overview of the dream metaphor in classical and modern film theory.

48. Massumi, *Parables for the Virtual*, 66.

49. Chris Rodley, *Lynch on Lynch* (Boston: Faber and Faber, 1997), 229.

50. Melissa McMahon, "'Fourth Person Singular'—Becoming Ordinary and the Void in the Critical Body Filmic," in *Kiss Me Deadly: Feminism and Cinema for the Moment,* ed. Laleen Jayamanne (Sydney: Power Publications, 1995), 126–46, 137.

51. Ibid., 137–38.

52. Bliss Cua Lim, "Spectral Times: The Ghost Film as Historical Allegory," *Positions* 9, no. 2: 287–329, 287.

53. Lim, *Translating Time*, 152. For an analysis of Lynch in terms of the fantastic, see Diane Stevenson, "Family Romance, Family Violence, and the Fantastic in Twin Peaks," in *Full of Secrets: Critical Approaches to Twin Peaks,* ed. David Lavery (Detroit, Mich.: Wayne State University Press, 1995), 70–81.

54. Ibid., 32.

55. Shaviro, *Post-Cinematic Affect.*

56. This, despite Lynch's decision not to include chapter markers on the DVD.

57. See Thain, "Rabbit Ears," 88.

58. Francois-Xavier Gleyzon, "Lynch, Bacon & the Formless," in Gleyzon, ed., *David Lynch in Theory,* 166–81.

59. *The Alphabet,* David Lynch, dir. (1968). 4 mins.

60. Guattari, *The Machinic Unconscious,* 51.

61. Lynch uses a skipping record during the murder of Maddy (Sheryl Lee), Laura Palmer's (also Sheryl Lee) cousin, in the television series *Twin Peaks*. It is another instance in which the failures of technology, not their invisible success, becomes associated with repetition, doubling, and a temporal loop.

62. Deleuze, *Cinema 2,* 3.

63. Deleuze, *Cinema 1,* 5.

64. This game of being in two places at once is one Lynch has played with before. In *Twin Peaks: Fire Walk with Me* (1991), Agent Cooper (Kyle McLachlan)

watches a monitor showing surveillance camera footage of a hallway just out-side as he waits for a man to arrive. Cooper repeatedly darts out into the hall to stand before the camera, and then back into the surveillance room to check the image. At one point, he comes back to find his own image on the monitor, frozen, as the awaited man (David Bowie) marches right through him in a doubling of the space of the hallway. It is Agent Cooper's displacement in time, being in both places at once and effected through the video camera, that "allows" the return of Bowie, who has been missing and who offers only an incoherent account of where he's been; temporal doubling mysteriously cre-ates an opening.

Nor is this a distinction between the analog and digital, which is sometimes mapped onto the distinction between film and video especially around the question of virtual reality. Massumi points out that "equating the digital with the virtual confuses the really apparitional with the artificial" in *Parables for the Virtual* (137). Film theorists such as Anne Friedberg have looked back to the nineteenth century to historicize the notion of the virtual in a way that untangles it from a technological determinism; see Friedberg's *Window Shop-ping: Cinema and the Postmodern* (Berkeley: University of California Press, 1993). Laura Marks also makes a useful distinction between indexical and non-indexical *practices* rather than indexical and non-indexical media. See Laura Marks, *The Skin of the Film: Intercultural Cinema, Embodiment and the Senses* (Durham, N.C.: Duke University Press, 2000).

65. Elsaesser and Hagener, *Film Theory through the Senses*.

66. Deleuze, *Cinema 2*, 3.

67. Ibid., 272.

68. Gregory Flaxman, "Introduction," in *The Brain Is the Screen*, 12.

69. Keith Ansell Pearson, *Germinal Life: The Difference and Repetition of Gilles Deleuze* (New York: Routledge, 1999), 69.

70. Mulvey, *Death 24x a Second*, 144.

71. Bergson, *Creative Evolution*, 302.

72. From the Victorian industrialism of *The Elephant Man* (1980) to the futuristic *Dune* (1984), all of Lynch's films obsessively figure electricity as dis-torting time and space. In *Eraserhead* (1977), electricity, usually hidden and only perceptible as itself in negative situations, becomes a dynamic force in the film; outlets are no longer simply tools for human use, but sites of poten-tial danger. Throughout the television series *Twin Peaks* (1990) and its film prequel *Twin Peaks: Fire Walk with Me* (1992), electrical wires and short cir-cuits become portals to other dimensions in which humans exist in a trans-formed state.

73. The scene was shot with tungsten lights, lit from the front to eliminate any detail on the actors' faces, and overexposed substantially (six and a half stops) to create the glow, Pizzello "Highway to Hell," 37.

74. *An Occurrence at Owl Creek Bridge*, Robert Enrico, dir. (1962).

75. Barry Gifford and David Lynch, *Lost Highway* (New York: Faber and Faber, 1997), 36.

76. Elsaesser and Hagener, *Film Theory through the Senses,* 165.

77. Participants speculated on the likely cause: that women's increased social power was no longer perceived as threatening in the same way as in the post–World War II period when noir first flourished; the teenage boy as today's privileged moviegoer, whose unsophisticated tastes couldn't stand up to the femme fatale's ferocious charms; and the proliferation of what they term the "new" chick flick, "different, dumber" films like *Sex and the City,* in which a character like Carrie Bradshaw might call to mind Christine Gledhill's lament about women in 1970s neo-noir as "less dangerous, more neurotic." Sheila Johnston, "Whatever Happened to the Femme Fatale?" *Independent,* February 7, 2009. The quote refers to Christine Gledhill, "Klute 2: Feminism and Klute," in E. Ann Kaplan, ed., *Women in Film Noir* (London: British Film Institute, 1998).

78. "Retrospective: Screen Seductresses: Vamps, Vixens and Femmes Fatales," Bird's Eye View Festival. http://www.birds-eye-view.co.uk/festival 2009/ retrospective.

79. We could actually go back to the "Beautiful Woman across the Hall" in *Eraserhead* and her ambiguous provocation of infanticide.

80. Rene Rodriguez, "Isabella Rossellini Revisits Blue Velvet," *Miami Herald,* November 12, 2009.

81. See, for example, Del Rio's reading of the Club Silencio scene in *Deleuze and the Cinemas of Performance* and Melissa McMahon's take on this scene in *Dreams of Difference, Songs of the Same,* 34–37, where she describes it as introducing a "suspended temporality" into the film.

82. Deleuze and Guattari, *What Is Philosophy?,* 69.

83. Rodowick, "Unthinkable Sex," 179.

84. Ibid., 180.

85. Ibid., 182.

86. George Toles, "Auditioning Betty in Mulholland Drive," *Film Quarterly* 58 (Fall 2004): 2–13, 13.

87. Del Rio, *Deleuze and the Cinemas of Performance,* 187.

88. Martha P. Nochimson, "*Inland Empire,*" *Film Quarterly* 60, no. 4 (Summer 2007): 10–14.

89. Julie Grossman, *Rethinking the Femme Fatale in Film Noir: Ready for her Close-Up* (London: Palgrave, 2009), 133.

90. Ibid., 54.

91. Toles, "Auditioning Betty," 9.

92. Ibid., 9.

93. Ibid., 13.

94. Ibid., 7–8.

95. Jennifer Pranolo, "Laura Dern's Eternal Return," *Screen* 52, no. 4 (Winter 2011): 490.

96. Ibid., 492.

97. Ibid., 491.

98. Deleuze, *Difference and Repetition*, 22

99. Ibid.

100. Deleuze, *Cinema 2*, 19.

101. Massumi, *Semblance and Event*, 17.

102. Mary Bryden "Être traitre à son propre regime: Deleuze's Aesthetics of Betrayal" in *Discernements*, ed. Joost de Bloois, Sjef Houppermans, and Frans-Willem Korsten (Amsterdam: Rodopi, 2004): 187–201.

103. Ibid., 190.

104. Ibid., 196.

105. Ibid., 198.

3. *Suzhou River* and the Movement-Vision of Love

1. "Sixth Generation" is a term widely used but loosely defined. In an interview with Stephen Teo, director Li Yang, often identified as Sixth Generation, argues that it does not in fact exist; each so-called member is rather defined by individual style rather than "revolt" against Fifth Generation filmmakers like Chen Kaige and Zhang Yimou; see Stephen Teo, "'There Is No Sixth Generation!': Director Li Yang on *Blind Shaft* and His Place in Chinese Cinema," *Senses of Cinema*, June 2003). Lou also expressed doubt about the legitimacy of the term, calling it an invention of Western critics; see Dennis Lim, "Lou Ye's Generation Next: Voyeur Eyes Only," *Village Voice* 7, November 11, 2000, 140. http://www.villagevoice.com/2000-11-07/film/lou-ye-s-generation-next/. Nevertheless, the term is widely used as a shorthand categorization.

2. Many Sixth Generation films are coproduced by foreign investors, and many are currently banned from screening in China.

3. Deleuze, *Cinema 2*, 82.

4. This form of time is discussed in *Difference and Repetition* and *The Logic of Sense*. The *Aion* (as empty form of time, it is both past and future, but not present) is opposed to *Chronos* (historical measurable time, within which events occur). Deleuze, *The Logic of Sense*, 77.

5. Ansell-Pearson, *Philosophy and the Adventure of the Virtual*, 35.

6. Deleuze, *Difference and Repetition*, 295.

7. Flaxman, *The Brain Is the Screen*, 43.

8. Deleuze, *Difference and Repetition*, 19.

9. Ibid., 86.

10. Ibid., 90, 89.

11. Andrew Horton and Stuart Y. McDougal, eds., *Play It Again, Sam: Retakes on Remakes* (Berkeley: University of California Press, 2004), 2.

12. Deleuze, *Cinema 2*, 22.

13. Bergson, *Creative Evolution*, 298.

14. Rodowick, *Gilles Deleuze's Time Machine*, 81.

15. Horton and McDougal, *Play It Again, Sam,* 4.

16. Leo Braudy, "Afterword: Rethinking Remakes," in *Play It Again, Sam,* 331.

17. Sven Lütticken, "Planet of the Remakes," *New Left Review* 25 (Jan/Feb 2004): 103–19, 115.

18. Deleuze, "The Simulacrum and Ancient Philosophy," in *The Logic of Sense,* 253–79.

19. Vivian Sobchack, *The Address of the Eye: A Phenomenology of the Film Experience* (Princeton: Princeton University Press, 1992), 220.

20. Ibid., 236.

21. Ibid., 244.

22. Ibid., 251.

23. Interestingly, Sobchack doesn't read this film as a "science fiction." The continual fascination with trying out its new body echoes a million sci-fi films where a robot is endowed with form and can't stop playing with itself.

24. In "Cinema Year Zero," Gregory Flaxman marks a shift in Bergson's writings between *Matter and Memory* to *Creative Evolution,* from a receptive perception acted upon by images to a perception that acts upon images to facilitate action. He quotes the later Bergson's "recourse to masculinity": "A man is so much more a 'man of action' as he can embrace in a glance a greater number of events: . . . He who grasps them as a whole will dominate them" (in *The Brain Is the Screen,* 100). I can't help but feel that despite claiming that the film body is not marked as a human body is, Sobchack's explicit gendering of the film body in *Lady in the Lake* as female is complemented by an implicit gendering of the ideal film body as male (and thus "unmarked").

25. Ibid., 205, 206.

26. Ibid., 218.

27. Ibid.

28. Deleuze, *Cinema 2,* 79, 82.

29. Deleuze, *Difference and Repetition,* 258.

30. Ibid., 261.

31. Flaxman, "Cinema Year Zero," 96.

32. Quoted in *James Turrell: A Retrospective,* ed. Michael Govan and Christine Y. Kim (Los Angeles: Prestel, 2013).

33. Massumi, *Parables for the Virtual,* 53.

34. Massumi, *Semblance and Event,* 113.

35. Massumi, *Parables for the Virtual,* 225.

36. Ibid., 232.

37. Dennis Lim, "Lou Ye's Generation Next: Voyeur Eyes Only," *Village Voice,* 2000.

38. For a relevant discussion of the mermaid in Chinese culture, see Sean Metzger, "The Little (Chinese) Mermaid: Importing 'Western' Femininity in Lou Ye's *Suzhou he (Suzhou River)*," in *How East Asian Films Are Reshaping*

National Identities: Essays on the Cinemas of China, Japan, South Korea, and Hong Kong, ed. Andrew David Jackson, Michael Gibb, and Dave White (Lewiston, N.Y.: Edwin Mellen Press, 2007), 135–54.

39. Massumi, *Parables for the Virtual*, 232.

40. Ibid., 214.

41. Damion Searls, "*Suzhou River*," *Film Quarterly* 55, no. 2 (Winter 2001): 55, 58.

42. Yunda Feng (2009) does precisely this, breaking the film into discrete segments to Lou's "complex storytelling" as a means of revitalizing the thriller genre. This approach's limitations, like that of "puzzle film" analyses, are revealed when Feng claims that the uncertainty around identity and the film's temporal instability are resolved beyond all doubt when Lou "literalizes" Mada and Mudan's tale by showing their dead bodies. I argue such "evidence" fails to account for uncertainty's *activity* throughout. See Y. Eddie Feng, "Revitalizing the Thriller Genre: Lou Ye's *Suzhou River* and *Purple Butterfly*," in *Puzzle Films: Complex Storytelling in Contemporary Cinema*, 187–202.

43. Deleuze, *Cinema 2*, 137.

44. Andres Kovacs, "The Film History of Thought," in *The Brain Is the Screen*, 163.

45. Barthes, *Image-Music-Text*, 119.

46. Searls, "*Suzhou River*," 59.

47. Deleuze, *Cinema 2*, 80.

48. Rodowick, *Virtual Life of Film*, 73.

49. Brian Massumi, "Deleuze, Guattari, and the Philosophy of Expression," *Canadian Review of Comparative Literature* 24, no. 3 (1997): 748.

50. Peter Canning, "The Imagination of Immanence: An Ethics of Cinema," in *The Brain Is the Screen*, 342, 343.

51. Deleuze, *Cinema 2*, 141.

52. Ibid., 139.

53. Sara Ahmed, "Happy Objects," in *The Affect Theory Reader*, ed. Melissa Greg and Gregory J. Seigworth (Durham, N.C.: Duke University Press, 2010), 41.

54. Friedrich Nietzsche, *On the Genealogy of Morals* (New York: Vintage Books, 1989), 57, 58, 62.

55. Deleuze, *Cinema 2*, 52, 290.

56. As with female names in *Vertigo* (the Proustian "Madeleine") and *Lost Highway* (Renée "reborn" though diegetically primary), there is again a curious inversion of temporalities. *Meimei* means "little sister" in Chinese; her character is older and more "experienced" than Mudan, but diegetically primary.

57. McMahon, "'Fourth Person Singular.'"

58. Deleuze, "Deleuze/Spinoza: Cours Vincennes," *lecture* (March 17, 1981). http://archives.skafka.net/alice69/doc/Deleuze%20-%20cours_vincennes _1978-1981.pdf

59. Massumi, *Parables for the Virtual*, 26.

60. Branigan, *Narrative Comprehension and Film*, 215.

61. Deleuze, *Cinema 1*, 81.

62. See Alain Robbe-Grillet, *For a New Novel: Essays on Fiction* (New York: Grove, 1965), especially "Time and Description in Fiction Today," 143–56, 147.

63. Deleuze, *Cinema 2*, 22.

64. Ibid., 143.

65. Chion's book was published in 1990, four years after Deleuze's *Cinema 2*. However, much of the work in Chion's book appeared previously in articles (as in the case of "La Voix Invisible" [1982], Chion's review of James Whale's 1933 film *The Invisible Man*, the basis for Chion's section "A Phantom Body: The Invisible Man," 126–29). These works develop ideas, like the *acousmêtre*, first explored in his earlier works.

66. Michel Chion, *Audio-Vision: Sound on Screen*, trans. and ed. Claudia Gorbman (New York: Columbia University Press, 1994), 125.

67. Ibid., 125. Chion notes this idea is found in Merleau-Ponty.

68. Ibid., 126.

69. Ibid. 129. Examples of *acousmêtres* include the Wizard of *The Wizard of Oz* and the mother in *Psycho*.

70. Ibid., 128, 130.

71. Massumi, *Semblance and Event*, 6.

72. Chion, *Audio-Vision*, 218.

73. Massumi, *Semblance and Event*, 133.

74. Marks, *The Skin of the Film*.

75. Searls, *"Suzhou River,"* 57.

76. Massumi, *Parables for the Virtual*, 23.

77. Ibid.,145.

78. Ibid., 156.

79. Bergson, *Creative Evolution*, 208.

80. Deleuze, *Cinema 2*, 200.

81. Ibid., 201.

82. Massumi, *Parables for the Virtual*, 131.

83. Deleuze, *Cinema 2*, 170.

4. Time Takings

1. See Linda Williams, "Discipline and Fun: Psycho and Postmodern Cinema" in *Alfred Hitchcock's Psycho: A Casebook*, ed. Robert Kolker (Oxford: Oxford University Press, 2004), 164–204.

2. Guattari, *Schizoanalytic Cartographies*, 29.

3. Ibid.

4. Siegfried Zielinski, "Backwards to the Future: Outline for an Investigation for Thinking Cinema as a Time Machine," in *Future Cinemas: The*

Cinematic Imaginary after Film, ed. Jeffrey Shaw and Peter Weibel (Cambridge: MIT Press, 2003), 566–69.

5. Ibid., 568.

6. The following discussion of the time machine in *Inland Empire* is adapted from a short section of Thain, "Rabbit Ears," 87–88.

7. See Alanna Thain, "Anarchival Cinemas," *Inflexions* 4 (2011). http://inflexions.org/n4_Anarchival-Cinemas-by-Alanna-Thain.pdf.

8. Guattari, *Schizoanalytic Cartographies,* 172.

9. Marshall McLuhan, *Understanding Media: The Extensions of Man* (Cambridge: MIT Press, 1994), 43.

10. Anna Munster, *Materializing New Media: Embodiment in Information Aesthetics* (Hanover, N.H.: Dartmouth University Press, 2006), 19.

11. Ibid., 33.

12. Michel Foucault, "Of Other Spaces," *Diacritics* 16 (1986): 22–27.

13. Deleuze and Guattari, *A Thousand Plateaus,* 37.

14. For a discussion of televisual preemptive narratives, including *Damages,* see Toni Pape, "Figures of Time: Preemptive Narratives in Contemporary Television Series," PhD thesis, Université de Montréal, 2013. Dillahunt was also doubly embodied in the TV series *Deadwood,* playing two different and unrelated characters in the series.

15. Guattari, *Schizoanalytic Cartographies,* 71.

16. Deleuze, *Cinema 2,* 142.

17. Barbara Filser, "Gilles Deleuze and a Future Cinema: Cinema 1, Cinema 2—and Cinema 3?" in *Future Cinemas,* 214–19, 218.

18. Rodowick, *The Virtual Life of Film,* 82.

19. Claire Colebrook, *Deleuze and the Meaning of Life* (New York: Continuum, 2010), 15.

20. "Michael Snow and Christian Marclay: A Conversation," in *Replay Marclay,* ed. Jean-Pierre Criqui (Dijon: Les Presses du reel, 2007), 126–36, 127.

21. Deleuze, *Foucault,* 47.

22. For a discussion of chronic collage, see Toni Pape, Noemie Solomon, and Alanna Thain, "Welcome to This Situation: Tino Sehgal's Impersonal Ethics," *Dance Research Journal* 46, no. 3 (December 2014): 89–100, 97–98.

23. Jean-Pierre Criqui, "The World According to Christian Marclay," in *Replay Marclay,* 68–79, 78.

24. Ibid, 68.

25. Massumi *Semblance and Event,* 45.

26. Ibid., 40.

27. Ibid, 42, 43.

28. Gilles Deleuze, *Pure Immanence: Essays on a Life* (New York: Zone, 2005).

29. See Raul Ruiz, *Poetics of Cinema: Volume 1* (New York: Distributed Art Pub, 1995), 113.

Conclusion

1. Andrei Tarkovsky, *Sculpting in Time: Reflections on the Cinema*, trans. Kitty Hunter-Blair (Austin: University of Texas Press, 1989), 8.

2. Ibid.

3. Ibid., 9.

4. Ibid., 10.

5. Ibid.

6. Ibid., 9.

7. Ibid., 10.

8. Ibid., 12.

9. Deleuze, *Cinema 2*, 146.

10. Deleuze, *Pure Immanence*.

11. Tarkovsky, *Sculpting in Time*, 108.

12. Ibid., 109.

13. Deleuze, *Pure Immanence*, 30.

14. Ibid., 31.

15. Massumi, *Parables for the Virtual*, 53.

16. Ibid., 225.

17. Deleuze, *Cinema 2*, 170.

18. Guattari, *Chaosmosis*, 90.

19. Deleuze and Guattari, *A Thousand Plateaus*, 102.

20. Ansell Pearson, *Germinal Life*, 69.

21. James Elkin, *The Object Stares Back: On the Nature of Seeing* (New York: Houghton Mifflin Harcourt, 2001), 11–12.

22. Ibid.

23. Massumi, *Semblance and Event*, 24.

24. Ibid., 2.

25. Ibid., 3.

26. Deleuze, *Cinema 2*, 130, and Rodowick, *The Virtual Life of Film*, 73–87.

Index

ALANNA THAIN is associate professor of English and world cinemas, and director of the Institute of Gender, Sexuality, and Feminist Studies, at McGill University.